THE ODYSSEY

Greenwich House Classics Library

Odysseus preparing to fight with Irus.

HOMER

THE ODYSSEY

TRANSLATED BY E.V. RIEU

ILLUSTRATIONS BY JOHN FLAXMAN

Greenwich House Classics Library

Greenwich House
Distributed by Crown Publishers, Inc.
New York

Compilation copyright © 1982 by Crown Publishers, Inc.
Translation copyright 1946 by E. V. Rieu.
All rights reserved.

This 1982 edition is published by Greenwich House, a Division of
Arlington House, Inc., distributed by Crown Publishers, Inc.
by arrangement with Penguin Books, Ltd.

Manufactured in the United States of America

h g f e d c b a

Library of Congress Cataloging in Publication Data

Homer.
The Odyssey.

(Greenwich House classics library)
Translation of: Odyssey.
Previously published: Harmondsworth, England: Penguin Books, 1946
(1981 printing) (Penguin classics)
I. Rieu, E. V. (Emile Victor), 1887–1972.
II. Title.   III. Series.   IV. Series: Penguin classics.
[PA4025.A5R5   1982]   883'.01   82-11794
ISBN: 0-517-39053-1

CONTENTS

The Greeks believed that the *Iliad* and the *Odyssey* were compiled by Homer, and seven Greek cities claim to be the place of his birth. Nothing is known of his life or date, nor can it be proved that the same person compiled both works at the same time, but the quality and unity of the structure in each book indicates one author, who may for convenience be called Homer. Modern scholarship now places him somewhere in Ionia in about 700 B.C.

E. V. RIEU, editor of the Penguin Classics from 1944 to 1964, was born in 1887 and was a scholar of St Paul's School and of Balliol College, Oxford. He was appointed Manager of the Oxford University Press in Bombay in 1912, and served in the Mahratta Light Infantry during the First World War. He worked as Educational Manager and Managing Director for Methuen & Co. until 1936, when he became their Academic and Literary Adviser. He was President of the Virgil Society in 1951, and Vice-President of the Royal Society of Literature in 1958. Among his publications are *The Flattered Flying Fish and other poems*, and translations of the *Odyssey*, the *Iliad*, Virgil's *Pastoral Poems*, the *Voyage of Argo* and *The Four Gospels*, in the Penguin Classics. E. V. Rieu died in 1972.

Editor: Betty Radice

INTRODUCTION

THIS version of the *Odyssey* is, in its intention at any rate, a genuine translation, not a paraphrase nor a retold tale. At the same time, and within the rules I have set myself, I have done my best to make Homer easy reading for those who are unfamiliar with the Greek world. Nevertheless, they are bound to find here much that is strange and I beg them to bear with me patiently through a few preliminary pages, so that I may provide them beforehand with the answers to some at least of the questions that will occur to them as they read.

Homer's *Iliad* and *Odyssey* have from time to time afforded a first-class battleground for scholars. In the nineteenth century in particular, German critics were at endless pains to show, not only that the two works are not the product of a single brain, but that each is a piece of intricate and rather ill-sewn patchwork. In this process Homer disappeared.

By now he has been firmly re-established on his throne and his readers may feel as sure that they are in one man's hands as they do when they turn to *As You Like It* after reading *King John*.* But this restoration depends on a judicious re-examination of the internal evidence and has brought little new to light about the man and his life. It is beyond question that he is the earliest surviving Greek writer; probable that he lived in the tenth century before Christ in one or other of those cities which the Greeks had established on the Aegaean coast of Asia Minor; and quite likely that he actually committed his poems to writing, though that art was still perhaps hardly known save to the

* This is not to say that in so ancient a text one or two lines here and there may not be later interpolations. Yet the only longer passage in the *Odyssey* which I find valid reasons for suspecting is that beginning at l. 67 of Book XX, where Penelope, in a prayer addressed to the goddess Artemis, tells her a story in which she, Artemis, is referred to in the third person.

minstrel fraternity to which he belonged. The rest, including his blindness, is legend or guesswork; and the reader who tries to glean from his poems something of the man, as apart from his art, will find himself baffled by the most impersonal and objective of authors.

The *Iliad* and *Odyssey* are twin aspects of a single theme – the story of the Trojan War and its aftermath. Together they constitute the first expression of the Western mind in literary form – the earliest, at all events, which we possess, for it will be obvious even to those who read them in translation that two such masterpieces could not have sprung into being without artistic antecedents. In form they are epic poems; but it will perhaps make their content clearer to the modern reader if I describe the *Iliad* as a tragedy and the *Odyssey* as a novel. It is in the *Iliad* that we hear for the first time the authentic voice of the Tragic Muse, while the *Odyssey*, with its well-knit plot, its psychological interest, and its interplay of character, is the true ancestor of the long line of novels that have followed it. And though it is the first, I am not sure that it is not still the best. Let the new reader decide for himself.

Each of the two poems is complete and independent as a work of art, with an atmosphere of its own, yet, as we have seen, they share a common background in the Trojan War; and of this war something must now be said.

The city of Troy or Ilium, which in Homer's account was besieged for ten years and finally sacked by the Greek king Agamemnon and his feudal supporters, has been identified by archaeologists with Hissarlik, an ancient settlement near the coast of the Aegaean in the north-west corner of Asia Minor, whose remains show traces of repeated demolition and rebuilding. It is quite likely that a marauding force from European Greece played a destructive part in its chequered life. But this is not to say that Homer's account is to be taken as history. Homer was neither a historian nor an archaeologist – the very ideas of history and archaeology were non-existent in his day – and we shall be far nearer to the truth if we regard him as having worked up a mass of legendary and mythical material, of very ancient date and well known to his hearers, into a seemingly historical tale. His heroes and heroines were the supposed ancestors of the nobles before whom he recited his poems. It flattered his audience to hear of their doughty deeds and, in the absence of genuine pedigrees and records, to imagine these divinely-descended and godlike beings as separated from themselves by only a few generations. But in my view,* at any rate, they are mythical, and Homer's historical value to us lies, not in his attempt to describe an actual past, but in the picture which, in the course of this attempt, he cannot help giving us of the life and manners of his own day.

Before introducing the reader to the scene he will meet with in the *Odyssey*, we must briefly describe the action of the *Iliad*, which is no more than an episode in the ten years' siege of Troy. The ships of the Greek expeditionary force are lined up on the beach; the troops are encamped in huts beside them; the fighting takes place on the rolling plain between these huts and the city walls. Agamemnon, son of Atreus, the Greek overlord, with his brother Menelaus of Sparta, has induced the princes who owe him allegiance to join forces with him against Troy and Priam, its king, because Paris, one of Priam's many sons, has abducted Menelaus' wife, the beautiful Helen. The narrative covers only the short period of Achilles' withdrawal from the fighting after a quarrel with Agamemnon, his resumption of arms, and the death at his hands of the Trojan prince, Hector, whose body is recovered from Achilles for burial by the personal efforts of his father, King Priam. With Hector's funeral the *Iliad* ends. Homer left it to the lesser epic poets who followed him to fill the story out at either end.

His own work he resumed† in the *Odyssey*, which, though with many a backward look at the actual fighting, starts at a point in the tenth year after its end and deals with the

---

* A view that I express with some diffidence, for I feel that I have many scholars against me.

† There are some slight suggestions that he wrote the *Iliad* first.

adventures of the Greek chieftains on their homeward way. All the principal heroes are carefully accounted for, but the fate of one of them, Odysseus, King of Ithaca, an island off the western coast of Greece, is for artistic purposes selected as the central theme. Menelaus, Agamemnon, and Nestor receive special treatment. The adventures of Menelaus, indeed, are given at such length in Book IV and bear so suggestive a resemblance to those of Odysseus that we are tempted to think that in the material at his disposal Homer found the legend of the Wandering Prince attached to the names of both Menelaus and Odysseus, and gave us two versions of the tale. At any rate there is a puzzle here for those who would have us believe that the pair are historical figures. Incidentally, it is noteworthy that apart from the death of Priam's daughter, Cassandra, Homer, who shows such meticulous care in winding up the Greek side of the business, concerns himself not at all with the destinies of the Trojans and their allies after the Sack.

But to return to the *Odyssey* – I am not going to spoil my readers' pleasure by an analysis of the plot. Homer is the world's best story-teller, and I can safely leave them in his hands. A few words, however, on the opening scenes may not come amiss. The tale begins with a council of the Olympian gods – of whom more anon – in the tenth year after the Fall of Troy. Zeus takes the chair, and comments first on the fate of Agamemnon, murdered on his return from Troy by Clytaemnestra, his wife, and her lover, Aegisthus; a tragic tale which Homer introduces here, and many times again, by way of pointing the contrast between Clytaemnestra's infamy and the sterling virtue of Penelope, Odysseus' queen. Next, Odysseus himself is discussed, and it is felt that this unhappy wanderer, who, mainly through the enmity of the sea-god Poseidon, has for ten years failed to reach his home in Ithaca, should be brought back to his kingdom. At the moment he is detained against his will in the remote island of Ogygia by the nymph Calypso, a lesser goddess who has for seven years exercised her charms in vain upon him; and it is there (in Book v) that we first meet him, and not till Book IX that we hear what he did in the first three years of his ten years' wanderings after the Sack of Troy.

Meanwhile, to return to Book I, after suggesting that Hermes, the Envoy of the gods, should be dispatched to release Odysseus, the goddess Athene, Odysseus' champion and protector, visits his palace in Ithaca to stir his young son Telemachus to take active steps towards the discovery of his long-lost father, or, failing this, to bring to an end the intolerable situation that has arisen during his long absence. For we find that his faithful wife Penelope is besieged in her own house by a host of amorous and ambitious princelings from Ithaca itself and the neighbouring isles, each eager to wed the still attractive queen and even more eager to step into King Odysseus' shoes. It is the doom of these Suitors that is slowly but surely worked up to in the magnificent climax of Book XXII.

But I undertook to introduce the reader only to the opening scene. Nor, having done this, do I propose to add one more to the many appreciations of the *Odyssey* that have been penned. I will content myself by drawing his attention to one or two aspects of Homer's genius which have struck me with even greater force during the long period of intimate study which translation involves than they did when I tackled him as a task at school.

I put first the extraordinary insight, delicacy, and truth with which he handles his hero's relations with members of the other sex – I cannot simply say women, for at least three goddesses are involved, though they are by no means the less feminine for being divine. The princess Nausicaa is a peculiarly attractive figure to modern readers. Some of us, steeped in the traditions of later fiction, may regret Homer's failure to pursue Nausicaa's romance to a more exciting conclusion, or may console ourselves by reading a broken heart into her last words with Odysseus. But Homer was neither a sex-ridden romantic nor a disillusioned realist, with the happy result that his picture of Nausicaa is as fresh and lovely now as when it was painted three thousand years ago.

Next, in an age which in spite of two savage wars is still too ready to look askance at the barbarity of its predecessors and to censure the occasional brutalities that Homer seems to condone, I cannot help dwelling on the tenderness which he expresses (or rather, in some subtle manner, causes *us* to feel) for all those whom fate or their own follies have afflicted or cast down. I am thinking of the luckless young Elpenor, 'not much of a fighting man, nor very strong in the head'; of the woman-slave grinding corn in the handmill, who was 'not so vigorous as the rest'; of the stricken Calypso's lament; of Odysseus' mother, pining in heartache 'for his wise and gentle ways'; of the great Otus and Ephialtes, destroyed 'before the down came curling on their cheeks'; of Cassandra's dying cry, which lingered so long in Agamemnon's ears; of the lonely Circe, 'decking herself out' in vain to meet Odysseus; of the faithful Eumaeus, braving the inclement night to sleep with his pigs; of his Phoenician nurse cut off in the midst of her successful crime by Artemis with her gentle darts; of the suitor Amphinomus, 'a thoroughly decent fellow', who had his warning but did not heed it; of the dog Argus, too old and weak to greet his master with more than a wag of the tail; of the netted birds, 'who meet death where they had only looked for sleep'; of the souls of the vanquished Suitors 'following the Deliverer down the dark paths of decay'; of Odysseus' old father, Laertes, expressing his misery in rustic clothes; and of the blinded Cyclops with his words of endearment to his darling ram – perhaps the most interesting case of all, for here Homer actually succeeds in enlisting our sympathy for a cruel and disgusting monster, and does so to the detriment of his own hero, much as in Shakespeare's *Tempest* the more our hearts are wrung for the unfortunate Caliban the more thoroughly do we dislike the ruthless master who 'works upon him'.

By now I have at least mentioned the chief human actors in the tale. It remains for me to repair an omission and say something of that galaxy of Olympian gods whom the reader is faced with at the very beginning of the poem and will meet as individuals on almost every page. This is no place for a disquisition on Greek religion, but it is worth while, before describing these gods and their functions, to pause for a moment and inquire what Homer's attitude towards them was.

The wrong conclusion to jump to, though I have often been tempted to make the mistake, is that Homer's attitude is detached and sophisticated. He does believe in his gods, and that very vividly, but whereas the Christian conception of godhead is based on our creation by God in his image and likeness, with imperfections introduced by Satan, Homer regards his gods, though immortal, as made in the image and likeness of man. Mixed with his deep respect for their almost unlimited powers and his aesthetic appreciation of their beauty, he betrays a very tolerant understanding of their motives and frailties. This leads quite often, as in the famous Lay of Demodocus in Book VIII, to a treatment that we can only regard as humorous. But it was neither flippant nor irreverent. These powerful beings, who were so intimately connected with men's passions and desires, were there to administer, not necessarily to obey, man's moral code. Christian apologists of a later age made a mistake when they suggested that the pagans had invented the gods and their iniquities as an excuse for themselves. Homer never censures a god nor lets a mortal use a god's misdeeds as a pretext for his own.

So much, however inadequate, about Homeric religion. It remains to touch briefly on the artistic use which Homer made of the superhuman realm. The most casual reader must at every page be struck by the contrast between the carefree happiness of the Olympian company and the toiling, anxious world of men. This contrast is woven into the very texture of the *Iliad* and *Odyssey*, and is nowhere turned to better account than when Odysseus refuses immortality as a gift from Calypso. To us the device may seem artificial. Yet how effective an artifice! Modern novelists might well envy Homer its use.

And now a few words on the individual gods who play a part in Odysseus' story. *Zeus*, son of Cronos, is supreme – the Father of gods and men. It is left a little doubtful to what extent he is independent of Fate,* but at all events it is he who administers the fate of men. Justice and the punishment of the transgressor are in his hands. So is mercy, and, perhaps because supreme power engenders confidence, he is more compassionate in his dealings than most of his fellow-Olympians. He was conceived by Greek artists as a handsome bearded man in early middle age. His consort, *Here*, is little more than mentioned in the *Odyssey*.

His brother *Poseidon*, the god of the earthquake, who rules the sea, as Zeus rules the heavens, is a far less attractive and imposing figure, at any rate in the *Odyssey*, where he is represented as persecuting the hero with implacable though not unjustified resentment.

Hades is another brother of Zeus. Remote from Olympus, he and his consort *Persephone* are the austere and dreaded powers that rule in the realm of the dead.

The youthful and attractive *Hermes* we have already met in his capacity as Ambassador of Zeus. He also serves as Guide to the dead. And Homer makes many references to his great exploit in slaying Argus, the monster with the hundred eyes.

Ares, the War-god; laughter-loving *Aphrodite*, the goddess of Love; and lame *Hephaestus*, the Master-craftsman, though frequently heard of in the *Iliad*, play only incidental parts in the *Odyssey* and may be summarily dealt with here. So may *Phoebus Apollo*, the Archer-king, and *Artemis*, the Virgin Huntress, though both are often mentioned in the poem as responsible for sudden deaths.

There are other and lesser deities whom we need not here describe, since Homer himself introduces them with sufficient clarity, but there remains one major figure, *Pallas Athene*, who commands our attention, since she plays a leading, if not the heroine's, part in the plot. Athene is a daughter of Zeus, and inherits many of his powers and qualities. She is not all-powerful nor all-wise. Her impetuosity is sometimes curbed by Zeus, and she dreads her uncle Poseidon; but subject to these Olympian limitations she stands in Homer for the intellectual and moral

* See the curious passage about Sarpedon, *Iliad*, XVI. 440 ff.

qualities which were most admired in man and with which he so liberally endows Odysseus – cunning, resolution, industry, and unfaltering courage. It is she too who has given Penelope her outstanding gifts, 'her skill in fine handicraft, her excellent brain, and that genius she has for getting her way'. When Homer does not describe the disguise she has for the moment adopted, we may think of her as a tall and beautiful woman, with brilliant eyes, clad in a white robe, with the *aegis*, a goatskin cloak, across her breast, a crested helmet on her head, and a long spear in her hand. Most vivid and alive of Homer's gods, she dominates the *Odyssey*. And this is true even though there are moments when we are at a loss to say whether the poet means us to imagine her actual presence or to understand only that his characters are exercising the mother-wit which she personifies. Finally, though the rest of Homer's gods are by no means distinguished for nicety in their ideas of fun, he has endowed his favourite goddess with a sense of humour as delicate as his own.

I do not propose to embarrass the reader with elaborate rules for the pronunciation of the names of these gods and the other proper names in Homer; but two hints may be useful. The final -*e* should be sounded (Athene has three syllables, Penelope four, Here two). And secondly, -*eus* is a diphthong (Zeus rhymes with *puce*, and Odysseus has three syllables only). Here too, while on the subject of names, I must point out that although I have talked, throughout this introduction, of *Greece* and the *Greeks*, the reader will not come across these names in the text. They were not used by Homer, nor were the terms *Hellas* and *Hellenes* applied by him to the whole of what we call Greece, except in one highly doubtful case. The people he describes were known to him as *Achaeans*, and their country as *Achaea*, though he calls them also *Argives* and *Danaans* with an apparent impartiality that we need not inquire into here.

The rest of what I have to say is addressed more especially to those who know Greek and are interested in the problems involved in the translation of Homer. It has been my aim to present the modern reader with a rendering of the *Odyssey* which

he may understand with ease and read with appreciation. I realize that in Homer, as in all greater writers, matter and manner
are inseparably blended, and I have sought, in so far as English
prose usage allowed it, not only to give what he says but to give
it in his own way. But style is one thing and idiom another. In
the very attempt to preserve some semblance of the original
effect, I have often found it necessary – in fact my duty as translator – to abandon, or rather to transform, the idiom and the
syntax of the Greek. Too faithful a rendering defeats its own
purpose; and if we put Homer straight into English words,
neither meaning nor manner survives.

Consider the following version of xxi, 402–3, by a pair of
scholarly translators whom I quote with awe, for my generation was brought up on their work: 'Oh, that the fellow may
get wherewith to profit withal, just in such measure as he shall
ever prevail to bend the bow!' That is a tolerably close translation, but quite apart from the fact that the modern reader can
scarcely get at the meaning without retranslating the sentence,
it cannot fail to suggest to him that Homer must have sounded
uncommonly turgid to his original audience. And this, we have
good reason to suppose, is not the fact.

Take, again, the famous phrase 'winged words'. I submit that
nobody knows what this means in English, though it may be
beautiful. Are we then to leave it at that, or should we seek to
discover and to reproduce the effect aimed at by the original
cliché? For such I believe it to have been; and an examination of
all the passages where it is used leads me to think that it indicates
an utterance delivered with particular care and emphasis, or
under the influence of some strong emotion – and I have tried
to translate accordingly.

Much the same applies to the expression 'What a word has
escaped you by the fence of your teeth!' This is intelligible, but
unidiomatic, English for 'What nonsense!' Must we flout English usage to preserve it, if we feel convinced, as I do, that Homer
took it over, as an idiom discounted by familiar use, from a long
line of bardic ancestors, much as he inherited the epithet 'fast'

for ships, and has, as a result, to talk of a 'swift fast ship' when he means a real clipper?

This brings me to the vexed question of the recurrent epithets. They are a marked feature of Homer's style, and as such I have endeavoured to deal with them faithfully (though not without an element of variety), since there are few cases* where English is altogether recalcitrant to their use. I think that, whether used for ornamental or for deictic purposes, they too were a legacy from the past. But genius has a way of its own with traditional material; and Homer not only added to his legacy but extended its use in several interesting and subtle ways. For instance, Odysseus and other princes are 'godlike' in right of their divine descent, and as a rule the word has no more significance than 'royal'. But in XXI. 254 the context surely gives it the full value of its original meaning: Odysseus is a superman. Then there are a number of curious cases in which, unless we credit him with self-conscious art, Homer must be regarded either as having used a stereotyped expression in a meaningless way, or as having 'nodded' – which would amount to the same thing for such a stylist. I take it as an axiom that Homer never nods, and I suggest that where (in XXIV. 57) he gives the Achaeans their usual epithet 'great-hearted', though they are behaving like cowards, he does so in order to produce an exactly opposite effect – and succeeds. Again, Phemius' lyre is called 'tuneful' on an occasion when it is not only silent (which would not matter) but likely to remain silent for ever as far as Phemius is concerned (XXII. 332). Or, if this is pushing the idea too far, consider the one occasion in the whole work when 'early' Dawn is late yet Homer persists in calling her 'early'. The artifice, if such it is, is untranslatable. But there is a kind of half-way usage where we can almost follow the Greek. Dogs are styled 'noisy', and rightly so in XIV. 29, where they bark at a stranger, but somewhat surprisingly also in XVI. 4 where they are greeting a friend and are expressly stated not to have barked. Here the meaning, and

* One occurs in XXII. 439, where the servants are *told* to use 'porous sponges'.

the translation 'usually so obstreperous', are easily arrived at.

I have cited these instances to make my point that Homer does a great deal with his adjectives and does not always use them in a conventional manner. In his handling of the personal epithets, in particular, we can see how Homer the novelist triumphed over Homer the traditional bard. Just as 'noisy' dogs, do not always bark, and all 'fast' ships are not clippers, so 'prudent' Penelope, the 'wise' Telemachus, and the 'stalwart' or 'resourceful' Odysseus are often found, as their characters evolve in the hands of their maker, to behave in a manner far removed from exemplary wisdom, patience, and sagacity. Indeed they are much too human and too well-drawn for such dull and uniform perfection.* And I feel that Homer often leaves them their epithets in cases where they do not apply, because their use will actually sharpen his hearers' perception of the characters he is building up. Nor, curiously enough, does his apparently inconsequent use of the epithets on inappropriate occasions detract from their effect when more pertinently used. I feel, at any rate, that there are cases where adverbial translation is justified, and I have acted accordingly, though I should be hard put to it if I were asked to lay down formal rules for such procedure.

Two points of detail, and I have done. Over the 'wine-dark' sea I have abandoned my own principles and thrown up my pen in despair. I know that it is wrong and ought to be 'wine-faced' or something to that effect. But the English language has failed me, just as it fails me, though for other reasons, when I am tempted to write of the 'fishy' sea. What a pity it is that so natural an epithet should have been reserved by us for such unsavoury uses.

But if there are some occasions when a translator of Homer may justly inveigh against the shortcomings of modern English, there are many more, I fear, when it is his own that are to blame.

---

* Apollonius Rhodius, always careful not to copy Homer, is more sparing in his use of laudatory epithets, but presents us with even greater contrasts between the traditional reputation of his characters and their actual behaviour. As often as not, Jason is left speechless and paralysed by situations that call for heroic action.

And I had better come to an end, rather than invite too close a scrutiny of these, or, worse still, fall into the most heinous crime that a translator can commit, which is to interpose the veil of his own personality between his original and the reader.

E. V. R.

May 1945

NOTE ON THE 14TH PRINTING, 1959

Michael Ventris' decipherment of Linear B in 1952 marks the beginning of a new era in Homeric studies. One of the leading pioneers in the field is Professor T. B. L. Webster, who in his brilliant work *From Mycenae to Homer*, London (Methuen) 1958 and New York (Praeger), has even proved able, through a minute examination of the Homeric poems, to give us some idea of the nature of Mycenaen poetry, none of which has as yet come to light. But though all who wrote about Homer before 1952 must already be feeling that their words will eventually stand in need of considerable revision, much work remains to be done; and at the moment I content myself by stating that on page 9 of the above Introduction I seem to have antedated Homer by at least a century.

E. V. R.

June 1959

THE
ODYSSEY

—

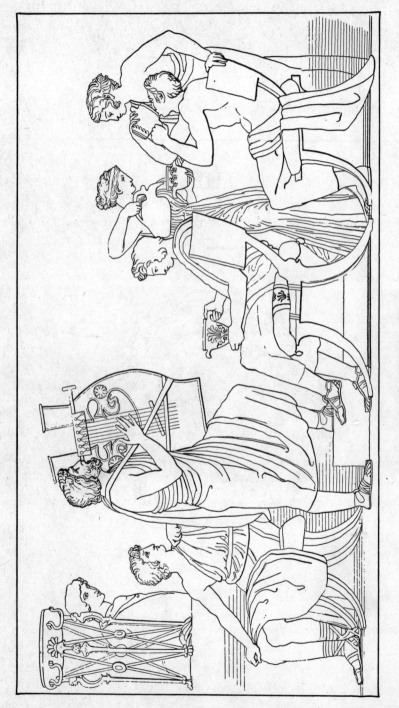

Phemius singing to the suitors.

I

ATHENE VISITS TELEMACHUS

The hero of the tale which I beg the Muse to help me tell is that resourceful man who roamed the wide world after he had sacked the holy citadel of Troy. He saw the cities of many peoples and he learnt their ways. He suffered many hardships on the high seas in his struggles to preserve his life and bring his comrades home. But he failed to save those comrades, in spite of all his efforts. It was their own sin that brought them to their doom, for in their folly they devoured the oxen of Hyperion the Sun, and the god saw to it that they should never return. This is the tale I pray the divine Muse to unfold to us. Begin it, goddess, at whatever point you will.

ALL the survivors of the war had reached their homes by now and so put the perils of battle and the sea behind them. Odysseus alone was prevented from returning to the home and wife he longed for by that powerful goddess, the Nymph Calypso, who wished him to marry her, and kept him in her vaulted cave. Not even when the rolling seasons brought in the year which the gods had chosen for his homecoming to Ithaca was he clear of his troubles and safe among his friends. Yet all the gods were sorry for him, except Poseidon, who pursued the heroic Odysseus with relentless malice till the day when he reached his own country.

Poseidon, however, was now gone on a visit to the distant Ethiopians, the farthest outposts of mankind, half of whom live where the Sun goes down, and half where he rises. He had gone to accept a sacrifice of bulls and rams, and there he sat and enjoyed the pleasures of the feast. Meanwhile the rest of the gods had assembled in the palace of Olympian Zeus, and the Father of men and gods opened a discussion among them. He had been thinking of that nobleman, Aegisthus, whom Agamemnon's son Orestes killed, to his own great renown; and it was with Aegisthus in his mind that Zeus now addressed the immortals:

'What a lamentable thing it is that men should blame the gods and regard *us* as the source of their troubles, when it is their own wickedness that brings them sufferings worse than any which Destiny allots them. Consider Aegisthus, who flouted Destiny by stealing Agamemnon's wife and murdering her husband when he came home, though he knew the ruin this would entail, since we ourselves had sent Hermes, the keen-eyed Giant-slayer, to warn him neither to kill the man nor to make love to his wife. For Orestes, as Hermes pointed out, was bound to avenge Agamemnon as soon as he grew up and thought with longing of his home. Yet with all his friendly counsel Hermes failed to dissuade him. And now Aegisthus has paid the final price for all his sins.'

The goddess of the flashing eyes, Athene, took him up at once:

'Father of ours, Son of Cronos, King of Kings; Aegisthus' end is just what he deserved. May all who act as he did share his fate! It is for Odysseus that my heart is wrung – the wise but unlucky Odysseus, who has been parted so long from all his friends and is pining on a lonely island far away in the middle of the seas. The island is well-wooded and a goddess lives there, the child of the malevolent Atlas, who knows the sea in all its depths and with his own shoulders supports the great columns that hold earth and sky apart. It is this wizard's daughter who is keeping the unhappy man from home in spite of all his tears. Day after day she does her best to banish Ithaca from his memory with false and flattering words; and Odysseus, who would give anything for the mere sight of the smoke rising up from his own land, can only yearn for death. Yet your Olympian heart is quite unmoved. Tell me, did the sacrifices he made you by the Argives' ships on the plains of Troy find no favour in your sight? Why so much bitterness against him, Zeus?'

'Nonsense, my child!' replied the Gatherer of the Clouds. 'How could I ever forget the admirable Odysseus? He is not only the wisest man alive but has been the most generous in his offerings to the immortals who live in heaven. It is Poseidon, Girdler of Earth, who is so implacable towards him on account of the great Polyphemus, the Cyclops whom Odysseus blinded. For Polyphemus is not only chief of his tribe but the son of the Nymph Thoosa, daughter of Phorcys, Warden of the Salt Sea Waves; and it was Poseidon who gave her this child when he slept with her in her cavern hollowed by the sea. That is why, ever since Polyphemus was blinded, Poseidon the Earthshaker has kept Odysseus in exile, though he stops short of killing him. But come now, let all of us here put our heads together and find a way to get him home. I am sure Poseidon will relent. For he cannot possibly hold out alone against the united will of the immortal gods.'

Bright-eyed Athene answered him: 'Father of ours, Son of Cronos, King of Kings; if it is really the pleasure of the blessed gods that the wise Odysseus shall return to Ithaca, let us send our messenger, Hermes the Giant-killer, to the isle of Ogygia, to tell the fair Calypso at once of our decision that her long-suffering guest must now set out for home. Meanwhile I myself will go to Ithaca to instil a little more spirit into Odysseus' son and to embolden him to call his long-haired compatriots to an assembly and speak his mind to that mob of suitors who spend their time in the wholesale slaughter of his sheep and fatted cattle. After which I shall send him off to Sparta and to sandy Pylos to seek news of his father's return. It is possible that he may hear of him; and the effort will redound to his credit.'

When Athene had finished she bound under her feet her lovely sandals of untarnishable gold, which carried her with the speed of the wind over the water or the unending land, and she seized her heavy spear with its point of sharpened bronze, the huge long spear with which she breaks the noble warriors' ranks, when she, the Daughter of the almighty Father, is roused to anger. Thus she flashed down from the heights of Olympus. On reaching Ithaca she took her stand on the threshold of the court in front of Odysseus' house; and to look like a visitor she assumed the appearance of a Taphian chieftain named Mentes, bronze spear in hand.

She found the insolent Suitors sitting in front of the door on the hides of oxen they themselves had slaughtered, and playing draughts, while their squires and pages were busy round them, the squires blending wine and water in the mixing-bowls, and the pages carving meat in lavish portions or washing the tables with sponges before they set them ready.

No one noticed her at first but Telemachus, who was sitting disconsolate among the Suitors, dreaming of how his noble father might come back from out of the blue, drive all these gallants pell-mell from the house, and so regain his royal honours and reign over his own once more. Full of these visions, which were natural in such company, he caught sight of Athene and set off at once for the porch, thinking it a shame that a stranger should be kept standing at the gates. He went straight up to his visitor, shook hands, relieved him of his bronze spear and gave him cordial greetings.

'Welcome, sir, to our hospitality!' he said. 'You can tell us what has brought you when you have had some food.'

With this he led the way and Pallas Athene followed. Once inside the lofty hall, he took her spear and put it away by one of the great pillars in a wooden rack with a number of other spears belonging to the stalwart Odysseus. He then conducted her to a carved chair, over which he spread a rug, and seated her there with a stool for her feet. For himself he drew up an inlaid easy-chair, well away from the crowd of Suitors, for fear that his guest might take offence at the uproar, and finding himself in such ill-mannered company turn with distaste from his meal. Moreover, he wished to question him about his absent father.

Presently a maid came with water in a handsome golden jug and poured it out over a silver basin so that they could rinse their hands. She then drew a polished table to their side, and the staid housekeeper brought some bread and set it by them with a choice of dainties, helping them liberally to all she could offer. Meanwhile a carver dished up for them on platters slices of various meats he had picked from his board, and put gold cups beside them, which a steward filled up with wine as he passed them on his frequent rounds.

The Suitors came swaggering in and took their seats in rows on the settles and chairs. Their squires poured water on their hands and the maids put piles of bread in baskets beside them, while the pages filled the mixing-bowls to the brim with drink. They helped themselves to the good things spread before them; and when all had satisfied their hunger and thirst, the Suitors turned their thoughts to other pleasures, to the music and dancing without which no banquet is complete. A herald brought a beautiful lyre and handed it to Phemius, the minstrel whom they had pressed into their service. He had just struck the first notes for some delightful song, when Telemachus leant across to the bright-eyed Athene, and whispered to her so that the others could not hear:

'I hope, sir, that I shall not embarrass you by my candour. How easy it is for that gang over there to think of nothing but music and songs! They are living scot-free on another man – a man whose white bones are rotting in the rain upon some distant land or rolling in the salt sea waves. One glimpse of him in Ithaca, and they'd give all they have for a faster pair of legs! But as it is, he has come to some dreadful end. No one on earth can bring us a spark of comfort by telling us that he'll come back. The day for that is gone for ever.

'However, do tell me who you are and where you come from. What is your native town? Who are your people? And since you certainly cannot have come on foot, what kind of vessel brought you here? How did the crew come to land you in Ithaca, and who did they claim to be? Then there's another thing I'd like to know. Is this your first visit to Ithaca, or have my people received you before – as is very likely, for my father used to entertain in our house just as much as he visited abroad?'

'I will tell you everything,' answered the bright-eyed goddess Athene. 'My father was the wise prince, Anchialus. My own name is Mentes, and I am chieftain of the sea-faring Taphians.

As for my arrival in Ithaca, I came with my own ship and crew across the wine-dark sea. We are bound for the foreign port of Temese with a cargo of gleaming iron, which we mean to trade for copper. My ship is not berthed near the city, but over there by the open country, in Reithron Cove, under the woods of Neion. As for our families, the ties between them go a long way back, as the old lord Laertes would tell you if you went and asked him. For I gather that he no longer comes to town, but lives a hard and lonely life on his farm with an old woman-servant, who puts his food and drink before him when he has tired himself out by dragging his legs up and down his vineyard on the hill.

'The reason for my presence here is this. I actually heard that *he* was home – I mean your father. And though it seems that the gods are putting every difficulty in his way, I still maintain that the good Odysseus is not dead, but alive somewhere on earth. I think he must be on some distant island out in the sea, in the hands of enemies, savages no doubt, who keep him there by force. Now I am no seer or soothsayer, but I will venture on a prophecy to you – one that I feel is inspired and will come true. Your father will not be exiled much longer from the land he loves so well, not even if he's kept in irons. Trust Odysseus to get free: he always finds a way.

'But tell me, are you really Odysseus' son? How you have grown! You certainly have his head and his fine eyes. The like-ness is startling to one who met him as often as I did, though that was before he embarked for Troy and the Argive captains all set out in their great ships. From that day to this, Odysseus and I have never set eyes on each other.'

Telemachus answered discreetly. 'My friend,' he said, 'I shall be candid too. My mother certainly says I am Odysseus' son; but for myself I cannot tell. It's a wise child that knows its own father. Ah, if only I were the son of some lucky man overtaken by old age in the midst of his belongings! As it is, and since you ask me, the man whose son they say I am is the most unfortunate that ever lived.'

'And yet,' said the goddess of the flashing eyes, 'with you as you are, and with Penelope for your mother, I cannot think that your house is doomed to an inglorious future. But here is another matter I should like you to explain. What is the meaning of this banquet? Who are all these people? And what is your concern in the affair? No sign of a subscription supper here! Perhaps it is a dinner-party or a wedding-feast? At any rate the banqueters appear to be making free of your house in a most improper way. Any decent man would be disgusted at the sight of such unseemly behaviour.'

'My friend,' Telemachus soberly replied, 'you may well ask what is going on. There was a time when this house was by way of being prosperous and respectable. That was when Odysseus, whom you mentioned just now, was still among us. But since then, the gods have had other and more sinister designs; and they have served him as they never served a man before: they have made him vanish. His death itself, if he had fallen among his men at Troy or died in friendly arms when all his fighting was done, would have caused me less distress. For in that case the whole Achaean nation would have joined in building him a mound, and he would have left a great name for his son to inherit. But there was to be no famous end for him; the Storm-Fiends have spirited him away. He has ceased to exist for us, and to me has left nothing but sorrow and tears. Nor is it only on his account that I am so anxious and unhappy, for the gods have gone on piling troubles on my head. Of all the island-chieftains in Dulichium, in Same, in wooded Zacynthus, or in rocky Ithaca, there is not one that isn't courting my mother and wasting my property. As for her, she neither refuses, though she hates the idea of remarrying, nor can she bring herself to take the final step. Meanwhile they are eating me out of house and home. And I shouldn't be surprised if they finished me myself.'

Pallas Athene gave vent to her indignation. 'For shame!' she cried. 'It is certainly high time your lost father came to grips with this impudent gang. If only he could show himself at this moment at the palace gates, with his helmet, his shield, and his two spears, just as he was when I first saw him, drinking and rollicking in our house, that time he came up from Ephyre after a visit to Ilus son of Mermerus. He had sailed there in search of a deadly poison to smear on the bronze tips of his arrows, and Ilus, a god-fearing man, refused to supply him; but my father, who loved him dearly, gave him what he wanted. Yes, if only Odysseus, as he then was, could get among these Suitors, there'd be a quick death and a sorry wedding for them all. But such matters, of course, lie on the knees of the gods. They must decide whether or no he's to come back and settle accounts in his palace. Meanwhile I do urge you to find some way of ridding the house of these Suitors. Listen carefully to what I suggest. Tomorrow morning call the Achaean lords to Assembly and make an announcement to them all, asking the gods to witness what you say. Tell the Suitors to be off, each to his own place. As for your mother, if she is set on marrying, let her go back to her father's house. He is a man of consequence, and the family will provide a marriage feast, and see that she has a generous dowry, as is only right for a daughter they value. For yourself, here is my advice. It is sound, and I hope you will take it. Choose your best ship, man her with twenty oars, and set out to discover why your father has been gone so long. Someone may be able to tell you about him, or you may pick up one of those rumours from heaven that so often spread the truth. Go to Pylos first and cross-examine the excellent Nestor; then on to Sparta to see red-haired Menelaus, since he was the last of the Achaeans to get home from the war. If you hear that your father is alive and on his way back, you might reconcile yourself to a year more of this wastage. But if you learn that he is dead and gone, return to your own country, build him a mound with all the proper funeral rites, and give your mother away to a new husband. This settled and done with, you must cudgel your own brains for some way of destroying this mob in your house, either by cunning or in open fight. You are no longer a child: you must put childish thoughts away. Have you not heard what a name

Prince Orestes made for himself in the world when he killed the traitor Aegisthus for murdering his noble father? You, my friend – and what a tall and splendid fellow you have grown! – must be as brave as Orestes. Then future generations will sing your praises.

'But my crew must be tired of waiting for me, and I'll be off now to my good ship. I leave the matter in your hands. Think over what I have said.'

'Sir,' said the wise Telemachus, 'you have spoken to me out of the kindness of your heart like a father talking to his son; and I shall never forget your words. I know you are anxious to be on your way, but I beg you to stay a little longer, so that you can bathe and refresh yourself. Then you can go to your ship in a happy frame of mind, taking with you as a keepsake from myself something precious and beautiful, the sort of present that one gives to a guest who has become a friend.'

'No,' said the bright-eyed goddess. 'I am eager to be on my way; please do not detain me now. As for the gift you kindly suggest, let me take it home with me on my way back. Make it the best you can find, and you won't lose by the exchange.'

The goddess spoke and the next moment she was gone, vanishing like a bird through a hole in the roof. But she left Telemachus full of spirit and daring, and concerned for his father even more than he had been before. He felt the change and was overcome with awe, for he realized that a god had been with him.

The young prince now rejoined the Suitors. He found them listening in silence to a song which their admirable bard was singing to them about the Achaeans' return from Troy and the disasters that Pallas Athene made them suffer. In her room upstairs, Penelope, wise daughter of Icarius, caught the words of his stirring ballad and came down from her quarters by the steep staircase, not alone, but with two waiting-women in attendance. Face to face with her suitors the great lady drew a fold of her bright head-dress over her cheeks and took her stand by a pillar of the massive roof, with one of her faithful maids on either side. Then, bursting into tears, she broke in on the worthy minstrel.

'Phemius,' she said, 'with your knowledge of the ballads that poets have made about the deeds of men or gods you could enchant us with many other tales than this. Choose one of those now for your audience here, and let them drink their wine in peace. But give us no more of your present song. It is too sad: it never fails to wring my heart. For in that catastrophe no one was dealt a heavier blow than I, who pass my days in mourning for the best of husbands, the man whose name rings through the land from Hellas to the heart of Argos.'

But Telemachus would not let Penelope have her way. 'Mother,' he said, 'why grudge our loyal bard the right to entertain us as the spirit moves him? Surely it is not the poets that are responsible for what happens, but Zeus himself, who deals with each of us toilers on earth as he sees fit? We cannot blame Phemius if he chooses to sing of the Danaans' tragic fate, for it is always the latest song that an audience applauds the most. You must be brave and nerve yourself to listen, for Odysseus is not the only one who has never returned from Troy. Troy was the end of many another man. So go to your quarters now and attend to your own work, the loom and the spindle, and tell the servants to get on with theirs. Talking must be the men's concern, and mine in particular; for I am master in this house.'

Penelope was taken aback; and she retired to her own apartments, for she was impressed by the good sense that her son had shown. Attended by her maids, she went upstairs to her bedroom, and there she wept for Odysseus, her beloved husband, till bright-eyed Athene closed her eyes in grateful sleep.

Meanwhile in the shadowy hall the Suitors burst into uproar, and each man voiced the hope that he might share her bed.

But the wise Telemachus called them to order. 'Gentleman,' he cried, 'from you who court my mother, this is sheer insolence. For the moment, let us dine and enjoy ourselves – quietly, I insist, for it is a lovely thing to listen to a minstrel such as we have here, with a voice like a god. But in the morning I propose that we all take our places in assembly, so that I can give you formal notice to quit my palace. Yes, you can feast yourselves elsewhere, and eat your own provisions in each other's homes. But if you think it a sounder scheme to destroy one man's estate and go scot-free yourselves, then eat your fill, while I pray to the immortal gods for a day of reckoning, when *I* can go scot-free though I destroy you in this house of mine.'

It amazed them all that Telemachus should have the audacity to adopt this tone, and they could only bite their lips. But at last Antinous, Eupeithes' son, spoke up in answer: 'It seems that the gods are already helping you, Telemachus, by teaching you this bold and haughty way of speaking. Being your father's son, you are heir to this island realm. Heaven grant that you may never be its king!'

But Telemachus was not at a loss. 'Antinous,' he answered, 'it may disappoint you to learn that I should gladly accept that office from the hands of Zeus. Perhaps you argue that nothing worse could happen to a man? I, on the contrary, maintain that it is no bad thing to be a king – to see one's house enriched and one's authority enhanced. However, the Achaeans are not short of princes; young and old they swarm in sea-girt Ithaca. And since the great Odysseus is dead, one of them must surely succeed him. But I intend at least to be master of my own house and the servants whom my royal father won for me in war.'

This time it was Eurymachus son of Polybus who answered him: 'Telemachus, the gods must of course decide who is to be our king in sea-girt Ithaca. But by all means keep your own belongings and rule your own house. God forbid that anyone should come and lay violent hands on your property, as long as Ithaca has people in it.

'But, my dear Telemachus, do tell us something about that guest of yours. Where did the man come from? What account does he give of his country? Who might his people be? And what is his native place? Does he bring news of your father's coming, or is he here on business of his own? He jumped up and was gone so suddenly that he gave one no time to get to know him, as I should gladly have done, for to judge by his looks he was a man of gentle birth.'

'Eurymachus,' the wise young prince replied, 'it is certain that my father will never come back. So I no longer believe any rumours, whatever their source, nor have I any use for the skill of such diviners as my mother may call in for consultation. As for my guest, he is an old friend of my father's from Taphos. He introduced himself as Mentes, the son of a wise man Anchialus, and chieftain of the sea-faring Taphians.' In this way Telemachus described the visitor whom in his heart he knew for an immortal goddess.

From then till dusk they gave themselves up to the pleasures of dancing and the delights of song. Night fell and found them making merry still; but at last they went off to bed, each to his own house. Telemachus, with much to turn over in his mind, retired to his own bedroom, a lofty chamber in the fine court-yard with a clear view on every side. He was escorted by Eury-cleia, who carried a blazing torch. This Eurycleia, daughter of Ops and granddaughter of Peisenor, was a servant of sterling character whom Laertes had procured at his own cost long ago, when she was still a girl, for the price of twenty oxen. He had treated her in his home with all the deference that is paid to a loyal wife, though for fear of his lady's displeasure he had re-spected her bed. It was she who now served as torch-bearer to his grandson; and she who of all the household women loved him most, for she had nursed him as a child.

Telemachus threw open the door of his comfortable room, sat down on the bed and took off his soft tunic, which he put in the wise old woman's hands. After folding and smoothing it out, she hung it on a peg by the wooden bedstead, and with-drew from the bedroom, pulling the door to by the silver handle and shooting the bolt home by means of its leather thong. And there, all the night long, under his woollen blanket, Telemachus lay planning in his mind the journey that Athene had pre-scribed.

II

THE DEBATE IN ITHACA

As soon as Dawn with her rose-tinted hands had lit the East, Odysseus' son put on his clothes and got up from his bed. He slung a sharp sword from his shoulder, bound a stout pair of sandals on his comely feet and strode from his bedroom looking like a god. He at once gave orders to the clear-voiced criers to call his long-haired compatriots to Assembly. The heralds cried their summons and the people quickly mustered. When all had arrived and the assembly was complete, Telemachus himself set out for the meeting-place, bronze spear in hand, escorted only by two dogs that trotted beside him. Athene endowed him with such magic charm that all eyes were turned on him in admiration when he came up. The elders made way for him as he took his father's seat.

Aegyptius, an old lord bent with years and rich in wisdom, was the first to speak. This was natural, for his own soldier son Antiphus had sailed with King Odysseus in the big ships to Ilium the city of horses, only to be killed by the savage Cyclops in his cavern home when he made the last of his meals off Odysseus' men. And although he had three other sons, Eurynomus, who forgathered with the Suitors, and two who worked steadily on their father's estate, Antiphus was always in his mind. His grief was inconsolable; and it was with tears for this lost son that he now rose to address the gathering:

'My fellow-countrymen, I beg your attention. Not once since the gallant Odysseus sailed have we been called to Assembly or held a session here. Who is it that has summoned us now, one of the young men or one of the older generation? And what emergency has made him take this step? Perhaps he has heard that the army is coming back, and may wish to share with us the early news he has received? Or is there some other

matter of public concern that he intends to raise for discussion?
"Good man!" I say, in any case. Our blessings on him! May
Zeus reward him with his heart's desire!'

His auspicious words brought comfort to Odysseus' son.
Eager to unburden himself, he left his seat without further ado
and took his stand in the middle of the assembly. The herald
Peisenor, who was an expert in debate, thrust the speaker's staff
into his hand; and Telemachus, turning first to old Aegyptius,
began:

'My venerable lord, you shall have the truth at once. The man
who summoned this gathering is not far to seek. It was I – suffering under a burden peculiar to myself. Of the army's return, I
have no prior news. I would share it with you if I had. Nor is it
some other question of national importance that I propose to
bring forward, but my own private business, the affliction – I
should say the double affliction – that has fallen on my house.
In the first place I have lost my good father, who was once king
among you here and gentle as a father to you all. But there was
a far greater calamity to follow, one which may well bring my
house to utter ruin and rob me of any livelihood I have. A mob
of hangers-on are pestering my mother with their unwanted
attentions, and these suitors are actually the sons of those who
are your leaders here. Too cowardly to present themselves at
her father's house, so that Icarius himself might make terms for
his daughter's hand with the claimant he preferred, they spend
the whole time in and out of our place. They slaughter our oxen,
our sheep, our fatted goats; they feast themselves and drink our
sparkling wine – with never a thought for all the wealth that is
being wasted. The truth is that there is no one like Odysseus in
charge to purge the house of this disease. You will understand
that we are not equipped like him for the task, and that the attempt would serve only to expose our miserable weakness. Yet
how gladly I should undertake my own defence, had I the force
at my command! For I tell you, the things they do are past all
bearing, and the way in which my wealth is being frittered
away has become an outrage to decency; which you, gentlemen,

should resent not only on your own behalf but as a scandal to our neighbours in the world around. Think of the gods! Have you no fear that they may requite these iniquities on your own heads? My friends, in the name of Olympian Zeus, in the name of Themis, who summons and dissolves the parliaments of men, I beg you to let me be and grant me leave to pine in solitary grief – unless by any chance you think that my good father was so cruel to your soldiers, whom he led, that you are trying to repay me with equal cruelty by the encouragement you give these parasites? If only it were you yourselves that were devouring our treasure and our flocks, I think we should be better off. For in that case we should not have far to look for compensation. We should simply dun you up and down the town for the restitution of our goods till every item was repaid. It is your present attitude that fills my heart with a bitterness for which I find no cure.'

As he spoke, his passion rose; and at the end he burst into tears and flung his staff on the ground. A wave of pity swept through the gathering. Nobody said a word or had the heart to give Telemachus a sharp reply, and the silence was unbroken till Antinous took it on himself to answer him:

'What rhetoric, Telemachus, and what an ugly show of spite! So you'd put us to shame, would you, and fix the blame on *us*? You are wrong. We suitors plead "Not guilty". It is your own mother, that incomparable schemer, who is the culprit. Listen. For three whole years – in fact for close on four – she has kept us on tenterhooks, giving us all some grounds for hope, and in her private messages to each making promises that she has not the slightest intention of keeping. And here's another example of her duplicity. On her loom at home she set up a great web and began weaving a large and delicate piece of work. She said to us: "I should be grateful to you young lords who are courting me, now that King Odysseus is dead, if you could restrain your ardour for my hand till I have done this work, so that the threads I have spun may not be utterly wasted. It is a winding-sheet for Lord Laertes. When he succumbs to the dread hand of Death that stretches all men out at last, I must not risk the scandal there would be among my countrywomen here if one who had amassed such wealth were put to rest without a shroud." That's how she talked; and we, like gentlemen, let her persuade us; with the result that by day she wove at the great web, but every night had torches set beside it and undid the work. For three years she fooled us with this trick. A fourth began, and the seasons were already slipping by, when one of her women, who knew all about it, gave her mistress away. We caught her un-ravelling her beautiful work, and she was forced reluctantly to complete it.

'This then, Telemachus, is the Suitors' answer to you. I'd have you note it well, and all the people too. Send your mother away and make her marry the man whom her father chooses and whom she prefers. She must beware of trying our young men's patience much further and counting too much on the matchless gifts that she owes to Athene, her skill in fine handicraft, her excellent brain, and that genius she has for getting her way. In that respect, I grant she has no equal, not even in story. For of all the Achaean beauties of former times, there is not one, not Tyro, nor Alcmene, nor Mycene of the lovely diadem, who had at her command such wits as she. Yet in the present case Penelope has used those wits amiss. For I assure you that so long as she main-tains this attitude that she has been misguided enough to adopt, the Suitors will continue to eat you out of house and home. She may be winning a great name for cleverness, but at what ex-pense to you! So I say again, we will not return to our own estates, nor go anywhere else, until she makes her choice and marries one of her countrymen.'

'Antinous,' the wise young prince replied, 'it is quite impos-sible for me to cast out the mother who bore me and who brought me up, with my father somewhere at the world's end and, as likely as not, still alive. Think, first, what I should have to pay Icarius if I took it into my head to send my mother back to him. Again, when that father of hers had done his worst to me, the gods would step in and let loose on me the avenging

Furies that my mother's curses would call up as she was driven from home. And finally my fellow-men would cry shame upon me. You may take it, then, that I shall never give the word. No; if a feeling of shame has any place in your own hearts, then quit my palace and feast yourselves elsewhere, eating your own provisions in each other's houses. But if you think it a sounder scheme to destroy one man's estate and go scot-free yourselves, then eat your fill, while I pray to the immortal gods for a day of reckoning, when *I* can go scot-free, though I destroy you in that house of mine.'

As though in answer to his words, Zeus, who was watching from afar, urged two eagles into flight from the mountain-top. For a while they sailed down the wind with outstretched pinions, wing to wing. But as soon as they were directly over the meeting-place, where the sound of voices filled the air, they began to flap their wings and wheel about, glancing down at the faces of the crowd with looks foreboding death. They then fell to work with their talons, ripping each other's cheeks and neck on either side, and so swooped eastward over the house-tops of the busy town. The people stared at the birds in amazement as this scene was enacted before their eyes, and asked themselves what was to come of such a portent. At last the old lord Haliserthes, Mastor's son, spoke out. He knew more of bird-lore and soothsaying than any man of his generation, and had his countrymen's welfare at heart when he rose now to harangue them:

'People of Ithaca, hear what I have to say. And it is to the Suitors in particular that I address my reading of these signs. For them, a great calamity is rolling up. Odysseus is not going to be parted from his friends much longer. At this very moment indeed he may be close at hand, sowing the seeds of a bloody doom for the Suitors one and all; which means disaster to many of the rest of us who live under the clear skies of Ithaca. Cannot we stop them before it happens? Or rather, won't they stop of their own accord – which I assure them they would find the better course? And I am not unskilled in prophecy: I speak from

ripe experience. Consider Odysseus. Has not everything fallen
out as I warned that self-reliant man when he embarked for
Ilium with the Argive army? I said it would be nineteen years
before he got home, after much suffering, with all his comrades
lost, and that no one would know him when he did. See how
my prophecies are coming true!'

It was Eurymachus son of Polybus who rose to deal with the
old man. 'Greybeard,' he said, 'enough! Run home and read
omens to your children, or they may be getting into mischief.
And leave me to interpret these signs. I am a better man than you
at that. After all, plenty of birds go about their business in the
sunny air, but it isn't every one that has a meaning. As for
Odysseus, he has met his fate abroad; and I wish you too had
perished with him. We should then have been spared this flood
of divination from your mouth, and the fuel you have added to
Telemachus' anger. No doubt you expect a handsome present
for your house, if he is in a generous mood. But let me tell you
this; and what I say holds good. If you, his senior, with the
wisdom of the ages at your disposal, misuse your eloquence to
incite this young man to violence, in the first place it will be all
the worse for him, and there will be nothing he can do about it;
and for you, old man, there will be the extremely unpleasant
consequence that we shall impose on you a fine that it will break
your heart to pay.

'For Telemachus, here is my own advice: I give it openly,
before you all. Let him tell his mother to remove to her father's
house, where they will make arrangements for her wedding and
see that she has a generous dowry, as is only right for a daughter
they value. Not till that is done, can I see the young lords giving
up their unwelcome suit. For we are afraid of no one at all – certainly not of Telemachus, for all his rhetoric. Nor, old gentleman, do we pay the slightest attention to these prophecies that
fall from your lips. They come to nothing and only get you
a worse name than you had. No; Telemachus must suffer and
see his wealth consumed without hope of restitution, so long
as Penelope keeps us kicking our heels in this matter of her

marriage. Meanwhile we stay, and instead of seeking other
brides, each according to his station, we feed our hopes from day
to day on the thought of the incomparable prize for which we
are competing.'

Telemachus now showed his good judgement. 'Eurymachus,'
he said, 'and the rest of you who pay my mother your distinguished attentions, I have done with entreaties and will discuss
the matter no further. The gods and the whole people here have
heard my case. All I ask for now is a fast ship and a crew of
twenty to see me to my journey's end and back. For I am going
to Sparta and to sandy Pylos to inquire after my father's return
from his long absence, in the hope that someone may be able to
tell me about him or that I may pick up one of those rumours
from heaven that so often spread the truth. If I hear that he
is alive and on his way back, then I might reconcile myself to
one more year of this wastage. But if I learn that he is dead
and gone, I shall come home, build him a mound with all the
proper funeral rites, and give my mother's hand to a new
husband.'

Telemachus resumed his seat and Mentor rose to speak.
Mentor was an old friend of Odysseus, to whom the king had
entrusted his whole household when he sailed, with orders to
defer to the aged Laertes and keep everything intact. He showed
his good will now by rising to admonish his compatriots.

'My fellow-citizens,' he said, 'the conclusion that I, for one,
have come to is that kindness, generosity, and justice should no
longer be the aims of any man who wields the royal sceptre – in
fact that he might just as well devote his days to tyranny and
lawless deeds, if one may judge by the case of Odysseus, that
admirable king, to whom not one of the people whom he once
ruled like a loving father gives a thought today. Mind you, I
pick no quarrel with these unruly Suitors for the crimes they
commit in the wickedness of their hearts. It is their own skins
they are risking when they wreck Odysseus' estate in the belief
that he is gone for ever. No, it is the rest of you sitting there in
abject silence that stir my indignation. They are a paltry few

and you are many. Yet not a word have they had from you in condemnation or restraint!'

Up sprang Leiocritus, Euenor's son. 'Mentor, you crazy fool,' he shouted at him, 'what sense is there in telling them to stop us? Odds or no odds, it would be hard on them to have to fight about a supper! Why, if Odysseus of Ithaca himself came up and took it into his head to drive us nobles from the palace because he found us dining in his hall, his wife would have no joy of his return, much as she may have missed him, but then and there he'd come to an ugly end, if he faced odds in such a cause. So what you suggest is nonsense. But enough of this. Break up the meeting, and each man go back to his own lands, while Mentor and Haliserthes, as old friends of his father's, forward the arrangements for Telemachus' expedition; though I, for one, have an idea that he will never bring this journey off, but will find himself sitting in Ithaca for many a long day, gathering news as best he can.'

The assembled people were quick to accept this dismissal and now scattered to their homes, while the Suitors made their way to King Odysseus' house.

In the meantime Telemachus sought the solitude of the sea-beach, where he washed his hands in the grey surf and lifted them in prayer to Athene:

'Hear me, you that in your godhead came yesterday to my house. It was your command that I should sail across the misty seas to find out whether my long-lost father is ever coming back. But see how my countrymen, and, above all those bullies that besiege my mother, are thwarting me at every point!'

Athene answered his prayer in person. She assumed the appearance of Mentor and seemed so like him as to deceive both eye and ear when she came up and addressed Telemachus in these inspiring words:

'Today has proved you, Telemachus, neither a coward nor a fool, nor destined to be such, if we are right in thinking that your father's manly vigour has descended to his son – and what a man *he* was in action and debate! No fear, then, that this journey of yours will end in farce or failure. It is only if you were not the true son of Odysseus and Penelope that I should think your plans might come to nothing. Few sons, indeed, are like their fathers. Generally they are worse; but just a few are better. And since we have seen that you are by no means lacking in Odysseus' wits, and that no fool's or coward's role awaits you in life, why then, you have every reason to feel that you will make a success of this undertaking. So forget the Suitors now and dismiss their plots and machinations from your mind. They are fools, and there is no sense or honour in them. Nor have they any inkling of the dark fate that is stalking so near and will strike them all down in a single day. You, meanwhile, will soon be off on this journey you have set your heart on. For am I not your father's friend, and ready to find you a fast ship and sail with you myself? Go home now and show yourself to the Suitors. Then get provisions ready and stow them all in vessels, the wine in jars, and the barley-meal, to keep your men fit, in well-sewn skins. Meanwhile, I will soon collect a crew of volunteers in the city. And there are plenty of ships, new and old, in sea-girt Ithaca. I myself will pick out the best for you, and we'll have her rigged in no time and launch her on the open sea.'

Athene, Daughter of Zeus, had spoken, and there was no loitering there for Telemachus when he heard the voice of the goddess, but he set off at once for home with a heavy heart. At the palace he found the ruffianly Suitors skinning goats and singeing fatted hogs in the courtyard. Antinous, with a laugh, ran up to him, seized his hand and spoke to him as man to man:

'Telemachus, my fiery young orator, enough now of hard words and thoughts of violence. Let me see you eat and drink with us as usual. And I'm sure our people will make all arrangements on your behalf for a ship and a picked crew to get you straight to sacred Pylos on your noble father's trail.'

But Telemachus was too wise to be deceived. 'Antinous,' he said, snatching his hand away, 'it is out of the question for a man to sit down to a quiet supper and take his ease with a set of rioters like you. Isn't it enough that all this time, under pretext of your suit, you have been robbing me of my best, while I was still too young to understand? I tell you, now that I'm old enough to learn from others what has happened and to feel my own strength at last, I will not rest till I have let hell loose upon you, whether I go to Pylos or manage here in Ithaca itself. And I shall not be balked of this journey I have spoken of. I am going, if only as a passenger, since it seems to have suited you better that I should not be allowed a ship or crew of my own.'

A storm of insults and derision greeted this speech. 'I do believe,' said one young ruffian, 'that Telemachus wants to cut our throats! And he's off to sandy Pylos to get help. Perhaps he'll go as far as Sparta and back, since he's so thirsty for our blood. Or it may occur to him that the fertile soil of Ephyre is worth a visit. He'll come home with a deadly poison, pop it in the wine-bowl, and lay us all out.'

And another of the young bloods chimed in: 'Ah, but who knows? If he too takes to seafaring, he may stray from home and be lost like Odysseus. And what a nuisance that would be for us! All the extra trouble of dividing his property between us and presenting his house to his mother and her bridegroom!'

Telemachus let them talk, and went along to his father's store-room, a big and lofty chamber stacked with gold and bronze, and with chests full of clothing, and stores of fragrant oil. There too, shoulder to shoulder along the wall, stood jars of mellow vintage wine, full of the true unblended juice, waiting for the day when Odysseus, for all he had suffered, should find his home again. There were locks to the closely-fitted, folding doors; and day and night the room and its treasures were in charge of the housekeeper, Eurycleia, daughter of Ops, Peisenor's son, a custodian who had all her wits about her.

Calling her now to the store-room, Telemachus said: 'Listen, nurse, will you draw me off some flagons of wine? And let it be good stuff, the best you have, next to the vintage you keep with such care for your unlucky king, always hoping that he may dodge his fate and walk in one day from heaven knows where. Fill me twelve flagons and put their stoppers on. And pour me out some barley-meal in strong leather bags – twenty measures, please, of mill-crushed grain. Not a word to anyone else! Get all the provisions together, and in the evening I shall fetch them myself when my mother has gone upstairs for the night. I am off to Sparta and sandy Pylos on the chance of finding out something about my dear father's return.'

At this, his fond old nurse, Eurycleia, burst into a wail of protest.

'Dear child,' she remonstrated with him, 'what on earth has put this idea into your head? What takes you that you must go wandering through the world, you an only son, the apple of your mother's eye; and King Odysseus dead and gone, far from his home in foreign parts? Why, the moment your back is turned those fellows will be plotting mischief against you; and when they've done you to death, they'll share all this between them. Sit tight where you are and guard your own property. There's no call for you to take to the hard life and wander round the barren seas.'

'Nurse, have no fears,' the wise Telemachus replied. 'There's a god's hand in this. But you must swear to me that you won't tell my good mother for at least a dozen days or till she misses me herself and finds I'm gone. We don't want tears to spoil her lovely cheeks.'

The old woman swore by all the gods that she would keep his secret, and when she had solemnly taken her oath she drew off the wine for him in flagons and ran the barley-meal into serviceable bags. Telemachus then rejoined the company in the hall.

Meanwhile another measure had suggested itself to the bright-eyed goddess Athene. Disguising herself as Telemachus, she went up and down through the city, picked out her twenty men and passed them each the word, instructing the whole company to forgather by the good ship at nightfall. The vessel itself she begged of Noemon son of Phronius, a prominent Ithacan, who was glad to let her have it.

The sun sank, and darkness fell in all the streets. The goddess now ran the good ship into the water and stowed in her all the

gear proper to a well-found galley. This done, she moored her
in the far corner of the haven. The gallant lads came up, and
when the full crew had gathered around, Athene gave each man
his orders.

The bright-eyed goddess then decided on a further step. She
made her way to King Odysseus' palace and lulled the Suitors
there into a state of pleasant drowsiness, bemusing them, as they
drank, till the wine-cups fell from their hands. Their eyelids
heavy with sleep, they loitered no more at table, but rose to seek
their various sleeping-quarters in the town. Then bright-eyed
Athene, borrowing Mentor's form and voice once more, called
Telemachus out of the palace building to her side.

'Telemachus,' she said, 'your gallant crew are sitting at their
oars, waiting for your word to be off. Come; we do not want
to delay their start.'

With this, Pallas Athene led the way at a smart pace and Telemachus followed in the footsteps of the goddess. When they
came down to the sea and reached the boat they found their
long-haired crew waiting on the beach and the young prince
took command.

'My friends, follow me,' he ordered: 'we must get the stores
on board. They are all stacked and ready at the palace. But I
must tell you that my mother knows nothing of this, nor any of
the servants either, except one woman whom I took into my
confidence.'

He led off and the crew fell in behind. They brought down all
the stores and stowed them in their well-built galley, taking
their orders from Odysseus' son. Telemachus then followed
Athene on board. She took her seat on the after-deck and he sat
down beside her. The sailors cast the hawsers off, climbed in, and
took their places on the benches. And now, out of the West,
Athene of the flashing eyes called up for them a steady following
wind and sent it singing over the wine-dark sea. Telemachus
shouted to the crew to lay hands on the tackle and they leapt to
his orders. They hauled up the fir mast, stept it in its hollow box,
made it fast with stays, and hoisted the white sail with plaited

oxhide ropes. Struck full by the wind, the sail swelled out, and a dark wave hissed loudly round her stem as the vessel gathered way and sped through the choppy seas, forging ahead on her course.

When all was made snug in the swift black ship, they got out mixing-bowls, filled them to the brim with wine and poured libations to the immortal gods that have been since time began, and above all to the Daughter of Zeus, the Lady of the gleaming eyes. And all night long and into the dawn the ship ploughed her way through the sea.

III

TELEMACHUS WITH NESTOR

LEAVING the waters of the splendid East, the Sun leapt up into the firmament to bring light to the immortals and to men who plough the earth and perish. The travellers now came to Pylos, the stately citadel of Neleus, where they found the people on the sea-beach sacrificing jet-black bulls to Poseidon, Lord of the Earthquake, god of the sable locks. There were nine companies in session, with five hundred men in each; and every company had nine bulls to offer. They had just tasted the victims' entrails and were burning the pieces from the thighs in the god's honour, as the trim ship came bearing down upon them. The crew brailed up the sail, moored their vessel, and disembarked. Athene followed; Telemachus was the last to leave the ship.

The goddess with the flashing eyes turned to him now and said: 'Telemachus, you must forget your diffidence: there is no occasion for it here at all. Why have you crossed the seas, if not to find out where your father's bones lie buried and how he met his end? Go straight up, then, to Nestor, the tamer of horses; for we are here to wring his secrets from him. But you yourself must approach him if you want the truth from his lips. Not that I think you will get anything else from so wise a man as he.'

But Telemachus was wary. 'Mentor,' he asked, 'how am I to go up to the great man? How shall I greet him? Remember that I have had no practice in making speeches; and a young man may well hesitate to cross-examine one so much his senior.'

'Telemachus,' replied Athene, 'where your native wit fails, heaven will inspire you. It is not for nothing that the gods have watched your progress ever since your birth.'

With this, Pallas Athene led off at a quick pace and Telemachus followed in the steps of the goddess till they reached the spot where the people of Pylos were assembled in session.

There sat Nestor with his sons, while their followers around them were piercing meat with skewers or roasting it in preparation for the banquet. But as soon as they caught sight of the strangers they all made a move in their direction, waving their hands in welcome, and beckoning the newcomers to join them. Nestor's son, Peisistratus, who was the first to reach them, took them both by the hand and gave them places at the banquet on downy fleeces spread over the sandy beach, near his brother Thrasymedes and his father. Then he helped them to the victims' inner parts, filled a gold cup with wine and proffered it with these words to Pallas Athene, Daughter of Zeus who wears the aegis:

'This feast that you find us holding is in the Lord Poseidon's honour. Pray to the god, my friend; and when you have made your drink-offering and your prayer, as our rites dictate, pass on the cup of mellow wine to your companion here, so that he may do the same. For he too must be a worshipper of the immortal gods, whom no man can neglect. And it is only because he is the younger, in fact a man of my own age, that I hand this golden beaker to you first.' And he placed the cup of sweet wine in Athene's hands.

The goddess was delighted at the tact and nicety which the young man had shown in giving her the golden beaker first, and at once began an earnest prayer to the Lord Poseidon:

'Hear me, Poseidon, Girdler of Earth, and do not begrudge us, your suppliants, the fulfilment of our wishes. First of all, vouchsafe success to Nestor and his sons. Consider next these others, and make a gracious return to all in Pylos for their sumptuous offerings. Grant, lastly, that Telemachus and I may successfully accomplish the task that brings us here in our black ship and afterwards get safely home.'

So the goddess prayed, and as each petition left her lips she herself made its fulfilment sure. Then she passed the fine two-handled beaker to Telemachus, and Odysseus' son repeated her prayers. The outer flesh from the victims was now roasted and drawn off the spits, portions were carved for all, and they fell to on their splendid feast. When they had satisfied their appetite and thirst, Nestor, the old charioteer of Gerenian fame, made himself heard:

'Now that our visitors have regaled themselves, it will be no breach of manners to put some questions to them and inquire who they may be.' And turning to his guests, 'Who are you, sirs? From what port have you sailed over the highways of the sea? Is yours a trading venture; or are you cruising the main on chance, like roving pirates, who risk their lives to ruin other people?'

Telemachus, inspired by Athene, who was anxious for him to catechize the old king about his father's disappearance, now plucked up the courage to make him a spirited reply:

'Nestor son of Neleus, I salute you whom the Achaeans love to honour. You ask where we hail from. I will tell you. We are from Ithaca, which lies at Neion's foot, and have come on private, not on public, business, as you will understand when I tell you that I am searching through the length and breadth of the land for any news that I can pick up of my royal father, the gallant Odysseus, who is said years ago to have fought by your side at the sack of Troy. We can account for all the others who took part in the war. We know where each man fell, and a sorry tale it is. But Zeus has wrapped Odysseus' fate up to his very death in utter mystery; and no one can tell us for certain when he died, whether he was the victim of some hostile tribe on land, or whether he was lost at sea in Amphitrite's waves. So I have come here to plead with you in the hope that you will tell me the truth about my father's unhappy end, if by any chance you witnessed it yourself or heard the story from some wanderer like him. For if ever a man was born for misery, it was he. Do not soften your account out of pity or concern for my feelings, but faithfully describe the scene that met your eyes. I beseech you, if ever my good father Odysseus in the hard years of war you had at Troy gave you his word to speak or act on your behalf, and made it good, remember what he did and tell me all you know.'

'Ah, my friend,' exclaimed Nestor, the Gerenian charioteer,

'what memories the name of Troy brings back! The miseries we fierce Achaeans put up with there – raid after raid across the misty seas in search of plunder at Achilles' beck and call, fight after fight around the very walls of royal Priam's town! And there our best men fell. There warlike Aias lies. There lies Achilles. There Patroclus, wise as the gods in counsel. There too Antilochus, my own dear son, as good as he was brave, the fastest runner of them all, and what a fighter too! Nor is *that* the full count of what the Achaean chivalry endured at Troy. There is no man on earth who could unfold to you the whole disastrous tale, not though you sat and questioned him for half a dozen years, by which time your patience would be gone, and you yourself be home.

'For nine long years we toiled to bring them down by every stratagem we could devise – even when the final victory came, Zeus seemed to grudge it to us. And all the time there was not a man that dared to match his wits against the admirable Odysseus, who in every kind of strategy proved himself supreme. I am speaking of your father, if you really are that great man's son. Indeed, I cannot help looking at you in amazement: you talk exactly as he did, and I should have sworn no youngster could so resemble him in speech. However, in all those years, whether at the general assembly or in the council of the kings, not once did Odysseus and I find ourselves speaking on opposite sides. We seemed to share a single mind, so well did we agree on the policy which in our good sense and ripe judgement we laid down for the successful conduct of the Argives' affairs.

'But not all of the Argives showed as much wisdom or honesty, and so, when we had brought Priam's city down in ruins and sailed away and had our fleet scattered by heaven's hand, Zeus planned disaster for them on the homeward run. As a result, many of them came to grief through the fatal anger of the bright-eyed Daughter of that mighty Sire. She began by making the two sons of Atreus quarrel. Acting on the spur of the moment and with no regard for form, they summoned the whole Achaean army to assemble at sunset, so that the troops rolled up sodden with wine; and then they delivered the harangues for which they had called them together. Menelaus put it to them all that their first concern should be to get to their distant homes across the seas. But this was not at all to Agamemnon's liking. He was for keeping them there and making ceremonial offerings to Athene, in the hope of appeasing her terrible wrath, not realizing in his folly how implacable she would prove; for it is not so easy to divert the immortal gods from their purpose. Well, the pair of them stood there bandying hard words, till their armed audience, themselves divided in opinion, broke up the assembly in indescribable uproar. That night our rest was spoilt by vindictive feelings against our comrades-in-arms; for Zeus was making ready to strike us the fatal blow. In the morning half of us ran our ships down into the tranquil sea, and stowed in them our spoils and the captive women with their girdles round their hips. Then, though the rest still held aloof and stayed where they were with Agamemnon the commander-in-chief, our party embarked and set out.

'Our ships went well, for luckily no swell was running and the sea was smooth. We soon made Tenedos, and there, all agog to be home, we sacrificed to the gods. But Zeus had no intention of letting us get home so soon, and for his own cruel purposes he set us all at loggerheads once more. As a result, one squadron swung the curved prows of their vessels round and turned back in their tracks. It was the followers of Odysseus, that wise and subtle king, who thus saw fit to renew their allegiance to Agamemnon son of Atreus. But I, well aware of the god's sinister designs, fled on with the massed ships that formed my company. Warlike Diomedes did the same, bringing his party with him, and late in our wake red-haired Menelaus followed too. He caught us up in Lesbos, where we were hesitating whether to choose the long passage outside the rugged coast of Chios and by way of Psyria, keeping that island on our left, or to sail inside Chios past the windy heights of Mimas. In this dilemma we prayed for a sign, and heaven made it clear that we should cut straight across the open sea to Euboea to get out of harm's way as quickly as possible. A whistling wind blew up, and our ships made splendid running down the highways of the fish, reaching Geraestus in the night. And many a bull's thigh we laid on Poseidon's altar after spanning that weary stretch of water.

'It was on the fourth day that the company of Diomedes the tamer of horses brought their fine craft to anchor in Argos. But I held on for Pylos, and the breeze never dropped from the moment when by god's will it had begun to blow. Consequently, my dear lad, I got back without any news of the men we had left behind, and have no idea who escaped or who was lost. But all the news that has come to me as I sit here at home you shall have, as is only right, and I'll keep nothing back. In the first place, they tell me that the Myrmidon spearmen reached home in safety under the great Achilles' noble son; and that Poeas' son, the brilliant Philoctetes, fared equally well. Again, Idomeneus brought all his men to Crete, all, that is, who had survived the war. The sea got none from him. As for Agamemnon, I know your home is far from his, yet even you must have heard how he had no sooner got back than he fell a wretched victim to Aegisthus' plot. And a grim reckoning there was for Aegisthus! Which shows what a good thing it is, when a man dies, for a son to survive him, as Orestes survived to pay the murderer out and kill that snake in the grass, Aegisthus, who had killed his noble father. You, my friend – and what a tall and splendid fellow you have grown! – must be as brave as Orestes. Then future generations will sing your praises.'

The wise young Telemachus replied: 'King Nestor, whom the Achaeans delight to honour, that was revenge indeed! Orestes' fame will travel through Achaean lands and live for generations still to come. Ah, if the gods would only give me strength like his, to cope with the insufferable insolence of my mother's suitors and settle accounts with those ruffians for their blackguardly tricks! But Fate has no such happiness in store for me, nor for my father either. I have to grin and bear things as they are.'

'My friend,' said Gerenian Nestor, 'now that your own remarks have put me in mind of it, I admit I have been told that a whole crowd of young gallants are courting your mother and running riot in your house as uninvited guests. Tell me, do you take this lying down, or have the people of Ithaca been listening to some heaven-fed rumour that has turned their hearts against you? Who knows whether some day Odysseus may not come back, alone perhaps, or with his following intact, and pay these Suitors out for all their violence? I only wish that bright-eyed Athene could bring herself to show on your behalf some of the loving care she devoted to your illustrious father in the course of those hard campaigns of ours at Troy. For never in my life have I seen the gods display such open affection as Pallas Athene showed in her championship of Odysseus. Ah, if only she would love and care for you like that, some of those gentlemen would soon have all thoughts of courtship knocked out of their heads for ever.'

'Sire,' said the wise Telemachus, 'I see no hope whatever of your forecast proving true. You have conjured up too marvellous a vision: I cannot bear to think of it. And I, for one, dare not expect such happiness, even if it proves to be god's will.'

But Athene rounded on the young man. 'Telemachus,' she exclaimed, 'what a thing to say! However far a man may have strayed, a friendly god could bring him safely home, and that with ease. And for myself I would rather live through untold hardships to get home in the end and see that happy day, than come back and die at my own hearth, as Agamemnon died by the treachery of Aegisthus and his wife. But there again, it is our common lot to die, and the gods themselves cannot rescue even one they love, when Death that stretches all men out lays its dread hand upon him.'

'Mentor,' the wise Telemachus replied, 'let us not discuss these painful matters any more. We can no longer count on my father's return. The gods who never die have already set his feet on the dark path that leads to death. But I should like now to bring up another question and put it to Nestor, whose knowledge of men's ways and thoughts is unrivalled. For they tell me he has been king through three generations, and when I look at him I seem to gaze on immortality itself.' Here Telemachus turned to his host: 'Will your majesty enlighten me again? How did imperial Agamemnon meet his end? Where was Menelaus, and by what cunning snare did that false knave Aegisthus contrive to kill a man far braver than himself? Was Menelaus away from Achaean Argos and wandering abroad? Is that why the coward plucked up the courage to strike?'

'My child,' Gerenian Nestor answered, 'I shall be glad to tell you the whole tale. You can imagine for yourself what would have happened had Agamemnon's brother, red-haired Menelaus, come back from Troy and caught Aegisthus in the house alive. No barrow would have honoured *his* remains! Flung on the plain outside the city walls, he'd have made meat for the dogs and birds of prey, and there's no woman in Achaea who would have shed a tear for him. His was indeed no petty crime. While we that were beleaguering Troy toiled at heroic tasks, he spent his leisured days, right in the heart of Argos where the horses graze, besieging Agamemnon's wife with his seductive talk. At first Queen Clytaemnestra turned a deaf ear to his dishonourable schemes. She was a sensible woman, and besides, she had a man with her, a minstrel by profession, to whom Agamemnon when he left for Troy had given strict orders to watch over his queen. But when the fatal day appointed for her conquest came, Aegisthus took this minstrel to a desert isle, left him there as carrion for the birds of prey and carried Clytaemnestra off to his own house, fond lover, willing dame. This doughty deed accomplished, he heaped the holy altars of the gods with sacrificial meat and plastered the temple walls with splendid gifts of gold brocade, thank-offerings for a success beyond his wildest dreams.

'Meanwhile we were sailing in company over the sea from Troy, Menelaus and I, the best of friends. But when we were abreast of the sacred cape of Sunium, where Attica juts out into the sea, Phoebus Apollo let fly his gentle darts at Menelaus' helmsman and struck him dead, with the steering-oar of the running ship in his hands. This man Phrontis son of Onetor had been the world's best steersman in a gale, and Menelaus, though anxious to proceed, was detained at Sunium till he could bury his comrade with the proper rites. But when he too had got away over the wine-dark sea in those great ships of his and had run as far as the steep bluff of Malea, Zeus, who is always on the watch, took it into his head to give them a rough time, and sent them a howling gale with giant waves as massive and as high as mountains. Then and there he split the fleet into two parts, one of which he drove towards Crete and the Cydonian settlements on the River Iardanus. Now where the lands of Gortyn end, out in the misty sea, there is a smooth rock that falls abruptly to the water, and the south-westerly gales drive the great rollers against a headland to the left, in towards Phaestus, with nothing but this puny reef to keep their violence in check. It was here that the one party made their landfall. The crews by a hair's breadth escaped destruction; their ships were splintered on the rocks by the fury of the seas. Meanwhile Menelaus with the remaining five vessels of his blue-prowed fleet was driven on by wind and wave to Egypt. And so it came about that he was cruising in those distant parts where people talk a foreign tongue, amassing a fortune in goods and gold, while Aegisthus schemed this wickedness at home. After he had killed Agamemnon, the usurper reigned in golden Mycenae and kept the people under his thumb for seven years. But the eighth brought him disaster, in the shape of Orestes; for that brave youth, returning from Athens, killed Aegisthus, his noble father's murderer, and so the slayer was slain. When Orestes had done the deed, he invited his friends to a funeral banquet for the mother he had loathed and the craven Aegisthus; and on the selfsame day he was joined by the veteran Menelaus bringing in all the treasures that had filled his holds.

'Be warned yourself, my friend! Don't stray too long from home, nor leave your wealth unguarded with such a set of scoundrels in the place, unless you want them to share it out, to eat up all you have and to make a farce of your expedition. I do

urge you, however, to pay Menelaus a visit. For he has only just
got back from abroad, and from a region so remote that one
might well give up all hope of return once the winds had blown
one astray into that wide expanse of sea, which is so vast and
perilous that even the birds cannot make their passage in the
year. So off you go now to Menelaus with your ship and crew;
or, if you prefer the land route, I have a chariot and horses at
your disposal and my sons are at your service too, to escort you
to lovely Lacedaemon where the red-haired Menelaus lives.
And see that you approach him in person if you want the truth
from his lips; not that I think you will get anything else from
so intelligent a man as Menelaus.'

As Nestor came to an end, the sun went down and darkness
fell. It was the bright-eyed goddess Athene who spoke next:

'We thank you, sire, for a tale well told. But come, sirs, cut
up the victims' tongues and mix the wine, so that we can pour
out offerings to Poseidon and the other immortals before we
think of sleeping. It is time for bed, now that the light has sunk
into the western gloom. Nor should one linger at a holy feast,
but make an early move.'

It was the Daughter of Zeus who had spoken; her words did
not fall on deaf ears. The squires sprinkled their hands with
water, while the young attendants filled the mixing-bowls to
the brim with drink, and then, after pouring a few drops first in
each man's cup, they served them all with wine. The tongues
were thrown into the flames; the company rose and sprinkled
libations on them. And when they had made their offerings and
drunk their fill, Athene and Prince Telemachus both made a
move to get back to the shelter of their ship. But Nestor stopped
them, protesting loudly:

'God forbid that you should go to your ship and turn your
backs on my house as though it belonged to some threadbare
pauper and there weren't plenty of blankets and rugs in the
place for host and guests to sleep between in comfort! Indeed, I
have good bedding for all; and I swear that the son of my friend
Odysseus shall not lie down to sleep on his ship's deck so long as

I am alive or sons survive me here to entertain all visitors that come to my door.'

'Nobly said, dear father,' replied the goddess of the flashing eyes; 'and Telemachus may well accept your invitation, for nothing could be more agreeable. Let him go off with you now and sleep in your palace, while I return to the black ship to reassure the men and tell them each their duties. For I am the only senior in the party; all the rest are young fellows of much the same age as our gallant Telemachus and follow him for love. I propose to sleep there by the black ship's hull tonight, and in the morning to set out on a visit to those enterprising people, the Cauconians, with whom I have an outstanding claim of some importance to settle. But since my friend here has become your guest, I suggest that you should send him on in a chariot with one of your sons and give him the fastest and strongest horses in your stable.'

As she finished, bright-eyed Athene took the form of a sea-eagle and flew off. They were all confounded at the sight. The old king marvelled as he took it in, and seizing Telemachus' hand saluted him.

'My friend,' he cried, 'no fear that you will ever be a dastard or a knave, when, young as you are, you already have your guardian gods. For of all that live on Olympus, this was no other than the Daughter of Zeus, the august Lady of Triton, who singled out your noble father too for honour among the Argives. My Queen, be gracious to your servant, and vouchsafe good repute to me and to my sons and to my faithful consort. In return you shall have a yearling heifer, broad in the brow, whom no one yet has broken in and led beneath the yoke. She shall be sacrificed to you with gold foil on her horns.'

His prayer reached the ears of Pallas Athene; and now the Gerenian charioteer Nestor led the way towards his stately home, followed by his sons and his daughters' husbands. When they came to the royal palace, they took their places on the settles and chairs, and the old man prepared a bowl of mellow wine for his guests, from a jar that had stood for ten years before

.the maid undid the cap and broached it. When the old king had mixed a bowl of this vintage, he poured a little out, with earnest prayers to Athene, Daughter of Zeus who wears the aegis.

They made their libations and quenched their thirst, after which the rest went off to their several quarters for the night. But the Gerenian horseman Nestor arranged for King Odysseus' son Telemachus to sleep at the palace itself, on a wooden bedstead in the echoing portico, with Peisistratus beside him; for that young spearman and captain was the only unmarried son left to him in the home. The king himself retired to rest in his room at the back of the high building, where the queen his wife made bed and bedding ready for him.

When tender Dawn had brushed the sky with her rose-tinted hands, Gerenian Nestor got up from his bed, went out, and seated himself on a smooth bench of white marble, which stood, gleaming with polish, in front of his lofty doors. Here Neleus once had sat and proved himself a rival of the gods in wisdom; but he had long since met his doom and gone to Hades' Halls. So now Gerenian Nestor sat there in his turn, sceptre in hand, a Warden of the Achaean race. His sons all came from their rooms and gathered round him, Echephron and Stratius, Perseus and Aretus, and the noble Thrasymedes. The young lord Peisistratus came last and made the sixth. Prince Telemachus was ushered to a seat at their side; and Nestor the Gerenian charioteer now made his wishes known:

'Bestir yourselves, my dear sons, and help me to pay my devotions to Athene, who of all gods has the first claim upon them, since it was she who made herself manifest to me at our sumptuous banquet. Go, one of you, to the meadows for a heifer, and get her here without delay, telling the man in charge of the herd to drive her up. And one go down to Prince Telemachus' ship and bring all his crew along but two; while another summons the goldsmith Laerces to the house to gild the heifer's horns. The rest of you stay with me here, and tell the servants indoors to prepare a feast in the palace and to fetch seats, and wood to go round the altar, and a supply of fresh water.'

They all hurried off to carry out his orders. The heifer was brought in from the meadows; Prince Telemachus' crew came up from his good ship; and the smith arrived, equipped with the tools of his trade, the anvil, the hammer, and the sturdy tongs he used for working gold. Athene too attended to accept the sacrifice. Then Nestor the old charioteer gave out the gold, which the smith worked into foil and laid round the heifer's horns by way of embellishment to please the goddess' eye. Next Stratius and Echephron led the heifer forward by the horns, and Aretus came out from the store-room, carrying in his right hand a flowered bowl of lustral water for their use, and in the other a basket with the barley-corns, while the stalwart Thrasymedes, gripping a sharp axe, stood by to cut the victim down, and Perseus held the dish to catch its blood.

The old charioteer Nestor now started the ritual with the lustral water and the scattered grain, and offered up his earnest prayers to Athene as he began the sacrifice by throwing a lock from the victim's head on the fire.

When they had made their petitions and sprinkled the barley-corns, Nestor's son Thrasymedes stepped boldly up and struck. The axe cut through the tendons of the heifer's neck and she collapsed. At this, the women raised their cry, Nestor's daughters and his sons' wives, and his loyal consort Eurydice, Clymenus' eldest daughter. But the men lifted the heifer's head from the trodden earth and held it up while the captain Peisistratus cut its throat. When the dark blood had gushed out and life had left the heifer's bones, they swiftly dismembered the carcass, cut slices off the thighs in ceremonial fashion, wrapped them in folds of fat and laid raw meat above them. These pieces the venerable king burnt on the faggots, while he sprinkled red wine over the flames, and the young men gathered round with five-pronged forks in their hands. When the thighs were burnt up and they had tasted the inner parts, they carved the rest into small pieces, pierced them with skewers and held the sharp ends of the spits to the fire till all was roasted.

In the meantime, the beautiful Polycaste, King Nestor's

youngest daughter, had given Telemachus his bath. When she had bathed him and rubbed him with olive oil, she gave him a tunic and arranged a fine cloak round his shoulders, so that he stepped out of the bath looking like an immortal god. He then went and sat down by Nestor, the shepherd of the people.

When they had roasted the outer flesh and drawn it off the skewers, they took their seats at table, with men of gentle birth to wait on them and fill their golden cups with wine. After they had satisfied their appetite and thirst, the Gerenian charioteer Nestor announced his wishes:

'Up with you now, my lads! Fetch Telemachus a pair of long-maned horses and harness them to a chariot so that he can be getting on his way.'

They obeyed him promptly and soon had a pair of fast horses harnessed to a car, in which the housekeeper packed bread and wine together with dainties of the kind that royal princes eat. Telemachus took his place in the handsome chariot and Nestor's son, the captain Peisistratus, got in beside him, took the reins in his hands, and flicked the horses with the whip to start them. The willing pair flew off towards the plains, putting the high citadel of Pylos behind them, and all day long they swayed the yoke up and down on their necks.

By sundown, when the roads grew dark, they had reached Pherae, where they drove up to the house of Diocles, son of Ortilochus, whose father was Alpheius. There they put up for the night and received the gifts that hospitality dictates. But tender Dawn had hardly touched the East with red when they were harnessing their horses once again and mounting the gaily-coloured chariot. Out past the sounding portico and through the gates they drove. A flick of the whip to make the horses go, and the pair flew on with a will. In due course they came to the wheat plains and attacked the last stage of their journey; such excellent going had their thoroughbreds made. And now the sun sank once more and darkness swallowed all the tracks.

IV

MENELAUS AND HELEN

AND SO they came to the rolling lands of Lacedaemon, deep in
the hills, and drove up to the palace of the illustrious Menelaus.
They found him entertaining a large company of retainers in
his house to celebrate the weddings of his son and of the princess
his daughter. He was sending the princess as a bride to the son of
Achilles, that breaker of the battle-line, for long ago at Troy he
had consented and had given his promise. So now the gods were
making these two man and wife, and Menelaus was dispatching
her with chariot and horses to the capital of the Myrmidons, of
whom her bridegroom was the king. But he had chosen Alec-
tor's daughter, a bride from Sparta itself, for his beloved son,
the gallant Megapenthes, whom a slave had borne to him, when
it was clear that he could hope for no other children from Helen
once she had given him Hermione, that lovely child with golden
Aphrodite's beauty.

They were banqueting then under the high roof of the great
hall, these neighbours and clansmen of the illustrious Menelaus,
and sitting in festive mood, while a minstrel in the company
sang divinely to the lyre, and a couple of acrobats, dancing to
the time he set with his tune, threw cart-wheels in and out
among the guests.

The two travellers, Prince Telemachus and Nestor's noble
son, came to a standstill in their chariot at the courtyard gate.
The lord Eteoneus, who had the arduous post of equerry to the
great Menelaus, happened to come out and see them there, and
he set off at once through the palace to inform the king, in whose
ear he urgently whispered the news:

'May it please your majesty, we have some strangers here
at the gates – a couple of men whom I take by their looks to
be of royal blood. Pray tell me whether we should unharness

their horses for them or send them on for someone else to entertain.'

Red-haired Menelaus answered him indignantly. 'My lord Eteoneus, you have not always been a fool; but at the moment you are talking nonsense like a child. Think of all the hospitality that you and I enjoyed from strangers before we reached our homes and could expect that Zeus might spare us from such pressing need again. Unyoke their horses at once, and bring our visitors into the house to join us at the feast.'

Eteoneus ran off through the hall, shouting to his assistants to look sharp and follow him. They led the horses sweating from the yoke and tied them up at the mangers in the stable, throwing down beside them a feed of spelt mixed with white barley. Then they tilted the chariot against the burnished wall by the gate and ushered the newcomers into the royal buildings. Telemachus and his friend opened their eyes in wonder at all they saw as they passed through the king's palace. It seemed to them that this lofty hall of the sublime Menelaus was lit by something of the sun's splendour or the moon's. When they had feasted their eyes on the sight, they went and bathed in polished baths, and after the maidservants had washed them, rubbed them with oil and dressed them in warm mantles and tunics, they took their places on high chairs at the side of Menelaus son of Atreus. A maid came with water in a beautiful golden ewer and poured it out over a silver basin so that they could rinse their hands. She also drew a wooden table to their side, and the staid house-keeper brought some bread and set it by them with a choice of delicacies, helping them liberally to all she had. Meanwhile a carver dished up for them on platters slices of various meats he had selected from his board, and put gold cups beside them.

Red-haired Menelaus now turned to the pair with a hospit-able gesture and said: 'Fall to, and welcome. After you've dined we shall inquire who you may be. Your pedigree has left a stamp upon your looks that makes me take you for the sons of kings, those sceptred favourites of Zeus, for no mean folk could breed such men as you are.'

As he spoke, he passed them with his own hands the rich piece of roast sirloin that had been given him as the portion of honour, and they helped themselves to the good things spread before them. When they had satisfied their appetite and thirst, Telemachus leant towards Nestor's son and whispered in his ear so that the rest might not hear him:

'Look round this echoing hall, my dear Peisistratus. The whole place gleams with copper and gold, amber and silver and ivory. What an amazing collection of treasures! I can't help thinking that the court of Zeus on Olympus must be like this inside. The sight of it overwhelms me.'

Red-haired Menelaus caught what he was saying and quickly interposed: 'No mortal can compete with Zeus, dear lads. His house and all his belongings are everlasting. But when it comes to men, I feel that few or none can rival me in wealth, considering all the hardships I endured and the journeys I made in the seven years that it took me to amass this fortune and to get it home in my ships. My travels took me to Cyprus, to Phoenicia, and to Egypt. Ethiopians, Sidonians, Erembi, I visited them all; and I saw Libya too, where the lambs are born with sprouting horns and their dams yean three times in the course of the year; where nobody from king to shepherd need go without cheese or meat, or fresh milk either, since all the year ewes have their udders full.

'But while I was wandering in those parts, making my fortune, an enemy of our house struck down my brother, caught off his guard through the treachery of his accursed wife. So it gives me little pleasure to call myself the lord of all this wealth, since, as you must have heard from your fathers, whoever they may be, I have had much sorrow in my life and have already seen the ruin of one lovely dwelling full of precious things. How happy I could be, here in my house, with even a third of my former estate, if those friends of mine were still alive who died long ago on the broad plains of Troy, so far from Argos where the horses graze! And yet, though I miss them all and often grieve for them as I sit here in our halls till sorrow finds relief in tears and the tears cease to fall (so soon does their chill comfort cloy), I do not mourn for that whole company, disconsolate as I am, so much as I lament one man among them, whose loss when I brood over it makes sleep and eating hateful things to me. For of all the Achaeans who toiled at Troy it was Odysseus who toiled the hardest and undertook· the most. Yet all that labour was to end in misery for him, and for me in the haunting consciousness that I have lost a friend, so long has he been gone and left us wondering whether he is dead or not; though I suppose his people are already mourning him for dead, the old man Laertes, clever Penelope, and Telemachus, whom he left a new-born baby in his home.'

Telemachus' grief for his father was made all the more poignant by Menelaus' lament, and when he heard Odysseus' name he let the tears roll down his cheeks to the ground and with both hands held up his purple cloak before his eyes. Menelaus observed him and was left in deep embarrassment, not knowing whether he should wait for the young man himself to mention his father or should cross-examine him forthwith. In the midst of his perplexity, Helen with her ladies came down from her lofty perfumed room, looking like Artemis with her golden distaff. Adreste drew up for her a comfortable chair; Alcippe brought a rug of the softest wool; while Phylo carried her silver work-basket, a gift from Alcandre, wife of Polybus, who lived in Egyptian Thebes, where the houses are furnished in the most sumptuous fashion. This man had given Menelaus two silver baths, a pair of three-legged cauldrons, and ten talents in gold; while in addition his wife gave Helen beautiful gifts for herself, including a golden spindle and a basket that ran on castors and was made of silver finished with a rim of gold. This was the basket that her lady, Phylo, brought and set beside her. It was full of fine-spun yarn, and the spindle with its deep blue wool was laid across it. Helen sat down on the chair, which had a stool below it for her feet, and proceeded at once to find out from her husband what was going on:

'Menelaus, my lord, have we been told the names of these

gentlemen who have come to our house? Shall I keep up a pretence of ignorance, or tell you what I really think? I feel that I must speak. For never in man or woman have I seen such a likeness before. I am so amazed that I cannot take my eyes off the young man. Surely this must be King Odysseus' son Telemachus, whom his father left as a new-born baby in his home, when you Achaeans boldly declared war and took the field against Troy for my sake, shameless creature that I was!'

'Lady,' replied the red-haired Menelaus, 'now that you point out the resemblance I notice it too. Odysseus' feet were just the same, and so were his hands, the way he moved his eyes about, his head and the very hair upon it. Why, only just now when I was talking of Odysseus as I remembered him and saying how much he had done and suffered for my sake, the tears came streaming down his cheeks and he covered his face with his purple cloak.'

Here Nestor's son Peisistratus intervened. 'Sire,' he said, 'your majesty is right in supposing that my friend here is Odysseus' son. But he is modest, and on a first visit like this it would go against the grain with him to thrust himself forward and hold forth before *you*, whose conversation gives us as much pleasure as we should get from listening to a god. So Nestor of Gerenia sent me with him for escort, as Telemachus was anxious to see you, in case you might help him with advice or suggest some line of action. For a son, when his father is gone, has many difficulties to cope with at home, especially if there is no one else to help him, as is the case with Telemachus, whose father is abroad and who has no other friends in the place to protect him from injustice.'

'Who would have thought it!' exlaimed the red-haired Menelaus. 'Here in my own house, the son of my best friend, the friend who undertook all those heroic tasks for love of me! I had meant to favour him above all others of our race when he came back, if an all-seeing Providence had allowed the two of us to get our good ships safely home across the sea. Yes, I'd have emptied one of the towns round here in my own dominions and given him a city in Argos to live in. I'd have built him a house and transplanted him from Ithaca with all his possessions and his son and his people too. We should have lived in the same country and continually met. Nor could anything have intervened to spoil our joy in one another's love, till the darkness of death had swallowed us up. But a jealous god must have thought otherwise, and so decreed that that unhappy man should be the only one who never reached his home.'

Menelaus' words brought them all to the brink of tears. Helen of Argos, child of Zeus, broke down and wept. Telemachus and Menelaus did the same. Nor could Nestor's son keep his eyes dry when he thought of his brother, the sterling Antilochus, whom the splendid son of the bright Dawn had killed. And this was the subject he led up to, as he turned to Menelaus now.

'Sire,' he said, 'whenever your name came up at home in the course of conversation, Nestor my old father used always to speak of you as the wisest of men. And I beg you to be persuaded now by me, if you can possibly contain your grief, since I for one take no delight in weeping as I dine – dawn will come soon enough for that. Not that I grudge the guerdon of a tear to any man who meets his fate and dies. Indeed, what other tribute can one pay to poor mortality than a lock of hair from the head and a tear on the cheek? I have my own dead too, a brother, not by any means the poorest soldier in the Argive camp. You must have met Antilochus, though I never knew him myself, nor even saw him. They say he was the finest man you had, a superb runner and a great fighter too.'

'My friend,' replied the red-haired Menelaus, 'in saying all you said just now, you spoke and acted with the discretion of a man of twice your years. In fact you show the sense I should have looked for in the son of such a father. Good breeding cannot be hidden when a man's father has himself been fortunate in birth and happy in his marriage, like Nestor, lucky from first to last through all his life, and now serenely ageing in his home, with sons about him who combine good spearmanship and brains. Well, let us forget the tearful mood that we had fallen into, and turn our thoughts once more to supper, when they have poured some water on our hands. In the morning Telemachus and I shall have many a long tale to tell one another.'

Asphalion, one of King Menelaus' busy squires, poured water on their hands, and they fell to again on the good fare that was spread before them. Helen, meanwhile, the child of Zeus, had had a happy thought. Into the bowl in which their wine was mixed, she slipped a drug that had the power of robbing grief and anger of their sting and banishing all painful memories. No one that swallowed this dissolved in wine could shed a single tear that day, even for the death of his mother and father, or if they put his brother or his own son to the sword and he were there to see it done. This powerful anodyne was one of many useful drugs which had been given to the daughter of Zeus by an Egyptian lady, Polydamna, the wife of Thon. For the fertile soil of Egypt is most rich in herbs, many of which are wholesome in solution, though many are poisonous. And in medical knowledge the Egyptian leaves the rest of the world behind. He is a true son of Paeeon the Healer.

When Helen had thrown the drug into the wine and seen that their cups were filled, she turned to the company once more and said: 'King Menelaus and my young and noble guests, each of us has his happy times, and each his spells of pain – Zeus sees to that in his omnipotence. Then why not be content to sit at dinner in this hall and see what pleasure we can get by telling tales? I shall begin myself with one that is to the point. It is, of course, beyond me to describe or even number all the daring feats that stand to the credit of the dauntless Odysseus. But here is one marvellous exploit which he had the nerve to conceive and carry through in Troy when you Achaeans were hard put to it at the front. By flogging his own body till it showed all the marks of ill-usage he made himself look like a slave, and with a filthy rag across his back he slunk into the enemy city and explored its streets. It was only by adopting this beggar's disguise that Odysseus, who cut so different a figure by the Achaean ships, could make his way into the town; but he did so, and the Trojans raised no hue and cry. I was the only soul who pierced through his disguise, but whenever I questioned him he was clever enough to evade me. However, the time came when he let me bathe and anoint him, and at last, after I had given him some clothes to wear and solemnly sworn that I would not disclose his name to the Trojans before he returned to the huts by the ships, he gave me full details of the Achaeans' plans. And after killing a number of Trojans with his long sword, he did get back to his friends with a harvest of information. The other women of Troy were loud in their lamentations, but I rejoiced, for I was already longing to go home again. I had suffered a change of heart, repenting the infatuation with which Aphrodite blinded me when she lured me to Troy from my own dear country and made me forsake my daughter, my bridal chamber, and a husband who had all one could wish for in the way of brains and good looks.'

'My dear,' said the red-haired Menelaus, 'your tale was well and truly told. I have wandered far in this world, I have looked into many hearts and heard the counsels of the great, but never have I set eyes on a man of such daring as the indomitable Odysseus. What he did in the Wooden Horse is another example of the man's pluck and resolution. I remember sitting inside it with the pick of the Argive army, waiting to bring havoc and slaughter on the Trojans, when you appeared on the scene, prompted, I can only suppose, by some god who wished to give the victory to Troy, for Prince Deiphobus came with you. Three times you made the circuit of our hollow ambuscade, feeling the outside with your hands, and you challenged all the Argive captains in turn, altering your voice, as you called out the name of each, to mimic that man's wife. Diomedes and I, who were sitting right in the middle with the good Odysseus, heard you calling and were both tempted to jump up and sally forth or give an instant answer from within. But Odysseus held us back and checked our impetuous movement. The rest of the warriors made not a sound, though Anticlus still seemed inclined to give you some reply. But Odysseus clapped his great hands relentlessly on the man's mouth, and saved the whole army thereby, for he held him tight till Pallas Athene had induced you to go away.'

Here Telemachus ventured to address the king: 'Your majesty, it only makes things worse to think that such qualities as these could not shield Odysseus from disaster. A heart of iron would have failed to save him. But now I beg leave for us to retire for the night. It is time that we went to bed and enjoyed a good sleep.'

Hereupon Helen of Argos instructed her maids to put two bedsteads in the portico and to furnish them with fine purple rugs, spread sheets over these, and add some thick blankets on top for covering. Torch in hand, the maids went out of the hall and made the beds, to which an equerry then conducted the guests. And so Prince Telemachus and Nestor's royal son spent the night there in the forecourt of the palace, while Menelaus slept in his room at the back of the high buildings and the lady Helen lay in her long robe by his side.

Dawn had just touched the East with crimson hands, when the warrior Menelaus put on his clothes and rose from bed. He slung a sharp sword from his shoulder, bound a fine pair of sandals on his shapely feet and strode from his bedroom looking like a god. He went straight to Telemachus and, with a word of greeting, took a seat beside him.

'And what,' he asked, 'was the real motive, my lord Telemachus, that brought you here over the wide seas to our pleasant land of Lacedaemon? Was it public business or private affairs? Tell me the truth.'

'King Menelaus,' the wise Telemachus replied, 'I came to find out whether you could give me any news of my father. I am eaten out of house and home, my rich estate has gone to ruin, and my place is packed with a set of scoundrels who spend their days in the wholesale slaughter of my sheep and fatted cattle, and in competing for my mother's hand with an utter disregard for decency. I am here to plead with you in the hope that you will tell me the truth about my father's unhappy end, if by any chance you witnessed it yourself or heard the story from some other wanderer like him. For if ever a man was born for misery, it was he. Do not soften your account out of pity or concern for my feelings, but faithfully describe the scene that met your eyes. I beseech you, if ever my good father Odysseus, in the hard years of war you had at Troy, gave you his word to speak or act on your behalf and made it good, remember what he did, and tell me all you know.'

Red-haired Menelaus was hot with indignation. 'For shame!' he cried. 'So the cowards want to creep into the brave man's bed? It's just as if a deer had put her little unweaned fawns to sleep in a mighty lion's den and gone to range the high ridges and the grassy dales for pasture. Back comes the lion to his lair, and hideous carnage falls upon them all. But no worse than Odysseus will deal out to that gang. Once, in the pleasant isle of Lesbos I saw him stand up to Philomeleides in a wrestling-match and bring him down with a terrific throw which delighted all his friends. By Father Zeus, Athene, and Apollo, that's the Odysseus I should like to see these Suitors meet. A swift death and a sorry wedding there would be for all!

'But to come to your appeal and the questions you asked me – I have no wish to deceive you or to put you off with evasive answers. On the contrary, I shall pass on to you without concealment or reserve every word that I heard myself from the infallible lips of the Old Man of the Sea.

'It happened in Egypt. I had been anxious for some time to get home, but the gods kept me dawdling there, for I had omitted to make them the correct offerings, and they never allow one to forget their rules. There is an island called Pharos in the rolling seas off the mouth of the Nile, a day's sail out for a well-found vessel with a roaring wind astern. In this island is a sheltered cove where sailors come to draw their water from a well and can launch their boats on an even keel into the deep sea. It was here that the gods kept me idle for twenty days; and all that time there was never a sign on the water of the steady breeze that ships require for a cruise across the open sea. All our supplies would have disappeared and the men's strength been exhausted, if one of the gods had not taken pity on me. It was Eidothee, the daughter of the mighty Proteus, the Old Man of the Sea, who came to my rescue. I must have made some special appeal to her compassion when she met me walking by myself, away from my men, whom the pangs of hunger scattered every day round the coast to angle with barbed hooks for fish. For she came right up and accosted me. "Sir," she asked, "are you an utter fool? Are you weak in the head? Or is it because you like hardships and prefer to let things slide that you allow yourself to be cooped up all this time in the island and can find no means of escape though your men are growing weaker day by day?" To which I replied, "I do not know what goddess you may be, but let me assure you that I have no wish to linger here. I can only think that I must have offended the immortals who live in the wide heavens. You gods know everything; so tell me which of you it is that has confined me here and cut my voyage short; and tell me also how I can get home across the playgrounds of the fish."

'The friendly goddess answered me at once: "Sir, I will tell you all you need to know. This island is the haunt of that immortal seer, Proteus of Egypt, the Old Man of the Sea, who owes allegiance to Poseidon and knows the sea in all its depths. He is my father too, so people say. If you could contrive somehow to set a trap and catch him, he would tell you about your journey and the distances to be covered, and direct you home along the highways of the fish. Not only that, but since you are a king he will tell you, if you want to know, all that has happened in your palace, good or bad, while you have been away on your long and arduous travels." "It is surely for you," I answered her, "to think of a way by which we can catch this mysterious old being. I am afraid that he might see me first, or know I am there and keep away. It is none too easy for a man to get the better of a god."

'Once more the kindly goddess undertook to enlighten me. "It is round about high noon," she said, "that the old seer emerges from his native salt, letting a cat's-paw from the West darken the surface to conceal his coming. Once out, he makes for his sleeping place in the shelter of a cave, and those children of the brine, the flippered seals, heave themselves up from the grey surf and go to sleep in herds around him, exhaling the pungent smell of the salt sea depths. Pick three men from your crew with care, the best you have on board, and at daybreak I will lead you to the spot and find you each a place to lie in. But I must tell you how the old sorcerer proceeds. First he will go his round and count the seals; then, when he has counted them and seen that all are there, he will lie down among them like a shepherd with his flocks of sheep. That is your moment. Directly you see him settled, summon all your strength and courage and hold him down however hard he strains and struggles to escape. He will try all kinds of transformations, and change himself not only into every sort of beast on earth, but into water too and blazing fire. But hold him fast and grip him all the tighter. And when he speaks at last and asks you questions in his natural shape, just as he was when you saw him lie down to rest, then, sir, you may relax your pressure, let the old man go, and ask him which god is your enemy and how to get home along the highways of the fish." After giving me this advice she disappeared into the rollers, and I took myself off to the spot where my ships were resting on the sand, with many dark forebodings as I walked along. When I had reached the sea and found my ship, we prepared our supper. The solemn night descended on us and we lay down to sleep on the surf-beaten strand.

'When the new Dawn had flecked the East with red, I set out, with many prayers to heaven, along the shore of the far-flung sea, accompanied by the three men from my crews whom I felt I could rely on most in any emergency.

'Eidothee had vanished under the wide waters of the sea, but she now reappeared, carrying in her arms the skins of four seals, all freshly flayed to decoy her father. She scooped out lairs for us

in the sandy beach and sat down to await our arrival. When we
came up to her, she ensconced us in our places and covered each
man with a skin, thus committing us to what might have been a
very painful ambuscade; for the vile smell of the sea-fed brutes
was peculiarly trying, and I should like to know who would
choose a monster of the deep for bed-fellow. However, the goddess herself thought of a sovran remedy and came to our rescue
with some ambrosia, which she applied to each man's nostrils. It
was sweet-smelling stuff and killed the stench of the seals. So
there we waited patiently right through the morning. And thick
and fast the seals came up from the sea and lay down in companies along the beach to sleep. At midday the old man himself emerged, found his fat seals already there, and went the
rounds to make his count. Entirely unsuspicious of the fraud,
he included us as the first four in his flock. When he had done,
he too lay down to sleep. Then, with a shout, we leapt upon
him and flung our arms round his back. But the old man's
skill and cunning had not deserted him. He began by turning
into a bearded lion and then into a snake, and after that a pan-
ther and a giant boar. He changed into running water too and
a great tree in leaf. But we set our teeth and held him like a
vice.

'When at last he had grown tired of his magic repertory, he
broke into speech and began asking me questions. "Tell me now,
Menelaus," he said, "which of the gods conspired with you to
waylay and capture me? And what have you done it for?" "Old
man," I answered, "this is mere prevarication. You know as
well as I do how long I have been a prisoner on this island, unable to escape and growing weaker every day. So tell me now,
in your divine omniscience, which god it is that has laid me by
the heels and cut my voyage short; and tell me also how I can
get home across the playgrounds of the fish." "You blundered,"
said the old man in reply. "Before embarking, you should have
offered rich sacrifice to Zeus and all the other gods, if you
wished to get home fast across the wine-dark sea. You have no
chance whatever of reaching your own country and seeing your

friends and your fine house again before you have sailed the heaven-fed waters of the Nile once more and made ceremonial offerings to the everlasting gods who live in the broad sky. When that is done, the gods will let you start this voyage that you are so keen to make."

'Now when I heard him tell me once again to make the long and weary trip over the misty seas to Egypt, I was heart-broken. Nevertheless I found my voice and made him this reply: "Old man, I shall do exactly what you advise. But there is something else I wish you to tell me. Did all of my countrymen whom Nestor and I left behind when we sailed from Troy reach home in safety with their ships, or were there any that came to grief in some accident at sea, or died in their friends' arms though the fighting was over?" "Son of Atreus," he replied, "why do you search·me with these questions when nothing compels you to find out and probe into my mind? I warn you that your tears will flow soon enough when you have listened to my tale. For many were killed, though many too were spared. Yet only two of the commanders of your armies lost their lives when home-ward bound – I need not speak of the fighting, since you took part yourself – but there is a third who, though still alive, is a prisoner somewhere in the vastness of the seas. Aias, to take him first, was wrecked in his long-oared galleys by Poseidon, who drove him onto the great cliff of Gyrae and then rescued him from the surf. In fact, he would have evaded his doom, in spite of Athene's enmity, if in his blind folly he had not talked so big, boasting that he had escaped from the hungry jaws of the sea in defiance of the gods. His loud-voiced blasphemy came to the ears of Poseidon, who seized his trident in his powerful hands, struck the Gyraean rock and split it into two. One half stood firm, but the fragment he had severed, where Aias had been resting when the mad impulse took him, crashed into the sea and carried him with it into the vast and rolling depths, where he gulped the salt water down and perished. But your brother contrived somehow to circumvent his fate, and slipped away in his great ships with the Lady Here's help. Yet when he was nearly up with the heights of Cape Malea, a hurricane caught him, and groaning in protest he found himself driven over the fish-infested seas towards the borderland where Thyestes in the old days and now his son Aegisthus had their home. But in due course he saw the chance of a safe return even from there. The wind, veering round as luck would have it, dropped to a breeze, and home they came.

' "Agamemnon set foot on the soil of his fathers with a happy heart, and as he touched it kissed his native earth. The warm tears rolled down his cheeks, he was so glad to see his land again. But his arrival was observed by a spy in a watch-tower, whom Aegisthus had had the cunning to post there with the promise of two talents of gold for his services. This man was on the lookout for a year in case the King should land unannounced, slip by, and himself launch an attack. He went straight to the palace and informed the usurper. Then Aegisthus set his brains to work and laid a clever trap. He selected twenty of the best soldiers from the town, left them in ambush, and after ordering a banquet to be prepared in another part of the building, set out in a horse-chariot to bring home the King, with his heart full of ugly thoughts. Agamemnon, never guessing that he was going to his doom, came up with him from the coast, and Aegisthus feasted and killed him as a man might fell an ox at its manger. Not a single one of the King's following was left, nor of Aegisthus' company either. They were killed in the palace to a man."

'This was his story, and it broke my heart. I sat down on the sands and wept. I had no further use for life, no wish to see the sunshine any more. But when I had had enough of tears and of writhing on the sands, the old Sea Prophet spoke to me again. "Menelaus," he said, "you have wept too long. Enough of this incontinent grief, which serves no useful end. Better bestir yourself to get back to your own land as quickly as you can. For either you will find Aegisthus still alive or Orestes will have forestalled you by killing him, and you may join them at the funeral feast." His words restored my manhood and in spite of my distress I felt once more a glow of comfort in my heart.

'There was one further point which I now insisted on his clearing up. "You have accounted for two," I said. "But who is the third, the one that is still alive but a prisoner somewhere in the vastness of the seas? Or is he dead by now? I wish to hear, whatever sorrow it may cause me." "The third," said Proteus, "is Odysseus, whose home is in Ithaca. I caught a glimpse of him on an island, in the Nymph Calypso's home, with the big tears rolling down his cheeks. She keeps him captive there, for without a galley and crew to carry him so far across the sea it is impossible for him to reach his home. And now, King Menelaus, hear your own destiny. You will not meet your fate and die in Argos where the horses graze. Instead, the immortals will send you to the Elysian plain at the world's end, to join red-haired Rhadamanthus in the land where living is made easiest for mankind, where no snow falls, no strong winds blow and there is never any rain, but day after day the West Wind's tuneful breeze comes in from Ocean to refresh its folk. That is how the gods will deal with Helen's husband and recognize in you the son-in-law of Zeus."

'The old man finished, and sank into the heaving waters of the sea, while I went off towards the ships with my heroic comrades, lost in the black night of my own thoughts as I walked along. Back at my ship beside the water's edge, we set to on our evening meal. Night in her mystery descended on us, and we lay down to sleep on the surf-beaten shore.

'In the first rosy light of Dawn, we got to work and ran our fleet down into the good salt water. We put the masts and sails on board, and trimmed the ships. The crews then climbed in, found their places on the benches, and struck the grey surf with their oars. And so I returned to the heaven-fed waters of the Nile, where I moored, made the proper ritual offerings, and after appeasing the deathless gods built a mound of earth to the everlasting memory of Agamemnon. When all this was done I set out for home, and the immortals sent me a

favourable wind and brought me quickly back to my own beloved land.

'And now, my friend, I invite you to stay on in my palace.
Stay for twelve days or so, and then I'll send you off in style. You
shall have glorious gifts from me – three horses and a splendid
chariot. Into the bargain, I'll give you a lovely cup, to remind
you of me all your life when you make drink-offerings to the
immortal gods.'

'My lord,' Telemachus replied with his usual wisdom, 'please
do not insist on my paying you a lengthy visit. It is true that your
tales and conversation so delight me that I could easily stop with
you for a year and never feel homesick for Ithaca or my people.
But I am afraid my friends must already be tired of waiting for
me in sacred Pylos; and now you are asking me to prolong my
stay. As for the gift you offer me, please make it a keepsake I can
carry. Horses I will not take to Ithaca. I'd rather leave them here
to grace your own stables. For your kingdom is a broad plain,
where clover grows in plenty and galingale is found, with wheat
and rye and the broad-eared white barley; whereas in Ithaca
there is no room for horses to run about in, nor any meadows at
all. It is a pasture-land for goats and more attractive than the sort
of land where horses thrive. None of the islands that slope down
to the sea are rich in meadows and the kind of place where you
can drive a horse. Ithaca least of all.'

These remarks made the warrior Menelaus smile. He patted
Telemachus with his hand and replied in the friendliest tone:
'I like the way you talk, dear lad: one can see that you have the
right blood in your veins. Very well, my liberality shall take another form: it is easily done. You shall have the loveliest and
most precious of the treasures that my palace holds. I'll give you
a mixing-bowl of wrought metal. It is solid silver with a rim of
gold round the top, and was made by Hephaestus himself. I had
it from my royal friend the King of Sidon, when I put up under
his roof on my journey home. That is the present I should like
you to take.'

During this talk of theirs, the guests began to arrive at the

great king's palace. They drove up their own sheep and brought
the wine that was to make them merry, while their bread was
sent in for them by their buxom wives. This was how they prepared for their banquet in Menelaus' hall.

Meanwhile, in front of Odysseus' palace, the Suitors in their
usual free and easy way were amusing themselves with quoits
and javelin-throwing on the levelled ground where we have
seen them at their sports before. Antinous and Prince Eurymachus, the boldest spirits in the gang and its acknowledged
leaders, were sitting by, when Phronius' son Noemon came up
to them with a question for Antinous.

'Have we any idea,' he asked him, 'when Telemachus comes
back from sandy Pylos, or don't we know? He has gone off with
my ship; and I happen to need it, to cross over to Elis, where the
fields are big and I keep a dozen mares. They have some unweaned mules not broken in yet to the work they'll have to do.
I want to drive one off and train him.'

His news filled them with secret consternation, for they had
no notion that Telemachus had gone to Pylos, but thought he
was somewhere in the neighbourhood on the farm, among the
flocks perhaps, or with the swineherd. So now it was Antinous'
turn to question Noemon.

'I want the truth,' he said. 'When did he leave and what young
fellows went with him? Did he pick men from the town or did
he make up a crew from his own serfs and servants, as he easily
might? And here's another point I must clear up; so answer me
carefully. Did he use force and go off with your ship against
your wishes? Or did you let him pitch you some yarn and take
her?'

'I gave her to him,' said Noemon, 'of my own accord. What
would anyone do when asked a favour by a man of his standing
with so much trouble on his mind? It would be very hard to
refuse him. As for the young fellows who went with him,
they're the best men in the place, next to ourselves. For captain,
they had Mentor. I saw him embark – him or some god.

Anyhow it was exactly like him. And that's what puzzles me. I saw the good Mentor here, only yesterday at dawn. Yet he certainly boarded my ship for Pylos that night.'

With this, Noemon went off to his father's house, leaving the two lords fuming with indignation. They made the rest sit round and stop their games, while Antinous, with his usual eloquence, held forth and gave vent to his fury. The man's heart was seething with black passion, and his eyes were like points of flame.

'Damnation take it!' he cried out. 'Here's a fine stroke Telemachus has had the impudence to bring off – this expedition that we swore should come to nothing. With all of us against him, the young puppy calmly sets out, after picking the best men in the place and getting them to launch him a ship! That lad is going to give us trouble by and by, unless the gods are kind to us and clip his wings before he gets much older. However, give me a fast ship and a crew of twenty, and I'll lie up for him in the straits between Ithaca and the bluffs of Samos, and catch him on his way. And a grim ending there'll be to this sea-trip of his in search of his father!'

The others welcomed the idea and abetted him. When all was settled, the meeting rose and they adjourned into the palace.

But it was not long before Penelope got wind of the plot that her lovers were hatching. It was Medon, the herald, who let her know. For while they were putting their heads together in the courtyard, he had been eavesdropping outside and heard all they said. He set straight off through the palace to tell Penelope, who accosted him as he crossed the threshold of her room.

'Herald,' she said, 'what errand have the young lords given you? Is it to tell King Odysseus' maids to drop their work and prepare them a feast? Oh how I hate their love-making and the way they swarm around! They'd never feast again in here, if I could stop them. Yes, the whole gang of you that come here day by day, plundering our larder and my thrifty son's estate. I suppose you never listened years ago when you were children and your fathers told you how Odysseus treated them – never a harsh word, never an injustice to a single person in the place. How different from the usual run of kings, who favour one man, only to oppress the next. Whereas Odysseus never wronged a soul. Which only serves to show up you and your infamy, and proves how easily past kindness is forgotten.'

'My Queen,' replied Medon, who was by no means a villain, 'I only wish that this were the worst of your troubles. Your suitors are planning a far greater and more heinous crime. God grant that they may not succeed! They are all set now on assassinating Telemachus as he comes home from this expedition of his. For I must tell you he has gone to Pylos and Lacedaemon to seek news of his father.'

When Penelope heard this her knees shook underneath her and her heart grew faint. For a long time she found it impossible to speak; her eyes filled with tears; the words stuck in her throat. At length she recovered and could make him some reply.

'But tell me, herald, why has my boy gone?' she asked. 'There was no call whatever for him to venture on these scudding ships that sailors use like chariots, to drive across the sea's immensities. Does he wish his very name to be forgotten in the world?'

The astute Medon replied: 'I do not know whether some god or his own feelings suggested this journey to Pylos, but his purpose was to find out about his father's return, or failing that to learn what end he met.'

Medon went off through the palace. But Penelope was overwhelmed by the anguish that racked her. She had not even the heart to seat herself on one of the many chairs in her apartments, but sank down on the threshold of her lovely room, weeping bitterly, while all the maids of her household young and old stood round her whimpering.

'Listen, my friends,' she said between her sobs. 'Is there a woman of my time whom Zeus has treated worse than me? I had a husband years ago, the best and bravest of our race, a lionhearted man, famous from Hellas to the heart of Argos. That husband I have lost. And now my dear son vanishes from home without a word. I was not even told that he had gone; not even by you, who must have known it well enough. How cruel of you all not to have thought of rousing me from bed when he went to his big black ship! For had I known that he had this journey in mind, I swear he should have stayed, however keen to go, or left me dead at home.

'But make haste, one of you, and call my old servant Dolius, whom my father gave me when I came here and who keeps my orchard now. He shall go straight to Laertes, sit down beside him, and tell him the whole story. Perhaps Laertes may hit upon some scheme and come out of his retreat to plead with the people, who seem intent on wiping out his and Odysseus' royal line.'

'Dear lady,' said Eurycleia, the fond old nurse, 'whether you kill me with the cruel knife or let me live in peace, I cannot hold my tongue. I knew the whole thing: it was I who gave him bread and wine and all he asked for. But he made me solemnly promise not to tell you for a dozen days or till you missed him yourself and found that he had started. He didn't want the tears to spoil your lovely cheeks.

'Come, wash yourself now and put some fresh clothes on. Then go to your room upstairs with your ladies-in-waiting and pray to Athene, Daughter of Zeus. She may still save him, even from the jaws of death. And don't pester an old man who has worries enough already. I cannot believe that the happy gods detest Laertes' line. I'm sure there will always be one of them left to own these lofty halls and the fat fields beyond.'

In this way Eurycleia hushed her sobs and cleared her eyes of tears. So Penelope, when she had washed herself and changed her clothes, went to her room upstairs with the ladies-in-waiting, filled a basket with sacrificial grains, and prayed to Athene:

'Hear me, unsleeping Daughter of Zeus who wears the aegis! If ever Odysseus in his wisdom burnt the fat thighs of a heifer or sheep to honour you in his halls, remember his offerings now, save my dear son for me, and guard him from outrage at the hands of these ruffians.'

At the end of her prayer she uttered a great cry. The goddess heard her petition, while in the shadowy hall the Suitors broke into uproar.

'I do believe,' one of the young roughs called out, 'that our much-courted Queen is going to give us a wedding. Little she knows that her son's death has been arranged.'

This was their boastful way, though it was they who little guessed how matters really stood. Antinous, however, rose up and silenced them.

'You fools!' he cried. 'None of this bragging, or somebody may go indoors and blab. Keep your mouths shut now and disperse. You know the plan we all agreed on. Let's carry it out.'

Without further ado he picked the twenty best men and they left for their ship and the sea-shore, where they began by running the black vessel down into deep water, then put the mast and sail on board, fixed the oars in their leather slings, all ship-shape, and spread the white sail out. Meanwhile their eager squires had brought down their armour. They moored the boat well out in the water and came on shore, where they had their supper and waited for evening to fall.

But prudent Penelope lay there in her upper room, fasting, without taste of sup or crumb, and wondering whether her innocent son would escape death or fall a victim to her arrogant lovers. Doubts and fears chased through her mind as they do through a lion's when he finds himself surrounded by the beaters and stands in terror as they stealthily close in. But at last a genial sense of drowsiness overcame her; she let herself sink back, she fell asleep, and all her limbs relaxed.

Once more, Athene of the flashing eyes seized the occasion to assist. There was another daughter of King Icarius, called Iphthime, who had married Eumelus and lived in Pherae. The goddess made a phantom now, exactly like this woman, and sent it to Odysseus' palace to save the woebegone and weeping queen from more distress and further floods of tears. It crept into her bedroom by the strap that worked the bolt, halted at the head of the bedstead and spoke to her:

'Are you asleep, Penelope, worn out with grief? I do assure you that the gods, who live such easy lives themselves, do not mean you to be so distressed, for it is settled that your son shall come home safe. They have no quarrel with the lad whatever.'

'Sister, what brings you here?' Penelope replied out of her sweet sleep at the Gate of Dreams. 'We are not used to seeing you with us, living as you do so far away. And so you think I should forget my sorrows and all these anxieties that give my mind and heart no rest from pain? As though I had not married and then lost the best and bravest of our race, my noble lion-hearted husband, famous from Hellas to the heart of Argos! And now my beloved son, for whom I grieve even more than for his father, has sailed away in a great ship – a child like him, untrained for action or debate. I tremble for him when I think what they may do to him where he has gone or what may happen to him on the sea. He has so many enemies plotting against him and thirsting to have his blood before he reaches home.'

'Be brave and conquer these wild fears,' said the dim figure in reply. 'He has gone with such escort as any man might pray to have beside him – Pallas Athene in all her power. And it is she who in pity for your grief has sent me here to bring this message to you.'

But the shrewd Penelope had not finished yet. 'If you are really divine,' she said, 'and have heard the voice of god, I beg you to tell me about his unhappy father too. Is he alive somewhere and can he see the sunshine still; or is he dead by now and down in Hades' Halls?'

'Of Odysseus, alive or dead,' said the shadowy phantom, 'I can give you no account. And it does no good to babble empty words.'

With that, it slipped past the bolt by the jamb of the door and was lost in the wind outside. But Icarius' daughter, waking with a start, drew a warm sense of comfort from the vividness of this dream that had flown to her through the early night.

Meanwhile her suitors had embarked and were sailing the

high seas with murder for Telemachus in their hearts. Out in the open strait, midway between Ithaca and the rugged coast of Samos, lies the rocky isle of Asteris, which, small as it is, can offer ships a harbour with two mouths. It was here that the Achaean lords set their ambush for Telemachus.

V

CALYPSO

WHEN Dawn had risen from the bed where she sleeps with the
Lord Tithonus, to bring daylight to the immortals and to men,
the gods sat down in assembly, and were joined by Zeus the
Thunderer, the greatest of them all. The imprisonment of Odysseus in Calypso's home was heavy on Athene's heart, and she
now recalled the tale of his misfortunes to their minds.

'Father Zeus,' she said, 'and you other happy gods who live
for ever, I have come to the conclusion that kindness, generosity, and justice should no longer be the aims of any man who
wields a royal sceptre – in fact that he might just as well devote
his days to tyranny and lawless deeds. Look at Odysseus, that
admirable king! Today, not one of the people he once ruled
like a loving father gives him a single thought. No, he is left to
languish on an island in misery. He is in the Nymph Calypso's
clutches; and she sees that he stays there. Not that he could reach
Ithaca in any case, for he has neither galley nor crew to carry
him so far across the sea. Meanwhile, his beloved son has gone to
sacred Pylos and blessed Lacedaemon for news of his father, and
they mean to murder him on his way back.'

'My child,' replied the Gatherer of the Clouds, 'I never
thought to hear such words from you. Did you not plan the
whole affair yourself? Was it not your idea that Odysseus should
return and settle accounts with these men? As for Telemachus,
you are well able to look after him: use your own skill to bring
him back to Ithaca safe and sound, and let the Suitors sail home
again in their ship with nothing accomplished.'

Zeus now turned to Hermes, his son. 'Hermes,' he said, 'in
your capacity as our Envoy, convey our final decision to that
dainty Nymph. Odysseus has borne enough and must now set
out for home. On the journey he shall have neither gods nor

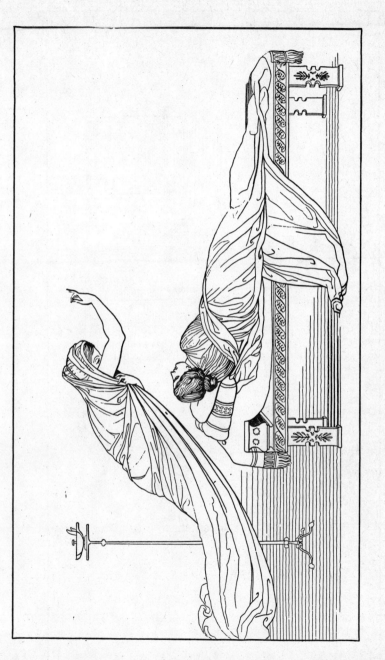

Penelope's dream.

Hermes's message to Calypso.

men to help him. He shall make it in hardship, in a boat put together by his own hands; and on the twentieth day he should
reach Scherie, the rich country of the Phaeacians, our kinsmen,
who will take him to their hearts and treat him like a god. They
will convey him by ship to his own land, giving him copper,
gold, and woven materials in such quantities as he could never
have won for himself from Troy, even if he had come away
unhurt with his share of the spoil. This is how it is ordained that
he shall reach his native land and there step under the high roof
of his house and see his friends once more.'

Zeus had spoken. His Messenger, the Giant-killer, obeyed at
once and bound under his feet the lovely sandals of untarnishable gold that carried him with the speed of the wind over the
water or the boundless earth; and he picked up the wand which
he can use at will to cast a spell upon our eyes or wake us from
the soundest sleep. With this wand in his hand, the mighty
Giant-slayer made his flight. From the upper air he dropped to
the Pierian range, and from there swooped down on the sea, and
skimmed the waves like a sea-mew drenching the feathers of its
wings with spray as it pursues the fish down desolate gulfs of the
unharvested deep. So Hermes rode the unending waves, till at
length he reached the remote island of Ogygia, where he
stepped onto the shore from the blue waters of the sea and
walked along till he reached the great cavern where the Nymph
was living. He found the lady of the lovely locks at home. A big
fire was blazing on the hearth and the scent from burning logs
of split juniper and cedar was wafted far across the island. Inside,
Calypso was singing in a beautiful voice as she wove at the loom
and moved her golden shuttle to and fro. The cave was sheltered
by a verdant copse of alders, aspens, and fragrant cypresses,
which was the roosting-place of feathered creatures, horned
owls and falcons and garrulous choughs, birds of the coast,
whose daily business takes them down to the sea. Trailing round
the very mouth of the cavern, a garden vine ran riot, with great
bunches of ripe grapes; while from four separate but neighbouring springs four crystal rivulets were trained to run this way and

that; and in soft meadows on either side the iris and the parsley flourished. It was indeed a spot where even an immortal visitor must pause to gaze in wonder and delight.

The Messenger stood still and eyed the scene. When he had enjoyed all its beauty, he passed into the great cavern. Calypso, a goddess herself, knew him the moment she raised her eyes to his face, for none of the immortal gods is a stranger to his fellows, even though his home may be remote from theirs. As for King Odysseus, Hermes did not find him in the cave, for he was sitting disconsolate on the shore in his accustomed place, tormenting himself with tears and sighs and heartache, and looking out across the barren sea with streaming eyes.

The divine Calypso invited Hermes to sit down on a brightly polished chair, and questioned her visitor. 'Hermes,' she asked, 'what brings you here with your golden wand? You are an honoured and a welcome guest, though in the past your visits have been few. Tell me what is in your mind, and I shall gladly do what you ask of me, if I can and if it is not impossible. But first follow me inside and let me offer you hospitality.'

The goddess now put some ambrosia on a table, drew it beside him, and mixed him a cup of red nectar. When he had dined and refreshed himself, he answered Calypso's questions:

'As one immortal to another, you ask me what has brought me here. Very well, since you command me, I shall tell you frankly. It was Zeus who sent me. Otherwise I should not have come. For who would choose to scud across that vast expanse of salt sea water? It seemed unending. And not a city on the way, not a mortal soul to offer an attractive sacrifice to a god. But when Zeus, who wears the aegis, makes up his mind, it is impossible for any other god to thwart him or evade his will. And he says that you have with you here a man who has been dogged by misfortune, more so indeed than any of those with whom he shared the nine years of fighting round the walls of Troy and left for home when they had sacked it in the tenth. It appears that in setting out they gave offence to Athene, who raised a gale of wind and heavy seas against them. His loyal followers were lost to a man but he himself was brought here in due course by the winds and waves. And now Zeus bids you send him off without delay. He is not doomed to end his days on this island, away from all his friends. On the contrary, he is destined to see them yet, to reach his native land, and to step beneath the high roof of his house.'

The divine Calypso listened in fear and trembling. When he had done, she unburdened her heart: 'A cruel folk you are, unmatched for jealousy, you gods who cannot bear to let a goddess sleep with a man, even if it is done without concealment and she has chosen him as her lawful consort. You were the same when Rose-fingered Dawn fell in love with Orion. Easy livers yourselves, you were outraged at her conduct, and in the end chaste Artemis rose from her golden throne, attacked him in Ortygia with her gentle darts and left him dead. And so again, when the lovely Demeter gave way to her passion and lay in the arms of her beloved Iasion in the thrice-ploughed fallow field, Zeus heard of it quickly enough and struck him dead with his blinding thunderbolt. And now it is my turn to incur that same divine displeasure for living with a mortal man – a man whom I rescued from death as he was drifting alone astride the keel of his ship, when Zeus had shattered it with his lightning bolt out on the wine-dark sea, and all his men were lost, but he was driven to this island by the wind and waves. I welcomed him with open arms; I tended him; I even hoped to give him immortality and ageless youth. But now, goodbye to him, since no god can evade or thwart the will of Zeus. If Zeus insists that he should leave, let him be gone across the barren water. But he must not expect *me* to transport him. I have no ship, no oars, no crew to carry him so far across the seas. Yet I do promise with a good grace and unreservedly to give him such directions as will bring him safe and sound to Ithaca.'

'Then send him off at once, as you suggest,' said Hermes, 'and so avoid provoking Zeus, or he may be annoyed and punish you one day.' With this the mighty Giant-slayer took his leave.

The Nymph at once sought out her noble guest, for the

message from Zeus had not fallen on deaf ears. She found Odysseus sitting on the shore. His eyes were wet with weeping, as they always were. Life with its sweetness was ebbing away in the tears he shed for his lost home. For the Nymph had long since ceased to please. At nights, it is true, he had to sleep with her under the roof of the cavern, cold lover with an ardent dame. But the days found him sitting on the rocks or sands, torturing himself with tears and groans and heartache, and looking out with streaming eyes across the watery wilderness.

The lovely goddess came and stood beside him now. 'My unhappy friend,' she said, 'as far as I am concerned there is no need for you to prolong your miseries or waste any more of your life on this island. For I am ready with all my heart to help you leave it. But you must be up and doing. Fell some tall trees for timber, make a big boat with the proper tools, and fit it with a deck high enough to carry you across the misty seas. I will stock it myself with bread and water and red wine, all to your taste, so that you need be in no fear of starvation; and I'll give you clothing too, and send you a following wind, so that you may reach your own country without accident, if it please the gods of the broad sky, who have more power to plan and to ordain than I have.'

The stalwart Odysseus shuddered at this and spoke his mind to Calypso. 'Goddess,' he said, 'it is surely not my safe conveyance but some other purpose that you have in mind when you suggest that I should cross this formidable sea, with all its difficulties, in such a craft. Even the fastest sailing-ships don't make the voyage, though they like nothing better than the winds of heaven. So you can take if from me that I shall not entrust myself to a boat, unless I can count on your goodwill. Could you bring yourself, goddess, to give me your solemn oath that you will not plot some new mischief against me?'

Lovely Calypso smiled and stroked him with her hand. 'Odysseus,' she protested, 'what a villain you are to think of such a thing to say! It shows the crafty way your own mind works. Now let Earth be my witness, with the broad Sky above, and the falling waters of Styx – the greatest and most solemn oath the blessed gods can take – that I harbour no secret plans for your discomfiture, but am thinking only of what I should do on my own behalf if I found myself in your plight. For I, after all, have some sense of what is fair; and *my* heart is not a block of iron. I know what pity is.' With these words the gracious goddess moved quickly away, and he followed her lead.

The goddess and the man reached the great cavern together and Odysseus seated himself on the chair that Hermes had just left, while the Nymph laid at his side the various kinds of food and drink that mortal men consume. Then she sat down herself facing her royal guest; her maids set ambrosia and nectar beside her, and the two helped themselves to the dainties spread before them. When they had enjoyed the food and drink, the Lady Calypso resumed their talk:

'So you are determined, Odysseus, my noble and resourceful lord, to leave at once for home and your beloved Ithaca? Well, even so I wish you happiness. Yet had you any inkling of the full measure of misery you are bound to endure before you reach your motherland, you would not move from where you are, but you would stay and share this home with me, and take on immortality, however much you long to see that wife of yours, I know that she is never out of your thoughts. And yet I claim to be by no means her inferior in looks or figure, for surely it would be most unseemly for a woman to compete with a goddess in elegance and looks.'

To this the nimble-witted Odysseus replied: 'My lady goddess, I beg you not to resent my feelings. I too know well enough that my wise Penelope's looks and stature are insignificant compared with yours. For she is mortal, while you have immortality and unfading youth. Nevertheless I long to reach my home and see the happy day of my return. It is my never-failing wish. And what if the powers above do wreck me out on the wine-dark sea? I have a heart that is inured to suffering and I shall steel it to endure that too. For in my day I have had many bitter and shattering experiences in war and on the stormy seas. So let this new disaster come. It only makes one more.'

By now the sun had set and it grew dark. So the two retired to a recess in the cavern and there in each other's arms they spent a night of love.

But the new Dawn had scarcely touched the East with red before Odysseus put his cloak and tunic on. The Nymph dressed herself too in a long silvery mantle of a light material charming to the eye, with a splendid golden belt round her waist, and a veil over her head. Then she turned her thoughts to the problem of her noble guest's departure. First she gave him a great axe of bronze. Its double blade was sharpened well, and the shapely handle of olive-wood fixed firmly in its head was fitted to his grip. Next she handed him an adze of polished metal; and then led the way for him to the farthest part of the island, where the trees grew tall, alders and poplars and firs that shot up to the sky, all withered timber that had long since lost its sap and would make buoyant material for his boat. When she had shown him the place where the trees were tallest the gracious goddess left for home, and Odysseus began to cut the timber down. He made short work of the task. Twenty trees in all he felled, and lopped their branches with his axe; then trimmed them in a workmanlike manner and trued them to the line. Presently Calypso brought him augers. With these he drilled through all his planks, cut them to fit across each other, and fixed this flooring together by means of dowels driven through the interlocking joints, giving the same width to his boat as a skilled shipwright would choose in designing the hull for a broad-bottomed trading vessel. He next put up the decking, which he fitted to ribs at short intervals, finishing off with long gunwales down the sides. He made a mast to go in the boat, with a yard fitted to it; and a steering-oar too, to keep her on her course. And from stem to stern he fenced her sides with plaited osier twigs and a plentiful backing of brushwood, as some protection against the heavy seas. Meanwhile the goddess Calypso had brought him cloth with which to make the sail. This he manufactured too; and then lashed the braces, halyards, and sheets in their places on board. Finally he dragged her down on rollers into the tranquil sea.

By the end of the fourth day all his work was done, and on the fifth beautiful Calypso saw him off from the island. The goddess had bathed him first and fitted him out with fragrant clothing. She had also stowed two skins in his boat, one full of dark wine, the other and larger one of water, besides a leather sack of corn and quantities of appetizing meats. And now a warm and gentle breeze sprang up at her command.

It was with a happy heart that the good Odysseus spread his sail to catch the wind and used his seamanship to keep his boat straight with the steering-oar. There he sat and never closed his eyes in sleep, but kept them on the Pleiads, or watched Bootes slowly set, or the Great Bear, nicknamed the Wain, which always wheels round in the same place and looks across at Orion the Hunter with a wary eye. It was this constellation, the only one which never bathes in Ocean's Stream, that the wise goddess Calypso had told him to keep on his left hand as he made across the sea. So for seventeen days he sailed on his course, and on the eighteenth there hove into sight the shadowy mountains of the Phaeacians' country, which jutted out to meet him there. The land looked like a shield laid on the misty sea.

But now Poseidon, Lord of the Earthquake, who was on his way back from his visit to the Ethiopians, observed him from the distant mountains of the Solymi. The sight of Odysseus sailing over the seas added fresh fuel to his anger. He shook his head and muttered to himself: 'So I had only to go to Ethiopia for the gods to change their minds about Odysseus! And there he is, close to the Phaeacians' land, where he is destined to bring his long ordeal to an end. Nevertheless I mean to let him have his bellyful of trouble yet.'

Whereupon he marshalled the clouds and seizing his trident in his hands stirred up the sea. He roused the stormy blasts of every wind that blows, and covered land and water alike with a canopy of cloud. Darkness swooped down from the sky. East Wind and South and the tempestuous West fell to on one another, and from the North came a white squall, rolling a great wave in its van. Odysseus' knees shook and his spirit quailed. In anguish he communed with that great heart of his:

'Poor wretch, what will your end be now? I fear the goddess prophesied all too well when she told me I should have my full measure of agony on the sea before I reached my native land. Every word she said is coming true, as I can tell by the sky, with its vast coronet of clouds from Zeus, and by the sea that he has raised with angry squalls from every quarter. There is nothing for me now but sudden death. They are the lucky ones, those countrymen of mine who fell long ago on the broad plains of Troy in loyal service to the sons of Atreus. If only I too could have met my fate and died that day the Trojan hordes let fly at me with their bronze spears over Achilles' corpse! I should at least have had my burial rites and the Achaeans would have spread my fame abroad. But now it seems I was predestined to a villainous death.'

As he spoke, a mountainous wave, advancing with majestic sweep, crashed down upon him from above and whirled his vessel round. The steering-oar was torn from his hands, and he himself was tossed off the boat, while at the same moment the warring winds joined forces in one tremendous gust, which snapped the mast in two and flung the sail and yard far out into the sea. For a long time Odysseus was kept under water. Weighed down by the clothes which the goddess Calypso had given him, he found it no easy matter to fight his way up against the downrush of that mighty wave. But at last he reached the air and spat out the bitter brine that kept streaming down his face. Exhausted though he was, he did not forget his boat, but raced after her through the surf, scrambled up, and squatting amidships felt safe from immediate death. The heavy seas thrust him with the current this way and that. As the North Wind at harvest-time tosses about the fields a ball of thistles that have stuck together, so did the gusts drive his craft hither and thither over the sea. Now the South Wind would toss it to the North to play with, and now the East would leave it for the West to chase.

But there was a witness of Odysseus' plight. This was the

daughter of Cadmus, Ino of the slim ankles, who was once a woman speaking like ourselves, but now lives in the salt depths of the sea, and, as Leucothoe, has been acknowledged by the gods. She took pity on the forlorn and woebegone Odysseus, rose from the water like a sea-mew on the wing, and settled on his boat.

'Poor man,' she said to him, 'why is Poseidon so enraged with you that he sows nothing but disasters in your path? At any rate he shall not kill you, however hard he tries. Now do exactly what I say, like the sensible man you seem to be. Take off those clothes, leave your boat for the winds to play with, and swim for your life to the Phaeacian coast, where deliverance awaits you. Here; take this veil and wind it round your waist. With its divine protection you need not be afraid of injury or death. But directly you touch the dry land with your hands, undo the veil and throw it far out from shore into the wine-dark sea; and as you do so turn your eyes away.'

As she spoke the goddess gave him the veil, and then like a mew she dived back into the turbulent sea and the dark waters swallowed her up. Stalwart Odysseus was left in perplexity and distress, and once more took counsel with his indomitable soul, asking himself with a groan whether this advice to abandon his boat was not some new snare that one of the immortals had set to catch him.

'No,' he decided; 'I will not leave the boat at once, for I saw with my own eyes how far the land is where she promised me salvation. Instead, I shall do what I myself think best. As long as the joints of my planks hold fast, I shall stay where I am and put up with the discomfort. But when the seas break up my boat, I'll swim for it, since, as far as I can see, there will be no better plan.'

As Odysseus was turning this over in his mind, Poseidon the Earthshaker sent him another monster wave. Grim and menacing it curled above his head, then hurtled down and scattered the long timbers of his boat, as a boisterous wind will tumble a parched heap of chaff and scatter it in all directions. Odysseus scrambled onto one of the beams, and bestriding it like a rider on horseback cast off the clothes that Calypso had given him. Then he wound the veil round his middle, and with arms outstretched plunged headlong into the sea and boldly struck out.

But the Lord Poseidon spied him again and once more shook his head and muttered low: 'So much for you! Now make your miserable way across the sea, until you come into the hands of a people whom the gods respect. Even though you reach them, I do not think you'll be in any mood to scoff at the buffeting you will have had.' With this, Poseidon lashed his long-maned horses and drove to Aegae, where he has his palace.

At this point Athene, Daughter of Zeus, decided to intervene. She checked all the other Winds in their courses, bidding them calm down and go to sleep; but from the North she summoned a strong breeze, with which she beat the waves down in the swimmer's path, so that King Odysseus might be rescued from the jaws of death and come into the hands of the sea-faring Phaeacians.

For two nights and two days he was lost in the heavy seas. Time and again he saw his end at hand. But in the morning of the third day, which Dawn opened in all her beauty, the wind dropped, a breathless calm set in, and Odysseus, keeping a sharp lookout ahead as he was lifted by a mighty wave, could see the land close by. He felt all the relief that a man's children feel when their father, wasted by long agonies abed in the malignant grip of some disease, passes the crisis by god's grace and they know that he will live. Such was Odysseus' happiness when he caught that unexpected glimpse of wooded land. He swam quickly on in his eagerness to set foot on solid ground. But when he had come within call of the shore, he heard the thunder of surf on a rocky coast. With an angry roar the great seas were battering at the ironbound land and all was veiled in spray. There were no coves, no harbours that would hold a ship; nothing but headlands jutting out, sheer rock, and jagged reefs. When he realized this, Odysseus' knees quaked and his courage ebbed. He groaned in misery as he summed up the situation to himself:

'When I had given up hope, Zeus let me see the land, and I have taken all the trouble to swim to it across those leagues of water, only to find no way whatever of getting out of this grey surf and making my escape. Off shore, the pointed reefs set in a raging sea; behind, a smooth cliff rising sheer; deep water near in; and never a spot where a man could stand on both his feet and get to safety. If I try to land, I may be lifted by a roller and dashed against the solid rock – in which case I'd have had my trouble for nothing. While, if I swim farther down the coast on the chance of finding a natural harbour where the beaches take the waves aslant, it is only too likely that another squall will pounce on me and drive me out to join the deep-sea fish, where all my groans would do no good. Or some monster might be inspired to attack me from the depths. Amphitrite has a name for mothering plenty of such creatures in her seas; and I am well aware how the great Earthshaker detests me.'

This inward debate was cut short by a tremendous wave which swept him forward to the rugged shore, where he would have been flayed and all his bones been broken, had not the bright-eyed goddess Athene put it into his head to dash in and lay hold of a rock with both his hands. He clung there groaning while the great wave marched by. But no sooner had he escaped its fury than it struck him once more with the full force of its backward rush and flung him far out to sea. Pieces of skin stripped from his sturdy hands were left sticking to the crag, thick as the pebbles that stick to the suckers of a squid when he is torn from his hole. The great surge passed over Odysseus' head and there the unhappy man would have come to an unpredestined end, if Athene had not inspired him with a wise idea. Getting clear of the coastal breakers as he struggled to the surface, he now swam along outside them, keeping an eye on the land, in the hope of lighting on some natural harbour with shelving beaches. Presently his progress brought him off the mouth of a fast-running stream, and it struck him that this was the best spot he could find, for it was not only clear of rocks but sheltered from the winds. The current told him that he was at a river's mouth, and in his heart he prayed to the god of the stream:

'Hear me, although I do not know your royal name; for in you I find the answer to all the prayers I have made for deliverance from the sea and from Poseidon's malice. Even the immortal gods do not rebuff a poor wanderer who comes to them for help, as I now turn to you after much suffering and seek the sanctuary of your stream. Take pity on me, royal River. I claim a suppliant's rights.'

In answer to his prayer the River checked its current, and holding back its waves made smooth the water in the swimmer's path, and so brought him safely to land at its mouth. Odysseus bent his knees and sturdy arms, exhausted by his struggle with the sea. All his flesh was swollen and streams of brine gushed from his mouth and nostrils. Winded and speechless he lay there too weak to stir, overwhelmed by his terrible fatigue. Yet directly he got back his breath and came to life again, he unwound the goddess' veil from his waist and let it drop into the river as it rushed out to sea. The strong current swept it downstream and before long it was in Ino's own hands. Odysseus turned his back on the river, threw himself down in the reeds and kissed the bountiful earth.

And now he grimly faced his plight, wondering, with a groan, what would happen to him next and what the end of this adventure would be. 'If I stay in the river-bed,' he argued, 'and keep awake all through the wretched night, the bitter frost and drenching dew together might well be too much for one who has nearly breathed his last through sheer exhaustion. And I know what a cold wind can blow up from a river in the early morning. If, on the other hand, I climb up the slope into the thick woods and lie down in the dense undergrowth to sleep off my chill and my fatigue, then, supposing I do go off into a sound sleep, there is the risk that I may make a meal for beasts of prey.'

However, in the end he decided that this was the better course and set off towards the wooded ground. Not far from the river he found a copse with a clear space all round it. Here he crept under a pair of bushes, one an olive, the other a wild olive, which grew from the same stem with their branches so closely inter-twined that when the winds blew moist not a breath could get inside, nor when the sun shone could his rays penetrate their shade, nor could the rain soak right through to the earth. Odys-seus crawled into this shelter, and after all he had endured was delighted to see the ground littered with an abundance of dead leaves, enough to provide covering for two or three men in the hardest winter weather. He set to work with his hands and scraped up a roomy couch, in the middle of which he lay down and piled the leaves over himself, covering his body as carefully as a lonely crofter in the far corner of an estate buries a glowing brand under the black ashes to keep his fire alive and save him-self from having to seek a light elsewhere. And now Athene filled Odysseus's eyes with sleep and sealed their lids – the surest way to relieve the exhaustion caused by so much toil.

VI

NAUSICAA

WHILE the noble, much-enduring Odysseus, conquered by sleep and worn out by his exertions, lay resting there, Athene came to the country of the Phaeacians and entered their city. These Phaeacians had once lived in the broad lands of Hypereie, and been neighbours to the Cyclopes, a quarrelsome people, who took advantage of their greater strength to plague them, till the day when their king, Nausithous, made them migrate and settled them in Scherie, far from the busy haunts of men. There he laid out the walls of a new city, built them houses, put up temples to the gods, and allotted the land for cultivation. But he had met his fate long since and gone to Hades' Halls; and it was now the divinely-inspired Alcinous who ruled them. To his palace the bright-eyed goddess Athene made her way, still intent on her plans for King Odysseus' restoration.

The good King Alcinous had a young daughter called Nausicaa, tall and beautiful as a goddess. She was asleep now in her richly-furnished room, with two of her ladies, both blest with beauty by the Graces, lying by the door-posts, one on either side. The polished doors were closed; but Athene swept through like a breath of air to the girl's bed, leant over the head of it and spoke to her disguising herself as the daughter of a ship's captain named Dymas, a woman of Nausicaa's own age and one of her bosom friends.

'Nausicaa,' said bright-eyed Athene, imitating her friend's voice, 'how did your mother come to have such a lazy daughter as you? Look at the lovely clothing you allow to lie about neglected, although you may soon be married and stand in need of beautiful clothes, not only to wear yourself but to provide for your bridegroom's party. It's this kind of thing that gives a girl a good name in the town, besides pleasing her father and her mother. Let us go and do some washing together the first thing in the morning. I offer to go with you and help, so that you can get yourself ready as soon as possible, for you certainly won't remain unmarried long. Why, every nobleman in the place wants you for his wife, you, a Phaeacian princess. Do ask your royal father in the morning to have a waggon made ready for you with a couple of mules. These waistbands and robes, and glossy wraps could go in it, and it would be much more comfortable for you yourself to drive than to go on foot, as it's a long way from the city to the washing-pools.'

When she had finished, Athene of the flashing eyes withdrew to Olympus, where people say the gods have made their everlasting home. Shaken by no wind, drenched by no showers, and invaded by no snows, it is set in a cloudless sea of limpid air with a white radiance playing over all. There the happy gods spend their delightful days, and there the Lady of the Bright Eyes went when she had explained her wishes to the girl.

Soon after, Dawn enthroned herself in the sky, and Nausicaa in her lovely gown awoke. She was amazed at her dream and set out at once through the palace to tell her father and her mother. She found them both in the house. Her mother was sitting at the hearth with her maids, spinning yarn stained with sea-purple; and she caught her father just as he was going out to join his princely colleagues at a conference to which he was called by the Phaeacian nobles. She went as close to him as she could and said:

'Father dear, I wonder if you could tell them to get me a big waggon with strong wheels, so that I can take all the fine clothes that I have lying dirty here to the river to wash? And indeed it is only decent for you yourself when you are discussing affairs of state with important people to have clean linen on your back. Then again, there are five sons of yours in the palace, two of them married, while three are merry bachelors who are always asking for clothes straight from the wash to wear at dances. It is I who have to think of all these things.'

She spoke in this way because she was too shy to mention her marriage to her father. But he understood her thoroughly and replied:

'I don't grudge you the mules, my child, or anything else. You may go; and the servants shall get you a fine big waggon with a hood to it.'

He called to his men and they set to work. While they prepared a smooth-running mule-cart outside the house, led the mules under the yoke and harnessed them to the vehicle, Nausicaa fetched the gay clothing from the store-room. She then packed it in the polished waggon, while her mother filled a box with various kinds of appetizing provisions and dainties to go with them, and poured some wine into a goatskin bottle. The girl climbed into the cart and her mother handed her a golden flask of soft olive-oil, so that she and her maids could anoint themselves after bathing. And now Nausicaa took the whip and the glistening reins, and flicked the mules to make them go. There was a clatter of hooves, and then they stepped out bravely, taking the clothes and their mistress along. But as her maids followed and kept her company, she was not left to go alone.

In due course they reached the noble river with its never-failing pools, in which there was enough clear water always bubbling up and swirling by to clean the dirtiest clothes. Here they turned the mules loose from under the yoke and drove them along the eddying stream to graze on the sweet grass. Then they lifted the clothes by armfuls from the cart, dropped them into the dark water and trod them down briskly in the troughs, competing with each other in the work. When they had rinsed them till no dirt was left, they spread them out in a row along the sea-shore, just where the waves washed the shingle clean when they came tumbling up the beach. Next, after bathing and rubbing themselves with olive-oil, they took their meal at the riverside, waiting for the sunshine to dry the clothes. And presently, when mistress and maids had all enjoyed their food, they threw off their headgear and began playing with a ball, while Nausicaa of the white arms led them in their song. It was just such a scene as gladdens Leto's heart, when her Daughter,

Artemis the Archeress, has come down from the mountain along the high ridge of Taygetus or Erymanthus to chase the wild boar or the nimble deer, and the Nymphs of the countryside join with her in the sport. They too are heaven-born, but Artemis overtops them all, and where all are beautiful there is no question which is she. So did this maiden princess stand out among her ladies.

When the time came for Nausicaa to set out for home after yoking the mules and folding up the clothes, the bright-eyed goddess Athene intervened once more and arranged for Odysseus to wake up and see this lovely girl who was to serve as his escort to the Phaeacian city. Accordingly, when the princess passed the ball to one of her maids, she missed her and dropped it instead into the deep and eddying current. At this they all gave a loud shriek. The good Odysseus awoke, and sitting up took counsel with himself.

'Alas!' he sighed. 'What country have I come to now? What people are there here? Some brutal tribe of lawless savages, or kindly and god-fearing folk? And what is this shrill echo in my ears, as though some girls were shrieking? Nymphs, I suppose – who haunt the steep hill-tops, the springs of rivers, and the grassy meadows. Or am I within hail, by any chance, of human beings who can talk as I do? Well, I must go and use my own eyes to find out.'

So the gallant Odysseus crept out from under the bushes, after breaking off with his great hand a leafy bough from the thicket to conceal his naked manhood. Then he advanced on them like a mountain lion who sallies out, defying wind and rain in the pride of his power, with fire in his eyes, to hunt the oxen or the sheep, to stalk the roaming deer, or to be forced by hunger to besiege the very walls of the homestead and attack the pens. The same urgent need now constrained Odysseus, naked as he was, to bear down upon these gentle girls. Begrimed with salt he made a gruesome sight, and one look at him sent them scuttling in every direction along the jutting spits of sand. Alcinous' daughter was the only one to stand firm. Emboldened by

Athene, who stopped her limbs from trembling, she checked herself and confronted him, while Odysseus considered whether he should throw his arms round the beautiful girl's knees and so make his prayer, or be content to keep his distance and beg her with all courtesy to give him clothing and direct him to the city. After some hesitation he decided that as the lady might take offence if he embraced her knees it would be better to keep his distance and politely plead his case. In the end, his address was not only disarming but full of subtlety:

'Mistress, I throw myself on your mercy. But are you some goddess or a mortal woman? If you are one of the gods who live in the sky, it is of Artemis, the Daughter of almighty Zeus, that your beauty, grace, and stature most remind me. But if you are one of us mortals who live on earth, then lucky indeed are your father and your gentle mother; lucky, your brothers too. How their hearts must glow with pleasure every time they see their darling join the dance! But he is the happiest of them all who with his wedding gifts can win you for his home. For never have I set eyes on such perfection in man or woman. I worship as I look. Only in Delos have I seen the like, a fresh young palm-tree shooting up by the altar of Apollo, when my travels took me there – with a fine army at my back, that time, though the expedition was doomed to end so fatally for me. I remember how long I stood spellbound at the sight, for no lovelier sapling ever sprang from the ground. And it is with just the same wonder and veneration that I look at you, my lady; with such awe, indeed, that I dare not clasp your knees, though my troubles are serious enough. Only yesterday, after nineteen days of it, I made my escape from the wine-dark sea. It took all that time for the waves and the tempestuous winds to carry me here from the island of Ogygia. And now some god has flung me on this shore, no doubt to suffer more disasters here. For I have no hope that my troubles are coming to an end: the gods have plenty in store for me before that can be. Pity me, my queen. You are the first person I have met after all I have been through, and I do not know a soul in this city or this land. I beg you to direct me to the town and to give me some rag to put round myself, if only the wrapper you may have brought for your linen when you came. And in return may the gods grant you your heart's desire; may they give you a husband and a home, and the harmony that is so much to be desired, since there is nothing nobler or more admirable than when two people who see eye to eye keep house as man and wife, confounding their enemies and delighting their friends, as they themselves know better than anyone.'

'Sir,' said the white-armed Nausicaa, 'your manners prove that you are no rascal and no fool; and as for these ordeals of yours, they must have been sent you by Olympian Zeus, who follows his own will in dispensing happiness to people whatever their merits. You have no choice but to endure. But since you have come to our country and our city here, you certainly shall not want for clothing or anything else that an unfortunate outcast has the right to expect from those he approaches. I will show you to the town and tell you who we are. This country and the city you will see belong to the Phaeacians. I myself am the daughter of King Alcinous, who is the head and mainstay of our state.'

Here she turned and called out her orders to the gentlewomen in attendance: 'Stop, my maids. Where are you flying to at the sight of a man? Don't tell me you take him for an enemy, for there is no man on earth, nor ever will be, who would dare to set hostile feet on Phaeacian soil. The gods are too fond of us for that. Remote in this sea-beaten home of ours, we are the outposts of mankind and come in contact with no other people. The man you see is an unfortunate wanderer who has strayed here, and now commands our care, since all strangers and beggars come under the protection of Zeus, and the charity that is a trifle to us can be precious to others. Bestir yourselves, girls, provide our guest with food and drink, and bathe him in the river where there's shelter from the wind.'

The rebuke from their mistress checked the women's flight. They called halt to each other, and then found Odysseus a seat in the sheltered spot that the Princess Nausicaa had pointed out.

On the ground beside him they laid a cloak and tunic for him to wear, and giving him some soft olive-oil in a golden flask they suggested that he should wash himself in the running stream. But the gallant Odysseus demurred.

'Ladies,' he said, 'be good enough to stand back over there and leave me to wash the brine myself from my shoulders and rub my body with olive-oil, to which it has long been a stranger. I am not going to take my bath with you looking on. I should be ashamed to stand naked in the presence of gentlewomen.'

At this the maids withdrew and told their young mistress what had occurred. Meanwhile Odysseus was cleaning himself with river-water of the salt that encrusted his back and his broad shoulders, and scrubbing his head free of the scurf left there by the barren brine. When he had thoroughly washed and rubbed himself with oil and had put on the clothes which the young girl had given him, Athene, Daughter of Zeus, made him seem taller and sturdier than ever and caused the bushy locks to hang from his head thick as the petals of the hyacinth in bloom. Just as a craftsman trained by Hephaestus and herself in the secrets of his art takes pains to put a graceful finish to his work by over-laying silver-ware with gold, she finished now by endowing his head and shoulders with an added beauty. When Odysseus retired to sit down by himself on the sea-shore, he was radiant with comeliness and grace. Nausicaa gazed at him in admiration and said to her fair attendants:

'Listen, my white-armed maids, while I tell you what I have been thinking. This man's arrival among the Phaeacians, who are so near the gods themselves, was not unpremeditated by the Olympian powers. For when first we met I thought he cut a sorry figure, but now he looks like the gods who live in heaven. That is the kind of man whom I could fancy for a husband, if he would settle here. I only hope that he will choose to stay. But come, girls, give the stranger something to eat and drink.'

Her maids at once carried out her orders and set food and drink before the stalwart Odysseus, who ate and drank with avidity, for it was a long time since he had tasted any food.

Meanwhile Nausicaa of the white arms had come to a decision. After folding up the clothing, she stowed it in her fine waggon, harnessed the sturdy mules, and herself climbed in. Then she called to Odysseus and gave him his instructions.

'Come, sir,' she said, 'it is time for you to make a move towards the city, so that I may direct you to my good father's house, where you can count on meeting all the Phaeacian nobility. But this is how you must manage – and I take you for a man of tact. So long as we are passing through the country and the farmers' lands, walk quickly with my maids behind the waggon and the mules, following my lead. But that will not do when we come to town.

'Our city is surrounded by high battlements; it has an excellent harbour on each side and is approached by a narrow causeway, where the curved ships are drawn up to the road and each owner has his separate slip. Here is the people's meeting-place, built up on either side of the fine temple of Poseidon with blocks of quarried stone bedded deeply in the ground. It is here too that the sailors attend to the rigging of the black ships, to their cables and their sails, and the smoothing of their oars. For the Phaeacians have no use for the bow and quiver, but spend their energy on masts and oars and on the graceful craft they love to sail across the foam-flecked seas.

'Now it is the possibility of unpleasant talk among these sailors that I wish to avoid. I am afraid they might give me a bad name, for there are plenty of vulgar fellows in the place, and I can well imagine one of the baser sort saying after he had seen us: "Who is this tall and handsome stranger Nausicaa has in tow? Where did she run across him? Her future husband no doubt! She must have rescued some shipwrecked foreigner who had strayed this way, since we have no neighbours of our own. Or perhaps some god has answered her importunate prayers and stooped from heaven to make her his for ever. And it is better so, better that she should venture out herself and find a husband from abroad. For she obviously despises her countrymen here, though so many of the best would like to marry her."

That is how they will talk, and my good name would suffer. Indeed I should blame any girl who acted so, with her parents alive, running away from her friends to consort with men before she was properly married.

'So you, sir, had best take note of my directions, if you wish to make sure of being sent home by my father with the least possible delay. You will see near the path a fine poplar wood sacred to Athene, with a spring welling up in the middle and a meadow all round. That is where my father has his royal park and vegetable garden, within call of the city. Sit down there and wait awhile till we get into the town and reach my father's house. When you think we have had time to do so, go into the city yourself and ask for the palace of my father, King Alcinous. It is quite easy to recognize: any little child could show it you. For the houses of the rest are not built in anything like the style of Lord Alcinous' mansion. Directly you have passed through the courtyard and into the buildings, walk quickly through the great hall till you reach my mother, who generally sits in the firelight by the hearth, weaving yarn stained with sea-purple, and forming a delightful picture, with her chair against a pillar and her maids sitting behind. My father's throne is close to hers, and there he sits drinking his wine like a god. Slip past him and clasp my mother's knees if you wish to make certain of an early and happy return to your home, however far you may have strayed. For, once you have secured her sympathy, you may confidently expect to get back to your motherland and to walk once more into your own fine house and see your friends again.'

When she had finished, Nausicaa used her glistening whip on the mules, and they soon left the flowing river behind them, swinging along at a steady trot. But the princess kept them to a pace which allowed the maids and Odysseus to keep up with her on foot, and used her judgement in laying on the whip. As the sun was setting they reached the well-known grove that bore Athene's name. Here the good Odysseus sat down and proceeded to offer up a prayer to the Daughter of almighty Zeus.

'Listen to me, unsleeping child of Zeus who wears the aegis, and hear my prayer this time, though you turned a deaf ear to me the other day, when I was shipwrecked and the great Earth-shaker broke me up. Grant that the Phaeacians may receive me with kindness and compassion.'

Pallas Athene heard his prayer but still refrained from appear-ing before him, out of deference to her Father's Brother, who persisted in his rancour against the noble Odysseus till the very day when he reached his own land.

VII

THE PALACE OF ALCINOUS

WHILE the much-enduring Odysseus was praying in Athene's grove, the two sturdy mules brought the princess to the city. When she reached her father's palace, she drew up at the entrance, and her handsome brothers gathered round her, unharnessed the mules from the cart, and carried the clothes indoors. She herself retired to her own apartments, where a fire was lit for her by the chambermaid Eurymedusa, an old Aperaean woman whom they had brought years before from Aperaea in their rolling ships and selected as a prize for Alcinous, the King of all Phaeacian folk and idol of the people. It was this woman who looked after the white-armed Nausicaa at home, and who now busied herself with the lighting of the fire and preparations for her mistress' supper in the inner room.

Meanwhile Odysseus started for the town. Athene, in her concern for his welfare, enveloped him in a thick mist, to ensure him against insult or challenge from any truculent Phaeacian who might cross his path. He was just about to go into the pleasant town when the bright-eyed goddess herself came to meet him, disguised as a young girl carrying a pitcher, and halted in his way.

'My child,' said Odysseus, 'I wonder if you could kindly direct me to the house of Alcinous, the king of this country. For you see I am a stranger here, who has come from a distant land and met with misfortune on the way; which accounts for my not knowing a single soul in the city or the country round.'

'Sir,' replied the bright-eyed Athene, 'I shall be pleased to take you to the house you are inquiring for, since it lies close to my good father's place. But you must follow my lead without a word, look at nobody as you come, and ask no questions. For the people here have little affection for strangers and do not welcome visitors with open arms. They pin their faith on the clippers that carry them across the far-flung seas, for Poseidon has made them a sailor folk, and these ships of theirs are as swift as a bird or as thought itself.'

With this Pallas Athene led the way at a quick pace and Odysseus followed in the goddess' steps. The Phaeacians, those famous seamen, failed to observe him as he passed them by on his way through the town. For the Lady Athene used her formidable powers to prevent it, shedding a magic mist round her favourite in her concern for his safety. As he walked, Odysseus marvelled at the harbours with their well-found ships, at the meeting-place of the sea-lords and at their long and lofty walls, which were surmounted by palisades and presented a wonderful sight.

When they reached the king's palace, the bright-eyed goddess Athene turned to him and said:

'Here, sir, you see the house that you asked me to show you. You will find highborn princes feasting there, but go straight in and have no qualms. For it is the bold man who every time does best, at home or abroad. Once in the palace make straight for the Queen. Her name is Arete and she comes from the same family as Alcinous the King. Nausithous, the first of the line, was the son of Poseidon the Earthshaker and of Periboea, the loveliest woman of her time. She was the youngest daughter of the great Eurymedon, who was once king of that haughty race, the Giants, but led his headstrong people to destruction, and himself came to an untimely end. Poseidon made Periboea his mistress and by her had a son, Nausithous the Magnificent, who was king of the Phaeacians. And Nausithous had two sons, Rhexenor and Alcinous. Rhexenor had not long been married and had as yet no son when he was killed by Apollo with his silver bow. But he left one daughter, Arete, in his palace. Alcinous made her his wife and gave her such homage as no other woman receives who keeps house for her husband in the world today. Such is the extraordinary and heartfelt devotion which she has enjoyed in the past and still enjoys, both from her children and Alcinous himself, and from the people, who worship her, and greet her when she walks through the town. For she is not only the Queen but a wise woman too, and when her sympathies are enlisted she settles even men's disputes. So if only you can secure her friendly interest, you may well hope to return to your native land, to step under the high roof of your own house and to see your friends once more.'

Athene finished, and now left the pleasant land of Scherie, crossed the barren seas, and came to Marathon and the broad streets of Athens, where she entered the great palace of Erechtheus.

Meanwhile Odysseus approached Alcinous' splendid dwelling. His heart was filled with misgivings and he hesitated before setting foot on the bronze threshold. For a kind of radiance, like that of the sun or moon, lit up the high-roofed halls of the great king. Walls of bronze, topped with blue enamel tiles, ran round to left and right from the threshold to the back of the court. The interior of the well-built mansion was guarded by golden doors hung on posts of silver which sprang from the bronze threshold. The lintel they supported was of silver too, and the door-handle of gold. On either side stood gold and silver dogs, which Hephaestus had made with consummate skill, to keep watch over the palace of the great-hearted Alcinous and serve him as immortal sentries never doomed to age. Inside the hall, high chairs were ranged along the walls on either side, right round from the threshold to the chamber at the back, and each was draped with a delicately woven cover that the women had worked. Here the Phaeacian chieftains sat and enjoyed the food and wine which were always forthcoming, while youths of gold, fixed on stout pedestals, held flaming torches in their hands to light the banqueters in the hall by night.

The house keeps fifty maids employed. Some grind the apple-golden corn in the handmill, some weave at the loom, or sit and twist the yarn, their hands fluttering like the tall poplar's leaves, while the soft olive-oil drips from the close-woven fabrics they have finished. For the Phaeacians' extraordinary skill in handling ships at sea is rivalled by the dexterity of their womenfolk at the loom, so expert has Athene made them in the finer crafts, and so intelligent.

Outside the courtyard but stretching close up to the gates, and with a hedge running down on either side, lies a large orchard of four acres, where trees hang their greenery on high, the pear and the pomegranate, the apple with its glossy burden, the sweet fig and the luxuriant olive. Their fruit never fails nor runs short, winter and summer alike. It comes at all seasons of the year, and there is never a time when the West Wind's breath is not assisting, here the bud, and here the ripening fruit; so that pear after pear, apple after apple, cluster on cluster of grapes, and fig upon fig are always coming to perfection. In the same enclosure there is a fruitful vineyard, in one part of which is a warm patch of level ground, where some of the grapes are drying in the sun, while others are gathered or being trodden, and on the foremost rows hang unripe bunches that have just cast their blossom or show the first faint tinge of purple. Vegetable beds of various kinds are neatly laid out beyond the farthest row and make a smiling patch of never-failing green. The garden is served by two springs, one led in rills to all parts of the enclosure, while its fellow opposite, after providing a watering-place for the townsfolk, runs under the courtyard gate towards the great house itself. Such were the beauties with which the gods had adorned Alcinous' home.

Stalwart Odysseus stood before the house and eyed the scene. When he had enjoyed all its beauty, he stepped briskly over the threshold and entered the palace. There he found the chieftains and counsellors of the Phaeacians pouring libations from their cups to the keen-eyed Giant-slayer, with an offering to whom it was their custom to finish before retiring to bed. But the stouthearted Odysseus marched straight up the hall, wrapped in the mist that Athene shed about him, till he reached Arete and King Alcinous and threw his arms around Arete's knees. At the same moment the magic mist that had hidden him rolled away, and at the sight of this man in their midst a silence fell on all the banqueters up and down the hall. They stared at Odysseus in amazement while he made his petition:

'Arete, daughter of divine Rhexenor, as one who has suffered much I seek refuge with your lord, I abase myself at your knees, and I appeal to these guests. May the gods grant them happiness for life and give each the joy of bequeathing to his sons the treasures of his house and the honours which the people have allotted him. As for myself, I beg you to arrange for my conveyance to my own country, as soon as may be, for I have had to live through many a long day of hardship since last I saw my friends.'

His petition made, he sat down in the dust by the hearth, close to the fire. And from that whole company there came not a sound, until at last the silence was broken by the venerable lord, Echeneus, a Phaeacian elder who was the most eloquent speaker among them and rich in the wisdom of his forefathers. At this juncture he made his friendly counsel heard:

'Alcinous, it is unseemly and unlike your royal ways to let a stranger sit in the dust at the hearth, while the guests around you must patiently await your lead. I beg you, sir, to let him rise and seat himself on one of the silver thrones, and to tell your squires to mix some wine so that we can make a fresh libation, to Zeus the Thunderer, who watches over suppliants that deserve respect. Also let the housekeeper fetch supper from the larder for our visitor.'

Thus reminded, the divine king, Alcinous, took the wise and subtle Odysseus by the hand, raised him from the hearth and seated him on a polished throne, which the gallant Laodamas, his favourite son, who sat next to him, vacated at his request. A maid came with water in a beautiful golden ewer and poured it out over a silver basin so that he could rinse his hands. Then she drew a wooden table to his side, and the staid housekeeper brought some bread and put it by him with a choice of dainties, helping him liberally to all she could offer. While the stalwart Odysseus ate and drank, King Alcinous gave an order to his squire:

'Pontonous, mix a bowl of wine and fill the cups of all the company in the hall, so that we may now make a drink-offering to Zeus the Thunderer, who watches over suppliants that deserve respect.'

So Pontonous prepared a bowl of mellow wine, from which after first pouring out a few drops in each man's cup he served the whole company. Then, when they had made their libations and drunk their fill, Alcinous addressed them:

'Captains and Counsellors of the Phaeacians, may I have your attention while I tell you what is in my mind? I suggest, now you have dined, that you should disperse to your homes for the night; and in the morning we will summon a fuller gathering of the elders for the entertainment of our visitor here and to sacrifice to the gods. We will then take up the matter of his passage so as to ensure him without trouble or anxiety the happiness of a quick return to his country under our escort, however far he may have wandered from it. And we will safeguard him on the way from any further hardship or accident till he sets foot in his own land. After which he must suffer whatever Destiny and the relentless Fates spun for him with the first thread of life when he came from his mother's womb. But if he turns out to be one of the immortals come down from heaven, then the gods must be playing some new trick upon us. For in the past they have always shown themselves to us without disguise when we have offered them their sumptuous sacrifices; and at our banquets they rub shoulders with us. Even when a traveller meets them on his lonely way, they make no concealment; for we are near to them, like the Cyclopes and the wild tribes of the Giants.'

'Alcinous,' Odysseus was quick to reply, 'on that score you may set your mind at rest. You can see that I have neither the looks nor the stature of the immortal gods who live in heaven, but am a human being. Think of the wretches who in your experience have borne the heaviest load of sorrow, and I will match my griefs with theirs. Indeed I think that I could tell an even longer tale of woe, if I gave you a full account of what I have been fated to endure. But all I ask of you now is your leave to eat my supper, in spite of all my troubles. For nothing in the world is so incontinent as a man's accursed appetite. However afflicted he may be and sick at heart, it calls for attention so loudly that he is bound to obey it. Such is my case: my heart is sick with grief, yet my hunger insists that I shall eat and drink. It makes me forget all I have suffered and forces me to take my fill. But at daybreak I beg you to make arrangements for landing this unfortunate guest of yours in his own country. I have had hard times indeed. Once let me see my own estate, my servants, and the high roof of my great house, and I shall be content to breathe my last.'

He had made good his case. They all applauded and voted that the stranger should be given his passage. Then, after making a libation and satisfying their thirst, they retired for the night to their several homes, leaving royal Odysseus sitting in the hall beside Arete and King Alcinous, while the maids cleared the dinner things away.

White-armed Arete was the first to break the silence. For in the fine cloak and tunic she saw him wearing she recognized some clothes that she herself had made with her women's help. Hence her pointed inquiries:

'Sir, I shall make so bold as to ask you some questions without further ado. Who are you? Where do you hail from? And who gave you those clothes? Didn't I gather from you just now that chance had brought you here across the seas?'

'My Queen,' Odysseus guardedly replied, 'it would be a wearisome business to tell you all I have been through from first to last, for I have had a long spell of evil luck. So I shall confine myself to your questions. Far out at sea there is an island called Ogygia, where Atlas' daughter, the wily Calypso, lives. She is a goddess, beautiful indeed, but to be feared. No god or man comes near her. And yet I had the misfortune to be brought by some power to her hearth. I was alone, for with one of his blinding bolts Zeus had smashed my good ship to pieces out in the wine-dark sea. My loyal company all lost their lives. But I got my arms round the curved ship's keel and for nine days kept afloat. In the blackness of the tenth night the gods washed me ashore on Ogygia, the home of Calypso, that formidable goddess with the beautiful locks. She took me in and looked after me with loving care. She even talked of making me immortal and immune from age for ever. But never for a moment did she win my heart. Seven years without a break I stayed, bedewing with my tears the imperishable clothes Calypso gave me. But at last, when the eighth came round in its course, she urged me to be gone, either in obedience to a message from Zeus or because her own feelings had changed. She sent me off in a boat I had put together, after providing me generously with bread and sweet wine, and clothing me in her imperishable stuffs. She also caused a warm and kindly wind to blow. So for seventeen days I sailed across the sea and on the eighteenth the shadowy mountains of your land hove in sight, and I rejoiced. Too soon, poor man, for Poseidon the Earthshaker was yet to send me plenty of troubles to face. Rousing the winds against me, he brought me to a standstill; and as I sat groaning there he stirred the sea to such unspeakable fury that my boat was unable to ride the waves. Before long, a squall had smashed her to pieces. However, I managed by swimming to make my way across that stretch of water, till the winds and the set of the current brought me to your coast. There I tried to land; but the swell would have driven me right up to a great cliff at a most inhospitable spot and dashed me on the rocks. So I sheered off and swam back from the shore. In the end I reached a river, which struck me as offering the best possible landing-place, clear of rocks and sheltered from the wind. I struggled out and lay where I fell till I could rally my strength. Meanwhile the solemn night came on. So after climbing up from the bed of that heaven-fed river I lay down in a thicket, heaped leaves over my body and by god's grace fell into a sound sleep. In my exhausted condition I slept there in the leaves all night and right through the morning into the middle of the day. In fact the sun was on his downward path when I awoke from my refreshing sleep to find your daughter's maids playing games on the beach. The princess herself was with them and I almost took her for a goddess. It was to her that I applied for help. And she proved what good sense she has, acquitting herself in a way you would not expect in one so young. For young people are thoughtless as a rule. But she not only gave me plenty of bread and sparkling wine, but made me bathe in the river and provided me with the clothes you see. That is the truth of the matter, though I am too sad at heart to make a story of it.'

Here Alcinous put in a word. 'Sir,' he said to Odysseus, 'in one respect I do find fault with my girl's judgement. She should have brought you straight home with her maids. After all, she was the first person you had applied to for help.'

'My lord,' replied the resourceful Odysseus, 'your daughter is not to blame for that, and I beg you not to take her to task. She did tell me to follow along with the servants. But in my modesty I shrank from doing so, thinking it possible that you might be annoyed at the sight. We men are jealous folk.'

'My friend,' replied Alcinous, 'I am not one to take umbrage at a trifle: we must always be fair. Now you are a man likeminded with myself, and that being so, I could wish for nothing better than for you to have my daughter and take your place here as my son-in-law, in a house I should provide and furnish for you. That is, if you were willing to stay. But if you wish to go, not one of us Phaeacians shall detain you. God forbid such a thing! And to set your mind at rest, I now appoint a day for your conveyance home: tomorrow, let us say. You shall lie there lapped in sleep, while they row you over tranquil seas, till you come to your own country and your house or anywhere else where you would like to go. Nor does it matter if the spot is even more remote than Euboea, which is said to be at the world's end by those of our sailors who saw it, that time they took redhaired Rhadamanthus to visit Tityos, the son of Earth. They not only got there, I must tell you, but finished the return trip also in one and the same day without fatigue. But you shall learn from your own experience the surpassing excellence of my ships and how good my young men are at churning up the sea water with their oars.'

Odysseus' patient heart was filled with happiness as he listened, and he raised his voice in prayer:

'O Father Zeus, grant that Alcinous may accomplish all that he has promised. His fame would never die wherever mankind till the soil, and I should come again to the land of my fathers.'

While they were conversing, white-armed Arete gave her maids instructions to put a bedstead in the portico and to furnish it with the finest purple rugs, spread sheets over these, and add warm blankets on top for covering. The servants, torch in hand, went out of the hall and busied themselves at this task. When they had spread the things on the well-made bedstead, they came up to Odysseus and invited him to retire. 'Up, sir, and come,' they said, 'for your bed is made.' And he realized then how glad he would be to get to sleep.

So the good Odysseus, after all his troubles, slept there in the echoing portico on a wooden bedstead, while Alcinous lay down for the night in his room at the back of the high building with his consort, who made and shared his bed.

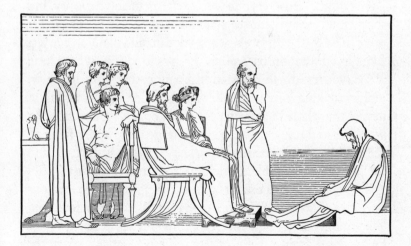

VIII

THE PHAEACIAN GAMES

As soon as the fresh Dawn had decked herself in crimson, the divine King Alcinous left his bed and conducted Odysseus, the royal sacker of cities, who had risen at the same time, to the place by the ships where the Phaeacians held their Assemblies; and there they sat down side by side on seats of polished marble. In the meantime Pallas Athene, pursuing her plans for the heroic Odysseus' return, went up and down the town disguised as a herald from the wise prince Alcinous. She accosted each of the Counsellors and gave them all this message:

'Captains and Counsellors of the Phaeacians, follow me to the Assembly, where you shall hear about the stranger who has just arrived at our wise prince's palace. He has wandered all over the seas, and he looks like an immortal god.'

Her news filled everyone with excitement and curiosity. In a short time not only the seats but all parts of the meeting-place were filled by the throng that crowded in; and many an eye was fixed in admiration on Laertes' keen-witted son, whose head and shoulders Athene invested with a more than human beauty, besides making him seem taller and broader, so that he might inspire the whole Phaeacian people not only with affection but with fear and respect, and might emerge successfully from all the tests they put him through. When everyone had arrived and the muster was complete, Alcinous rose to address them:

'Captains and Counsellors of the Phaeacians, I beg for your attention. There is a matter here that I wish to put before you. The stranger at my side – I do not know his name, nor whether he has come from Eastern or from Western lands – has in the course of his travels become my guest. He asks for his passage home and begs us to assure him this favour. I propose, in accordance with our custom, that we make immediate arrangements for his conveyance. For there never has been a time when one who has come to my house has had to complain of his detention here for lack of escort. So let us run a black ship down into the friendly sea for her maiden voyage, and from the town pick fifty-two young oarsmen who have proved their excellence. This crew, when they have all made their oars fast at the benches, may leave the ship and repair to my house, where they can fall to and take a hasty meal: I will make ample provision for all. These are my orders for the ship's company.

'As for the rest, I invite you that are sceptred kings to my palace with a view to entertaining our visitor indoors. I shall accept no refusal. And let our glorious bard, Demodocus, be summoned. For no other singer has his heavenly gift of delight-ing our ears whatever theme he chooses for his song.'

When Alcinous had finished speaking he made a move, and the sceptred kings went with him. His equerry set out in search of the excellent minstrel, and meanwhile fifty-two young men were chosen and made their way, as he had directed, to the shore of the barren sea. When they had reached the ship and come down to the beach, they dragged the black vessel into deep water, put the mast and sails on board, fixed the oars in their leather loops, all ship-shape, and hauled the white sail up. Then they moored her well out in the water, and proceeded to the great house of their wise king, where the galleries, the courts, and the apartments themselves were filled with a throng of people. The young men and the old together made up a numerous com-pany, for whose benefit Alcinous sacrificed a dozen sheep, eight white-tusked boars, and a couple of shambling oxen. These they flayed and made ready for the table, and so prepared a goodly feast.

The equerry now came up, leading their favourite bard, whom the Muse loved above all others, though she had mingled good and evil in her gifts, robbing him of his eyes but lending sweetness to his song. Pontonous placed a silver-studded chair for him in the centre of the company, with its back to one of the great pillars, and the equerry hung his tuneful lyre on a peg just above his head and showed him how to lay his hand upon it. At his side he put a basket and a handsome table, together with a cup of wine to drink when he was thirsty. Then they all helped themselves to the good fare that was spread before them.

When they had satisfied their appetite and thirst, the bard was inspired by the Muse to sing of famous men. He chose a passage from a lay well known by then throughout the world, the Quarrel of Odysseus and Achilles, telling how these two had fallen out at a rich ceremonial banquet and dismayed the rest by the violence of their language, though King Agamemnon was secretly delighted to see the Achaean chieftains at loggerheads. He was reminded of the prophecy that Phoebus Apollo had made to him in sacred Pytho when he crossed the marble threshold to consult the oracle, in those days when almighty Zeus was conjuring up the great wave of disasters that was to overwhelm Trojans and Danaans alike.

This was the theme of the famous minstrel's lay. It caused Odysseus to lift his purple mantle with his sturdy hands and draw it down over his head to hide his comely face, for he was ashamed to be caught weeping by the Phaeacians. But in the intervals of the worthy minstrel's song, he wiped the tears away and removing the cloak from his head reached for his two-handled cup and made libations to the gods. Yet whenever Demodocus started singing again, encouraged by the Phaeacian lords, who were enjoying the tale, Odysseus once more hid his face and wept. He managed to conceal his tears from everyone except Alcinous. But the King could not help observing his condition, as he was in the next seat to Odysseus and could hear his heavy sighs. He spoke up before long and said to the Phaeacian sea-captains:

'My Lords and Counsellors, we have had our fill of the good things we have shared, and of the banquet's boon companion, the harp. Let us go out of doors now and try our hands at various sports, so that when our guest has reached his home he can tell his friends that at boxing, wrestling, jumping, and running there is no one who could beat us.'

With these words he led the way and was followed by the rest. The equerry hung Demodocus' tuneful lyre on its peg, took the bard's hand and guided him out of the palace, in the wake of the Phaeacian nobility as they set out to see the games. They all made for the place of assembly and were followed there by a gathering many thousands strong.

There was no lack of young noblemen to compete – Acroneos, Ocealus, Elatreus, Nauteus, Prymneus, Anchialus, Eretmeus, Ponteus, Proreus, Thoon, and Anabesineos, Amphialus son of Polyneus and grandson of Tecton, and Euryalus too, the son of Naubolus, who looked a match for the man-killing Wargod and was the most handsome and stalwart of all the Phaeacians next to the peerless Laodamas. Good King Alcinous' three sons, Laodamas, Halius, and Prince Clytoneus, also took part.

The first event was a race. They ran all out from scratch, raising a cloud of dust on the track as they flew along in a serried mass. But there was no doubt about the fastest man. The excellent Clytoneus shot ahead, and when he reached the crowd at the post had left the rest behind by as much as the width of fallow that mules plough in a day. Wrestling came next – a tougher sport; and here it was Euryalus' turn to beat all the champions. Amphialus won the jump; at throwing the disk, Elatreus carried all before him; and in the boxing, Laodamas, Alcinous' worthy son. When they had all enjoyed the games, it occurred to the same Laodamas to make a suggestion to the rest:

'Come along, you fellows, and let us ask our visitor here if he's an expert in any form of sport. He is well enough built: look at his thighs and legs, look at the pair of hands he has on him, and that great neck. The man is mighty strong, and he's not so old, either. What has broken him down is his hard life. For I tell you, there's nothing like the sea to break the stoutest heart.'

'Laodamas,' said Euryalus, 'I like your idea. Go and have a word with the man yourself and challenge him.'

Thus encouraged Alcinous' worthy son made his way to the centre and addressed Odysseus:

'Come, sir, won't you take a hand with us in our games, if you're good at any sport? You must surely be an athlete, for nothing makes a man so famous for life as what he can do with his hands and feet. Come along then and have a try, casting your cares aside; for it won't be long before you are off on your journey. Your ship is launched already and the crew are standing by.'

Odysseus answered him promptly: 'Laodamas, why vex me with your challenges, you and your friends? I am too sick at heart to think of games. I have been through many bitter and exhausting experiences, and all I seek now is my passage home, which is why I am sitting here in your assembly to plead my suit with your king and your whole nation.'

Euryalus now saw fit to interpose and insult him to his face: 'You are quite right, sir. I should never have taken you for an athlete such as one is accustomed to meet in the world. But rather for some skipper of a merchant crew, who spends his life on a hulking tramp, worrying about his outward freight, or keeping a sharp eye on the cargo when he comes home with the profits he has snatched. No; one can see you are no sportsman.'

With a black look the nimble-witted Odysseus retorted: 'That, sir, was an ugly speech, and you must be a fool to have made it. It shows that we cannot all hope to combine the pleasing qualities of good looks, brains, and eloquence. A quite insignificant-looking fellow may yet be a heaven-born orator watched with delight as he advances confidently and with persuasive modesty from point to point, the one man who stands out in the gathering and is stared at like a god when he passes through the town. Another may be as handsome as an immortal, yet quite deficient in the graceful art of speech. You yourself, sir, present a most distinguished exterior to the world – the gods themselves could not improve it – but you have the brains of a dolt. You have stirred me to anger with your inept remarks, and I'd have you realize that I am no novice at sport, as you suggest, but consider myself to have been in the first rank so long as I was able to rely on the strength of my youth. But as things are, all the misfortunes and hardships I have endured in warfare and in fighting my way through hostile seas weigh heavily upon me. All the same, and in spite of what I have gone through, I'll try my luck at the sports. For words can sting, and yours have put me on my mettle.'

With this he leapt to his feet and, not even troubling to remove his cloak, picked up the biggest disk of all, a huge weight, more massive by far than those used in their regular matches. With one swing he launched it from his mighty hand, and the stone hummed on its course. The Phaeacians, lords of the sea and champions of the long oar, cowered down as it hurtled through the air; and so lightly did it fly from his hand that it overshot the marks of all the other throws. Athene, pretending to be one of the crowd, marked the distance of the cast, and saluted the thrower.

'Look, sir,' she called, 'even a blind man could pick out your peg, by feeling with his hands. The others are all in a bunch, but yours stands right out in the front. As far as this event is concerned, you can set your mind at rest. None of the Phaeacians will make as good a throw, let alone a better.'

Her announcement delighted the much-enduring Odysseus, who was happy to find a real friend in the lists and now addressed the Phaeacians in lighter vein:

'Reach that, my young friends, if you can, though I shouldn't be surprised if presently I sent along another just as far or even farther. And since you have thoroughly roused me, come out, if any of you fancy the idea and have the pluck, come out and take me on – at boxing, wrestling, or even running, I don't care which. Laodamas, whose guest I am, is the only one among you all whom I except, for who would fight his host? A man must be out of his senses or an utter fool to challenge the friend who is entertaining him in a strange country. He would only wreck his own prospects by doing so. But of the rest of you, there is no one I'm too proud to take on; in fact I'm ready to meet and match myself against all comers. For I am not a bad hand all round at any kind of manly sport. I can handle well the polished

bow, and I should be the first to pick off my man with an arrow
in the enemy ranks, however many of my side might be standing by and shooting at their marks. Philoctetes was the only one
who used to beat me with the bow when we Achaeans practised
archery at Troy. Of all others now alive and eating their bread
on the face of the earth, I claim to be by far the best, though I
should not care to compete with the men of the past, with
Heracles, for instance, or Eurytus of Oechalia, who as bowmen
were a match even for the gods. In fact that was why the great
Eurytus came to a sudden end and never lived to see old age in
his home, but was killed by Apollo, whom he had offended by
challenging him to a match. As for the javelin, I can throw it
farther than anyone else can shoot an arrow. It is only in running
that I am afraid some of you might outstrip me. I was too badly
knocked about by the rough seas, for in that boat of mine all
comfort soon gave out, and as a result my limbs have lost their
power.'

Odysseus came to an end, and they all held their tongues,
leaving it to Alcinous to make him a reply.

'My friend,' said the King, 'we can take no exception to what
you say. Angered as you are at the way this fellow came up and
insulted you in the lists, you naturally wish to prove your native
mettle. No one who knew how to talk sense would thus have
belittled your prowess. But listen now to what I have to say.
When you are banqueting in your own home with your wife
and your children beside you, and the talk turns on what the
Phaeacians excel in, I want you to be able to tell your noble
friends that Zeus has given us too a certain measure of success,
which has held good from our forefathers' time to the present
day. Though our boxing and wrestling are not beyond criticism, we can run fast and we are first-rate seamen. But the things
in which we take a perennial delight are the feast, the lyre, the
dance, clean linen in plenty, a hot bath, and our beds. So forward
now, my champion dancers, and show us your steps, so that
when he gets home our guest may be able to tell his friends how
far we leave all other folk behind in seamanship, in speed of foot,

in dancing, and in song. And let one of you run and fetch Demodocus the lyre that is so tuneful in his hands. They left it lying somewhere in my house.'

At the King's word, an equerry set off to fetch the well-made instrument from the palace, and the official stewards, a committee of nine, took matters in hand. These were public servants who supervised all the details on such occasions. They now swept the dancing-floor and cleared a ring wide enough for the performance. Meanwhile the equerry came up to Demodocus and handed him his tuneful lyre. The minstrel then moved forward to the centre; a band of expert dancers, all in the first bloom of youth, took up their positions round him; and their feet came down on the sacred floor with a scintillating movement that filled Odysseus with admiration as he watched.

Presently the bard's fine voice was heard above the music of his lyre. His theme was the love of Ares and Aphrodite of the beautiful crown. He sang of their first and stealthy meetings in Hephaestus' palace; of the many gifts Ares made her, and of the dishonour he did to King Hephaestus' bed. But the Sun – his lay went on to tell – had witnessed their loving embraces and came to inform Hephaestus, who, when he heard the galling truth, went straight to his workshop with his heart full of evil thoughts, laid his great anvil on the stithy and forged a chain network that could neither be broken nor undone, so as to keep them prisoners for ever. His fury with Ares inspired him as he worked, and when the snare was finished he went to the room where his bed was laid and threw the netting right round the bedposts. A number of further lengths were attached to the rafters overhead and hung down light as gossamer and quite invisible even to the blessed gods. It was a masterpiece of cunning work.

When he had thus surrounded the bed and set his trap, he made a pretence of leaving for the pleasant town of Lemnos, his favourite spot on earth. Meanwhile Ares of the Golden Reins had not kept watch for nothing. Directly he saw the Mastercraftsman leave, he made his way to the great god's house, filled with a passionate desire for Cythereia of the lovely crown. Now she had lately returned from a visit to her mighty Father, Zeus, and had just sat down when Ares came in at the door, grasped her hand and saluted her fondly.

'Come, my beloved,' he said, 'let us go to bed and lie in each other's arms, for Hephaestus is no longer about. He has gone to Lemnos, I think, to visit his Sintian friends and listen to their barbarous talk.'

Aphrodite desired nothing better than to sleep with him; so the two went to the bed and lay down. Whereupon the netting which Hephaestus' ingenuity had contrived fell around them in such a way that they could not move or lift a limb. They found too late that there was no escape. And now they were faced by the great lame god himself. For the Sun, acting as his spy, had given him word; and he had turned back before reaching the island of Lemnos and hurried home in anguish. Standing there in the entrance he was seized by a spasm of rage and raised his voice in a terrible shout, so that all the gods might hear him:

'Father Zeus and you other happy gods who live for ever, come here and see a comic and cruel thing. Zeus' Daughter Aphrodite has always despised me for my lameness, and now she has given her heart to this butcher, Ares, just because he is good-looking and sound of limb, while I was born a cripple. And whom have I to blame for that, if not my father and my mother? I wish they had never begotten me! But you shall see how these two have crept into my bed and are sleeping in each other's loving arms. The sight cuts me to the quick. Yet I have an idea that they won't be eager to prolong that embrace, no, not for a moment, not for all their love. Theirs is a sleep that both will soon be tired of. But my cunning meshes are going to keep them just where they are, till her Father hands me back every one of the gifts I made him to win this brazen-faced hussy, who may be his Daughter and a lovely creature but is the slave of her passions.'

His shouts brought the gods trooping to the house with the bronze floor. Up came Poseidon the Earthshaker; Hermes,

the bringer of luck; and the archer king, Apollo; but the goddesses, constrained by feminine modesty, all stayed at home.
There they stood, then, in front of the doors, the immortals
who are the source of all our blessings; and when they caught
sight of Hephaestus' clever device a fit of uncontrollable
laughter seized these happy gods.

'Bad deeds don't prosper,' said one of them with a glance at
his neighbour; 'the tortoise catches up the hare. See how our
slow-moving Hephaetus has caught Ares, though no god on
Olympus can run as fast. Hephaestus may be lame, but his
craft has won the day. And now Ares will have to pay him an
adulterer's fine.'

This was the kind of comment that was made, and King
Apollo, Son of Zeus, turned to Hermes and said:

'Hermes, you that are Son of Zeus, Ambassador and Giver
of good things, would you care, though held in those unyield-
ing shackles, to lie in bed by golden Aphrodite's side?'

To which the Giant-slayer replied: 'Apollo, my royal
Archer, there is nothing I should relish more. Though the
chains that kept me prisoner were three times as many, though
all you gods and all the goddesses were looking on, yet would
I gladly sleep by golden Aphrodite's side.'

His jest raised another laugh from all the gods except Poseidon, who was not amused, but kept urging the great smith
Hephaestus to free Ares from the net.

'Let him go,' he insisted: 'and I promise you that he himself
shall make full and proper atonement, as required by you, in
the presence of the immortal gods.'

'Poseidon, Girdler of the Earth,' replied the illustrious lame
god, 'I beg you, do not press me. Even a surety for a scoundrel
is a poor thing to hold in hand. How could I subject you to
public arrest if Ares were to shuffle out of his debt as well as
out of his chains?'

'Hephaestus,' said Poseidon the Earthshaker, 'if Ares does
repudiate his debt and abscond, I myself will pay you the
fine.'

'To such an offer from you,' replied the great lame god, 'I cannot and I must not answer no.'

With that the mighty Hephaestus undid the chains, and the two of them, freed from the shackles that had proved so strong, leapt up and fled, Ares to Thrace, and laughter-loving Aphrodite to Paphos in Cyprus, where she has her sacred precinct and an altar fragrant with incense. There the Graces bathed her and anointed her with the imperishable oil that the immortals use. And when they had decked her out in her lovely clothes she was a marvel to behold.

This was the song that the famous minstrel sang, to the delight of Odysseus and the rest of his audience, the Phaeacian sea-lords, those lovers of the oar.

After this Alcinous commanded Halius and Laodamas to dance by themselves, since no one could compete with them. Polybus, a skilled craftsman, had made them a beautiful purple ball, which they took in their hands, and one of them, bending right back, would throw it up towards the shadowy clouds, and the other, leaping up from the ground, would catch it deftly in his turn before his feet touched earth again. After showing their skill at this high play, they began tossing the ball quickly to and fro as they moved in their dance on the bountiful earth, while the other youths stood at the ringside beating time, till the air was filled with sound, and the good Odysseus turned to his host with a compliment:

'Alcinous, my royal and most worshipful prince, you boasted just now that your dancers are supreme. Your claim is made good. I marvel at the sight of them.'

His praise delighted the august Alcinous, who turned at once to his sea-faring subjects and said:

'Listen, Princes and Elders of the Phaeacians, I find a nice discernment in this guest of ours. Let us make him a friendly donation, as is only proper. Our folk have for their chiefs and rulers twelve eminent princes, or thirteen if you count myself. I suggest that each one of us present him with a fresh mantle, a tunic, and a talent of sterling gold. Let us quickly gather all our

gifts together, so that the stranger can take possession and come
to supper in a happy frame of mind. As for Euryalus, he must
make amends to him by a personal apology, and a present as
well, for his incivility was marked.'

His suggestions found favour with all and were adopted.
Each of the princes dispatched his equerry to fetch the gifts,
and Euryalus spoke up in answer to the king's rebuke:

'Alcinous, my royal and most worshipful prince, I am ready
to obey you and make atonement to the stranger. I will give
him this sword of bronze, which has a silver hilt and a sheath of
fresh ivory to hold it – a gift he will value.'

He then laid the sword with its silver mounting in Odysseus'
hands, and addressed him with studied courtesy:

'Father and stranger, I salute you. If some offensive words
escaped my lips, let the storm-winds blow them hence; and
may the gods give you the joy of getting home again and
seeing your wife, since you have been away from your friends
and lived a hard life for so long.'

'Friend,' said the wise Odysseus, 'I return your kindly greeting. May the gods bless you! And I only hope you will not one
day miss the sword you have given me here with such con-
ciliatory words.' And as he spoke he slung the silver weapon
from his shoulder.

By sunset he was in possession of all their noble gifts, which
were carried to Alcinous' palace by their well-born equerries.
There the good king's sons took charge of them and placed the
magnificent collection at their worthy mother's feet. Meanwhile King Alcinous brought the rest of the company to his
house, where they seated themselves on high chairs, and Alcinous called to Arete.

'My dear,' he said, 'bring a good coffer here, the best we
have, and put a fresh mantle and a tunic in it on your own
account. Then see that they heat a copper over the fire and
make some water warm for our guest, so that when he has had
his bath and seen that all the gifts which the Phaeacian nobles
have brought him here are properly packed, he can dine at his

ease and enjoy the minstrel's lay that he will hear. And see, I'll give him this beautiful golden chalice of mine, so that he may have me in mind for the rest of his days when he makes drink-offerings in his house to Zeus and to the other gods.'

Arete told her maid-servants to put a large three-legged cauldron on the fire at once. They set the cauldron for the bath-water on the glowing fire, filled it with water, and brought faggots, which they kindled beneath it. The flames began to lick round the belly of the cauldron and the water was heated. Meanwhile Arete brought out from the inner chamber a fine coffer for their guest, in which she packed the splendid gifts of clothing and of gold which the Phaeacians had made him. To these, on her own account, she added a mantle and a tunic of good quality, and then gave Odysseus a word of advice.

'You had better see to the lid yourself, now,' she said, 'and tie it up at once with a knot, so that you may not be robbed on your journey when you're enjoying a good sleep by and by as the black ship carries you along.'

Stalwart Odysseus took her advice and fixed the lid on at once, fastening it neatly with a complicated knot that the Lady Circe had once taught him. No sooner was the task completed than the housekeeper invited him to get into his bath and wash. It was a pleasure to him to see a hot bath again, for he had not been used to such comforts since leaving the home of the refined Calypso, though while he was there he had received constant attention like a god. When the maids had bathed and anointed him, and had clothed him in a fine cloak and a tunic, he left the bath to join the men at their wine.

Now Nausicaa, in all her heaven-sent beauty, was standing by one of the pillars that supported the massive roof. Filled with admiration as her eyes fell on Odysseus, she greeted him warmly:

'Good luck, my friend,' she said, 'and I hope that when you are in your own country you will remember me at times, since it is to me before all others that you owe your life.'

'Princess Nausicaa,' answered the wise Odysseus, 'I do indeed pray Zeus the Thunderer and Lord of Here to let me see the day of my return and reach my home. If he does, then even there I will never fail to worship you all the rest of my days. For it was you, lady, who gave me back my life.'

With this he took a chair by the side of King Alcinous, for they were already serving the portions and mixing the wine. An equerry now came in leading their beloved bard Demodocus, the people's favourite. He seated him in the centre of the company with his back against one of the high columns, and at once the thoughtful Odysseus, carving a portion from the chine of a white-tusked boar, which was so large that more than half was left, with plenty of rich fat on either side, called to a serving-man and said:

'Here, my man, take this helping to Demodocus and let him eat it, with kindly wishes from my unhappy self. No one on earth can help honouring and respecting the bards, for the Muse has taught them the art of song and she loves the minstrel fraternity.'

The man took the meat and handed it to the lord Demodocus, who accepted the attention with pleasure. The company now helped themselves to the good fare that was spread before them, and when they had satisfied their thirst and hunger, Odysseus turned to the minstrel and said:

'Demodocus, I give you the highest possible praise. Either Zeus' Child, the Muse, or Apollo must have been your teacher. For it is remarkable how well you sing the tale of the Achaeans' fate and of all their achievements, sufferings, and toils. It is almost as though you had been with them yourself or heard the story from one who was. But I ask you now to change your theme and sing to us of the making of the Wooden Horse, which Epeius built with Athene's help, and which my lord Odysseus contrived to introduce one day into the citadel of Troy as an ambuscade, manned by the warriors who then sacked the town. If you can satisfy me in the telling of this tale I shall be ready to acknowledge to the world how generously the god has endowed you with the heavenly gift of song.'

The bard took his cue from Odysseus and beginning with an invocation to the god unfolded the tale. He took it up at the point where the Argives after setting fire to their huts had embarked on their galleys and were sailing off, while the renowned Odysseus and his party were already sitting in the place of assembly at Troy, concealed within the Horse, which the Trojans had themselves dragged into the citadel. There stood the Horse, with the Trojans sitting round it and indulging in a war of words. Three policies emerged. Some were for piercing the wooden frame with a bold stroke of the spear; others would have dragged it to the edge of the heights and hurled it down the rocks; while others again wished to let it stand as a signal offering to appease the gods – and that was just what happened in the end. For it was destiny that they should fall when Troy received within her walls that mighty Wooden Horse, laden with the pick of the Argive chivalry bringing doom and slaughter to the Trojans. He went on to sing how the Achaean warriors, deserting their hollow ambuscade, poured out from the Horse to ravage Troy; how they scattered through the steep streets of the city leaving ruin in their wake; and how Odysseus, looking like Ares himself, went straight to Deiphobus' house with the gallant Menelaus. And there, sang the bard, he rushed into the most terrible of all his fights, which in the end he won with Athene's magnanimous aid.

Odysseus broke down as the famous minstrel sang this lay, and his cheeks were wet with the tears that ran down from his eyes. He wept as a woman weeps when she throws her arms round the body of her beloved husband, fallen in battle before his city and his comrades, fighting to save his home-town and his children from disaster. She has found him gasping in the throes of death; she clings to him and lifts her voice in lamentation. But the enemy come up and belabour her back and shoulders with spears, as they lead her off into slavery and a life of miserable toil, with her cheeks wasted by her pitiful grief. Equally pitiful were the tears that now welled up in Odysseus' eyes, and though he succeeded in hiding them from all but the King, Alcinous could not help observing his condition, for he was sitting next to him and heard his heavy groans. He spoke up at once and said to the Phaeacian sea-captains:

'Pray silence, my noble and honourable lords. And let the music of Demodocus' lyre be stilled, for it appears that the theme of his song is not to everybody's liking. Since we have been sitting at supper and our worthy minstrel struck up, our guest here has been weeping bitterly without a pause. Some poignant sorrow must have overwhelmed his feelings. Let the bard stop playing, so that we can all be merry, hosts and guest alike. How much pleasanter that would be! For it was on account of our worthy guest that all this has been arranged, this farewell banquet and these friendly gifts that show the warmth of our hearts. To any man with the slightest claim to common sense, a stranger and suppliant is as good as a brother.

'And now, sir, I beg you to be equally friendly, and not, for some subtle purpose, to withhold the answers to the questions I may ask. 'Twould be more courteous on your part to be frank. Tell me the name by which you were known at home to your mother and father and your friends in the town and country round. No one, after all, whether of low or high degree, goes nameless once he has come into the world; everybody is named by his parents the moment he is born. You must also tell me where you come from, to what state and to what city you belong, so that my ships as they convey you there may plan the right course in their minds. For the Phaeacians have no steersmen, nor steering-oars such as other craft possess. Our ships know by instinct what their crews are thinking and propose to do. They know every city, every fertile land, and hidden in mist and cloud they make their swift passage over the sea's immensities with no fear of damage and no thought of wreck. At the same time, I must tell you of a warning I had from my father Nausithous, who used to say that Poseidon grudged us our privilege of giving safe-conduct to all comers. He prophesied that some day the god would wreck one of our well-found vessels out on the misty sea as she came home from a convoy, and would overshadow our city with a great mountain-wall. That is what the old king used to say; and the god may do it, or may let things be. It is for him to decide at his pleasure.

'And now I call upon you for a true account of your wanderings. To what parts of the inhabited world did they take you? What lovely cities did you see; what people in them? Did you meet hostile tribes and lawless savages, or did you fall in with some friendly and god-fearing folk? Explain to us also what secret sorrow makes you weep as you listen to the tragic story of the Argives and the fall of Troy. Were not the gods responsible for that, weaving catastrophe into the pattern of events to make a song for future generations? Perhaps one of your kinsmen by marriage fell before Ilium, a good man, your son-in-law possibly or your wife's father, to mention those nearest after one's own blood and stock? Or perhaps it was a comrade, some true friend who knew his way to your heart? For a sympathetic friend can be quite as dear as a brother.'

IX

THE CYCLOPS

IN answer to the King, this is how Odysseus, the man of many resources, began his tale:

'Lord Alcinous, my most worshipful prince, it is indeed a lovely thing to hear a bard such as yours, with a voice like the gods'. I myself feel that there is nothing more delightful than when the festive mood reigns in a whole people's hearts and the banqueters listen to a minstrel from their seats in the hall, while the tables before them are laden with bread and meat, and a steward carries round the wine he has drawn from the bowl and fills their cups. This, to my way of thinking, is something very like perfection.

'You, however, have made up your mind to probe into my troubles and so to intensify my grief. Well, where shall I begin, where end, my tale? For the list of woes which the gods in heaven have sent me is a long one. I had better start by giving you my name: I wish you all to know it so that in the days to come, if I escape the cruel hand of fate, I may be counted as a friend of yours, however far away I live.

'I am Odysseus, Laertes' son. The whole world talks of my stratagems, and my fame has reached the heavens. My home is under the clear skies of Ithaca. Our landmark is the wooded peak of windswept Neriton. For neighbours we have many peopled isles with no great space between them, Dulichium and Same and wooded Zacynthus. But Ithaca, the farthest out to sea, lies slanting to the west, whereas the others face the dawn and rising sun. It is a rough land, but a fit nurse of men. And I, for one, know of no sweeter sight for man's eyes than his own country. The divine Calypso certainly did her best to keep me yonder in her cavern home because she wished to be my wife, and with the same object Circe, the Aeaean witch, detained me in her castle; but never for a moment did they win my heart. So true it is that his motherland and his parents are what a man holds sweetest, even though he may have settled far away from his people in some rich home in foreign lands. However, it is time I told you of the disastrous voyage Zeus gave me when I started back from Troy.

'The same wind as wafted me from Ilium brought me to Ismarus, the city of the Cicones. I sacked this place and destroyed the men who held it. Their wives and the rich plunder that we took from the town we divided so that no one, as far as I could help it, should go short of his proper share. And then I said we ought to be off and show a clean pair of heels. But my fools of men refused. There was plenty of wine, plenty of livestock; and they kept on drinking and butchering sheep and · fatted cattle by the shore. Meanwhile the Cicones went and raised a cry for help among other Cicones, their up-country neighbours, who are both more numerous and better men, trained in fighting from the chariot and on foot as well, as the occasion requires. At dawn they were on us, thick as the leaves and flowers in their season, and it certainly looked as though Zeus meant the worst for my unhappy following and we were in for a very bad time. A pitched battle by the ships ensued, and volleys of bronze spears were interchanged. Right through the early morning and while the blessed light of day grew stronger we held our ground and kept their greater force at bay; but when the sun began to drop, towards the time when the ploughman unyokes his ox, the Cicones gained the upper hand and broke the Achaean ranks. Six of my warriors from each ship were killed. The rest of us contrived to dodge our fate and got away alive.

'We made off from Ismarus with heavy hearts, for the joy we felt at our own reprieve was tempered by grief for our dear comrades-in-arms; and I would not let the curved ships sail before each of our poor friends who had fallen in action against the Cicones had been three times saluted. Zeus, who marshals the clouds, now sent my fleet a terrible gale from the north. He covered land and sea alike with a canopy of cloud; and darkness swept down on us from the sky. Our ships were driven sidelong by the wind, and the force of the gusts tore their sails to rags and tatters. With the fear of death upon us, we lowered these onto the decks, and rowed the bare ships landward with all our might. Thus we lay for two days and two nights on end, with exhaustion and anxiety gnawing at our hearts. But on the third morning, which a beautiful dawn had ushered in, we stepped the masts, hauled up the white sails, and sat down, leaving the wind and the helmsmen between them to keep our vessels straight. In fact I should have reached my own land safe and sound, had not the swell, the current, and the North Wind combined, as I was doubling Malea, to drive me off my course and send me drifting past Cythera.

'For nine days I was chased by those accursed winds across the fish-infested seas. But on the tenth we made the country of the Lotus-eaters, a race that live on vegetable foods. We disembarked to draw water, and my crews quickly set to on their midday meal by the ships. But as soon as we had a mouthful and a drink, I sent some of my followers inland to find out what sort of human beings might be there, detailing two men for the duty with a third as messenger. Off they went, and it was not long before they were in touch with the Lotus-eaters. Now it never entered the heads of these natives to kill my friends; what they did was to give them some lotus to taste, and as soon as each had eaten the honeyed fruit of the plant, all thoughts of reporting to us or escaping were banished from his mind. All they now wished for was to stay where they were with the Lotus-eaters, to browse on the lotus, and to forget that they had a home to return to. I had to use force to bring them back to the ships, and they wept on the way, but once on board I dragged them under the benches and left them in irons. I then commanded the rest of my loyal band to embark with all speed on their fast ships, for fear that others of them might eat the lotus and think no more of home. They came on board at once, went to the benches, sat down in their proper places, and struck the white surf with their oars.

'So we left that country and sailed on sick at heart. And we came to the land of the Cyclopes, a fierce, uncivilized people who never lift a hand to plant or plough but put their trust in Providence. All the crops they require spring up unsown and untilled, wheat and barley and the vines whose generous clusters give them wine when ripened for them by the timely rains. The Cyclopes have no assemblies for the making of laws, nor any settled customs, but live in hollow caverns in the mountain heights, where each man is lawgiver to his children and his wives, and nobody cares a jot for his neighbours.

'Not very far from the harbour on their coast, and not so near either, there lies a luxuriant island, covered with woods, which is the home of innumerable goats. The goats are wild, for man has made no pathways that might frighten them off, nor do hunters visit the island with their hounds to rough it in the forests and to range the mountain-tops. Used neither for grazing nor for ploughing, it lies for ever unsown and untilled; and this land where no man goes makes a happy pasture for the bleating goats. I must explain that the Cyclopes have nothing like our ships with their crimson prows; nor have they any shipwrights to build merchantmen that could serve their needs by plying to foreign ports in the course of that overseas traffic which ships have established between the nations. Such craftsmen would have turned the island into a fine colony for the Cyclopes. For it is by no means a poor country, but capable of yielding any crop in due season. Along the shore of the grey sea there are soft water-meadows where the vine would never wither; and there is plenty of land level enough for the plough, where they could count on cutting a deep crop at every harvest-time, for the soil below the surface is exceedingly rich. Also it has a safe harbour, in which there is no occasion to tie up at all. You need neither cast anchor nor make fast with hawsers: all your crew have to do is to beach their boat and wait till the spirit moves them and the right wind blows. Finally, at the head of the harbour there is a stream of fresh water, running out of a cave in a grove of poplar-trees.

'This is where we came to land. Some god must have guided us through the murky night, for it was impossible to see ahead. The ships were in a thick fog, and overhead not a gleam of light came through from the moon, which was obscured by clouds. In these circumstances not a man among us caught sight of the island nor did we even see the long rollers beating up to the coast, before our good ships ran aground. It was not till they were beached that we lowered sail. We then jumped out on the shore, fell asleep where we were and so waited for the blessed light of day.

'When the fresh Dawn came and with her crimson streamers lit the sky, we were delighted with what we saw of the island and set out to explore it. Presently, in order that my company might have something to eat, the Nymphs, those Children of Zeus, set the mountain goats on the move. Directly we saw them we fetched our curved bows and our long spears from the ships, separated into three parties, and let fly at the game; and in a short time Providence had sent us a satisfactory bag. There were twelve ships in my squadron: nine goats fell to each, while to me they made a special allotment of ten. So the whole day long till the sun set we sat and enjoyed this rich supply of meat, which we washed down by mellow wine, since the ships had not yet run dry of our red vintage. There was still some in the holds, for when we took the sacred citadel of the Cicones, every member of the company had drawn off a generous supply in jars. There we sat, and as we looked across at the neighbouring land of the Cyclopes, we could not only see the smoke from their fires but hear their voices and the bleating of their sheep and goats. The sun went down, night fell, and we slept on the sea-shore.

'With the first rosy light of Dawn, I assembled my company and gave them their orders. "My good friends," I said, "for the time being I want you to stay here, while I go in my own ship with my own crew to find out what kind of men are over there, and whether they are brutal and lawless savages or hospitable and god-fearing people."

'Then I climbed into my ship and told my men to follow me and loose the hawsers. They came on board at once, went to the benches, sat down in their places and churned the grey water with their oars. It was no great distance to the mainland coast. As we approached its nearest point, we made out a cave there, close to the sea, was a high entrance overhung by laurels. Here large flocks of sheep and goats were penned at night, and round the mouth a yard had been built with a great wall of stones bedded deep between tall pines and high-branched oaks. It was the den of a giant, the lonely shepherd of sequestered flocks, who had no truck with others of his kind but lived aloof in his own lawless way. And what a formidable monster he was! No one would have taken him for a man who ate bread like ourselves; he reminded one rather of some wooded peak in the high hills, lifting itself in solitary state.

'At this point, I told the rest of my loyal following to stay there on guard by the ship while I myself picked out the twelve best men in the company and advanced. I took with me in a goatskin some dark and mellow wine which had been given to me by Maron son of Euanthes, the priest of Apollo (who was patron-deity of Ismarus), because we had protected him and his child and wife out of respect for his office, when we came upon his home in a grove of trees sacred to Phoebus Apollo. This man made me some fine presents: he gave me seven talents of wrought gold, with a mixing-bowl of solid silver, and he drew off for me as well a full dozen jars of mellow unmixed wine. And a wonderful drink it was. It had been kept secret from all his serving-men and maids, in fact from everyone in the house but himself, his good wife, and a single stewardess. When they drank this red and honeyed vintage, he used to pour one cupful of wine into twenty of water, and the sweet fumes that came up from the bowl were irresistible – those were occasions when abstinence could have no charms.

'Well, I filled a big bottle with this wine and took some food in a wallet along with me also; for I had an instant foreboding, though I am no coward, that we were going to find ourselves face to face with some being of colossal strength and ferocity, to whom the law of man and god meant nothing. It took us very little time to reach the cave, but we did not find its owner at home: he was tending his fat sheep in the pastures. So we went inside and had a good look round. There were baskets laden with cheeses, and the folds were thronged with lambs and kids, each class, the firstlings, the summer lambs, and the little ones, being separately penned. All his well-made vessels, the pails and bowls he used for milking, were swimming with whey.

'Now my men's idea was first to make off with some of the cheeses, then come back, drive the kids and lambs quickly out of the pens down to the good ship, and so set sail across the salt water. They pleaded with me; but though it would have been far better so, I was not to be persuaded. I wished to see the owner of the cave and had hopes of some friendly gifts from my host. As things fell out, my company were to have an unpleasant surprise when he did put in an appearance.

'We lit a fire, killed a beast and made offerings, took some cheeses just for ourselves, and when we had eaten, sat down in the cave to await his arrival. At last he came up, shepherding his flocks and carrying a huge bundle of dry wood to burn at supper-time. With a great din he cast this down inside the cavern, giving us such a fright that we hastily retreated to an inner recess. Meanwhile he drove his fat sheep into the wider part of the cave – I mean all the ewes that he milked: the rams and he-goats he left out of doors in the walled yard. He then picked up a huge stone, with which he closed the entrance. It was a mighty slab, such as you couldn't have budged from the ground, not with a score of heavy four-wheeled waggons to help you. That will give you some idea of the monstrous size of the rock with which he closed the cave. Next he sat down to milk his ewes and bleating goats, which he did methodically, putting her young to each mother as he finished. He then curdled half the white milk, gathered it all up, and stored it in wicker baskets; the remainder he left standing in pails, so that it would be handy at supper-time and when he wanted a drink. When he had done with his business and finished all his jobs, he lit up the fire, spied us, and began asking questions.

'"Strangers!" he said. "And who may you be? Where do you hail from over the highways of the sea? Is yours a trading venture; or are you cruising the main on chance, like roving pirates, who risk their lives to ruin other people?"

'Our hearts sank within us. The booming voice and the very sight of the monster filled us with panic. Still, I managed to find words to answer him.

'"We are Achaeans," I said, "on our way back from Troy, driven astray by contrary winds across a vast expanse of sea. Far from planning to come here, we meant to sail straight home; but we lost our bearings, as Zeus, I suppose, intended that we should. We are proud to belong to the forces of Agamemnon, Atreus' son, who by sacking the great city of Ilium and destroying all its armies has made himself the most famous man in the world today. We, less fortunate, are visiting you here as suppliants, in the hope that you may give us friendly entertainment or even go further in your generosity. You know the laws of hospitality: I beseech you, good sir, to remember your duty to the gods. For we throw ourselves on your mercy; and Zeus is there to avenge the suppliant and the guest. He is the travellers' god: he guards their steps and he invites them with their rights."

'So said I, and promptly he answered me out of his pitiless heart: "Stranger, you must be a fool, or must have come from very far afield, to preach to me of fear or reverence for the gods. We Cyclopes care not a jot for Zeus with his aegis, nor for the rest of the blessed gods, since we are much stronger than they. It would never occur to me to spare you or your men against my will for fear of trouble from Zeus. But tell me where you moored your good ship when you came. Was it somewhere up the coast, or near by? I should like to see her."

'He was trying to get the better of me, but I knew enough of the world to see through him and I met him with deceit.

' "As for my ship," I answered, "it was wrecked by the Earth-shaker Poseidon on the confines of your land. The wind had carried us onto a lee shore. He drove the ship up to a headland and hurtled it on the rocks. But I and my friends here managed to escape with our lives."

'To this the cruel brute made no reply. Instead, he jumped up, and reaching out towards my men, seized a couple and dashed their heads against the floor as though they had been puppies. Their brains ran out on the ground and soaked the earth. Limb by limb he tore them to pieces to make his meal, which he devoured like a mountain lion, never pausing till entrails and flesh, marrow and bones, were all consumed, while we could do nothing but weep and lift up our hands to Zeus in horror at the ghastly sight, paralysed by our sense of utter helplessness. When the Cyclops had filled his great belly with this meal of human flesh, which he washed down with unwatered milk, he stretched himself out for sleep among his flocks inside the cave. And now my manhood prompted me to action: I thought I would draw my sharp sword from the scabbard at my side, creep up to him, feel for the right place with my hand and stab him in the breast where the liver is supported by the midriff. But on seconds thoughts I refrained, realizing that we should have perished there as surely as the Cyclops, for we should have found it impossible with our unaided hands to push aside the huge rock with which he had closed the great mouth of the cave. So for the time being we just sat groaning there and waited for the blessed light of day.

'No sooner had the tender Dawn shown her roses in the East, than the Cyclops lit up the fire and milked his splendid ewes, all in their proper order, putting her young to each. This business over and his morning labours done, he once more snatched up a couple of my men and prepared his meal. When he had eaten, he turned his fatted sheep out of the cave, removing the great doorstone without an effort. But he replaced it immediately, as easily as though he were putting the lid on a quiver. Then, with many a whistle, he drove his rich flocks off towards the high pasture, while I was left, with murder in my heart, beating about for some scheme by which I might pay him back if only Athene would grant me my prayer. The best plan I could think of was this. Lying by the pen, the Cyclops had a huge staff of green olive-wood, which he had cut to carry in his hand when it was seasoned. To us it looked more like the mast of some black ship of twenty oars, a broad-bottomed freighter such as they use for long sea voyages. That was the impression which its length and thickness made on us. On this piece of timber I set to work and cut off a fathom's length, which I handed over to my men and told them to smooth down. When they had dressed it, I took a hand and sharpened it to a point. Then I poked it into the blazing fire to make it hard, and finally I laid it carefully by, hiding it under the dung, of which there were heaps scattered in profusion throughout the cave. I then told my company to cast lots among themselves for the dangerous task of helping me to lift the pole and twist it in the Cyclops' eye when he was sound asleep. The lot fell on the very men that I myself should have chosen, four of them, so that counting myself we made a party of five.

'Evening came, and with it the Cyclops, shepherding his woolly sheep, every one of which he herded into the broad part of the cave, leaving none out in the walled yard, either because he suspected something or because a god had warned him. He raised the great doorstone, set it in its place, and then sat down to milk his ewes and bleating goats, which he did in an orderly way, giving each mother its young one in due course. When this business was over and his work finished, he once more seized upon two of us and prepared his supper. Then came my chance. With an ivy-wood bowl of my dark wine in my hands, I went up to him and said: "Here, Cyclops, have some wine to wash down that meal of human flesh, and find out for yourself what kind of vintage was stored away in our ship's hold. I brought it for you by way of an offering in the hope that you would be charitable and help me on my homeward way. But your savagery is more than we can bear. Cruel monster, how can you expect ever to have a visitor again from the world of men, after such deeds as you have done?"

'The Cyclops took the wine and drank it up. And the delicious draught gave him such exquisite pleasure that he asked me for another bowlful.

' "Be good enough," he said, "to let me have some more; and tell me your name, here and now, so that I may make you a gift that you will value. We Cyclopes have wine of our own made from the grapes that our rich soil and timely rains produce. But this vintage of yours is nectar and ambrosia distilled."

'So said the Cyclops, and I handed him another bowlful of the ruddy wine. Three times I filled up for him; and three times the fool drained the bowl to the dregs. At last, when the wine had fuddled his wits, I addressed him with disarming suavity.

' "Cyclops," I said, "you wish to know the name I bear. I'll tell it to you; and in return I should like to have the gift you promised me. My name is Nobody. That is what I am called by my mother and father and by all my friends."

'The Cyclops answered me with a cruel jest. "Of all his company I will eat Nobody last, and the rest before him. That shall be your gift."

'He had hardly spoken before he toppled over and fell face upwards on the floor, where he lay with his great neck twisted to one side, conquered, as all men are, by sleep. His drunkenness made him vomit, and a stream of wine mixed with morsels of men's flesh poured from his throat. I went at once and thrust our pole deep under the ashes of the fire to make it hot, and meanwhile gave a word of encouragement to all my men, to make sure that no one should play the coward and leave me in the lurch. When the fierce glow from the olive stake warned me that it was about to catch alight in the flames, green as it was, I withdrew it from the fire and brought it over to the spot where my men were standing ready. Heaven now inspired them with a reckless courage. Seizing the olive pole, they drove its sharpened end into the Cyclop's eye, while I used my weight from above to twist it home, like a man boring a ship's timber with a drill which his mates below him twirl with a strap they hold at either end, so that it spins continuously. In much the same way we handled our pole with its red-hot point and twisted it in his eye till the blood boiled up round the burning wood. The fiery smoke from the blazing eyeball singed his lids and brow all round, and the very roots of his eye crackled in the heat. I was reminded of the loud hiss that comes from a great axe or adze when a smith plunges it into cold water – to temper it and give strength to the iron. That is how the Cyclops' eye hissed round the olive stake. He gave a dreadful shriek, which echoed round the rocky walls, and we backed away from him in terror, while he pulled the stake from his eye, streaming with blood. Then he hurled it away from him with frenzied hands and raised a great shout for the other Cyclopes who lived in neighbouring caves along the windy heights. These, hearing his screams, came up from every quarter, and gathering outside the cave asked him what ailed him:

'"What on earth is wrong with you, Polyphemus? Why must you disturb the peaceful night and spoil our sleep with all this shouting? Is a robber driving off your sheep, or is somebody trying by treachery or violence to kill you?"

'Out of the cave came Polyphemus' great voice in reply:"O my friends, it's Nobody's treachery, no violence, that is doing me to death."

'"Well then," they answered, in a way that settled the matter, "if nobody is assaulting you in your solitude, you must be sick. Sickness comes from almighty Zeus and cannot be helped. All you can do is to pray to your father, the Lord Poseidon."

'And off they went, while I chuckled to myself at the way in which my happy *notion* of a false name had taken them in. The Cyclops, still moaning in agonies of pain, groped about with his hands and pushed the rock away from the mouth of the cave. But then he sat himself down in the doorway and stretched out both arms in the hope of catching us in the act of slipping out among the sheep. What a fool he must have thought me! Meanwhile I was cudgelling my brains for the best possible course, trying to hit on some way of saving my friends as well as my own skin. Plan after plan, dodge after dodge, passed through my mind. It was a matter of life or death: we were in mortal peril. And this was the scheme I eventually chose. There were in the flock some well-bred, thick-fleeced rams, fine, big animals in their coats of black wool. These I quietly lashed together with the plaited withes which the savage monster used for his bed. I took them in threes. The middle one in each case was to carry one of my followers, while its fellows went on either side to protect him. Each of my men thus had three sheep to bear him. But for myself I chose a full-grown ram who was the pick of the whole flock. Seizing him by the back, I curled myself up under his shaggy belly and lay there upside down, with a firm grip on his wonderful fleece and with patience in my heart. Thus in fear and trembling we waited for the blessed Dawn.

'As soon as she arrived and flecked the East with red, the rams of the flock began to scramble out and make for the pastures, but the ewes, unmilked as they were and with udders full to bursting, stood bleating by the pens. Their master, though he was worn out by the agonies he had gone through, passed his hands along the backs of all the animals as they came to a stand before him; but the idiot never noticed that my men were tied up under the breasts of his own woolly sheep. The last of the flock to come up to the doorway was the big ram, burdened by his own fleece and by me with my teeming brain. As he felt him with his hands the great Polyphemus broke into speech:

' "Sweet ram," he said, "what does this mean? Why are you the last of the flock to pass out of the cave, you who have never lagged behind the sheep, you who always step so proudly out and are the first of them to crop the lush shoots of the grass, first to make your way to the flowing stream, and first to turn your head homewards to the sheepfold when the evening falls? Yet today you are the last of all. Are you grieved for your master's eye, blinded by a wicked man and his accursed friends, when he had robbed me of my wits with wine? Nobody was his name; and I swear that he has not yet saved his skin! Ah, if only you could feel as I do and find a voice to tell me where he's hiding from my fury! Wouldn't I hammer him and splash his brains all over the floor of the cave, till that miserable Nobody had eased my heart of the suffering I owe to him!"

'So he passed the ram out; and when we had put a little distance between ourselves and the courtyard of the cave, I first freed myself from under my ram and next untied my men from theirs. Then, quickly, though with many a backward look, we drove our long-legged sheep right down to the ship – and a rich, fat flock they made. My dear companions were overjoyed when they caught sight of us survivors, though their relief soon changed to lamentation for their slaughtered friends. I would have none of this weeping, however, and with a nod made clear my will to each, bidding them make haste instead to tumble all the fleecy sheep on board and put to sea. So in they jumped, ran to the benches, sorted themselves out, and plied the grey water with their oars.

'But before we were out of earshot, I let Polyphemus have a piece of my mind. "Cyclops!" I called. "So he was not such a weakling after all, the man whose friends you meant to overpower and eat in that snug cave of yours! And your crimes came home to roost, you brute, who have not even the decency to refrain from devouring your own guests. Now Zeus and all his fellow-gods have paid you out."

'My taunts so exasperated the angry Cyclops that he tore the top off a great pinnacle of rock and hurled it at us. The rock fell just ahead of our blue-painted bows. As it plunged in, the water rose and the backwash, like a swell from the open sea, swept us landward and nearly drove us on the beach. Seizing a long pole, I succeeded in punting her off, at the same time rousing my crew with urgent nods to dash in with their oars and save us from disaster. They buckled to and rowed with a will; but when they had brought us across the water to twice our previous distance I was for giving the Cyclops some more of my talk, though from all parts of the ship my men's voices were raised in gentle remonstrance.

' "Aren't you rash, sir," they said, "to provoke this savage? The rock he threw into the sea just now drove the ship back to the land, and we thought we were done for then and there. Had he heard a cry, or so much as a word, from a single man, he'd have smashed in our heads and the ship's timbers with another jagged boulder from his hand. You have seen how he can throw!"

'But all this went for nothing with me. My spirit was up, and in my rage I called to him once more:

' "Cyclops, if anyone ever asks you how you came by your unsightly blindness, tell him your eye was put out by Odysseus, Sacker of Cities, the son of Laertes, who lives in Ithaca."

'The Cyclops gave a groan. "Alas!" he cried. "So the old prophecy has come home to me with a vengeance! We had a prophet with us once, a fine, upstanding man, Telemus son of Eurymus, who was an excellent seer and grew old among us in the practice of his art. All that has now happened he foretold, when he warned me that a man called Odysseus would rob me of my sight. But I always expected some big and handsome fellow of tremendous strength to come along. And now, a puny, good for nothing, little runt fuddles me with wine and then puts out my eye! But come here, Odysseus, so that I may make you some friendly gifts and prevail on the great Earthshaker to see you safely home. For I am his son, and he is not ashamed to call himself my father. He is the one who will heal me if he's willing – a thing no other blessed god nor any man on earth could do."

'To which I shouted in reply: "I only wish I could make as sure of robbing you of life and breath and sending you to Hell, as I am certain that not even the Earthshaker will ever heal your eye."

'At this the Cyclops lifted up his hands to the heavens that hold the stars and prayed to the Lord Poseidon: "Hear me, Poseidon, Girdler of Earth, god of the sable locks. If I am yours indeed and you accept me as your son, grant that Odysseus, who styles himself Sacker of Cities and son of Laertes, may never reach his home in Ithaca. But if he is destined to reach his native land, to come once more to his own house and see his friends again, let him come late, in evil plight, with all his comrades dead, and when he is landed, by a foreign ship, let him find trouble in his home."

'So Polyphemus prayed; and the god of the sable locks heard his prayer. Then once again the Cyclops picked a boulder up – bigger by far, this time – and hurled it with a swing, putting such boundless force into his throw that the rock fell only just astern of our blue-painted ship, missing the end of the steering-oar by inches. The water heaved up as it plunged into the sea; but the wave that it raised carried us on toward the farther shore. And so we reached our island, where the rest of our good ships were awaiting us in a body, while their crews sat round disconsolate and kept a constant watch for our return. Once there, we beached our ship, jumped out on the shore, and unloaded the Cyclops' sheep from the hold. We then divided our spoil so that no one, as far as I could help it, should go short of his proper share. But my comrades-in-arms did me the special honour, when the sheep were distributed, of presenting me with the big ram in addition. Him I sacrificed on the beach, burning slices from his thighs as an offering to Zeus of the Black Clouds, the Son of Cronos, who is lord of us all. But Zeus took no notice of my sacrifice; his mind must already have been full of plans for the destruction of all my gallant ships and of my trusty band.

'So the whole day long till sundown we sat and feasted on our rich supply of meat washed down by mellow wine. When the sun set and darkness fell, we lay down to sleep on the sea-shore. But as soon as Dawn first showed her rosy fingers in the East, I roused my men and ordered them to get on board and let the hawsers go. Climbing in at once, they went to the benches, sorted themselves out, and struck the grey water with their oars. Thus we left the island and sailed on with heavy hearts, for the joy we felt at our escape from death was tempered by grief for the dear friends we had lost.

Odysseus giving wine to Polyphemus.

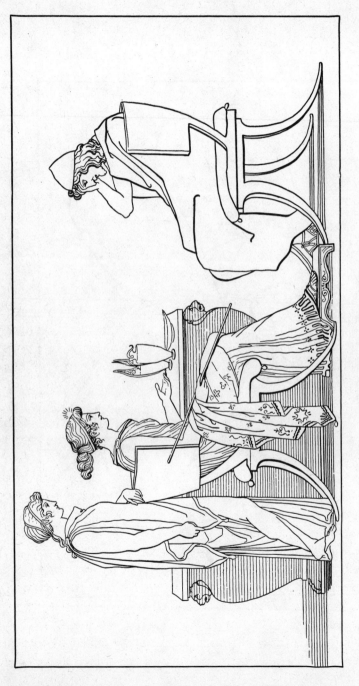

Odysseus at the table of Circe.

X

CIRCE

'OUR next landfall was the floating island of Aeolia, the home of Aeolus son of Hippotas, who is a favourite of the immortal gods. All round this isle there runs an unbroken wall of bronze, and below it the cliffs rise sheer from the sea. Aeolus shares his house with his family of twelve, six daughters and six grown-up sons; and I must tell you that he has given his daughters to his sons in marriage. With their father and their estimable mother they spend their days in feasting. Of luxuries they have a never-failing store. All day long the house is fragrant with the roasting of meat, and the courtyard echoes to the sounds of banqueting within. At night they sleep in blankets by their loving wives on well-made wooden beds.

'To this domain of theirs and this palatial home we found our way. For a whole month Aeolus was my kind host and I was able to satisfy his thirst for news by giving him a full account of the Argive expedition to Ilium and the Achaeans' start for home. Nor was he less obliging when it came to my turn and I asked him whether I might now continue my journey and count on his help. He gave it willingly and presented me with a leather bag, made from the flayed skin of a full-grown ox, in which he had imprisoned the boisterous energies of all the Winds. For you must know that Zeus has made him Warden of the Gales, with power to lay or rouse them each at will. This pouch he stowed in the hold of my ship, securing it tightly with a burnished silver wire so as to prevent the slightest leakage. Then, for my present purpose, he called up a breeze from the west to blow my ships and their crews across the sea. But his measures were doomed to failure, for we came to grief, through our own criminal folly.

'For the next nine days we sailed on, day and night; and on the tenth we were already in sight of our homeland, and had actually come near enough to see the people tending their fires, when I fell fast asleep. I was utterly exhausted, for in my anxiety to make a quick run home I had refused to let any of my men handle the sheet of my ship and had managed it myself without a break.

'The crew seized this chance to discuss matters among themselves, and word went round that I was bringing home a fortune in gold and silver which the generous Aeolus son of Hippotas had given me. You can imagine the glances and comments that were exchanged: "What a captain we have, welcomed wherever he goes and popular in every port! Back he comes from Troy with a splendid haul of plunder, though we who have gone every bit as far come home with empty hands – and what must Aeolus do but give him all this into the bargain, just for friendship's sake! Come on; let's find out all about it and see what gold and silver is hidden in that bag."

'A few speeches in this vein – and evil counsels carried the day. They undid the bag, the Winds all rushed out, and in an instant the tempest was upon them, carrying them headlong out to sea. They had good reason for their tears: Ithaca was vanishing astern. As for myself, when I awoke to this, my spirit failed me and I had half a mind to jump overboard and drown myself in the sea rather than stay alive and quietly accept such a calamity. However, I steeled myself to bear it, and covering my head with my cloak I lay where I was in the ship. So the whole fleet was driven back again to the Aeolian Isle by that accursed storm, and in it my repentant crews.

'Once there, we disembarked and watered. The men fell to and took a quick meal by the ships. But as soon as we had had something to eat and drink I detailed a messenger and one sailor to accompany me and set out for the palace of Aeolus, whom we found at dinner with his wife and family. We went in and sat down on the threshold by the pillars of the door.

'Our friends were astounded at the sight of us. "Odysseus?" they exclaimed. "How do *you* come to be here? What evil power is to blame for this? Surely, when we sent you off, we thought of all you could possibly need to get you home to Ithaca or to any port you might choose?"

'I was utterly downcast. I could only explain that two things had combined to bring me to this pass, a rascally crew and a fatal sleep. "But my friends," I went on, "won't you put things right for me? You easily could."

'My humble appeal had no effect. The sons held their tongues. Their father answered only to denounce me. "Begone from this island instantly!" he cried. "The world holds no greater sinner than you, and I am not one to entertain and equip a man detested by the blessed gods. Your very presence here is proof of their enmity. Be off!"

'Thus he dismissed me from his palace, and all my protests went for nothing. We left the island and resumed our journey in a state of gloom; and the heart was taken out of my men by the wearisome rowing, though it was certainly through our own folly that the friendly breeze we had before enjoyed now failed us.

'For six days we forged ahead, never lying up even at night, and on the seventh we came to Telepylus, Lamus' stronghold in the Laestrygonian land, where shepherds bringing in their flocks at night hail and are answered by their fellows driving out at dawn. For in this land nightfall and morning tread so closely on each other's heels that a man who could do without sleep might earn a double set of wages, one as a neatherd and the other for shepherding white flocks of sheep. Here we found an excellent harbour, closed in on all sides by an unbroken ring of precipitous cliffs, with two bold headlands facing each other at the mouth so as to leave only a narrow channel in between. The captains of my squadron all steered their craft straight into the cover and tied up in the sheltered waters within. They remained close together, for it was obvious that the spot was never exposed to a heavy or even a moderate sea, and the weather outside was bright and calm. But I did not follow them. Instead I brought my ship to rest outside the cove and made her fast with a cable to a rock at the end of the point. I then climbed the headland to get a view from the top, and took my bearings. No ploughed fields or other signs of human activities were to be seen: all we caught sight of was a wisp of smoke rising up from the countryside. So I sent a party inland to find out what sort of people the inhabitants were, for which duty I detailed two of my sailors, together with a messenger.

'When they had left the ships they found a well-worn track which had been used by waggons bringing timber down from the high mountains to the settlement. Presently they fell in with a girl who was drawing water outside the village and for this purpose had come down to a bubbling spring called Artacie, which supplied the place. This strapping young woman proved to be the daughter of Antiphates, the Laestrygonian chief. When they went up and asked her who was the ruler of the country and what his people were called, she pointed at once to the high roof of her father's dwelling. So they made their way to his house, and had no sooner gone in than they were confronted by Antiphates' wife, a creature of mountainous proportions, one glance at whom was enough to fill them with horror. The woman rushed off to the market-place to call her husband, Antiphates himself. And he gave my men a murderous reception, pouncing on one of them at once with a view to eating him for supper. The other two beat a hasty retreat and managed to make their way to the ships. Meanwhile Antiphates raised a hue and cry through the place, which brought the Laestrygonians running up from every side in their thousands – huge fellows, more like giants than men. Standing at the top of the cliffs they began pelting my flotilla with lumps of rock such as a man could barely lift; and the din that now rose from the ships, where the groans of dying men could be heard above the splintering of timbers, was appalling. One by one they harpooned their prey like fish and so carried them off to make their loathsome meal. But while this massacre was still going on in the depths of the cover, I drew my sword from my hip, slashed through the hawser of my vessel, and yelled to the crew to dash in with their oars if they wished to save their skins. With the fear of death upon them they struck the water like one man, and with a sigh of relief we shot out to sea and left those frowning cliffs behind. My ship was safe. But that was the end of all the rest.

'We travelled on in utter dejection, thankful to have escaped alive, but grieving for the good comrades we had lost. In due course we came to the island of Aeaea, the home of the beautiful Circe, a formidable goddess, though her voice is like a woman's. She is the sister of the wizard Aeetes, both being children of the Sun who lights the world, by the same mother, Perse the Daughter of Ocean. We approached the coast of this island and brought our ship into the shelter of the haven without making a sound. Some god must have guided us in. And when we had disembarked, for two whole days and nights we lay on the beach, suffering not only from exhaustion but from the horrors we had been through. The third day was heralded by a lovely Dawn. When the sun was up I took my spear and sword, slipped away from the ship, and struck inland, making for a coign of vantage from which I might look out for signs of human industry or hear men's voices. I climbed a rocky height which promised a wide view, and on reaching the top I was able to see the smoke rising from the distant spot where Circe's house lay screened by the dense oak-scrub and forest trees. That glimpse I had of ruddy smoke left me in two minds whether or not to press forward and reconnoitre. After some hesitation I thought the better course would be to return first to my ship on the beach, give my men a meal, and send out an exploring party. And here some god must have been moved to pity by my forlorn condition. For when I had almost got back to the ship, I fell in with a great antlered stag, right across my path. The fierce heat of the sun had brought him down from the forest pastures to drink at a stream, and as he came up from the water I caught him on the spine half-way down his back. The bronze point of my spear went right through him, and with a groan he fell in the dust and was dead. With one foot on his carcass I dragged the spear out of the wound, laid it on the ground, and left it there while I plucked myself some withes and willow-twigs, which I twisted into a fathom's length of rope carefully plaited from end to end. With this I tied his feet together, and since he was far too big for me to carry on one shoulder and steady with a single hand, I slung the great beast round my neck, and using my spear as a staff I set off for my ship. When I reached it, I threw the stag down by the hull, made the round of all my men, and roused them with the cheerful news.

' "My friends," I said, "we may be miserable, but we are not going down below just yet, not till our time has come. Up you get, and while there's food and drink on board, let us have something to eat instead of dying here of starvation."

'This was a hint they took readily enough. All heads were at once unmuffled, and there on the desolate sea-beach they saw the stag. They had good reason to stare; for he really was a monster. When they had feasted their eyes on the sight they washed their hands and prepared a glorious meal. So the whole day long till sundown we sat and banqueted on our rich supply of meat washed down by mellow wine. When the sun set and darkness fell, we lay down for sleep on the sea-shore. But as soon as Dawn had flecked the sky with red, I gathered my men round me and made them a speech.

' "My friends," I said, "East and West mean nothing to us here. Where the Sun is rising from when he comes to light the world, and where he is sinking, we do not know. So the sooner we decide on a sensible plan the better – if one can still be found (which I doubt). For when I climbed a crag to reconnoitre I found that this is an island, and for the most part low-lying, as all round it in a ring I saw the sea stretching away to the horizon. What I did catch sight of, right in the middle, through dense oak-scrub and forest, was a wisp of smoke."

'When they heard my report they broke down completely. They could not help remembering what Antiphates the Laestrygonian had done, and the unbridled savagery of the man-eating Cyclops. They burst into sobs and the tears streamed down their cheeks. But they might have spared themselves their lamentations for all the good they did.

'In the end I numbered them off into two well-armed parties with a commander for each. Of one, I myself took charge; the other I gave to an officer of noble birth called Eurylochus; and without more ado we shook lots in a bronze helmet. Out came the gallant Eurylochus' lot, and so he went off with his two-and-twenty men, a tearful company, leaving us, who stayed behind, in no better case. In due course they came upon Circe's house, which was built of dressed stone and stood in the middle of a clearing in a forest dell. Prowling about the place were mountain wolves and lions, actually the drugged victims of Circe's magic, for they not only refrained from attacking my men, but rose on their hind legs to caress them, with much wagging of their long tails, like dogs fawning on their master, as he comes from table, for the tasty bits they know he always brings. But these were wolves and lions with great claws that were gambolling in this way round my men. Terrified at the sight of the formidable beasts, they shrank away and took refuge in the porch of the fair goddess' castle. From there they could hear Circe within, singing in her beautiful voice as she went to and fro at her great and everlasting loom, on which she was weaving one of those delicate, graceful, and dazzling fabrics that goddesses love to make.

'Polites, one of my captains and the man in my party whom I liked and trusted most, now took the lead. "Friends," he said, "there is someone in the castle working at a loom. The whole place echoes to that lovely voice. It's either a goddess or a woman. Let us waste no more time, but give her a shout."

'So they shouted to attract attention, and the next moment Circe came out, opened the polished doors, and invited them to enter. In their innocence, the whole party except Eurylochus followed her in. But he suspected a trap and stayed outside. Circe ushered the rest into her hall, gave them settles and chairs to sit on, and then prepared them a mixture of cheese, barley-meal, and yellow honey flavoured with Pramnian wine. But into this dish she introduced a powerful drug, to make them lose all memory of their native land. And when they had emptied the bowls in which she had served them, she struck them with her wand, drove them off, and penned them in the pigsties. For now to all appearance they were swine: they had pigs' heads and bristles, and they grunted like pigs; but their minds were as human as they had been before the change. Indeed, they shed tears in their sties. But Circe flung them some mast, acorns, and cornel-berries, and left them to eat this pigs' fodder and wallow in the mud.

'Meanwhile Eurylochus came back to the good black ship to report the catastrophe his party had met with. He was in such anguish that for all his eagerness to tell us he could utter not a single word; his eyes were filled with tears, and the rising sobs stuck in his throat. Aghast at the sight, we all bombarded him with questions, till at length the story of his comrades' fate came out.

' "My lord Odysseus," he said, "we followed your orders. We made our way through the oaklands and in a clearing in a glade we came to a well-built castle of dressed stone. Someone was working at a great loom inside and singing in a clear voice— either a goddess or a woman. My men gave a shout to attract her attention. In a moment she came out, opened the polished doors, and invited us in. Not knowing better, the men followed her into the house in a body. But I stayed where I was, for I thought it might be a trap. And now the whole party have vanished. Not a single man showed up, though I sat there a long time and kept a sharp lookout."

'When I heard this story I slung my bow over my shoulder, and my big bronze sword in its silver scabbard, and I told Eurylochus to take me back with him by the way he had come. But he threw his arms round my knees in supplication and broke into a pitiful appeal.

' "My king," he said, "leave me behind and don't force me to go with you there. You will never come back yourself and you won't rescue a man of your crew. I am certain of it. Let us get away quickly with those that are left here. We might still save our skins."

'"Very well, Eurylochus," I replied; "stay where you are, and eat and drink by the black ship's hull. But I shall go. It is my plain and bounden duty."

'With this, I turned my back on the ship and the sea, and struck inland. But as I was threading my way through the enchanted glades that led to the witch's castle, whom should I fall in with but Hermes, god of the golden wand, who came up to me just before I reached the house, looking like a young man at that most charming age when the beard first starts to grow. He took my hand in his and greeted me amiably.

'"Where are you off to now, my poor fellow," he said, "wandering alone through the wilds in unknown country, with your friends there in Circe's house penned like pigs in their crowded sties? I suppose you have come here to free them, though I think you are more likely to stay with them yourself and never see your home again. However, I am coming to the rescue and will see you through. Look; here is a drug of real virtue that you must take with you into Circe's palace to save yourself from disaster. But I must explain how she works her black magic. She will begin by mixing you a pottage, into which she will put her poison. But even with its help she will be unable to enchant you, for this antidote that I am going to give you and describe will rob it of its power. When Circe strikes you with her long wand, you must draw your sword from your side and rush at her as though you meant to take her life. She will shrink from you in terror and invite you to her bed. Nor must you hesitate to accept the goddess' favours, if you want her to free your men and treat you kindly. But make her swear a solemn oath by the blessed gods not to try on you any more of her tricks, or when she has you stripped she may rob you of your courage and your manhood."

'Then the Giant-killer handed me a herb he had plucked from the ground, and showed me what it was like. It had a black root and a milk-white flower. The gods call it Moly, and it is an awkward plant to dig up, at any rate for a mere man. But the gods, after all, can do anything.

'Hermes went off through the island forest, making for high Olympus, while I with a heart oppressed by many dark forebodings pursued my way to Circe's home, till I found myself at the doors of the lovely goddess' palace. Here I halted and gave a shout. Circe heard my call, came out at once, and opening the polished doors invited me in. Filled with misgivings, I followed her indoors and was asked to sit down on a beautiful chair with silver decorations and a stool for my feet, while she prepared some pottage in a golden bowl for me to drink and for her own evil purposes threw in some poison. When I had taken the bowl from her and drained it, but without suffering any magic effects, she touched me with her wand and sharply ordered me to be off to the pigsties and lie down with my friends. Whereupon I snatched my sword from my hip and rushed on Circe as though I meant to kill her. But with a shriek she slipped below my blade, fell at my knees and burst into tears.

' "Who on earth are you?" she asked. "What parents begot, what city bred such a man? I am amazed to see you take my poison and suffer no magic change. For never before have I known a man who could resist that drug once he had taken it and swallowed it down. You must have a heart in your breast that is proof against all enchantment. I am sure you are Odysseus, the man whom nothing defeats, the man whom the Giant-slayer with the golden wand always told me to expect here on his way back from Troy in his good black ship. But I beg you now to put up your sword and come with me to my bed, so that in love and sleep we may learn to trust one another."

' "Circe," I answered her, "how can you expect me to be gentle with you, who have turned my friends into pigs here in your house, and now that you have me too in your clutches are inveigling me to your bedroom and inviting me to your bed, to make a coward and a weakling of me when you have me stripped? Nothing, goddess, would induce me to sleep with you, unless you can bring yourself to swear a solemn oath that you have no other mischief in store for me."

'Circe complied and swore that she had no evil intentions. So when she had given me her word with due solemnity, I went with the goddess to her beautiful bed.

'Meanwhile the four maids who do the housework for Circe were busying themselves in the palace. They are the daughters of Springs and Groves and the sacred Rivers that flow out into the sea. One of them threw covers over the chairs and spread fine purple rugs on top. Another drew silver tables up to the chairs and placed golden baskets upon them; while the third was mixing the sweet and mellow wine in a silver bowl and setting out the golden cups; and the fourth fetched water and lit up a great fire under the big cauldron so that the water grew warm.

'When the bright copper was boiling, she sat me down in a bath and washed me with water from the great cauldron mixed with cold to a comfortable heat, sluicing my head and shoulders till all the painful weariness was gone from my limbs. My bath done, she rubbed me with olive oil, clothed me in a tunic and a splendid cloak, and conducted me to the hall, where she seated me in a beautiful chair with silver decorations and a footstool below. Next came another maid with water in a splendid golden ewer. She poured it out over a silver basin so that I could rinse my hands, and then drew up a polished table to my side. A staid housekeeper brought some bread, which she put by me with a variety of dainties; and after helping me liberally to all she had brought she invited me to fall to. But I had no heart for eating. I sat there heedless, engrossed in my cares.

'When Circe saw me sitting so quiet and not helping myself to the food, she knew that I had some serious trouble on my mind. So she faced me and came straight to the point.

'"Odysseus," she said, "why are you sitting here like this as though you were dumb, and feeding on your own thoughts instead of helping yourself to meat and wine? Do you suspect another trap? You need have no fears: I have given you my solemn word to do you no more harm."

'"Circe," I answered her, "could any honest man in my position bear to taste food and drink before he had freed his men and seen them face to face? If you really mean me to eat and drink, give them their liberty and let me set eyes on my loyal followers."

'Wand in hand, Circe went straight out of the hall, threw open the pigsty gate, and drove them out, looking exactly like full-grown swine. And there they stood and faced her. She went in among them and smeared them each in turn with some new salve she had. Whereupon the bristles which her first deadly potion had made them sprout dropped off their limbs, and they not only became men again but looked younger and much handsomer and taller than before. They recognized me now, and one after the other ran up and seized my hand. We were so moved that we all wept for happiness. It was a strange sound for those walls to echo. Even the goddess was touched.

'Presently she came up to me and said: "Royal son of Laertes, you have shown your infinite resource. Go down now to your ship and the sea-shore, drag her straight up onto dry land, stow your belongings and all the ship's tackle in a cave, and then come back yourself with the rest of your loyal company."

'I could not refuse this challenge to my adventurous spirit. So off I went to the ship and the sea-shore. I found my good fellows by the ship in a woebegone state, with the tears streaming down their cheeks. Indeed I was reminded of the scene at a farm when a drove of cows come home full-fed from the pastures to the yard and are welcomed by all their frisking calves, who burst out from the pens to gambol round their mothers and fill the air with the sound of their lowing. For my men no sooner caught sight of me than they were all round me in a weeping throng. They were as deeply moved as if they had reached their homeland and were standing in the streets of their own town in rugged Ithaca, where they were born and bred.

' "Royal master," they said between their sobs, "we are as happy to see you back as we should be to set foot in our own island of Ithaca. But tell us how our comrades met their end."

'I gave them a cheerful reply. "Our first business," I said, "is to drag up the ship on dry land and stow our cargo and the tackle in a cave. Then you must get ready and all come along with me yourselves, if you wish to see your friends eating and drinking in Circe's enchanted palace, where I tell you they have enough to last them for ever."

'The rest were quick to fall in with my suggestion. But not Eurylochus, who, by infecting them with his fears, did his best to keep the whole company back.

' "Where are we poor wretches off to now?" he cried. "Are you so keen on trouble that you must seek out the Witch in her stronghold, and all be turned into pigs or wolves or lions, and forced to keep watch in that great house of hers? We have had all this before, with the Cyclops, when our friends found their way into his fold with this dare-devil Odysseus for company. It was this man's reckless folly that cost *them* their lives."

'Now when Eurylochus said that, I had half a mind, though he was a close kinsman of my own, to draw the long sword from my side and lop his head off to roll in the dust. But I was checked by a chorus of remonstrance from my men, who took a milder view.

' "Sir," they said, "it is for you to give the order; but why not leave this fellow here by the ship on guard, while we follow your lead to Circe's enchanted castle?"

'So we turned our backs on the ship and the sea and struck inland. And Eurylochus came with us after all. He was not going to be left by the ship, and was afraid of the stinging rebuke I might give him.

'Circe had been spending the interval in hospitable care for the party in her house. She bathed and anointed them with olive-oil, and gave them all tunics and warm cloaks to wear, so that on our arrival we found them enjoying a comfortable dinner in the hall. When the two companies came face to face and each man recognized his friends, they burst into tears and the whole house echoed to their sobs, till the goddess herself, coming up and addressing me by my royal titles, appealed to me to check this fit of weeping.

' "I know as well as you," she said, "all you have gone through on the fish-infested seas and suffered at the hands of savages on land. But now I want to see you enjoying your food and putting down your wine, till you are once more the men you were when first you sailed from your homes in rugged Ithaca. You are worn out now and depressed: you cannot forget the buffetings you have had. And your sufferings have been so continuous that you don't know what it is to have a merry heart.'

'My gallant company were not difficult to persuade. In fact we stayed on day after day for a whole year, feasting on meat galore and mellow wine. But when the year was out, and the seasons began to repeat their round, my good friends called me aside one day and said reproachfully: "Master, if you are ever going to escape and get back to your old home in your own country, it's high time you thought of Ithaca again." This was enough: my proud heart was convinced.

'For the rest of that day till sunset we sat and banqueted on the meat and mellow wine that were provided in such abundance. When the sun sank and night fell, my men settled down for sleep in the darkened hall. But I went to the beautiful bed where Circe lay and there clasped the goddess' knees in prayer, while she listened to my eager words:

' "Circe," I said, "I beseech you to keep that promise which you made me once to send me home. I am eager now to be gone, and so are all my men. They wear me out and pester me with their complaints whenever you are not about."

' "Royal son of Laertes, Odysseus of the nimble wits," the goddess answered me, "I am not going to keep you in my house against your wishes. But before I can send you home you have to make a journey of a very different kind, and find your way to the Halls of Hades and Persephone the Dread, to consult the soul of Teiresias, the blind Theban prophet, whose understanding even death has not impaired. For dead though he is, Persephone has left to him, and him alone, a mind to reason with. The rest are mere shadows flitting to and fro."

'This news broke my heart. I sat down on the bed and wept. I had no further use for life, no wish to see the sunshine any more. But when at last I grew tired of tears and of tossing about on the bed, I began to question her:

' "But tell me, Circe, who is to guide me on the way? No one has ever sailed a black ship into Hell."

' "Odysseus," the goddess answered me, "don't think of lingering on shore for lack of a pilot. Set up your mast, spread the white sail and sit down in the ship. The North Wind will blow her on her way; and when she has brought you across the River of Ocean, you will come to a wild coast and to Persephone's Grove, where the tall poplars grow and the willows that so quickly shed their seeds. Beach your boat there by Ocean's swirling stream and march on into Hades' Kingdom of Decay. There the River of Flaming Fire and the River of Lamentation, which is a branch of the Waters of Styx, unite round a pinnacle of rock to pour their thundering streams into Acheron. This is the spot, my lord, that I bid you to seek out. Once there, dig a trench about a cubit long and a cubit in breadth. Around this trench pour offering to all the dead, first with honey mixed with milk, then with sweet wine, and last of all with water. Over all this sprinkle white barley and then begin your prayers to the helpless ghosts of the dead. Promise them that once you are in Ithaca you will sacrifice in your palace a barren heifer, the best that you have, and will heap the pyre with treasures and make Teiresias a separate offering of the finest jet-black sheep to be found in your flock. When you have finished your invocations to the glorious fellowship of the dead, sacrifice a young ram and a black ewe, holding their heads down towards Erebus while you turn your own aside, as though about to recross the River of Ocean. Then the souls of the dead and departed will come up in their multitudes and you must bid your men make haste to flay the sheep that are lying there slaughtered by your blade, and burn them up while they pray to the gods, to mighty Hades and august Persephone. Sit still yourself meanwhile, with your drawn sword in your hand, and do not let any of the helpless ghosts come near the blood till you have had speech with Teiresias. Presently the prophet himself will come to you, my lord king. And he will lay down for you your journey and the distances to be covered, and direct you home across the fish-delighting seas."

'Circe finished, and soon after the Dawn enthroned herself in gold. The Nymph clothed me in my tunic and cloak and dressed herself in a long robe of silvery sheen, light in fabric and charming to the eye. She put a veil on her head, and round her waist she fastened a splendid golden belt. Then I walked through the palace and made the round of my men, rousing them each with a cheerful word.

' "Wake up," I said, "and bid your pleasant dreams farewell. We must be off. My lady Circe has given me our sailing orders."

'My gallant band made no demur. But not even now did I get them all off without a casualty. There was one called Elpenor, the youngest of the party, not much of a fighting man nor very strong in the head. This young fellow of mine had got drunk, and longing for fresh air had left his friends in the enchanted palace and gone to sleep by himself. Roused in the morning by the bustle and din of the departure, he leapt up suddenly, and forgetting to go to the long ladder and take the right way down, he toppled headlong from the roof. He broke his neck and his soul went down to Hades.

'When the rest of the party joined me I took them into my confidence. "You no doubt imagine," I said, "that you are bound for home and our beloved Ithaca. But Circe has marked out for us a very different route, to the Halls of Hades and Persephone the Dread, where we must seek advice of the soul of Theban Teiresias."

'When I told them this they were heart-broken. They sat down where they were and wept and tore their hair. But they might have spared themselves their lamentations for all the good they did.

'We made our way to our ship and the beach in a sorry mood and with many tears. Meanwhile Circe, after taking leave of us, had tethered a young ram and a black ewe by the ship. She had slipped past us with ease; and when a god wishes to remain unseen, what eye can observe his coming or his going?

XI

THE BOOK OF THE DEAD

'OUR first task, when we came down to the sea and reached our ship, was to run her into the good salt water and put the mast and sails on board. We then picked up the sheep we found there and stowed them in the vessel. After which we ourselves embarked. And a melancholy crew we were. There was not a dry cheek in the company. However, Circe of the lovely tresses, human though she was in speech, proved her powers as a goddess by sending us the friendly escort of a favourable breeze, which sprang up from astern and filled the sail of our blue-prowed ship. All we had to do, after putting the tackle in order fore and aft, was to sit still, while the wind and the helmsman kept her straight. With a taut sail she forged ahead all day, till the sun went down and left her to pick her way through the darkness.

'Thus she brought us to the deep-flowing River of Ocean and the frontiers of the world, where the fog-bound Cimmerians live in the City of Perpetual Mist. When the bright Sun climbs the sky and puts the stars to flight, no ray from him can penetrate to them, nor can he see them as he drops from heaven and sinks once more to earth. For dreadful Night has spread her mantle over the heads of that unhappy folk.

'Here we beached our boat and after disembarking the sheep made our way along the banks of the River of Ocean till we reached the spot that Circe had described. There, while Perimedes and Eurylochus caught hold of the victims, I drew my sharp sword from my side and dug a trench about a cubit long and a cubit wide. Around this trench I poured libations to all the dead, first with mingled honey and milk, then with sweet wine, and last of all with water. Over all this I sprinkled some white barley, and then began my prayers to the helpless ghosts of the dead, promising them that directly I got back to Ithaca I should sacrifice a barren heifer in my palace, the best I had in my possession, and heap the pyre with treasures, and make Teiresias a separate offering of the finest jet-black sheep to be found in my flocks. When I had finished my prayers and invocations to the communities of the dead, I took the sheep and cut their throats over the trench so that the dark blood poured in. And now the souls of the dead who had gone below came swarming up from Erebus – fresh brides, unmarried youths, old men with life's long suffering behind them, tender young girls still nursing this first anguish in their hearts, and a great throng of warriors killed in battle, their spear-wounds gaping yet and all their armour stained with blood. From this multitude of souls, as they fluttered to and fro by the trench, there came a moaning that was horrible to hear. Panic drained the blood from my cheeks. I turned to my comrades and told them quickly to flay the sheep I had slaughtered with my sword and burn them, while they prayed to the gods, to mighty Hades and august Persephone. But I myself sat on guard, bare sword in hand, and prevented any of the feckless ghosts from approaching the blood before I had speech with Teiresias.

'The first soul that came up was that of my own man Elpenor, for he had not yet had his burial in the wide bosom of Earth. So urgent had we felt our other task to be that we had left his corpse unburied and unwept in Circe's house. Now, when I saw him, tears started to my eyes and I was stirred with pity for him.

'I called across to him at once: "Elpenor! How did you come here, under the western gloom? You have been quicker on foot than I in my black ship!"

'I heard him sigh, and then his answer came: "My royal master, Odysseus of the nimble wits, it was the malice of some evil power that was my undoing, and all the wine I swilled before I went to sleep in Circe's palace. For I clean forgot to go to the long ladder and take the right way down, and so fell headlong from the roof. My neck was broken and my soul came down to Hades. And now, since I know that when you leave this kingdom of the dead you will put in with your good ship at the Isle of Aeaea, I beseech you, my prince, by all the absent friends we left behind, by your wife, by the father who supported you as a child, and by Telemachus, your only son, whom you left at home – by all these I beg you to remember me then and not to sail away and forsake me utterly nor leave me there unburied and unwept, or the gods may turn against you when they see my corpse. So burn me there with all my arms, such as they are, and raise a mound for me on the shore of the grey sea, in memory of an unlucky man, to mark the spot for future voyagers. Do this for me, and on my barrow plant the oar I used to pull when I was alive and on the benches with my mates."

'To which I answered: "All this, my poor Elpenor, I will do. Nothing shall be forgotten."

'Thus we two faced each other across the trench in solemn colloquy, I on the one side, with my sword stretched out above the blood, and on the other the ghost of my comrade pouring out his tale.

'Next came the soul of my dead mother, Anticleia, the daughter of the great Autolycus, who had still been alive when I said farewell and sailed for sacred Ilium. My eyes filled with tears when I saw her there, and I was stirred to compassion. Yet, deeply moved though I was, I would not allow her to approach the blood out of turn, before I had had speech with Teiresias. And the soul of the Theban prophet now came up, with a gold rod in his hand, saw who I was, and saluted me.

' "Royal son of Laertes, Odysseus of the nimble wits, what has brought you, the man of misfortune, to forsake the sunlight and to visit the dead in this mirthless place? Step back now from the trench and hold your sword aside, so that I can drink the blood and prophesy the truth to you."

'I backed away, driving my sword home in its silver scabbard. And when Teiresias spoke, after drinking the dark blood, it was the voice of the authentic seer that I heard.

' "My lord Odysseus," he began, "you are in search of some easy way to reach your home. But the powers above are going to make your journey hard. For I cannot think that you will slip through the hands of the Earthshaker, who has by no means forgotten his resentment against you for blinding his beloved son. Notwithstanding that, you and your friends may yet reach Ithaca, though not without mishap, if only you determine to keep a tight hand on yourself and your men from the moment when your good ship leaves the deep blue seas and approaches the Isle of Thrinacie, and you see there at their pasture the cattle and the fat sheep of the Sun-god, whose eye and ear miss nothing in the world. If you leave them untouched and fix your mind on getting home, there is some chance that all of you may yet reach Ithaca, though not in comfort. But if you hurt them, then I warrant you that your ship and company will be destroyed, and if you yourself do manage to escape, you will come home late, in evil plight, upon a foreign ship, with all your comrades dead. You will find trouble too in your house – a set of scoundrels eating up your stores, making love to your royal consort, and offering wedding gifts. It is true that you will pay out these men for their misdeeds when you reach home. But whichever way you choose to kill them, whether by stratagem or in a straight fight with the naked sword, when you have cleared your palace of these Suitors, you must then set out once more upon your travels. You must take a well-cut oar and go on till you reach a people who know nothing of the sea and never use salt with their food, so that our crimson-painted ships and the long oars that serve those ships as wings are quite beyond their ken. And this will be your cue – a very clear one, which you cannot miss. When you fall in with some other traveller who speaks of the 'winnowing-fan' you are carrying on your shoulder, the time will have come for you to plant your shapely oar in the earth and offer Lord Poseidon the rich sacrifice of a ram, a bull, and a breeding-boar. Then go back home and make ceremonial offerings to the immortal gods who live in the broad heavens, to all of them, this time, in due precedence.

'"As for your own end, Death will come to you out of the sea, Death in his gentlest guise. When he takes you, you will be worn out after an easy old age and surrounded by a prosperous people. This is the truth that I have told you."

' "Teiresias," I answered him, "I cannot doubt that these are the threads of destiny which the gods themselves have spun. But there is another matter that I wish you to explain. I see the soul of my dead mother over there. She sits in silence by the blood and cannot bring herself to look her own son in the face or say a single word to him. Tell me, my prince, is there no way to make her know that I am he?"

' "There is a simple rule," said Teiresias, "which I will explain. Any ghost to whom you give access to the blood will hold rational speech with you, while those whom you reject will leave you and retire."

'These were the last words I heard from Prince Teiresias. He had spoken his prophecies and now withdrew into the Halls of Hades. But I kept steady at my post and waited till my mother came up and took a draught of the black blood. She recognized me then at once, and the pitiful words fell fast enough from her lips:

' "My child, how did you come here under the western gloom, you that are still alive? This is no easy place for living eyes to find. For between you and us flow the wide waters of the Rivers of Fear, and the very first barrier is Ocean, whose stream a man could never cross on foot, but only in a well-found ship. Have you come here now from Troy and been wandering over the seas with your comrades ever since you left? Have you not been to Ithaca yet, nor seen your wife and home?"

' "Mother," I answered her, "I had no choice but to come down to Hades and consult the soul of Theban Teiresias. For I have never yet been near to Achaea, nor set foot on our own land, but have been a wretched wanderer from the very day when I sailed with King Agamemnon for Ilium to fight the Trojan charioteers. But tell me your own story. What was your fate; what death overtook you? Had you some lingering disease? Or did Artemis the Archeress visit and kill you with her gentle darts? And tell me of my father and the son I left behind.

Is my royal prerogative safe in their hands, or did it fall to some other man when it was assumed that I should never return? And what of my good wife? How does she feel and what does she intend to do? Is she still living with her son and keeping our estate intact? Or has the likeliest of her countrymen already married her?"

"There is no question of her not staying in your house," my royal mother replied. "She has schooled her heart to patience, though her eyes are never free from tears as the slow nights and days pass sorrowfully by. Your princely rights have not yet passed into other hands, but Telemachus is in peaceful possession of the royal lands and attends all public banquets such as the magistrates are expected to give, for every one of them invites him. But your father has made a recluse of himself in the country and never goes down to the city. He has given up sleeping in laundered sheets and blankets on a proper bed. Instead, he lies down in the winter-time with the labourers at the farm in the dust by the fire, and goes about in rags. But when the summer and the mellow autumn days come round, he makes himself a humble couch of fallen leaves anywhere on the high ground of his vineyard plot. There he lies in his misery, nursing his grief and yearning for you to come back, while to make things worse old age is pressing hard upon him. That was my undoing too; it was that that brought me to the grave. It was not that the keen-eyed Archeress sought me out in our home and killed me with her gentle darts. Nor was I attacked by any of the malignant diseases that so often make the body waste away and die. No, it was my heartache for you, my glorious Odysseus, and for your wise and gentle ways that brought my life and all its sweetness to an end."

'As my mother spoke, there came to me out of the confusion in my heart the one desire, to embrace her spirit, dead though she was. Thrice, in my eagerness to clasp her to me, I started forward with my hands outstretched. Thrice, like a shadow or a dream, she slipped through my arms and left me harrowed by an even sharper pain.

' "Mother," I cried in my despair, "why do you avoid me when I try to reach you, so that even in Hell we may throw our loving arms around each other's necks and draw cold comfort from our tears? Or is this a mere phantom that grim Persephone has sent me to accentuate my grief?"

' "My child, my child!" came her reply. "What man on earth has more to bear than you? This is no trick played on you by Persephone, Daughter of Zeus. You are only witnessing here the law of our mortal nature, when we come to die. We no longer have sinews keeping the bones and flesh together, but once the life-force has departed from our white bones, all is consumed by the fierce heat of the blazing fire, and the soul slips away like a dream and flutters on the air. But you must hasten back now to the light of day. And bear in mind all you have learnt here, so that one day you can tell your wife."

' Such was the talk that we two had together. And now, impelled by dread Persephone, there came up all the women who had been the wives or the daughters of princes, and gathered round the black blood in a throng. I cast about me for a way to question each in turn, and in the end I solved the problem by drawing my long sword from my side and preventing them from drinking the dark blood all together. So they came forward and announced their lineage one by one, and thus I was able to question them all.

' The first I saw was highborn Tyro, who told me she was the daughter of the noble Salmoneus, and had married Cretheus, Aeolus' son. She fell in love with the god of the River Enipeus, the loveliest river that runs on earth, and often wandered on the banks of his beautiful stream, until one day the Lord of the Earthquake, the Girdler of the World, disguised himself as the river-god and lay with her where the river rushes out to sea. A dark wave gathered mountain-high, curled over them, and hid the woman and the god. He then unclasped her virgin belt and sealed her eyes in sleep. But when his love had had its way, he took her hand in his; and now he spoke. "Lady," he said, "be happy in this love of ours, and as the year completes its course, since a god's embrace is never fruitless, you will give birth to beautiful children, whom you must nurse and rear with care. But now go home, and guard your tongue. Tell no one; but I wish you to know that I am Poseidon, the Shaker of the Earth." The god then disappeared under the heaving sea. Tyro conceived, and gave birth to Pelias and Neleus, who both rose to power as servants of almighty Zeus. Pelias lived in the spacious lands of Iolcus, and his wealth lay in his flocks; while Neleus had his home in sandy Pylos. Nor were these the only children of this queen among women. To Cretheus she bore three other sons, Aeson and Pheres and Amythaon, that gallant charioteer.

'The next I saw was Antiope, the daughter of Asopus; and it was in the arms of Zeus that she claimed to have slept. She had two sons, Amphion and Zethus, the founders of Thebes of the Seven Gates, who first fortified its site with towers, since for all their prowess they could not establish themselves in the open lands of Thebes without a wall to their city.

'After Antiope I saw Alcmene, Amphitryon's wife, who lay in the loving arms of almighty Zeus and brought the all-daring lion-hearted Heracles into the world. Megare I also saw, proud Creon's daughter, who married that indomitable son of Amphitryon.

'Then I met Oedipus' mother, the lovely Epicaste. She in her ignorance committed the sin of marrying her son. For Oedipus killed his father and took his mother to wife. But the gods soon let the truth come out. For Oedipus they then conceived a cruel punishment: they left him to suffer the tortures of remorse as king of the Cadmeians in his beloved Thebes. But Epicaste, obsessed by anguish at her deed, hanged herself with a long rope she made fast to the roof-beam overhead, and so came down to the Halls of Hades, the mighty Warden of the Gates, leaving Oedipus to suffer all the horrors that a mother's curses can inflict.

'Next, and loveliest of all, came Chloris, the youngest daughter of Amphion son of Iasus, who once lorded it in Orchomenus as King of the Minyae. Neleus married her for her beauty and paid a fortune for her hand. So she was Queen in Pylos, and bore him glorious children, Nestor and Chromius and princely Periclymenus; and besides these the stately Pero, the wonder of her age, whom all their neighbours wished to marry. But Neleus announced that he would give her hand to no one but the man who should succeed in lifting from Phylace the cattle of the mighty Iphicles. It was a dangerous task to round up these shambling broad-browed cattle. A certain chivalrous seer was the only man who undertook the adventure. And the gods were against him. Misfortune dogged his steps; and he was left a wretched prisoner in the savage herdsmen's hands. The days passed and mounted up into months. But it was not until a year had run its course and the seasons came round once more, that the mighty Iphicles set him free in return for all the oracles he had uttered. Thus the will of Zeus was done.

'Then I saw Lede, wife of Tyndareus, who bore him those stout-hearted twins, Castor the trainer of horses, and Polydeuces the great boxer, both of whom are still alive, though the fruitful earth has received them in her lap. For even in the world below they have been singled out by Zeus; each is a living and a dead man on alternate days, and they are honoured like the gods.

'My eyes fell next on Iphimedeia, the consort of Aloeus, who claimed that she had slept with Poseidon, and was the mother of those short-lived twins, the godlike Otus and Ephialtes famed in story, the tallest men Earth ever nourished on her bread, and finer by far than all but the glorious Orion. In their ninth year they were nine cubits across the shoulders and nine fathoms tall. It was this pair that threatened to confound the very gods on Olympus with the din and turmoil of battle. It was their ambition to pile Mount Ossa on Olympus, and wooded Pelion on Ossa, so as to make a stairway up to heaven. And this they would have accomplished had they reached their full stature. But the son whom Leto of the lovely tresses bore to Zeus destroyed them both before the down came curling on their cheeks and decked their chins with its fleecy mantle.

'Phaedre I also saw, and Procris, and the lovely Ariadne, that daughter of the wizard Minos whom Theseus once attempted to carry off from Crete to the sacred soil of Athens, though he had no joy of her, for before their journey's end Dionysus brought word to Artemis, and she killed her in sea-girt Dia.

'Maera too, and Clymene I saw, and the hateful Eriphyle, who bartered her own husband's life for lucre. Indeed I could not tell you the tales, nor even give you the names, of all the great men's wives and daughters whom I saw, for before I had done the livelong night would have slipped away.

'But now the time has come for me to go and sleep, whether I join my crew on board or remain in your palace. As for my journey, I leave the arrangements in the gods' hands and in yours.'

Odysseus came to a stop. And such was the spell he had cast on the entire company that not a sound was heard in the whole length of that shadowy hall, till white-armed Arete broke the silence at last.

'Phaeacians,' she said, 'what is your verdict, now that you have seen the looks and stature of our guest and have sampled his wisdom? *My* guest, I should have said. But each of you shares in the honour. So do not send him on his way with undue haste, nor stint your generosity to one who stands in such sore need. For heaven has filled your homes with riches.'

The venerable lord Echeneus, the oldest man among them, followed this up. 'My friends,' he said, 'our wise queen's advice goes straight to the mark and is just what we might have expected. I think you should follow it. But it rests with Alcinous here to say the word and take the appropriate action.'

Alcinous replied without hesitation: 'As I live and rule this sailor folk, it shall be so. But our guest must curb his eagerness to get home and make up his mind to stay till tomorrow, so as to give me time to fulfil my generous plans. Meanwhile his passage home shall be the concern of the whole people, and my own in particular, since I am monarch here.'

'Lord Alcinous, my most worshipful prince,' Odysseus discreetly put in, 'nothing would suit me better than that you should press me to stay among you even for a year, provided you saw me safely back and loaded me with your splendid gifts. It would be a great advantage to me to arrive in my own country with fuller coffers. For thus enriched I should win a kindlier welcome and greater respect from everyone I met after returning to Ithaca.'

'Odysseus,' said Alcinous, 'we are far from regarding you as one of those impostors and humbugs whom this dark world brings forth in such profusion to spin their lying yarns which nobody can test. On the contrary, not only is your speech a delight but you have sound judgement too, and you have told us the stories of your compatriots and your own grievous misadventures with all the artistry that a ballad-singer might display. I beg you now to continue and let us know whether you also saw any of those heroic comrades of yours who joined you on the expedition to Ilium and fell in action there. The night is still long, too long for reckoning; and the time has not yet come for us to seek our sleeping-quarters. Tell me more of your marvellous doings. I could hold out till the blessed dawn, if only you could bring yourself to stay in this hall and continue the tale of your misfortunes.'

In response to this the resourceful Odysseus went on with his story.

'Lord Alcinous, my most worshipful prince,' he began, 'there is a time for long tales, but there is also a time for sleep. However, if you really wish to hear me further, far be it from me to deny you an even more tragic tale than you have heard already. I will tell you the sad fate of my comrades-in-arms who perished after the sack and escaped from the perils and turmoil of the Trojan war only to lose their lives when homeward bound, all through the whim of one unfaithful wife.

'In the end, holy Persephone drove off the women's ghosts. They scattered in all directions, and I was approached by the soul of Agamemnon son of Atreus. He came in sorrow, and round about him were gathered the souls of all those who had met their doom and died with him in Aegisthus' palace. As soon as he had drunk the dark blood, he recognized me, uttered a loud cry and burst into tears, stretching his arms out in my direction in his eagerness to reach me. But this he could not do, for all the strength and vigour had gone for ever from those once supple limbs. Moved to compassion at the sight, I too gave way to tears and spoke to him from my heart:

' "Illustrious son of Atreus, Agamemnon, King of men, tell me what mortal stroke of fate it was that laid you low. Did Poseidon rouse the winds to fury and overwhelm your ships? Or did you fall to some hostile tribe on land as you were rounding up their cattle and their flocks or fighting with them for their town and women?"

' "Royal son of Laertes, Odysseus of the nimble wits," he answered me at once, "Poseidon did not wreck my ships; nor did I fall to any hostile tribe on land. It was Aegisthus who plotted my destruction and with my accursed wife put me to death. He invited me to the palace, he feasted me, and he killed me as a man fells an ox at its manger. That was my most miserable end. And all around me my companions were cut down in ruthless succession, like white-tusked swine slaughtered in the mansion of some great and wealthy lord, for a wedding, a club-banquet, or a sumptuous public feast. You, Odysseus, have witnessed the deaths of many men in single combat or the thick of battle, but none with such horror as you would have felt had you seen us lying there by the wine-bowl and the laden tables in the hall, while the whole floor swam with our blood. Yet the most pitiable thing of all was the cry I heard from Cassandra, daughter of Priam, whom that foul traitress Clytaemnestra murdered at my side. As I lay on the ground, I raised my hands in a dying effort to grip her sword. But the harlot turned her face aside, and had not even the grace, though I was on my way to Hades, to shut my eyes with her hands or to close my mouth. And so I say that for brutality and infamy there is no one to equal a woman who can contemplate such deeds. Who else could conceive so hideous a crime as her deliberate butchery of her husband and her lord? Indeed, I had looked forward to a rare welcome from my children and my servants when I reached my home. But now, in the depth of her villainy, she has branded not herself alone but the whole of her sex and every honest woman for all time to come."

' "Alas!" I exclaimed. "All-seeing Zeus has indeed proved himself a relentless foe to the House of Atreus, and from the beginning he has worked his will through women's crooked ways. It was for Helen's sake that so many of us met our deaths, and it was Clytaemnestra who hatched the plot against her absent lord."

' "Let this be a lesson to you also," replied Agamemnon. "Never be too gentle even with your wife, nor show her all that is in your mind. Reveal a little of your counsel to her, but keep the rest of it to yourself. Not that *your* wife, Odysseus, will ever murder you. Icarius' daughter is far too sound in heart and brain for that. The wise Penelope! She was a young bride when we said goodbye to her on our way to the war. She had a baby son at her breast. And now, I suppose, he has begun to take his seat among the men. The lucky lad! His loving father will come home and see him, and he will kiss his father. That is how things should be. Whereas that wife of mine refused me even the satisfaction of setting eyes on my son. She could not wait so long before she killed his father. And now let me give you a piece of advice which I hope you will take to heart. Do not sail openly into port when you reach your home-country. Make a secret approach. Women, I tell you, are no longer to be trusted. But to go back to my son, can you give me the truth about him? Do you and your friends happen to have heard of him as still alive, in Orchomenus possibly, or sandy Pylos, or maybe with Menelaus in his spreading city of Sparta? For I know that my good Orestes has not yet died and come below."

' "Son of Atreus," I answered him, "why ask me that? I have no idea whether he is alive or dead. And it would be wrong of me to give you idle gossip."

' Such was the solemn colloquy that we two had as we stood there with our sorrows and the tears rolled down our cheeks. And now there came the souls of Peleus' son Achilles, of Patroclus, of the noble Antilochus, and of Aias, who in stature and in manly grace was second to none of the Danaans but the flawless son of Peleus. It was the soul of Achilles, the great runner, who recognized me. In mournful, measured tones he greeted me by my titles, and went on: "What next, Odysseus, dauntless heart? What greater exploit can you plan to cap your voyage here? How did you dare to come below to Hades' realm, where the dead live on without their wits as disembodied ghosts?"

'"Achilles," I answered him, "son of Peleus and flower of Achaean chivalry, I came to consult with Teiresias in the hope of finding out from him how I could reach my rocky Ithaca. For I have not managed to come near Achaea yet, nor set foot on my own island, but have been dogged by misfortune. How different from you, Achilles, the most fortunate man that ever was or will be! For in the old days when you were on earth, we Argives honoured you as though you were a god; and now, down here, you are a mighty prince among the dead. For you, Achilles, Death should have lost his sting."

'"My lord Odysseus," he replied, "spare me your praise of Death. Put me on earth again, and I would rather be a serf in the house of some landless man, with little enough for himself to live on, than king of all these dead men that have done with life. But enough. Tell me what news there is of that fine son of mine. Did he follow me to the war and play a leading part or not? And tell me anything you have heard of the noble Peleus. Does the Myrmidon nation still do him homage, or do they look down on him in Hellas and Phthie now that old age has made a cripple of him? For I am not up there in the sunlight to protect him with the mighty arms that once did battle for the Argives and laid the champions of the enemy low on the broad plains of Troy. If I could return for a single hour to my father's house with the strength I then enjoyed, I would make those who injure him and rob him of his rights shrink in dismay before my might and my unconquerable hands."

'"Of the noble Peleus," I answered Achilles, "I have heard nothing. But of your dear son Neoptolemus I will give you all the news you ask for, since it was I who brought him from Scyros in my own fine ship to join the Achaean army. And there in front of the city of Troy, when we used to discuss our plans, he was always the first to speak and no words of his ever missed their mark. King Nestor and I were his only betters in debate. Nor, when we Achaeans gave battle on the Trojan plain, was he ever content to linger in the ranks or with the crowd. That impetuous spirit of his gave place to none, and he would sally out beyond the foremost. Many was the man he brought down in mortal combat. I could not tell you of all the people he killed in battle for the Argives, nor give you their names; but well I remember how the lord Eurypylus son of Telephus fell to his sword, and how many of his Hittite men-at-arms were slaughtered at his side, all on account of a bribe that a woman had taken. He was the handsomest man I ever saw, next to the godlike Memnon. Then again, when we Argive captains took our places in the wooden horse Epeius made, and it rested solely with me to throw our ambush open or to keep it shut, all the other Danaan chieftains and officers were wiping the tears from their eyes and every man's legs were trembling beneath him, but not once did I see your son's fine colour change to pallor nor catch him brushing a tear from his cheek. On the contrary he begged me time and again to let him sally from the Horse and kept fumbling eagerly at his sword-hilt and his heavy spear in his keenness to fall on the Trojans. And when we had brought Priam's city tumbling down in ruins, he took his share of the booty and his special prize, and embarked safe and sound on his ship without a single wound either from a flying dart or from a sword at close quarters. The War-god in his fury is no respecter of persons, but the mischances of battle had touched your son not at all."

'When I had done, the soul of Achilles, whose feet had been so fleet on earth, passed with great strides down the meadow of asphodel, rejoicing in the news I had given him of his son's renown.

'The mourning ghosts of all the other dead and departed

pressed round me now, each with some question for me on matters that were near his heart. The only soul that stood aloof was that of Aias son of Telamon, still embittered by the defeat I had inflicted on him at the ships when defending my claim to the arms of Achilles, whose divine mother had offered them as a prize, with the Trojan captives and Pallas Athene for judges. Would to god I had never won such a prize – the arms that brought Aias to his grave, the heroic Aias, who next to the peerless son of Peleus was the finest Danaan of all in looks and the noblest in action. I called to him now, using his own and his royal father's names, and sought to placate him:

' "So not even death itself, Aias, could make you forget your anger with me on account of those accursed arms! Yet it was the gods that made them a curse to us Argives, who lost in you so great a tower of strength and have never ceased to mourn your death as truly as we lament Achilles, Peleus' son. No one else is to blame but Zeus, that bitter foe of the Danaan army, who brought you to your doom. Draw near, my prince, and hear me tell our story. Curb your resentment and conquer your pride."

'But Aias gave me not a word in answer and went off into Erebus to join the souls of the other dead, where, for all his bitterness, he might yet have spoken to me, or I to him, had not the wish to see the souls of other dead men filled my heart.

'And indeed I there saw Minos, glorious son of Zeus, sitting gold sceptre in hand and delivering judgement to the dead, who sat or stood all round the King, putting their cases to him for decision within the wide portals of the House of Hades.

'My eyes fell next on the giant hunter Orion, who was rounding up the game on the meadow of asphodel, the very beasts his living hands had killed among the lonely hills, armed with a club of solid bronze that could never be broken.

'And I saw Tityos, son of the majestic Earth, prone on the ground and covering nine roods as he lay. A pair of vultures sat by him, one on either side, and plucked at his liver, plunging their beaks into his body; and his hands were powerless to drive them off. This was his punishment for assaulting Leto, the glorious consort of Zeus, as she was travelling to Pytho across the pleasant lawns of Panopeus.

'I also saw the awful agonies that Tantalus has to bear. The old man was standing in a pool of water which nearly reached his chin, and his thirst drove him to unceasing efforts; but he could never get a drop to drink. For whenever he stooped in his eagerness to lap the water, it disappeared. The pool was swallowed up, and all he saw at his feet was the dark earth, which some mysterious power had parched. Trees spread their foliage high over the pool and dangled fruits above his head – pear-trees and pomegranates, apple-trees with their glossy burden, sweet figs and luxuriant olives. But whenever the old man tried to grasp them in his hands, the wind would toss them up towards the shadowy clouds.

'Then I witnessed the torture of Sisyphus, as he tackled his huge rock with both his hands. Leaning against it with his arms and thrusting with his legs, he would contrive to push the boulder up-hill to the top. But every time, as he was going to send it toppling over the crest, its sheer weight turned it back, and the misbegotten rock came bounding down again to level ground. So once more he had to wrestle with the thing and push it up, while the sweat poured from his limbs and the dust rose high above his head.

'Next after him I observed the mighty Heracles – his wraith, that is to say, since he himself banquets at ease with the immortal gods and has for consort Hebe of the slim ankles, the Daughter of almighty Zeus and golden-sandalled Here. From the dead around him there rose a clamour like the call of wild fowl, as they scattered in their panic. His looks were sombre as the blackest night, and with his naked bow in hand and an arrow on the string he glanced ferociously this way and that as though at any moment he might shoot. Terrible too was the golden strap he wore as a baldric over his breast, depicting with grim artistry the forms of bears, wild boars, and glaring lions, with scenes of conflict and of battle, of bloodshed and the massacre of men. That baldric was a masterpiece that no one should have made, and I can only hope that the craftsman who conceived the work will rest content.

'One look was enough to tell Heracles who I was, and he greeted me in mournful tones. "Unhappy man!" he exclaimed, after reciting my titles. "So you too are working out some such miserable doom as I was a slave to when the sun shone over my head. Son of Zeus though I was, unending troubles came my way. For I was bound in service to a master far beneath my rank, who used to set me the most arduous tasks. Once, being unable to think of anything more difficult for me to do, he sent me down here to bring away the Hound of Hell. And under the guiding hands of Hermes and bright-eyed Athene, I did succeed in capturing him and I dragged him out of Hades' realm."

'Heracles said no more, but withdrew into the House of Hades, while I stuck to my post, in the hope that I might yet be visited by other men of note who had perished long ago. And now I should have gone still further back in time and seen the heroes whom I wished to meet, Theseus, for instance, and Peiri-thous, those glorious children of the gods. But before that could happen, the tribes of the dead came up and gathered round me in their tens of thousands, raising their eerie cry. Sheer panic turned me pale, gripped by the sudden fear that dread Perse-phone might send me up from Hades' Halls some ghastly mon-ster like the Gorgon's head. I made off quickly to my ship and told my men to embark and loose the hawsers. They climbed in at once and took their seats on the benches, and the current carried her down the River of Ocean, helped by our oars at first and later by a friendly breeze.

XII

SCYLLA AND CHARYBDIS

'FROM the flowing waters of the River of Ocean my ship passed into the wide spaces of the open sea, and so reached Aeaea, the Island of the Rising Sun, where tender Dawn has her home and her dancing-lawns. Here we beached her on the sands and climbed out on to the sea-shore, where we fell into a sound sleep that lasted till daybreak.

'At the first sight of Dawn's red streamers in the East, I sent off a party to Circe's house to fetch the dead body of Elpenor. We quickly hewed some billets of wood, and then, with the tears streaming down our cheeks, gave him solemn burial on the summit of the boldest headland of the coast. When the corpse was burnt, and with it the dead man's arms, we built him a barrow, hauled up a stone for monument, and planted his shapely oar on the top of the mound.

'We had just dispatched the last details of our task, when Circe, who was well aware of our return from Hades and had decked herself out to meet us, came hurrying up with a train of servants laden with bread, a plentiful supply of meat, and sparkling ruddy wine.

' "What hardihood," said the goddess, as we gathered round her, "to descend alive into the House of Hades! One death is enough for most men; but you will now have two. However, forget these things, spend the rest of the day where you are, enjoying this food and wine, and at the first peep of dawn you shall sail. I myself will give you your route and make every landmark clear, to save you from the disasters you would suffer if you ran into the snares that may be laid for you on sea or land."

'We were not difficult to persuade. So the whole day long till sunset we sat and feasted on our rich supply of meat washed down by mellow wine. When the sun sank and darkness fell, my men settled down for the night by the hawsers of the ship; but Circe took me by the hand, led me away from my good friends, and made me sit down and tell her all my news as she lay beside me. When I had given her the whole tale from first to last the goddess said:

' "Very well; all that is done with now. But listen while I tell you what follows – and the gods themselves will see that my words keep fresh in your mind. Your next encounter will be with the Sirens, who bewitch everybody that approaches them. There is no home-coming for the man who draws near them unawares and hears the Sirens' voices; no welcome from his wife, no little children brightening at their father's return. For with the music of their song the Sirens cast their spell upon him, as they sit there in a meadow piled high with the mouldering skeletons of men, whose withered skin still hangs upon their bones. Drive your ship past the spot, and to prevent any of your crew from hearing, soften some beeswax and plug their ears with it. But if you wish to listen yourself, make them bind you hand and foot on board and stand you up by the step of the mast, with the rope's ends lashed to the mast itself. This will allow you to listen with enjoyment to the twin Sirens' voices. But if you start begging your men to release you, they must add to the bonds that already hold you fast.

' "When your crew have carried you past this danger, you will have reached a point beyond which I cannot fully guide you. Two ways will lie before you, and you must choose between them as you see fit, though I will tell you both. One leads to those sheer cliffs which the blessed gods know as the Wandering Rocks. Here blue-eyed Amphitrite sends her great breakers thundering in, and the very birds cannot fly by in safety. Even from the shy doves that bring ambrosia to Father Zeus the beetling rock takes toll each time they pass, and the Father has to send one more to make their number up; while for such sailors as bring their ship to the spot, there is no escape whatever. They end as flotsam on the sea, timbers and corpses tossed in confusion by the waves or licked up by tempestuous and destroying flames.

Of all ships that go down to the sea one only has made the passage, and that was the celebrated Argo, homeward bound from Aeetes' coast. And she would soon have been dashed upon those mighty crags, if Here, for love of Jason, had not helped her past.

'"In the other direction lie two rocks, the higher of which rears its sharp peak up to the very sky and is capped by black clouds that never stream away nor leave clear weather round the top, even in summer or at harvest-time. No man on earth could climb it, up or down, not even with twenty hands and feet to help him; for the rock is as smooth as if it had been polished. But half-way up the crag there is a misty cavern, facing the West and running down to Erebus, past which, my lord Odysseus, you must steer your ship. The strongest bowman could not reach the gaping mouth of the cave with an arrow shot from a ship below. It is the home of Scylla, the creature with the dreadful bark. It is true that her yelp is no louder than a new-born pup's, but she is a horrible monster nevertheless, and one whom nobody could look at with delight, not even a god if he passed that way. She has twelve feet, all dangling in the air, and six long necks, each ending in a grisly head with triple rows of teeth, set thick and close, and darkly menacing death. Up to her middle she is sunk in the depths of the cave, but her heads protrude from the fearful abyss, and thus she fishes from her own abode, scouting around the rock for any dolphin or sword-fish she may catch, or any of the larger monsters which in their thousands find their living in the roaring seas. No crew can boast that they ever sailed their ship past Scylla without loss, since from every passing vessel she snatches a man with each of her heads and so bears off her prey.

'"The other of the two rocks is lower, as you, Odysseus, will see, and the distance between them is no more than a bowshot. A great fig-tree with luxuriant foliage grows upon the crag, and it is below this that dread Charybdis sucks the dark waters down. Three times a day she spews them up, and three times she swallows them down once more in her horrible way. Heaven keep you from the spot when she is at her work, for not even the

Earthshaker could save you from disaster. No: you must hug Scylla's rock and with all speed drive your ship through, since it is far better that you should have to mourn the loss of six of your company than that of your whole crew."

'"Yes, goddess," I replied, "but there is more I wish to know. Could I not somehow steer clear of the terrors of Charybdis, yet tackle Scylla when she comes at my crew?"

'But the goddess only cried out at me as an obstinate fool, always spoiling for a fight and welcoming trouble. "So you are not prepared," she said, "to give in even to immortal gods? I tell you, Scylla was not born for death: the fiend will live for ever. She is a thing to shun, intractable, ferocious, and impossible to fight. No; against her there is no defence, and valour lies in flight. For if you waste time by the rock in putting on your armour, I am only afraid she may dart out once more, catch you again with all six heads and snatch another half-dozen of your crew. So drive your ship past with all your might, and call on Cratais, Scylla's mother, who brought her into the world to prey on men. She will prevent her from making a second sally.

'"Your next landfall will be the island of Thrinacie, where the Sun-god pastures his large herds and well-fed sheep. There are seven herds of cattle and as many flocks of beautiful sheep, with fifty head in each. These animals were not born into the world nor are they subject to a natural death. And to shepherd them they have goddesses, the lovely Nymphs, Phaethusa and Lampetie, children of Hyperion the Sun-god by the divine Neaera, whom their mother, when she had brought them up, carried off to this new and distant home in Thrinacie to watch over their father's sheep and fatted cattle. Now if you leave these animals untouched and fix your mind on getting home, there is some chance that all of you may yet reach Ithaca, though not in comfort. But if you hurt them, then I swear to you that your ship and your company will be destroyed. And if you yourself contrive to escape, you will come home late, in evil plight, with all your comrades lost."

'As Circe came to an end, Dawn took her golden throne. The

gracious goddess left me and made her way inland, while I went
to my ship and ordered my men to embark and loose the hawsers. They did so promptly, went to the benches, sat down in
their places and struck the grey surf with their oars. Then the
fair Circe, that formidable goddess with a woman's voice, sent
us the friendly escort of a favourable wind, which sprang up
from astern and filled the sail of our blue-painted ship. We set
the tackle in order fore and aft and then sat down, while the
wind and the helmsman kept her on her course.

'I was much perturbed in spirit and before long took my men
into my confidence. "My friends," I said, "it is not right that
only one or two of us should know the prophecies that Circe, in
her divine wisdom, has made to me, and I am going to pass them
on to you, so that we may all be forewarned, whether we die or
escape the worst and save our lives. Her first warning concerned
the mysterious Sirens. We must beware of their song and give
their flowery meadow a wide berth. I alone, she suggested,
might listen to their voices; but you must bind me hard and
fast, so that I cannot stir from the spot where you will stand me,
by the step of the mast, with the rope's ends lashed round the
mast itself. And if I beg you to release me, you must tighten and
add to my bonds."

'I thus explained every detail to my men. In the meantime our
good ship, with that perfect wind to drive her, fast approached
the Sirens' Isle. But now the breeze dropped, some power lulled
the waves, and a breathless calm set in. Rising from their seats
my men drew in the sail and threw it into the hold, then sat
down at the oars and churned the water white with their blades
of polished pine. Meanwhile I took a large round of wax, cut it
up small with my sword, and kneaded the pieces with all the
strength of my fingers. The wax soon yielded to my vigorous
treatment and grew warm, for I had the rays of my Lord the
Sun to help me. I took each of my men in turn and plugged their
ears with it. They then made me a prisoner on my ship by bind-
ing me hand and foot, standing me up by the step of the mast
and tying the rope's ends to the mast itself. This done, they sat

down once more and struck the grey water with their oars.

'We made good progress and had just come within call of the shore when the Sirens became aware that a ship was swiftly bearing down upon them, and broke into their liquid song.

' "Draw near," they sang, "illustrious Odysseus, flower of Achaean chivalry, and bring your ship to rest so that you may hear our voices. No seaman ever sailed his black ship past this spot without listening to the sweet tones that flow from our lips, and none that listened has not been delighted and gone on a wiser man. For we know all that the Argives and Trojans suffered on the broad plain of Troy by the will of the gods, and we have foreknowledge of all that is going to happen on this fruitful earth."

'The lovely voices came to me across the water, and my heart was filled with such a longing to listen that with nod and frown I signed to my men to set me free. But they swung forward to their oars and rowed ahead, while Perimedes and Eurylochus jumped up, tightened my bonds and added more. However, when they had rowed past the Sirens and we could no longer hear their voices and the burden of their song, my good companions were quick to clear their ears of the wax I had used to stop them, and to free me from my shackles.

'We had no sooner put this island behind us than I saw a cloud of smoke ahead and a raging surf, the roar of which I could already hear. My men were so terrified that the oars all dropped from their grasp and fell with a splash in the wash of the ship; while the ship herself, now that the hands that had pulled the long blades were idle, was brought to a standstill. I made a tour of the vessel, and with a soothing word for each man I tried to put heart into my company.

' "My friends," I said, "we are men who have met trouble before. And I cannot see that we are faced here by anything worse than when the Cyclops used his brutal strength to imprison us in his cave. Yet my courage and presence of mind found a way out for us even from there; and I am sure that this too will be a memory for us one day. So now I appeal to you all to do exactly as I say. Oarsmen, stick to your benches, striking hard with your blades through the broken water, and we may have the luck to slip by and for once avoid disaster. Helmsman, your orders are these. Get them by heart, for the good ship's steering-oar is under your control. Give a wide berth to that smoke and surf you see, and hug these cliffs, or before you can stop her the ship may take it into her head to make a dash over there and you'll wreck us."

'The crew obeyed me readily enough. Trouble from Scylla seemed inevitable, so I did not mention her, fearing that in their panic my men might stop rowing and hide in the hold. But now I allowed myself to forget Circe's irksome injunction not to arm myself in any way. I put my fine harness on, seized a couple of long spears, and took my stand on the forecastle deck, hoping from that post to get the first view of Scylla, the monster of the rocks, who wrought such havoc on my crew. But I could not catch a glimpse of her anywhere, though I searched the sombre face of the cliff in every part till my eyes were tired.

'Thus we sailed up the straits, groaning in terror, for on the one side we had Scylla, while on the other the mysterious Charybdis sucked down the salt sea water in her dreadful way. When she vomited it up, she was stirred to her depths and seethed over like a cauldron on a blazing fire; and the spray she flung on high rained down on the tops of the crags at either side. But when she swallowed the salt water down, the whole interior of her vortex was exposed, the rocks re-echoed to her fearful roar, and the dark sands of the sea bottom came into view.

'My men turned pale with fear; and now, while all eyes were fixed on Charybdis and the quarter from which we looked for disaster, Scylla snatched out of my boat the six ablest hands I had on board. I swung round, to glance at the ship and run my eye over the crew, just in time to see the arms and legs of her victims dangled high in the air above my head. "Odysseus!" they called out to me in their agony. But it was the last time they used my name. For like an angler on a jutting point, who with a long rod casts his ox-horn lure into the sea as bait for the little fish below, gets a bite, and whips his struggling prize to land, Scylla had whisked my comrades up and swept them struggling to the rocks, where she devoured them at her own door, shrieking and stretching out their hands to me in their last desperate throes. In all I have gone through as I made my way across the seas, I have never had to witness a more pitiable sight than that.

'From the peril of the Rocks, from Scylla, and from the terrors of Charybdis we had now escaped; and it was not long before we reached the Sun-god's favoured isle, where Hyperion kept his splendid broad-browed cattle and his flocks of sturdy sheep. From where I was on board, right out at sea, I could hear the lowing of cows as they were stalled for the night, and the bleating of sheep. And there came into my mind the words of Teiresias, the blind Theban prophet, and of Circe of Aeaea, who had each been so insistent in warning me to avoid this Island of the Sun, the comfort of mankind. So in spite of my own disappointment I decided to inform the others.

' "My men," I said, "forget your troubles for a moment, and listen to me while I tell you of the oracles I had from Teiresias and Circe of Aeaea. They warned me repeatedly to keep clear of the Island of the Sun, the comfort of mankind, for there, they said, our deadliest peril lurks. So drive the ship past and put the island astern."

'My men were heart-broken when they heard this, and Eurylochus weighed in at once in a truculent vein. "Odysseus," he said, "you are one of those hard men whose spirit never flags and whose body never tires. You must be made of iron through and through to forbid your men, worn out by labour and by lack of sleep, to set foot on dry land, with the chance of cooking themselves a cheerful supper on this sea-girt isle. Instead, you expect us, just as we are, to go blindly on through the night that is overtaking us and put leagues of fog and sea between the island and ourselves. What of the high winds that spring up at night and do such harm to shipping? What port could we make to save ourselves from foundering, if we were hit by a sudden squall from the south or the west? There's nothing like the South Wind or the wicked West for smashing up a ship. And they don't ask leave of our lords the gods! No, let us take our cue now from the evening dusk and cook our supper. We won't stray from the ship, and in the morning we can get on board once more and put out into the open sea."

'This speech of Eurylochus was greeted by applause from all the rest, and it was brought home to me now that heaven really had some calamity in store for us. I answered him gravely: "Eurylochus, I am one against many, and you force my hand. Very well. But I call on every man of you to give me his solemn promise that if we come across a herd of cattle or some great flock of sheep, he will not kill a head of either in a wanton fit of folly. Instead, you will sit in peace and eat the rations that the goddess Circe has provided."

'The crew agreed and promised to abstain. Accordingly, when all had solemnly taken the oath, we brought the good ship to anchor in a sheltered cove, with fresh water at hand, and the men disembarked and proceeded to prepare their supper in the proper style. When they had satisfied their hunger and thirst, their thoughts returned to their dear comrades whom Scylla had snatched from the ship's hold and devoured; and they wept for them till sweet sleep overtook them in their tears.

'In the third watch of the night, when the stars had passed their zenith, Zeus the Cloud-gatherer sent us a gale of incredible violence. He covered land and sea with clouds, and in a moment the black sky had blotted out the world. So at the first peep of day we beached our ship and dragged her up into the shelter of a cave, a pleasant spot which the Nymphs used as a dancing-ground and meeting-place. I then ordered all my men to gather round, and gave them their warning. "My friends," I said, "since we have plenty of food and drink on board, let us keep our hands off these cattle, or we shall come to grief. For the cows and the fine sheep you have seen belong to that formidable god, the Sun, whose eyes and ears miss nothing in the world."

'My company accepted this with no sign of a rebellious spirit.

And now for a whole month the South Wind blew without a pause, and after that we had nothing but southerly and easterly winds. The men, so long as their bread and red wine lasted, kept their hands off the cattle as they valued their lives. But when the provisions in the ship gave out and the pangs of hunger sent them wandering with barbed hooks in quest of game, fishes or birds, or anything that might come to hand, I went off inland to pray to the gods in the hope that one of them might show me a way of escape. When I had gone far enough across the island to be clear of the rest, I found a spot that was sheltered from the wind, washed my hands, and made my supplications to the whole company on Olympus. But all they did was to cast me into a pleasant sleep. And in the meantime Eurylochus was broaching a wicked scheme to his mates.

' "My poor long-suffering friends," he said, "listen to what I have to say. To us wretched men all forms of death are abominable, but death by starvation is the most miserable end that one can meet. So I suggest that we round up the best of the Sun's cows and slaughter them in honour of the immortals who live in the broad sky. If ever we reach our homeland in Ithaca, our first act shall be to build Hyperion the Sun-god a rich temple and fill it with precious offerings. If, on the other hand, he shows annoyance at this treatment of his straight-horned herds and chooses to wreck our ship, with the other gods to back him, I would sooner make one gulp at the sea and give up the ghost than be pinched to death by slow degrees upon a desert isle."

'His ideas found favour with the rest, and they proceeded at once to round up the pick of the Sun's cattle. They had not far to go, for the fine fatted cows with their broad foreheads were often to be seen at their pasture in the neighbourhood of our blue-prowed ship. The men gathered round the cattle and made their prayers to the gods, using for the ceremony some full-grown leaves they stripped from a tall oak-tree, since they had no white barley in the ship. Their prayers done, they slit the cows' throats and flayed them, then cut out slices from the thighs, wrapped them in folds of fat and laid raw meat above them. And since they had no wine to pour over the burning sacrifice, they made libations with water as they roasted all the entrails. When the thighs were burnt up and they had tasted the inner parts, they carved the rest into small pieces and spitted them on skewers.

'They had reached this point when I suddenly awoke from my deep sleep, and started on my way back to the vessel and the coast. Directly I came near my good ship the sweet smell of roasting meat was wafted to my nostrils. I exclaimed in horror and called on the immortal gods to hear me. "Father Zeus," I cried, "and you other blessed gods who live for ever! So it was to ruin me that you lulled me into that cruel sleep, while the men I left conceived and did this hideous thing!"'

'The news that we had killed his cattle was promptly conveyed by Lampetie of the long robes to the Sun-god Hyperion; and he was quick to voice his outraged feelings to the immortals.

' "Father Zeus and you other happy gods who live for ever, I call on you to punish the followers of Odysseus son of Laertes. They have had the insolence to kill my cattle, the cattle that gave me such joy every day as I climbed the sky to put the stars to flight and as I dropped from heaven and sank once more to earth. If they do not repay me in full for my slaughtered cows, I will go down to Hades and shine among the dead."

' "Sun," the Cloud-gatherer answered him, "shine on for the immortals and for mortal men on the fruitful earth. As for the culprits, I will soon strike their ship with a blinding bolt out on the wine-dark sea and break it to bits."'

'This part of the tale I had from the fair Calypso, who told me that she herself had heard it from Hermes the Messenger.

'When I had come down to the sea and reached the ship, I confronted my men one after the other and rebuked them. But we could find no way of mending matters: the cows were dead and gone. And the gods soon began to visit my crew with portents. The hides crawled; the meat, roast and raw, groaned on the spits; and a sound as though of lowing cattle could be heard.

'For six days those good men of mine feasted on the pick of

the Sun's cattle they had driven in. But when Zeus brought the seventh day round, the fury of the gale abated, and we quickly embarked and put out into the open sea after stepping the mast and hauling the white sail up.

'When we had left the island astern and no other land, nor anything but sky and water was to be seen, Zeus brought a sombre cloud to rest above the ship so that the sea was darkened by its shadow. Before she had run very far, a howling wind suddenly sprang up from the west and hit us with hurricane force. The squall snapped both forestays together. As the mast fell aft, all the rigging tumbled into the bilge, and the mast itself, reaching the stern, struck the helmsman on the head and smashed in all the bones of his skull. He plunged like a diver from the poop, and his brave soul left his body. Then at one and the same moment Zeus thundered and struck the vessel by lightning. The whole ship reeled to the blow of his bolt and was filled with sulphur. My men were flung overboard and tossed round the black hull like sea-gulls on the waves. There was no homecoming for them: the god saw to that.

'Meanwhile I kept shifting from one part of the ship to another, till a great wave tore her sides from her keel, which the seas then swept along denuded of its ribs. They even snapped the mast off close to the keel, but as the backstay, which was a leather rope, had fallen across the mast, I used it to lash mast and keel together, and astride these two timbers I became the sport of the furious winds.

'The storm that had blown up from the west subsided soon enough, but was quickly followed by more wind from the south, to my great distress, for this meant that I should have once more to run the gauntlet of the dread Charybdis. All through the night I was swept along, and at sunrise found myself back at Scylla's rock and that appalling whirlpool. Charybdis was beginning to suck the salt water down. But as she did so, I was flung right up to the great fig-tree, on which I got a tight grip and clung like a bat. I could find no foothold to support me, nor any means of climbing into the tree, for its roots were far away below, and the great long branches that overshadowed Charybdis stretched high above my head. However, I stuck grimly on until such time as she should spew me up my mast and keel once more. My hope was justified, though they came up very late, in fact not till the time when a judge with a long list of disputes to settle between obstinate litigants rises from court for his evening meal. Then at last the timbers reappeared on the surface of the pool. I flung my arms and legs down for a plunge, and with a splash fell in the water clear of the great logs, which I then bestrode and rowed along with my hands. And thanks to the Father of men and gods I was spared another sight of Scylla. Otherwise nothing could have saved me from certain death.

'Nine days of drifting followed; but in the night of the tenth the gods washed me up on the Isle of Ogygia, the home of the fair Calypso, that formidable goddess with a woman's voice; and she received me kindly and looked after me. But why go again through all this? Only yesterday I told you and your noble consort the whole story here in your house, and it goes against the grain with me to repeat a tale already plainly told.'

XIII

ODYSSEUS LANDS IN ITHACA

ODYSSEUS' tale was finished, and such was the spell he had cast
on the whole company that not a sound was heard throughout
the shadowy hall, till at last Alcinous turned to his guest and
said: 'Odysseus, you have suffered much. But now that you
have set foot on the bronze floor of my great house I feel assured
that you will reach your home without any further wanderings
from your course. As for you, sirs, here are my wishes – let them
stand as an order to every one of you that frequent my palace to
drink the sparkling wine of the elders and enjoy the minstrel's
song. I know that the clothing, gold ornaments, and other presents that our counsellors brought in are already laid by for our
guest in a wooden strong-box. I now suggest that we each give
him a large tripod and a cauldron. Later we will recoup ourselves by a tax on the people, since it would be hard on us singly
to have to make so generous a donation.'

His proposal was approved and all went home to their beds.
But as soon as Dawn had flecked the morning sky with red, they
came bustling down to the ship with their welcome bronze-
ware gifts, and the great King Alcinous himself went up and
down the vessel, stowing them carefully under the benches, so
as not to hamper any of the ship's hands as they tugged at the
oars. This done, they repaired for a banquet to Alcinous' house,
and for their entertainment the divine king sacrificed a bullock
to Zeus of the Black Cloud, the son of Cronos, who is lord of all.
They burnt the thighs and settled down happily to a splendid
feast, while in their midst the people's favourite, Demodocus,
that admirable bard, sang to the music of his harp. But Odysseus
kept turning his face toward the blazing sun, as though to hasten
its descent, for he was longing to be off. And as the ploughman,
whose two dun oxen have pulled the ploughshare through the

fallow all day long, yearns for his supper and welcomes the sunset that frees him to seek it and drag home his weary legs, so did Odysseus welcome the setting of the sun that day. No sooner was it down than he appealed to his sailor hosts, and to Alcinous in particular:

'Lord Alcinous, my most worshipful prince, make your drink-offerings now and see me safely off. And may every blessing be yours! For now my dearest wish has been fulfilled: I have secured your escort and I have your friendly gifts. May the gods in heaven allow me to enjoy them, and may I find my wife and dear ones safe and sound in my home when I reach it. As for you that I leave here, may you all bring happiness to your good wives and to your children; and may the gods prosper you in every way and keep your people from harm!'

This speech of Odysseus pleased the whole company. They felt the justice of his claim and held that their guest should now be sent on his way. King Alcinous called to his squire. 'Pontonous,' he said, 'mix a bowl of wine and serve everyone in the hall so that we can make a drink-offering to Father Zeus before seeing our visitor off to the land of his birth.' Pontonous mixed the mellow wine, went his rounds and served each of the guests, who then made libations to the blessed gods that live in the far-flung heavens. All remained seated for this ritual except the gallant Odysseus, who rose from his chair, put his two-handled beaker in Arete's hands, and made her this cordial adieu: 'My Queen, here's fortune all your life, until man's common lot, old age and death, comes on you! I take my leave of you now. May your house be blessed, and may you be happy in your children, your people, and Alcinous your king!'

With this the noble Odysseus stepped across the threshold. King Alcinous ordered an equerry to accompany him and lead him to the good ship and the sea-shore, while Arete sent with him a party of serving-women, one with a clean mantle and a tunic, and another to carry his strong-box, while a third conveyed his bread and the red wine.

When they had come down to the ship and the sea, the young

nobles who were to escort him took charge of his baggage, including all the food and drink, and stowed it in the hold. For Odysseus himself they spread a rug and sheet on the ship's deck, well aft, so that he might enjoy unbroken sleep. Then he too climbed on board and quietly lay down, while the crew found their seats on the benches like men drilled to their work and untied the cable from the pierced stone that held it. But no sooner had they swung back and struck the water with their blades than sweet oblivion sealed Odysseus' eyes in sleep delicious and profound, the very counterfeit of death. And now, like a team of four stallions on the plain who start as one horse at the touch of the whip and break into their bounding stride to make short work of the course, the ship lunged forward, and above the great dark wave that the sea sent roaring in her wake her stern began to rise and fall. With unfaltering speed she forged ahead, and not even the wheeling falcon, the fastest thing that flies, could have kept her company. Thus she sped lightly on, cutting her way through the waves and carrying a man wise as the gods are wise, who in long years of war on land and wandering across the cruel seas had suffered many agonies of spirit but now was lapped in peaceful sleep, forgetting all he had once endured.

When the brightest of all stars came up, the star which often ushers in the tender light of Dawn, the ship's voyage was done and she drew near to Ithaca. Now in that island is a cove named after Phorcys, the Old Man of the Sea, with two bold headlands squatting at its mouth so as to protect it from the heavy swell raised by rough weather in the open and allow large ships to ride inside without so much as tying up, once within mooring distance of the shore. At the head of the cove grows a long-leaved olive-tree and near by is a cavern that offers welcome shade and is sacred to the Nymphs whom we call Naiads. This cave contains a number of stone basins and two-handled jars, which are used by bees as their hives; also great looms of stone where the Nymphs weave marvellous fabrics of sea-purple; and there are springs whose water never fails. It has two mouths. The one that looks north is the way down for men. The other, facing south, is meant for the gods; and as immortals come in by this way it is not used by men at all.

It was here that the Phaeacians put in, knowing the spot; and such was the headway of the ship, rowed by those able hands, that when she drove against the shore a full half of her keel's length mounted the beach. They rose from the benches, jumped out, and made it their first task to lift Odysseus, sheet, glossy rug and all, out of the gallant ship and deposit him on the sand still fast asleep. Next they took out all the treasures which Athene's generous impulse had caused their noble countrymen to give him when he left for home. These they stacked in a pile by the trunk of the olive-tree, well away from the path, lest some passer-by should happen to come upon them before he awoke and rob him. This done, they set out for home.

Meanwhile the Lord of the Earthquake, who had by no means forgotten the threats he had once uttered against the noble Odysseus, tried to find out what purpose was in Zeus' mind. 'Father Zeus,' he said, 'the immortal gods will think nothing of me, flouted as I am by mortal men, by these Phaeacians, I mean, who after all are sprung from my own stock. *I* said that Odysseus should suffer much before he reached his home, though I never put a final ban on his return, once you had promised it and nodded your assent. But now these people have brought him over the sea in their good ship and landed him asleep in Ithaca, after showering gifts upon him, gifts of copper, gold, and woven stuffs in such profusion as he could never have won for himself from Troy, even if he had come back unhurt with his fair share of the spoils.'

'Imperial Earthshaker,' replied the Gatherer of the Clouds, 'your fears are preposterous! The gods are innocent of all irreverence towards you. Indeed it would be an abominable thing for them to scoff at the eldest and best of their company. As for mankind, if anyone thinks himself powerful enough to slight you, you have all the future in which to take your revenge. You are free to please yourself: act as you see fit.'

'Lord of the Black Cloud,' Poseidon answered him, 'I should promptly have done as you say but for my ingrained deference to your will and dread of your resentment. Now, however, I propose to wreck that fine ship of the Phaeacians on the high seas as she comes back from her mission, to teach them to hold their hands and give up this habit of escorting travellers. And I will also fence their town with a ring of high mountains.'

'My friend,' said the Gatherer of the Clouds, 'this is what I think best. Choose the moment when all eyes in the city are fixed on the ship's approach to turn her into a rock off-shore, and let this rock look like a ship, so that all the world may wonder. Then throw a circle of high mountains round their city.'

With this encouragement from Zeus, Poseidon made for Scherie, where the Phaeacians live; and there he bode his time till the approaching ship, making good headway, showed in the offing. The Earthshaker then went up to her and with one blow from the flat of his hand turned her into stone and rooted her to the sea-bottom, where he left her.

The Phaeacian spectators, oarsmen themselves and seamen of repute, looked at each other and cried out in their amazement. 'Who in heaven's name,' they asked, 'has stopped our good ship out at sea as she was making port? Only a moment ago we could see every spar.'

They might well ask, for they had no inkling of what had happened till Alcinous explained.

'Alas!' he cried. 'My father's prophecy of long ago has indeed come home to me! He used to maintain that Poseidon resented our giving safe-conduct to all and sundry, and he foretold that one day he would wreck one of our fine ships on the high seas as she was returning from such a mission, and would overshadow our city with a ring of high mountains. Now all these prophecies of the old king's are coming true! But listen: I have remedies to suggest, which I hope you will all accept. For the future give up your custom of seeing home any traveller who comes to our city; and for the present let us sacrifice twelve picked bulls to Poseidon. He may take pity on us and refrain from hemming in our town with a long mountain range.' They were filled with consternation and at once prepared the bulls for sacrifice.

Thus the chieftains and counsellors of the Phaeacian people were gathered round the altar and interceding with the Lord Poseidon at the moment when the good Odysseus awoke from sleep on his native soil. After so long an absence, he failed to recognize it; for the goddess, Pallas Athene, Daughter of Zeus, had thrown a mist over the place to give herself time to make plans with Odysseus and disguise him, so that he would not be recognized by his wife and friends or the people of the town before the Suitors had paid for all their crimes. As a result everything in Ithaca, the long hill-paths, the quiet bays, the beetling rocks, and the green trees, seemed unfamiliar to its King. He leapt to his feet and stood staring at his native land. Then he groaned, and slapping his thighs with the flat of his hands gave vent to his disappointment:

'Alas! Whose country have I come to now? Are they some brutal tribe of lawless savages, or a kindly and god-fearing people? Where shall I put all these goods of mine, and where on earth am I myself to go? If only I had stayed there with the Phaeacians! Then I could have gone on to some other powerful prince, who might have received me well and seen me on my way. As it is, I have not the least idea where to stow them, and I certainly can't leave them here, or someone else will make free with my property. And what a blow to find that those Phaeacian lords and chieftains are not exactly the wise and honest men I took them for! They say they will put me down in my own sunny Ithaca, and then they carry me off to this outlandish spot. A broken promise – for which I pray they may be punished by Zeus, the suppliants' god, who watches all mankind and punishes offenders. But now I had better count my belongings and make sure that the crew have not robbed me and carried something off in the hold of their ship.'

He proceeded to check his fine tripods and cauldrons, his gold and his splendid woven fabrics, and found not a single item missing. But this did not console him for the homeland he had sought, and weeping bitterly he dragged his feet along the shore of the sounding sea.

Athene now appeared upon the scene. She had disguised herself as a young shepherd, with all the delicate beauty that marks the sons of kings. A handsome cloak was folded back across her shoulders, her feet shone white between the sandal-straps, and she carried a javelin in her hand. She was a welcome sight to Odysseus, who came forward at once and accosted her eagerly. 'Good-day to you, sir,' he said. 'Since you are the first person I have met in this place, I hope to find no enemy in you, but the saviour of my treasures here and of my very life; and so I pray to you as I should to a god and kneel at your feet. But what I beg of you first is to tell me exactly where I am. What part of the world is this? What is the country called and who live here? Is is one of the sunny islands or is it one of those coastal tracts that run down from the rich mainland to meet the sea?'

'Sir,' said the goddess of the gleaming eyes, 'you must be a simpleton or have travelled very far from your home to ask me what this country is. It has a name by no means so inglorious as that. In fact it is known to thousands, to all the peoples of the dawn and sunrise and all that live on the other side toward the western gloom. I grant that it is rugged and unfit for driving horses, yet narrow though it may be it is very far from poor. It grows abundant corn and wine in plenty. The rains and the fresh dews are never lacking; and it has excellent pasturage for goats and cattle, timber of all kinds, and watering-places that never fail. And so, my friend, the name of Ithaca has travelled even as far as Troy; and that, they say, is a good long way from Achaea.'

Odysseus' patient heart leapt up as the divine Pallas Athene told him this, and he revelled in the knowledge that he was on his native soil. He answered her readily enough, but not with the truth. It had been on the tip of his tongue, but loyal as ever to his own crafty nature he contrived to keep it back.

'Of course,' he said, 'I heard tell of Ithaca even over there across the seas in the spacious land of Crete. And now I have come here myself with all these goods of mine, leaving the other half of my fortune to my children. For I had to take to my heels. I had killed Idomeneus' son, the great runner Orsilochus, who was faster on his feet than any living man in the whole island of Crete. He tried to fleece me of all the spoil I had won at Troy, my wages for the long-drawn agonies of war and all the miseries that sea-travel means, merely because I refused to curry favour with his father by serving as his squire at Troy and preferred to lead my own command. So with a friend at my side I laid an ambush for him close to the road, and let fly at him with my bronze spear as he was coming in from the country. There was a pitch-black sky that night and not a soul saw us; so no one knew that it was I who'd killed him. However, with the man's blood fresh on my hands, I hastily sought out a Phoenician ship, threw myself on the mercy of its honest crew, and with a liberal donation from my booty persuaded them to take me on board and set me down in Pylos or the good land of Elis, where the Epeians rule. But as things turned out, the wind was too strong for them and drove them off their course, much to their distress, for they had no wish to disappoint me. We beat about for a time, and in the night we made this island and rowed the ship helter-skelter into harbour. And though we stood in sore need of it, not a man among us thought of his supper; we all tumbled out of the ship and lay down just as we were. I was so exhausted that I fell sound asleep. Meanwhile the crew fetched my goods out of the good ship and dumped them down on the sand where I lay. After which they embarked once more and set sail for their own fine city of Sidon, leaving me and my troubles behind.'

The bright-eyed goddess smiled at Odysseus' tale and caressed him with her hand. Her appearance altered, and now she looked like a woman, tall, beautiful, and accomplished. And when she replied to him she abandoned her reserve.

'What a cunning knave it would take,' she said, 'to beat

you at your tricks! Even a god would be hard put to it.

'And so my stubborn friend, Odysseus the arch-deceiver, with his craving for intrigue, does not propose even in his own country to drop his sharp practice and the lying tales that he loves from the bottom of his heart. But no more of this: we are both adepts in chicane. For in the world of men you have no rival as a statesman and orator, while I am pre-eminent among the gods for invention and resource.

'And yet you did not know me, Pallas Athene, Daughter of Zeus, who always stand by your side and guard you through all your adventures. Why, it was I who made all the Phaeacians take to you so kindly. And here I am once more, to plan your future course with you; to hide the treasures that the Phaeacian nobles, prompted by me, gave to you when you left for home, and to warn you of all the trials you will have to undergo within the walls of your palace. Bear these with patience, for bear them you must. Tell not a single person in the place, man or woman, that you are back from your wanderings; but endure all vexations in silence and submit yourself to the indignities that will be put upon you.'

Odysseus was ready with his answer. 'Goddess,' he said, 'it is hard for a man to recognize you at sight, however knowledgeable he may be, for you have a way of donning all kinds of disguises. But this I know well, that you were gracious to me in the old days so long as we Achaeans were campaigning at Troy. Yet when we had sacked Priam's lofty citadel and gone on board our ships, and a god had scattered the Achaean fleet, I did not notice you then, Daughter of Zeus, nor see you set foot on my ship to save me from any of my ordeals. No; I was left to wander through the world with a stricken heart, till the gods put a term to my sufferings and the day came, in the rich land of the Phaeacians, when you comforted me with your talk and yourself guided me to their city. But now I beseech you in your Father's name – since I cannot think that I have come to my bright Ithaca but feel that I must be at large in some foreign country and that you must have said what you did in a spirit of mockery to lead me astray – I bcsccch you to tell me, am I really back in my own beloved land?'

'How like you to be so wary!' said Athene. 'And that is why I cannot desert you in your misfortunes: you are so civilized, so intelligent, so self-possessed. Any other man on returning from his travels would have rushed home in high spirits to see his children and his wife. You, on the contrary, are in no hurry even to ask questions and to learn the news. No; with your own eyes you must first make sure of your wife – who, by the way, does nothing but sit at home with her eyes never free from tears as the slow nights and days pass sorrowfully by.

'As for your home-coming, I myself was never in any doubt: I knew in my heart that you would get back with the loss of all your men. But you must understand that I was not prepared to oppose my uncle Poseidon, who was highly incensed when you blinded his own son and has cherished his grudge against you. And now, to convince you, let me show you the Ithacan scene. Here is the harbour of Phorcys, the Old Man of the Sea; and there at the head of the haven is the long-leaved olive-tree with the cave near by, the pleasant shady spot that is sacred to the Nymphs whom men call Naiads. Over there you can see its vaulted roof – it will put you in mind of many a solemn sacrifice you have made there to the Nymphs – while the forest-clad slopes behind are those of Mount Neriton.'

As she spoke the goddess dispersed the mist, and the countryside stood plain to view. And now joy came at last to the gallant long-suffering Odysseus. So happy did the sight of his own land make him that he kissed the generous soil, then with uplifted hands invoked the Nymphs: 'And I had thought, you Nymphs of the Springs, you Daughters of Zeus, that I should never set my eyes on you again! Accept my greetings and my loving prayers. Gifts too will follow as in days gone by, if through the kindness of this warrior Child of Zeus I am allowed to live and see my son grow up.'

'Be bold,' said Athene of the flashing eyes, 'and dismiss all such doubts from your heart. Our immediate task is to hide your goods in some corner of this haunted cave where they may lie in safety. After that we must decide on our best course for the future.'

The goddess now plunged into the gloom of the cavern to explore it for a hiding-place, while Odysseus made haste to bring in all his belongings, the gold, the indestructible copper and the fine fabrics the Phaeacians had given him. After he had stowed them carefully away, Pallas Athene, Daughter of Zeus, closed the entrance with a stone.

The pair then sat down by the trunk of the sacred olive-tree to scheme the downfall of the presumptuous Suitors, and the bright-eyed goddess put the case to Odysseus. 'Royal son of Laertes,' she said, 'you are a man of resource. Consider now how you will come to grips with this gang of profligates who for three whole years have been lording it in your palace, paying court to your incomparable wife and tempting her with marriage settlements. All this time she has pined for your homecoming, and though she has given them all some grounds for hope and doled out promises in private messages to each, her real wishes are very different.'

'Alas!' cried Odysseus of the nimble wits. 'It seems to me that I should have come to the same miserable end as King Agamemnon directly I set foot in my home, if you, goddess, had not made all this clear to me. I beseech you to think of some way by which I could pay these miscreants out. And take your stand at my side, filling me with the spirit that dares all, as you did on the day when we pulled down Troy's shining diadem of towers. Ah, Lady of the bright eyes, if only you would aid me with such vehemence as you did then, I could fight against three hundred, with you beside me, sovran goddess, and with your whole-hearted help to count on!'

'Indeed I will stand at your side,' Athene answered. 'I shall not forget you when the time comes for this task of ours. As for those Suitors who are wasting your fortune, I can already see them staining your broad floors with their own blood and brains. But now to work! I am going to change you beyond recognition. I shall wither the smooth skin on those supple limbs of yours and rob your head of its auburn locks; I shall clothe you in rags from which people will shrink in disgust; and I shall take all the light out of those fine eyes that you have – all this to make the whole gang of Suitors and even your wife and the son you left at home take you for a disreputable vaga-bond. And now for your part – the first man you must approach is the swineherd in charge of your pigs. His loyal heart is on your side as firmly as ever, and he loves your son and your wise queen Penelope. You will find him watching over his swine out at their pastures by the Raven's Crag and at the Spring of Arethusa, where they find the right fodder to make them fat and healthy pigs, feeding on the acorns they love and drinking water from deep pools. Stay there, sit down with the old man, and question him about the whole affair. Meanwhile I shall go to Sparta, the city of fair women, to summon Telemachus, your own son, Odysseus, who, I must tell you, has travelled to the broad vale of Lacedaemon and visited Menelaus in the hope of getting on your track and finding out if you are still alive.'

Odysseus replied with a shrewd question: 'But why, in your omniscience, did you not tell him the truth? Do you want him too to scour the barren seas in misery while strangers eat him out of house and home?'

'You need not be alarmed for him,' the bright-eyed goddess answered. 'I myself arranged the journey for him, feeling that the adventure would redound to his credit. He is in no diffi-culties, but is sitting quite at ease in Menelaus' palace, in the lap of luxury. It is true that those young men in their black ship have laid an ambush for him on his journey home, with murder in their hearts. But I have an idea that they will not succeed. No; sooner than that, the earth will close over some of these gallants who are wasting your wealth.'

Athene touched him now with her wand. She withered the smooth skin on his supple limbs, robbed his head of its auburn locks, covered his whole body with the wrinkles of old age, and dimmed the light that shone in his beautiful eyes. His clothing too she changed into a shabby cloak and tunic, filthy rags begrimed by smoke. Over his back she threw the great bald hide of a nimble stag; and finally she gave him a staff and a mean and tattered knapsack with a shoulder-strap.

Their plans prepared, the two parted company, and Athene went off to the sacred land of Lacedaemon to fetch Odysseus' son.

XIV

IN EUMAEUS' HUT

MEANWHILE Odysseus turned his back on the harbour and followed a rough track leading up into the woods and through the hills towards the spot where Athene had told him he would meet the worthy swineherd, who of all the royal servants had shown himself to be his most faithful steward.

He found him sitting in front of his homestead in the farm-yard, whose high walls, perched on an eminence and protected by a clearing, enclosed a fine and spacious court. The herdsman had made it himself for his absent master's swine, without help from his mistress or the aged Laertes, building the wall of quarried stone with a hedge of wild-pear on top. As an additional protection outside he had fenced the whole length on either hand with a closely set stockade made of split oak which he had taken from the dark heart of the logs. Inside the yard, to house the pigs at night, he had put twelve sties, all near to one another, in each of which fifty sows slept on the ground and had their litters. The boars lay outside the yard; and of these there were far fewer, since their numbers suffered constant inroads at the banquets of the courting noblemen, for whom the swineherd used at regular intervals to send down the pick of his fatted hogs. Yet there were three hundred and sixty of them still. They were guarded every night by four fierce and powerful dogs, trained by the swineherd's master hand.

He himself was busy cutting a piece of good brown leather and fitting a pair of sandals to his feet, while his mates had gone afield in various directions with the pigs to their pastures – three of them, that is to say, for he had been obliged to send the fourth to town with a hog for the rollicking Suitors to slaughter so that they might gorge themselves with pork.

The noisy dogs suddenly caught sight of Odysseus and flew at him, barking loudly. He had the presence of mind to sit down and drop his staff; yet he would have come to grief then and there, at his own farm, if the swineherd had not intervened. Letting the leather fall from his fingers in his haste, he dashed through the gateway, shouted at the dogs and sent them flying with a shower of stones.

'Old man,' he said to his master, 'that was a narrow escape! The dogs would have made short work of you, and the blame would have fallen on me. As though the gods hadn't done enough already to pester and torment me! Here I sit, yearning and mourning for the best of masters and fattening his hogs for others to eat, while he himself, starving as like as not, is lost in foreign lands and tramping through strange towns – if indeed he is still alive and can see the light of day. However, follow me, sir, to my cabin, to join me in my meal. When you have had all the bread and wine you want, you shall tell me where you come from and what your troubles are.'

The friendly herdsman led the way to his cabin, ushered Odysseus in and bade him be seated on some brushwood that he piled up for him and covered with the shaggy skin of a wild goat, large and thick enough to serve as his own mattress. Odysseus was delighted by this welcome and did not hide his pleasure.

'My good host,' he said, 'I hope Zeus and the other gods will reward you with your heart's desire for receiving me so kindly.'

'Sir,' said the swineherd Eumaeus, 'my conscience would not let me turn away a stranger in a worse state even than yourself, for strangers and beggars all come in Zeus' name, and a gift from folk like us is none the less welcome for being small. Serfs, after all, can do no better, so long as they go in fear of their lords and masters. I mean these new ones; for as for my old master, the gods have fixed it that he shan't get home. *He* would have looked after me properly and pensioned me off with a cottage and a bit of land, and an attractive wife, as a kind master does for a servant who has worked hard for him and whose work heaven has prospered, as it prospers the job I toil at here. Yes, the King would have rewarded me well for this, had he grown old in Ithaca. But he is dead and gone. And I wish I could say the same of Helen and all her breed, for she brought many a good man to his knees. My master too was one of those who went to Ilium to fight the Trojan charioteers in Agamemnon's cause.'

The swineherd broke off, hitched up his tunic in his belt, and went out to the sties where the young porkers were penned in batches. He selected two, carried them in, and slaughtered them both. Next he singed them, chopped them up, and skewered the meat. When he had roasted it all, he served it up piping hot on the spits, set it in front of Odysseus, and sprinkled it with white barley-meal. He then mixed some mellow wine in a bowl of olive-wood, took a seat facing his guest, and invited him to eat.

'Stranger,' he said, 'fall to on these porkers, which are all we serfs can offer you. For our fatted hogs are eaten up by the Suitors, who have no fear of the wrath to come and no compunction in their hearts. Yet the blessed gods don't like foul play. Decency and moderation are what they respect in men. Even bloodthirsty pirates, when they've raided a foreign coast and had the luck to carry off some loot, are haunted by the fear of retribution as they make for home with their ships full of plunder. So I can't help thinking that these Suitors have somehow discovered, maybe through some heaven-sent rumour, that my master has come to a disastrous end – which explains why they will neither pay court to his widow in the regular way nor go home and mind their own business, but sit there instead at their ease and eat up all his livelihood in this high-handed style with no thought for economy. For I tell you they slaughter beasts every blessed day and night, never contenting themselves with one or even two at a time; while the amount of wine they draw and waste is disgraceful. My master, you see, was enormously wealthy; there wasn't a lord on the black continent or in Ithaca itself to touch him. He's worth more than twenty others rolled into one. Let me give you some idea. On the mainland, twelve herds of cattle, as many flocks of sheep, as many droves of pigs and as many scattered herds of goats, all tended by hired labour or his own herdsmen; while here in Ithaca eleven herds of goats graze up and down the coast with reliable men to look after them. And every one of these men has day by day to choose the likeliest of his fatted goats and drive it in for the Suitors; while I, who tend and keep these swine, carefully pick out the best and send it down to them.'

While Eumaeus was talking, Odysseus devoted himself to the meat and wine, which he consumed greedily and in silence, his brain teeming with thoughts of what he would do to the Suitors. When he had finished supper and refreshed himself, Eumaeus filled his own drinking-bowl and handed it to his master brimful of wine. Odysseus accepted with pleasure and now put a direct question to his host:

'Tell me, my friend, who was the man who bought you with his wealth, this lord whom you describe as so exceedingly rich and powerful? You said he had lost his life in Agamemnon's cause. Tell me his name. I may find that I can recognize him by your description. Heaven only knows whether I can tell you I've met him; but I've certainly seen a great deal of the world.'

'My dear sir,' answered this prince among swineherds, 'no wanderer who comes here and claims to bring news of Odysseus could convince his wife and son. Beggars in need of creature comforts find lying easy, and to tell a true tale is the last thing they wish. Whenever a tramp comes to Ithaca on his rounds he goes straight to my mistress with his artful talk. She welcomes him graciously and makes him tell his tale from first to last, while the tears of distress stream down her cheeks, as is natural for a woman whose husband has met his end abroad. Why, sir, you yourself would be quick enough to invent a tale if someone gave you a cloak and tunic to put on! As for my master, he is dead and gone: the dogs and the birds of the air must by now have torn the flesh from his bones; or the fish have eaten him in the sea, and his bones lie there on the shore with the sand piled high above them. Yes, that is how he met his end, and his death has meant nothing but trouble for his friends and for myself above all. For I shall never find so kind a master again wherever

I may go, not even if I return to my parents' house, where I was born and where they brought me up themselves. And much as I should like to be back in my own country and set eyes on them again, my longing for them has given place in my heart to overwhelming regret for the lost Odysseus. Yes, sir, even though he is not here, I hesitate to use his name. He loved me and took thought for me beyond all others. And so, though he is far away, I still think of him as my beloved lord.'

'Friend,' said the patient Odysseus in reply, 'since you'll have none of what I say, and since you have so little faith that you cannot believe he will ever return, I will not content myself by merely stating that Odysseus is coming back, but I will swear it. Directly he comes and sets foot in his own house I claim the reward for the good news and you can dress me properly in a new cloak and tunic. But till that moment, destitute as I am, I will accept nothing; for I loathe like Hell's Gates the man who is driven by poverty to lie. I swear now by Zeus before all other gods, and by the board of hospitality, and by the good Odysseus' hearth, which I am approaching, that everything will happen as I say. This very year Odysseus will be here. Between the waning of the old moon and the waxing of the new, he will come back to his home and will punish all that offer outrage there to his consort and his noble son.'

What answer did Eumaeus make to this? 'Old man,' he said, 'that reward I shall never have to pay, nor will Odysseus ever come home again. But drink in peace and let us pass to other topics. Don't remind me of my troubles, for I tell you my heart is wrung within me when anyone puts me in mind of my true king. As for your oath, let us forget it. And may Odysseus still come home, as I pray he will, and as Penelope does, and old Laertes and Prince Telemachus. Ah, there's another cruel anxiety for me – Odysseus' son Telemachus. The gods made him grow like a young sapling, and I had hoped to see him play no meaner a part in the world than his father, a paragon of manly beauty, when suddenly some god deprived him of his wits – or perhaps it was a man who fooled him – and off he went to holy

Pylos on his father's trail. And now my lords the Suitors are lying in ambush for him on his way home, so that King Arceisius' line may be wiped out of Ithaca and the very name be forgotten. Well, we must leave him to his fate, whether they get him, or whether by god's help he saves his skin.

'But now, my ancient friend, you must tell me about your own troubles and satisfy my curiosity. Who are you and where do you come from? What is your city? Who are your family? And since you certainly can't have come on foot, what kind of vessel brought you here? How did its crew come to land you in Ithaca; and who did they claim to be?'

'I will enlighten you on all these points,' replied Odysseus, with his usual cunning. 'But even supposing that you and I had an endless supply of food and wine, here in the hut, and so could eat in peace while the rest got on with the work, I should still find it easy to talk to you for a whole twelvemonth without coming to the end of my grievances and of all the hardships that heaven has made me endure.

'I am a native of the broad lands of Crete, and the son of a wealthy man. He had a number of other sons who, like me, were born and brought up in the house; but they were the lawful issue of his wife, whereas my mother was a concubine he had bought. In spite of this difference, Castor son of Hylax, to give my father his name, put me on an equal footing with his legitimate sons. The Cretans of his day respected and envied him for his good fortune, his riches, and his splendid children; but his time came, and Death bore him off to Hades' Halls. His sons then split up the estate in their high-handed way and cast lots for the shares, assigning to me a meagre pittance and a house to match. However, I won a wife for myself from a rich family on the strength of my own merits, for I was neither a fool nor a coward. My glory has departed now, yet I think you will still be able to see by the stubble what the harvest was like. Since then I have been overwhelmed by troubles, but in the old days Ares and Athene had endowed me generously with the daring that sweeps all before it; and when it came to planning a bold stroke

against the enemy and I had picked my men for an ambush, my
ardent spirits were never dashed by any foreboding of death,
but I would leap out before all the rest and cut down with my
spear any foeman who was slower on his feet than I. That was
the kind of man I was in battle. But I did not like work, nor the
domestic pursuits that make for a fine family. What I always
loved was a ship with oars, and fighting, and polished javelins
and arrows – terrible things, which make other people shudder.
I suppose that in making such a choice I just followed my natural
bent, for different men take kindly to very different ways of
earning a living. Anyhow, before the Achaean expedition ever
set foot on the coasts of Troy, I had nine times had my own
command and led a well-found fleet against a foreign land. As a
result, large quantities of loot fell into my hands. From these I
used to select what I liked, and a great deal more came my way
in the subsequent distributions. Thus my estate increased rapidly
and my fellow-countrymen soon learned both to fear and respect me. The time came, however, when Zeus, who never
takes his eyes off the world, let us in for that deplorable adventure which brought so many men to their knees; and they
pressed me and the famous Idomeneus to lead the fleet to Ilium.
There was no way of avoiding it: public opinion was too much
for us. So for nine years we Achaeans campaigned at Troy; and
after sacking Priam's city in the tenth we sailed for home and
our fleet was scattered by a god. But the inventive brain of Zeus
was hatching more mischief than that for my unhappy self. I
had spent only a month in the delights of home life with my
children, my wife, and my wealth, when the spirit moved me to
fit out some ships and sail for Egypt with a picked company. I
got nine vessels ready and the crews were soon mustered. For
six days my good men gave themselves up to festivity and I provided beasts in plenty for their sacrifices and their own table. On
the seventh we embarked, said goodbye to the broad acres of
Crete and sailed off with a fresh and favourable wind from the
north, which made our going as easy as though we were sailing
down stream. Not a single one of my ships came to harm: we

sat there safe and well while the wind and the steersmen kept them on their course. On the fifth day we reached the great River of Egypt, and there in the Nile I brought my curved ships to. And now I ordered my good men to stay by the ships on guard while I sent out some scouts to reconnoitre from the heights. But these ran amuck and in a trice, carried away by their own violence, they had plundered some of the fine Egyptian farms, borne off the women and children and killed the men. The hue and cry soon reached the city, and the towns-folk, roused by the alarm, turned out at dawn. The whole place was filled with infantry and chariots and the glint of arms. Zeus the Thunderer struck abject panic into my party. Not a man had the spirit to stand up to the enemy, for we were threatened on all sides. They ended by cutting down a large part of my force and carrying off the survivors to work for them as slaves. As for myself, a sudden inspiration saved me – though I still wish I had faced my destiny and fallen there in Egypt, for trouble was waiting for me yet with open arms. I quickly doffed my fine helmet, let the shield drop from my shoulder, and threw away my spear. Then I ran up to the king's chariot and embraced his knees. Moved to pity, he spared my life, gave me a seat beside him, and so drove his weeping captive home. Many of his people, of course, were lusting for my blood and made at me with their ashen spears, for they were thoroughly roused; but he kept them away, for fear of offending Zeus, the Strangers' god, whose special office it is to call cruelty to account.

'I passed seven years in the country and made a fortune out of the Egyptians, who were liberal with me one and all. But in the course of the eighth, I fell in with a rascally Phoenician, a thiev-ing knave who had already done a deal of mischief in the world. I was prevailed on by this specious rogue to join him in a voyage to Phoenicia, where he had a house and estate; and there I stayed with him for a whole twelvemonth. But when the days and months had mounted up, and a second year began its round of seasons, he put me on board a ship bound for Libya, on the pre-text of wanting my help with the cargo he was carrying, but really in order that he might sell me for a handsome sum when he got there. Full of suspicions but having no choice I followed him on board. With a good stiff breeze from the north the ship took the central route and ran down the lee side of Crete. But Zeus had their end in store for them. When we had put Crete astern and no other land, nor anything but sky and water, was to be seen, he brought a dark cloud to rest above the ship. The sea below it was blackened. Zeus thundered and in the same moment struck the vessel by lightning. The whole ship reeled to the blow of his bolt and was filled with sulphur. The men were all flung overboard and tossed round the black hull like sea-crows on the waves. There was no home-coming for them – the god saw to that. But in this hour of my affliction Zeus himself brought into my arms the great mast of the blue-prowed ship, so that I might even yet escape the worst. I coiled myself round it and became the sport of the accursed winds. For nine days I drifted, and on the tenth night, in pitch darkness, a great roller washed me up on the coast of Thesprotia, where my lord Pheidon, King of the Thesprotians, gave me free hospitality. His own son found me fainting from exposure and exhaustion, lent me a hand to help me up, and took me home with him to his father's palace, where he gave me a cloak and tunic to put on.

'It was there that I heard of Odysseus. The king told me that he had entertained and befriended him on his homeward way and showed me what a fortune in copper, gold, and wrought iron Odysseus had amassed. Why, the amount of treasure stored up for him there in the king's house would keep a man and his heirs to the tenth generation! He added that Odysseus had gone to Dodona to learn the will of Zeus from the great oak-tree that is sacred to the god, and to discover how he ought to approach his own rich island of Ithaca after so long an absence, whether to return openly or in disguise. Moreover, he swore in my presence over a drink-offering in his own house that a ship was waiting on the beach with a crew standing by to convey Odysseus to his own country. But he sent me off before him. For a

Thesprotian ship happened to be starting for the corn island of
Dulichium, and he told its crew to carry me there, with every
attention, and take me to Acastus, the King.

'The crew, however, saw fit to hatch a plot against me, so that
I might drain the cup of misery to the dregs. When the ship's
course over the sea had brought her well away from land they
set about their scheme for reducing me to slavery. They stripped
me of my own cloak and tunic and supplied their place with a
filthy set of clothes, the very rags, in fact, which you see before
you now.

'The evening sun was shining on the fields of Ithaca when
they reached the island. They lashed me down tightly under the
ship's benches with a stout rope, disembarked, and hastily took
their supper on the beach. But the gods found no difficulty in
untying my knots for me. I covered my head with my rags,
slipped down the smooth lading-plank, gently breasted the
water, and struck out with both hands. Nor had I far to swim
before I was out of the sea at a safe distance from my foes. I then
made my way inland to a thicket in full leaf and crouched down
in hiding. They raised a great outcry and beat about, but soon
decided that nothing was to be gained by prolonging their
search, and so climbed on board their ship once more. The gods
made it quite easy for me to remain unseen and ended by guiding my steps to the homestead of a decent man. From which I
conclude that I am not yet meant to die.'

'My poor friend!' exclaimed the swineherd. 'You have certainly touched my heart with your long tale of hardships and
wandering. It is when you come to Odysseus that you go
wrong, to my way of thinking; you won't get me to believe
that. What call is there for a man like you to pitch such silly
yarns? As though *I* didn't know all about my master's disappearance, and how the gods showed their utter detestation of
the man by allowing him neither to fall in action against the
Trojans nor to die in his friends' arms when all the fighting was
over. Had he done so, the whole Achaean nation would have
joined in building him a mound, and he would have left a great

name for his son to inherit. But there was to be no glorious end for him: the Storm-Fiends have spirited him away.

'As for myself, I am a hermit here with my swine and never go to town, except perhaps when someone has blown in with news and the wise Penelope sees fit to invite me. On such occasions they all gather round the newcomer and ply him with questions, whether they belong to the party who are pining for their long-lost king or to those who have the satisfaction of feeding gratis at his expense. But I personally have lost all interest in such cross-examinations since the day when a fellow from Aetolia took me in with his tale. He had killed a man, and after roaming all over the world found his way to my doors. I received him kindly and was told by him that he had seen Odysseus with Idomeneus in Crete, repairing the damage his fleet had suffered in a gale. "He will be back," said he, "either in the summer or by autumn, bringing a fortune with him, and his gallant company too." Take note of that, my distressful old friend, since the powers above have brought you here, and don't try to wheedle your way to my heart with any falsehoods. It isn't that sort of thing that will win you my regard or my favours, but the respect I have for the laws of hospitality and the pity that I feel for you.'

But the cunning Odysseus persisted. 'Surely,' he said, 'you have a very suspicious nature, if not even a sworn statement from me can bring you round and convince you of the truth. Come, let us make a bargain – with the gods of Olympus to see that both parties carry out its terms. If your master comes back to this house, you shall give me a cloak and tunic to wear and send me on to Dulichium, where I wanted to go. If on the other hand he does not return as I say he will, you shall set your men on me and have me thrown down from a precipice, just to teach the next beggar not to cheat.'

'Yes,' cried the worthy swineherd, 'and what a fine name I should win for myself in the world, once and for all, if the first thing I did after taking you into my cabin and showing you hospitality was to rob you of your precious life! I should certainly have to put all I know into my prayers, if I did that. However, it's supper-time, and I hope my men will be in before long, so that we can get a square meal cooked in the house.'

While the two were engaged in this conversation the herdsmen came up with their swine. The men drove the animals in batches into their sties to sleep and the air was filled with the grunting of pigs settling down for the night. The worthy swineherd gave a shout to his men. 'Bring in the best of your hogs,' he called. 'I want to slaughter it, for a guest I have here from abroad. And we'll enjoy it ourselves, after the way we've toiled and moiled for the porkers all this time, with other people living scot-free on our work.'

He then chopped some firewood with his sharp axe, while his men dragged in a fatted five-year-old hog and brought it up to the hearth. The swineherd, who was a man of sound principles, did not forget the immortals, but began the ritual by throwing a tuft of hair from the white-tusked victim into the fire and praying to all the gods that the wise Odysseus might come back to his home. Then he drew himself up and struck the animal with a billet of oak which he had left unsplit. The hog fell dead. They slit its throat, singed its bristles, and deftly cut the carcass up. The swineherd took a first cut from all the limbs, laid the raw flesh on the rich fat, cast the whole into the flames and sprinkled barley-meal on top. Then they chopped up the rest of the meat, pierced it with skewers, roasted it thoroughly, and after drawing it off the spits heaped it up on platters. And now the swineherd, who had a nice judgement in such matters, stood up to divide it into helpings. He carved and sorted it all out into seven portions, of which he set aside one, with a prayer, for the Nymphs and for Hermes, Maia's son, and distributed the rest to the company. But he paid Odysseus the honour of helping him to the tusker's long chine. This courtesy warmed the heart of his master, who turned to him and said: 'Eumaeus, I hope Father Zeus will look on you as kindly as I do for picking out the best portion for a poor fellow like me.' To which the swineherd Eumaeus replied: 'Fall to, my worthy guest, and enjoy such fare as we can offer. It's the way of the gods to bestow or withhold their favours according to their own sweet will – and there's nothing to prevent them.' Then he sacrificed the first cuts to the everlasting gods, and after making a libation of sparkling wine handed the cup to Odysseus, the sacker of cities, and sat down to his own portion. They were served with bread by Mesaulius, a servant whom Eumaeus had procured for himself during his master's absence, acting without help from his mistress or the old Laertes and buying the man from the Taphians with his own resources. All fell to on the good fare spread before them, and when they had satisfied their hunger and thirst Mesaulius cleared away the food. Sated by now with bread and meat they began to think kindly of their beds.

Foul weather set in with the dusk. There was no moon, rain fell all night, and a high wind blew from the west, always the wet quarter. So Odysseus decided to put the swineherd to the test and see whether his host's very real consideration for him might not induce him either to part with his own cloak and let him have it, or to suggest this self-denial to one of his men. 'Listen to me,' he said. 'Eumaeus and you men of his. I am going to put a wish of mine into the form of a story. This is the effect of your wine – for wine is a crazy thing. It sets the wisest man singing and giggling like a girl; it lures him on to dance and it makes him blurt out what were better left unsaid. However, I've set my tongue wagging now and I might as well go on.

'Ah, I wish I were still as young and strong as I was when we led that surprise attack against Troy! Odysseus and Menelaus were in charge, and at their own request I went in with them as third in command. When we came up to the frowning city walls we lay down round the place, crouching under our armour in the dense undergrowth of marshland reeds. The North wind dropped and a cruel frosty night set in. From overhead the snow came down like hoar-frost, bitterly cold, and the ice formed thick on our shields. All the rest had cloaks and tunics and they slept in comfort with their shields drawn up over their shoulders. But when I started I was stupid enough to leave my cloak with my men, thinking that even so I shouldn't suffer from cold; and thus I joined the party with nothing but my shield and a light kilt.

'In the third watch of the night, when the stars had passed their zenith, I decided to have a word with Odysseus, who was my neighbour. I nudged him with my elbow. He was all attention. "King Odysseus," I said, "bring your wits to the rescue. I shall be a dead man soon. This frost is killing me, for I have no cloak. I was misguided enough to put on nothing but a tunic. And now there's no way out of my plight." When I put this to him, Odysseus turned it over in his mind and, like the schemer and soldier that he was, he had an idea, as you will see. "Quiet!" he whispered in my ear. "Don't let any of the others hear you." Then he raised his head on his elbow and called to the rest: "Wake up, my friends. The gods have sent me a dream in my sleep. I feel we have come too far from the ships, and I want someone to take a message to Agamemnon, the commander-in-chief. He might send us reinforcements from the base." The response was immediate. A man called Thoas, Andraimon's son, jumped up, threw off his purple cloak, and set out for the ships at the double – leaving me to lie in his clothes with a grateful heart till Dawn appeared on her golden throne. Ah, I wish I were still as young and strong as I was then!'

'Old man,' said the swineherd Eumaeus to Odysseus, 'that is an excellent story you have told us. Every word went home, and you shall have your reward. Tonight you shan't want for clothing or anything else that an unfortunate outcast has the right to expect from those he approaches. But in the morning you'll have to knock about in your own rags once more. We have no stock of cloaks here nor extra tunics to put on: each man has to manage with a single cloak. But when Odysseus' son arrives, you can count on *him* to give you a cloak and tunic to wear, and to send you wherever you have set your heart on going.'

The swineherd sprang up, placed a bed for him by the fire and spread on it the skins of sheep and goats. Odysseus lay down and

Eumaeus covered him with a great thick mantle, which he kept laid by to change into when an exceptionally cold spell came on.

So there Odysseus slept, with the young farm-hands beside him. But the swineherd was not content to sleep there and desert his boars. On the contrary, he got himself ready for a night outside, and Odysseus was delighted to see how careful a steward he was of his absent master's property. He began by slinging a sharp sword from his sturdy shoulders. He then wrapped himself in a good thick cloak to keep out the wind, picked up the fleece of a big full-grown goat, and finally took a sharp javelin with which to ward off dogs and men. And so he went off to pass the night where the white-tusked porkers slept, under an overhanging rock sheltered from the northerly winds.

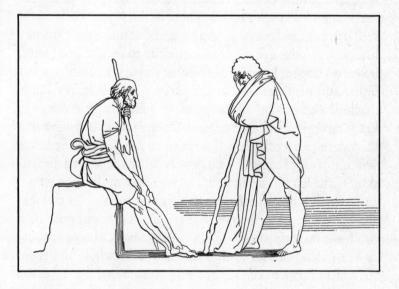

XV

TELEMACHUS RETURNS

PALLAS ATHENE, meanwhile, went to the broad vale of Lacedaemon to warn King Odysseus' noble son that it was time for him to return, and to hasten his departure.

She found Telemachus and Prince Peisistratus sleeping in the great Menelaus' portico. Nestor's son, at all events, was lying sound asleep; but Telemachus was enjoying no rest, for anxiety on his father's behalf kept him wakeful all the livelong night. The bright-eyed goddess came up to his bed. 'Telemachus,' she said, 'it is wrong of you to linger abroad and leave your property unguarded with such a rabble in the place. They might well share out and eat up all you have, and so make your journey futile. Urge your gallant host, Menelaus, to let you go at once, if you wish to find your noble mother still in the palace. For her father and brothers are already pressing her to marry Eurymachus, who outdoes all the rest of her Suitors in generosity and keeps raising his bid for her hand. There is also the danger that she might carry off some of your own things from the house without your permission. You know what a woman's disposition is. She likes to bring riches to the house of the man who is marrying her, while, as for her former husband and the children she has borne him, she never gives him a thought once he is dead, nor inquires after *them*. So when you reach home I should like to see you take the lead and hand over the whole household to whichever woman-servant you trust most, until heaven sends you a wife worthy of your rank. And here's another matter for you to digest. The leading spirits among the Suitors are lying in ambush in the straits between Ithaca and the rugged coast of Samos, intent on murdering you before you can get home. Not that I think they will succeed. No; sooner than that, the earth will close over some of these love-lorn gentlemen who are wasting your wealth. However, give the islands a wide berth, and sail on through the night; your guardian god will send you a following breeze. Land in Ithaca at the first point you reach and send the ship and the whole ship's company round to the port; but before you yourself do anything else, visit the swineherd in charge of your pigs, who is loyal to you despite all. Stay there for the night and send him to the city to give your wise mother, Penelope, the news that you are in from Pylos and that she has you safely back.'

Her message delivered, Athene withdrew to the heights or Olympus. But Telemachus roused Nestor's son from his pleasant dreams with a touch of his foot and said: 'Wake up, Peisistratus, and harness the horses to the chariot, so that we may be getting on our way.'

'Telemachus,' his friend replied, 'however eager we may be to start, we cannot possibly drive in complete darkness. It'll soon be dawn. Why not wait and give the brave Menelaus, our royal host, the chance of putting some presents for us in the chariot and bidding us a civil farewell? A guest never forgets the host who has treated him kindly.'

They had not long to wait before Dawn took her golden throne and the warrior Menelaus rose from sleep beside the lovely Helen and made his way towards them. When Odysseus' son saw him coming he hastily drew his shining tunic on, threw his great cloak across his sturdy shoulders, and, dressed like a prince, went out to Menelaus and greeted him by his titles. 'Sire,' he said, 'I beg leave of you now to return to my own country, for I find myself longing to be home.'

'Telemachus,' the warrior king replied, 'far be it from me to keep you here for any length of time, if you wish to get back. I condemn any host who is either too kind or not kind enough. There should be moderation in all things, and it is equally offensive to speed a guest who would like to stay and to detain one who is anxious to leave. What I say is, treat a man well while he's with you, but let him go when he wishes.

'However, do give me time to bring you some presents and

pack them in your chariot – they will be fine ones, as you will see for yourself. And let me tell the women to get a meal ready in the hall. There's plenty of food in the larder, and it is a point of honour and decency for us, and a question of comfort for you, that you should lunch before starting on your long trip overland. Perhaps you would like to make a tour through Hellas and the Argive country, letting *me* take your companion's place; in which case I should provide the car and horses and serve as your guide to the various cities? Nobody will send us away empty-handed: we can count on each of our hosts for at least one gift, a copper tripod or a cauldron, a pair of mules or a golden cup.'

'My lord Menelaus,' the wise Telemachus answered, 'I really am anxious to return at once to my own place. For when I set out I left no custodian in charge of my property. I must see that this journey in search of my royal father does not end in my own destruction, and that the house isn't robbed of any of my valuables.'

When the gallant Menelaus heard this, he at once told his wife and the servants to prepare a meal in the hall from the plentiful supplies they would find in the larder. At this moment, Boethous' son Eteoneus, who lived near by and had just got up, drew near and was told by Menelaus to light the fire and roast some meat. Eteoneus hastened to carry out his instructions, while Menelaus, in company with Helen and Megapenthes, went down to his scented store-room. When they had reached the spot where the treasure was kept, Menelaus picked out a two-handled cup and told his son Megapenthes to take a silver mixing-bowl. Helen, meanwhile, went to the chests which contained her embroidered dresses, the work of her own hands, and from them, great lady that she was, she lifted out the longest and most richly decorated robe, which had lain underneath all the rest, and now glittered like a star. They then made their way through the house and found Telemachus, to whom red-haired Menelaus said: 'It is my earnest hope, Telemachus, that Zeus the Thunderer and Lord of Here will grant you a safe journey and make your home-coming all that you desire. By way of presents you shall have the loveliest and most precious of the treasures that my palace holds. I am giving you a mixing-bowl of wrought metal. It is solid silver, with a rim of gold round the top, and was made by Hephaestus himself. I had it from my royal friend, the King of Sidon, when I put up under his roof on my journey home. And now I wish it to be yours.'

The lord Menelaus then handed him the two-handled cup, while his valiant son Megapenthes brought forward the shining silver bowl he had described and set it before him. Helen of the lovely cheeks stood by with the robe in her hands and made him her own adieu: 'Look, dear child, I too have a gift for you here, a keepsake from Helen, made by her own hands. It is for your bride to wear when the longed-for day of your wedding arrives. Till then let it lie at home in your mother's care. And now I wish you a happy return to your own country and your pleasant house.'

With that, Helen handed the robe to Telemachus, who accepted it joyfully. Prince Peisistratus took charge of the gifts and noted their excellence with silent admiration as he stowed them in the body of the chariot. Red-haired Menelaus then led the way for them into the house and the two young men sat down. A maid brought water in a fine golden jug and poured it out over a silver basin so that they could rinse their hands. Next she drew a polished table to their side, and the staid housekeeper brought some bread and set it by them with a choice of dainties, helping them liberally to all she could offer. Eteoneus stood by and carved the meat into helpings, while the great Menelaus' son poured out their wine. And so they fell to on the good things spread before them.

When they had satisfied their hunger and thirst, Telemachus and Nestor's noble son yoked their horses, mounted their gaily painted chariot, and drove out by the gateway and its echoing portico. Red-haired Menelaus walked along after them with a golden cup of mellow wine in his right hand, to enable his guests to make a drink-offering before they left. He went up to their chariot and drank their health. 'Goodbye, my young friends,' he said; 'and give King Nestor my respects. He was like a kind father to me when we were in the field at Troy.'

'Your Majesty,' Telemachus replied, 'we will certainly give him your message when we arrive. I only wish I were as sure of finding Odysseus at home when I reach Ithaca, so that I could tell him how I have met with nothing but kindness at your hands during my stay and have come away laden with precious gifts.'

As though in answer to his words, a bird came flying to the right. It was an eagle, carrying in its talons a great white goose, a tame bird from the yard. Some men and women were noisily giving chase, and when the eagle reached the car he sheered off toward the right in front of the horses, to the delight of the whole party, whose spirits rose at the sight. Nestor's son Peisistratus was the first to speak. 'Your Majesty,' he said to Menelaus, 'here is a problem. Did heaven send this omen for us two or for you?'

Menelaus, for all his warlike qualities, was at a loss to give him the correct interpretation, and his beautiful wife forestalled him. 'Listen,' she said, 'while with such inspiration as I have I explain this omen and what I feel sure that it portends. Just as this eagle came down from his native mountains and pounced on our home-fed goose, so shall Odysseus, after many hardships and many wanderings, reach his home and have his revenge. Why, at this very moment he may be there and sowing trouble for the whole pack of Suitors!'

'May Zeus the Thunderer and Lord of Here,' cried Telemachus, 'make what you say come true, and in my distant home I shall treat you as a goddess in my prayers.'

Then he gave the horses a touch of his whip. They set off smartly and pressed forward through the town towards the open country, where throughout the long day they swayed the yoke up and down on their necks.

By sundown, when the roads grew dark, they had reached Pherae, where they drove up to the house of Diocles, son of Ortilochus, whose father was Alpheius. There they put up for the night and were hospitably entertained. But tender Dawn had hardly touched the East with red, when they were harnessing their horses once again and mounting the gaily-coloured chariot. Out past the sounding portico and through the gates they drove. A flick of the whip to make the horses go, and the pair flew on, with such a will that before very long the high citadel of Pylos came into view.

At this point Telemachus turned to Nestor's son and said: 'Peisistratus, I want you, if you can, to undertake something on my behalf. We may well claim that our fathers' friendship makes a lasting bond between us. Besides which, we are of the same age and this journey will have served to bring us even closer together. So I beg you, my dear prince, not to drive me past my ship, but to drop me there and thus save me from being kept at the palace against my will by your old father's passion for hospitality. For I must get home quicker than that.'

Nestor's son turned the problem over in his mind. How could he honourably consent and oblige his friend? After some hesitation he made up his mind. Turning his horses, he drove down to the ship on the sea-shore, unloaded the chariot, and stowed Menelaus' fine presents of clothing and gold in the ship's stern. He then impressed on Telemachus the need for haste. 'Embark at once,' he said, 'and order all your men on board before I reach home and tell the old man. In my own mind I am convinced that he is far too obstinate to let you go, but will come down here himself to fetch you – and I do not see him going back alone. For whatever your excuse, he'll be very much annoyed.'

Peisistratus left him without more ado and drove his long-maned horses back to the city of Pylos, where he soon reached his home. Meanwhile Telemachus spurred on his crew. 'Men,' he called to them, 'see that the tackle is properly stowed on board, and let's get in ourselves. I wish to make a start.'

The crew leapt to his orders, climbed on board, and took their places on the benches. Telemachus had just supervised their embarkation and was praying and sacrificing to Athene by the ship's stern when he was accosted by a stranger from a distant state. This man, who had fled from Argos after committing manslaughter, was a prophet descended from Melampus. His ancestor had at one time lived in Pylos, mother of sheep, and been known among his fellow-citizens as a wealthy man with a magnificent house. But a time came when he had to fly the country and venture abroad to escape from the great but tyrannical King Neleus. The king seized his rich estate and kept it for a whole year. Melampus meanwhile was a wretched prisoner in the castle of Phylacus, reaping untold miseries, for Neleus' daughter's sake, from the fit of infatuation into which that irresistible goddess the Fury had cast him. However, he escaped alive and managed to drive the lowing cattle from Phylace to Pylos, where he had his revenge on King Neleus for the injustice done to him and secured the hand of the princess for his brother. As for himself, he withdrew abroad, to the plains of Argos, where he was destined to make his home and establish his rule over a large part of the people. There he married, built himself a splendid palace, and had two sturdy sons, Antiphates and Mantius. Antiphates became the father of the doughty Oicles, and Oicles, in his turn, of that great leader Amphiaraus, a man whom Zeus and Apollo loved and blessed with every mark of their favour. Even so he never came within sight of old age, but fell at Thebes, the victim of a woman's avarice. His sons were Alcmaeon and Amphilochus, while his brother Mantius was the father of Polypheides and Cleitus – Cleitus, who was so lovely that Dawn of the golden throne carried him off to forgather with the immortals, and the magnanimous Polypheides, who was made a seer by Apollo, and after Amphiaraus' death succeeded him as the leading prophet in the world. A quarrel with his father led him to migrate to Hyperesie, where he settled and practised his profession.

It was his son, Theoclymenus by name, who now appeared and came up to Telemachus, whom he found engaged in libations and prayers by his black ship. 'Friend,' he said to him eagerly, 'since I find you sacrificing here, I adjure you by your sacrifice and the god you are honouring, and again by your own life and the lives of these friends who are with you, to be open with me and tell me the truth. Who are you? Where do you hail from? And what is your native town?'

'Sir,' answered Telemachus, 'I am quite ready to give you the facts. Ithaca is my native place, and my father is Odysseus, or certainly was. But I have come to think that he has long since met with some unhappy end. That is what brings me here with my ship and my crew. I am trying to find out what has happened to my long-lost father.'

'Like you,' said the noble Theoclymenus, 'I have left my country. I killed a man of my own blood, and the plains of Argos are full of his brothers and kinsmen, who form the most powerful family in the land. It was to avoid the certainty of death at their hands that I ran away and embraced my new destiny as a wanderer on the face of the earth. As I have sought sanctuary with you, I beg you to take me on board and prevent them from killing me, for I believe they are on my track.'

'I shall certainly not forbid you my good ship, if you wish to use her,' said the sensible young man. 'Come along then; and in Ithaca you shall be welcome to such hospitality as we can offer.'

He took Theoclymenus' bronze spear and laid it on the curved ship's deck. Then he stepped on board the gallant vessel himself, sat down in the stern, and gave Theoclymenus a place beside him. The hawsers were cast off and Telemachus shouted to the crew to lay hands on the tackle. They obeyed with a will, hauled up the fir mast, stept it in its hollow box, made it fast with stays, and hoisted the white sail with plaited leather ropes. And Athene of the gleaming eyes sent a boisterous wind through the clear weather to buffet them from astern, so that their ship might make the shortest possible work of her run across the open sea. Thus they sailed past Crouni and Chalcis with its lovely streams, and when the sun set and they had to pick their way through the darkness, they stood for Pheae with the wind still at their backs, and ran past the good land of Elis where the Epeians rule. After which Telemachus set a course for the Pointed Isles, wondering whether he would get through alive or be caught.

Meanwhile Odysseus and the worthy swineherd, with the farm-hands for company, were taking supper in the hut. When they had eaten and drunk their fill, Odysseus put out a feeler to discover whether he could count on the swineherd's continued hospitality and an invitation to stay there at the farm, or would be sent off to the city. 'Listen to me,' he said, 'Eumaeus and you men of his. I intend to leave you in the morning and go to the town to beg, so that I may not be a burden to you and your mates. But I should be glad of your best advice and the company of a trustworthy guide to show me the way. Once there I shall be thrown on my own resources and shall have to wander about the place in the hope that someone will give me a cup of water and a crust of bread. I propose also to go to King Odysseus' palace and deliver my news to his wise queen, Penelope. Nor do I see why I shouldn't approach those ill-conditioned Suitors you speak of. They have such an abundance of good things that they might well spare me a meal. I should be ready to make an excellent job of whatever work they wanted done. For I tell you frankly, and you can take it from me, that by favour of Hermes the Messenger, to whom the labour of men's hands owes all the grace and the success that it achieves, there's not a man to touch me at servants' work, at laying a fire well, at splitting dry faggots, as a carver, a cook, a wine-steward, in short at anything that humble folk do by way of serving their betters.'

But the swineherd was most indignant. 'My good sir,' he exclaimed, 'what on earth put such a scheme into your head? You will simply be courting sudden death, if you insist on attaching yourself to a set of men whose profligacy and violence have outraged heaven itself. *Their* servants are not at all your kind, but smartly dressed young fellows, who always grease their hair and keep their pretty faces clean. That is the kind that wait on them – at polished tables, groaning under their load of bread and meat and wine. No, sir, stay with me, where nobody finds you a nuisance. I certainly don't, nor does any of my mates here. And when Odysseus' son arrives, he'll fit you out in a cloak and tunic and send you on wherever you would like to go.'

'Eumaeus,' replied the good and gallant Odysseus, 'may Father Zeus look on you as kindly as I do for putting a term to my wandering and hopeless want. Surely a tramp's life is the worst thing that anyone can come to. Yet exile, misfortune, and sorrow often force a man to put up with its miseries for his wretched stomach's sake. However, since you press me to stay and await the prince's arrival, perhaps you'll be so good as to give me the news about King Odysseus' mother, and his father, whom he left on the threshold of old age when he went abroad. Are they still in the land of the living? Or are they dead by now and in the Halls of Hades?'

'My friend,' said the admirable swineherd, 'I shall be glad to answer your questions. Laertes, to take him first, is still alive, but every day he prays to Zeus that death may visit his house and release the spirit from his flesh. For he grieves inconsolably for his lost son and for that wise lady, his wife, whose death was the heaviest blow he has suffered, and left him an old man before his time. As for her, it was pining for her brilliant son that brought her to the grave – a dreadful death – heaven spare my friends and patrons here in Ithaca from the like. So long as the unhappy woman was still alive, I used always to make a point of asking after her and hearing the news, for it was she who brought me up, together with that fine girl of hers, the lady Ctimene, her youngest. Yes, we were educated together and her mother treated me almost as her equal. But when we two young things had reached the age when love will have its way, they married her off to someone in Same – and what a price he paid them! As for me, her mother fitted me out in a fine mantle and tunic, with a new pair of sandals for my feet, and packed me off to the farm. But she always kept a tender place for me in her heart. Ah, I have long missed kindness such as hers! I'm not complaining about my work here. The blessed gods have prospered it, so that it brings me in enough to eat and drink and to give to such as have a claim upon me. But from my mistress there's never a gentle word to be had, nor a kind deed either. For the house has come on evil days and fallen into ruffians' hands. Yet servants do miss it mightily when they can't talk face to face with their mistress, and find out all the news, and have a bite and a sup, and carry off a titbit to the farm as well. That is the sort of thing that always warms a servant's heart.'

'You surprise me,' said Odysseus. 'You must have been quite a little fellow, Eumaeus, when you came all that way from your parents and your home! Won't you tell me what happened? Were you stolen in the streets when they sacked the city where your parents lived; or did some band of buccaneers catch you alone with the flocks or herds, bring you by ship to the palace here and get a good price from your master?'

'My friend,' replied the admirable swineherd, 'you have asked for the story of my capture. Very well, give me your ear and enjoy the tale as you sit there and drink your wine. There's no end to these nights. They give one time to listen and be entertained as well as time to sleep. Nor is there any need for you to go early to bed. Even where sleep is concerned, too much is a bad thing. But any of the rest, if the spirit moves them, can go out and sleep. For at the first sign of dawn they must break their fast and sally out with the royal pigs. Meanwhile let us two, here in the hut, over our food and wine, regale ourselves with the unhappy memories that each can recall. For a man who has been through bitter experiences and travelled far can enjoy even his sufferings after a time.

'You were asking me about my early days. Let me give you the tale. There is an island called Syrie – you may have heard the name – out beyond Ortygie, where the Sun turns in his course. It's not so very thickly peopled, though the rich land is excellent for cattle and sheep and yields fine crops of grapes and corn. Famine is unknown there and so is disease. No dreadful scourges spoil the islanders' happiness, but as the men of each generation grow old in their homes, Apollo of the Silver Bow comes with Artemis, strikes them with kindly darts, and lays them low. There are two cities in the island, which is divided between them. My father, Ctesius son of Ormenus, was king of them both and ruled them like a god.

'One day the island was visited by a party of those notorious Phoenician sailors, greedy rogues, with a whole cargo of gew-gaws in their black ship. Now there happened to be a woman of their race in my father's house, a fine strapping creature and clever too with her hands. But the double-dealing Phoenicians soon turned her head. One of them began it by making love to her when she was washing clothes, and seducing her by the ship's hull – and there's nothing like love to lead a woman astray, be she never so honest. He asked her who she was and where she came from. She replied by pointing out to him the high roof of my father's house, and to this she added: "I come from Sidon, where they deal in bronze. I am the daughter of Arybas, and a rich man he was. But some Taphian pirates carried me off as I was coming in from the country, brought me here to this man's house and sold me. He gave a good price for me, too!"

' "And how would you like," said her seducer, "to come home again with us and to see the high roof of your *own* house, and your parents in it? For I tell you they are still alive and have the name of wealthy folk."

' "I would jump at the chance," said the woman, "if you sailors would swear to bring me safe and sound to my home."

'They were quite willing to promise what she asked; and solemnly took their oaths. But the woman had something more for their ears. "Keep your mouths shut," she said, "and don't let any of your party say a word to me if you meet me in the street or at the well. Someone might go to the house and blab to the old man, who would clap me into irons if his suspicions were roused, and see what he could do to kill you all. No; keep the idea to yourselves, and buy your homeward freight as fast as you can. When the ship is fully victualled quickly send word to me up at the house. For I shall bring away some gold with me – all I can lay my hands on. And there's something else I should gladly give you in payment for my passage. I'm nurse there in the house to a nobleman's child – a clever little scamp, who trots along at my side when we go out. I'm quite ready to bring him on board with me, and he'd fetch you a fortune in any foreign port where you might put him up for sale." With this the woman left them and returned to our comfortable home.

'The traders stayed with us for a whole year, during which they bought and took on board a vast store of goods. When the hold was full and their ship ready for sea, they sent up a messenger to pass the word to the woman. The cunning rascal came to my father's home with a golden necklace strung at intervals with amber beads. While my mother and the women-servants in the house were handling and bargaining for the necklace, and all eyes were fixed upon it, he quietly nodded to my nurse, and, his signal delivered, slipped off to the ship. Meanwhile the woman took me by the hand and dragged me out through the door, and there in the entrance-hall she saw the wine-cups and tables that had been used for a banquet given to my father's retainers. The guests themselves had gone out to attend a public debate in the meeting-place. So she quickly hid three goblets in her bosom and carried them off. And in my childish innocence I followed her.

'The sun had set by now, and we ran down through darkened streets to the great harbour where the fast Phoenician ship was lying. They put us on board at once, climbed in themselves and made for the open sea, with a following wind, as luck would have it. For six days and nights we sailed steadily on, but on the seventh day Artemis the Archeress struck the woman and she crashed headlong into the hold like a gannet diving into the sea. They threw her corpse overboard as carrion for the seals and fish, and I was left alone in my misery. In due course the winds and currents drove us in to Ithaca, where Laertes parted with some of his wealth to buy me. That, sir, is how I first came to set eyes on this land.'

'Eumaeus,' said King Odysseus, 'this vivid account of your misfortunes has moved me deeply. But you must admit that heaven sent you some good luck too, to set off the bad, since after all these misadventures you came to the house of a kind master, who has obviously been careful to see that you have plenty to eat and drink; so that the life you live is a good one, whereas I have tramped through half the cities in the world before reaching this refuge.'

In this way they entertained each other with talk; and when at last they lay down, it was not for a long night's sleep: only a little time was left before Dawn was on her golden throne.

Meanwhile Telemachus had reached the coast of Ithaca, and his men were striking sail. Down came the mast, and they rowed her into her berth, where they dropped anchor and made the hawsers fast. Then they jumped out on the beach, prepared their breakfast, and mixed the sparkling wine. Telemachus wisely let them eat and drink their fill before he gave them their orders. 'You will now take the ship round to the port,' he said, 'while I pay a visit to the farms and see the herdsmen. This evening, when I've looked round my estate, I shall come down to the city. And tomorrow morning I propose to pay you your wages for the voyage – a good feast of meat with mellow wine to wash it down.'

'And what is to become of me, dear child?' asked his noble passenger, Theoclymenus. 'Which of your chieftains' homes is to be my refuge in this rugged land of yours? Or shall I go straight to your mother and your own house?'

'In other circumstances,' answered the prudent Telemachus, 'I should invite you to go to our own house, where there is no lack of hospitality. But as things stand, for your own sake I do not recommend that course, since you won't have me at your side and my mother wouldn't see you. She seldom shows herself to her Suitors in the hall, but keeps away from them and works at the loom in her room upstairs. However, there *is* a man you might go to, and I'll give you his name – Eurymachus, the noble son of a wise father, Polybus, who at the moment is my countrymen's idol. He is certainly by far the best man there, as well as the keenest bidder for my mother's hand and for my father's rights. But Olympian Zeus in his heaven is the only one who knows whether he hasn't a bad time in store for them all before it comes to weddings!'

This speech of Telemachus was greeted by a happy omen, a

bird flying to the right. It was a hawk, Apollo's winged herald, holding a dove in its talons, which it plucked so that the feathers fluttered down to earth half-way between the ship and Telemachus himself. Theoclymenus beckoned him away from his men, seized his hand, and congratulated him. 'Telemachus,' he said, 'this bird that passed to your right was certainly a sign from heaven. Directly I set eyes on him I knew him for a bird of omen. In all Ithaca there is no more royal house than yours. No; yours is the power for all time.'

'My friend,' said Telemachus, 'may what you say prove true! If it does, you shall learn from my liberality what my friendship means, and the world will envy you your luck.' Then he turned to his loyal friend Peiraeus son of Clytius and said: 'Peiraeus, of all who joined me on this trip to Pylos I have always found you the most reliable. Will you oblige me now by taking charge of this guest of ours and treating him with every kindness and attention in your own house till I come back?'

To which the gallant Peiraeus replied: 'Stay here as long as you like, Telemachus, and I will look after him. He shall not complain of any lack of hospitality.'

Peiraeus then went on board the ship and ordered the rest to cast off the hawsers and embark. They quickly got in and took their seats on the benches. Meanwhile Telemachus fastened his sandals on his feet and picked up his powerful bronze-pointed spear from the ship's deck. The men untied the cables, thrust her off, and sailed for the city, as ordered by Telemachus, the son of Odysseus their king. But Telemachus set out on foot and walked at a good pace till he reached the yard where his large droves of pigs were kept and the swineherd slept among them, loyal heart, with none but kindly feelings for his masters' house.

XVI

ODYSSEUS MEETS HIS SON

WHEN Telemachus arrived, Odysseus and the worthy swineherd were preparing their breakfast in the hut by the light of
dawn, after stirring up the fire and sending the herdsmen off
with the pigs to the pastures. The dogs, usually so obstreperous,
not only did not bark at the newcomer but greeted him with
wagging tails. Odysseus heard footsteps and at the same moment observed the dogs' friendly behaviour. Immediately alert,
he turned to his companion and said: 'Eumaeus, you have a
visitor: I can hear his steps. He must be a friend of yours or someone familiar here, for the dogs are wagging their tails instead
of barking.'

The last words were not out of his mouth when his own son
appeared in the gateway. Eumaeus jumped up in amazement
and the bowls in which he had been busy mixing the sparkling
wine tumbled out of his grasp. He ran forward to meet his
young master, he kissed his forehead, kissed him on both his
lovely eyes, and then kissed his right hand and his left, while the
tears streamed down his cheeks. Like a fond father welcoming
back his son after nine years abroad, his only son, the apple of his
eye and the centre of all his anxious cares, the admirable swineherd threw his arms round Prince Telemachus and showered
kisses on him as though he had just escaped from death.

'So you are back, Telemachus, light of my eyes!' he said in a
voice filled with emotion. 'And I thought I should never see you
again, once you had sailed for Pylos! Come in, come in, dear
child, and let me feast my eyes on the wanderer just home. We
herdsmen see little of you here on the farm: you are too fond of
the town. It seems as though you found it amusing to watch that
crew of wreckers at their work!'

'I'll come in with pleasure. uncle.' said Telemachus. 'In fact it

was for you I came here. I wanted to see you myself and find out
from you whether my mother is still in the palace or whether
she has married again and Odysseus' bed is hung with cobwebs
for lack of occupants.'

'Of course she's still at home,' said the excellent swineherd.
'She has schooled her heart to patience, though her eyes are
never free from tears as the slow nights and days pass sorrowfully by.'

As he spoke he relieved his visitor of his bronze spear, and
Telemachus crossed the stone threshold into the house. At his
entrance, Odysseus his father rose to give him his seat. But Telemachus from the other side of the room checked him with a
gesture and said: 'Keep your seat, sir. I am sure that in our own
farmhouse we can find a seat elsewhere; and here is someone to
provide it.'

So Odysseus resumed his chair, while the swineherd made a
pile of green brushwood for his son, with a fleece spread on top,
and there Telemachus sat down. Eumaeus then put beside them
platters of roast meat that had been left over from their meal on
the previous day, and with eager hospitality piled baskets high
with bread and mixed them some sweet wine in an ivy-wood
bowl. This done, he himself sat down opposite King Odysseus,
and they fell to on the good fare before them. When they had
satisfied their hunger and thirst, Telemachus turned to the
worthy swineherd and said: 'Uncle, where does this guest of
yours hail from? I am quite sure he didn't walk to Ithaca. Some
ship's crew must have brought him here. How did it happen
and who may they have been?'

'My child,' Eumaeus replied, 'you shall have nothing but the
truth from me. He claims to be a native of the large island of
Crete and says he has tramped as an outcast through half the
towns in the world, for that seems the kind of life that heaven
has let him in for. But quite recently he managed to escape from
a Thesprotian ship and came to my homestead here. I propose
to make him over to you, to deal with as you like, for he has
decided to throw himself on your mercy.'

'Eumaeus, this is very mortifying to me,' Telemachus thoughtfully replied. 'How can I possibly receive the stranger in my house? In the first place I myself am young and I doubt whether I yet have the physical strength to cope with anyone who might care to pick a quarrel with me. Then again my mother is in two minds whether to stay at home and keep house for me, in deference to her husband's bed and to public opinion, or whether to choose among the nobles in the palace who are candidates for her hand and go off with the likeliest and most generous bidder. However, as the stranger has sought refuge in your house, I will fit him out in a good cloak and tunic, give him a two-edged sword and sandals for footwear, and see that he reaches his destination, wherever that may be. But I should be glad if you could agree to keep him at the farm and look after him. I'll send you the clothes and all the food he'll need, so that he shan't be a burden to you and your mates. But I will not permit him to come down to the palace and meet the Suitors. For their brutality goes beyond all bounds, and if they insult him, as I fear is likely, I should take it very much to heart. But it is extremely difficult for a man to do anything single-handed against a crowd, however strong he may be. They have an overwhelming advantage.'

'I feel sure, my dear sir,' the gallant Odysseus interposed, 'that there can be no objection to my joining in your discussion. My indignation has been deeply stirred by what I have learnt from you of the outrageous conduct of these Suitors, which you, a gentleman, have had to put up with in your house. Tell me, do you take this lying down; or have the people of Ithaca been turned into enemies of yours by some wave of irrational feeling? Or again, is it your brothers who cannot be trusted to stand by you as they should through thick and thin? Ah, I wish I had the youth, as I have the stomach, for this work; that I were the noble Odysseus' son, or that Odysseus himself had come back from his travels – as there is still reason to hope that he may! I should be ready here and now to let anyone cut my head off, if I didn't go straight down to the palace of Laertes' heir and make myself a curse to every man in that crowd. And what if they did over-whelm me by numbers, single-handed as I should be? I would rather die by the sword in my own house than witness the perpetual repetition of these outrages, the brutal treatment of visitors, men hauling the maids about for their foul purposes in that lovely house, wine running like water, and those rascals gorging themselves, just for the sport of the thing, with no excuse, no rational end in sight!'

'My friend,' said the wise Telemachus, 'let me explain the situation to you. I cannot say that the people as a whole have fallen out with me and taken up a hostile attitude. Nor can I complain of any disloyalty in the brothers I should normally rely on to stand by me through thick and thin. For Zeus has made only sons the rule in our family. Laertes was the only son of Arceisius, and Odysseus of Laertes, while I was the only son who had been born to Odysseus when he left his home – and little joy he had of me. As a result, the house is infested by our enemies. Of all the island chieftains in Dulichium, in Same, in wooded Zacynthus, or in rocky Ithaca, there is not one that isn't courting my mother and wasting my property. As for her, she neither refuses, though she hates the idea of remarrying, nor can she bring herself to take the final step. Meanwhile they are eating me out of house and home. And I shouldn't be surprised if they finished me myself. However, the issue of all this is on the knees of the gods. And now, uncle, will you go quickly down and tell my wise mother, Penelope, that she has me safely back from Pylos. I myself propose to wait here till you return after deliver-ing your message – which is for her ears alone. Let none of the men in the place hear it. There are plenty of them eager to do me a mischief.'

'I know; I understand,' said the swineherd Eumaeus. 'You've chosen a man who can think for himself. But what do you say to my making one journey of it and telling Laertes also the news? The poor man, for all his great grief for Odysseus, used till lately to take a look round the fields and eat and drink with the hands at the farm when he felt disposed to do so. But ever since you

sailed for Pylos, they say that he has not so much as taken a bite
or sup, nor cast an eye over the work on the farm, but sits there
moaning and groaning in his misery, with the flesh withering
on his bones.'

'So much the worse,' said the cautious Telemachus, 'but all
the same we will let him be. Not that I do not sympathize; for if
men could have anything for the asking, my father's return
would be *my* first choice. However, deliver your message and
come straight back. Don't go wandering about the countryside
after Laertes, but ask my mother to send out one of her waiting-
women, quickly and secretly. *She* could tell the old man.'

So Telemachus gave him his errand, and Eumaeus picked up
his sandals, bound them on his feet and set off for the town. His
departure from the farm was not unobserved by Athene, who
now approached, to all appearance a tall, beautiful, and accomplished woman, and halting opposite the door of the hut made
herself visible to Odysseus, though Telemachus could neither
see her nor become conscious of her presence, since it is by no
means to everyone that the gods grant a clear sight of themselves. Thus, only Odysseus and the dogs saw her, and the dogs
did not bark but ran whimpering in panic to the other side of the
farm. Athene frowned and nodded to Odysseus, who caught
her signal, and leaving the house passed along by the great wall
of the yard and presented himself before her. Athene spoke to
him. 'The time has come,' she said, 'royal son of Laertes,
Odysseus of the nimble wits, to let Telemachus into your secret,
so that the pair of you may plot the downfall and death of the
Suitors and then make your way to the famous city. I will not
leave you two alone for long: I am eager for the fight.'

As she spoke, Athene touched him with her golden wand,
and behold, a clean mantle and tunic hung from his shoulders;
his stature was increased and his youthful vigour restored; his
bronze tan returned; his jaws were filled out; and the beard
grew black on his chin. Her work done, Athene disappeared;
and Odysseus went back into the hut. His son gave him one look
of amazement, then withdrew his eyes for fear that he might be

a god, and in an awestruck tone said: 'Stranger, you are not the same now as the man who just went out. Your clothes are different; your complexion is changed. I can only think that you are one of the gods who live in the broad sky. Be gracious to us, and we will make you pleasing sacrifices and offerings of wrought gold. Have mercy upon us.'

'Why do you take me for an immortal?' said the noble and patient Odysseus. 'Believe me, I am no god. But I *am* your father, on whose account you have endured so much sorrow and trouble and suffered persecution at men's hands.'

With that he kissed his son and let a tear roll down his cheek to the ground, though hitherto he had kept himself under strict control. But Telemachus could not yet accept the fact that it was his father, and once more put his feelings into words. 'You are not my father,' he said: 'you are not Odysseus; but to make my grief all the more bitter some power is playing me a trick. No mortal man unaided by a god has wizardry like this at his command, though I know that any god who wished could easily bring about these alterations between youth and age. Why, only a moment ago you were an old man in shabby clothes, and now you look like one of the gods who live in the wide heavens.'

'Telemachus,' replied Odysseus, never at a loss, 'there is no reason why you should feel any excessive surprise at your father's home-coming, or be so taken aback. Be quite certain of this, that you will see no second Odysseus return. No, I am the man, just as you see me here, back in my own country after nineteen years of misfortune and wandering. As for these changes in me, they are the work of the warrior goddess Athene, who can do anything, and makes me look as she wishes, at one moment like a beggar and at the next like a young man finely dressed. It is easy for the gods in heaven to make or mar a man's appearance.'

Odysseus sat down, but Telemachus, softened at last, flung his arms round his noble father's neck and burst into tears. And now they both broke down and sobbed aloud without a pause like birds bereaved, like the sea-eagle or the taloned vulture when villagers have robbed the nest of their unfledged young. So did these two let the piteous tears run streaming from their eyes. And sunset would have found them still in tender mood, if Telemachus had not suddenly thought of asking his father a question. 'But, father dear,' he said, 'what ship can have brought you just now to Ithaca, and who were the men on board? It is obvious that you didn't come on foot.'

'My boy,' said Odysseus, 'you shall have the whole story. The Phaeacians brought me here. You know their name for seamanship and how they provide any stranger who lands on their coasts with his passage home. Well, they brought me across the sea on one of their fast ships and landed me in Ithaca – I was asleep the whole time. They gave me splendid presents too, copper and gold in plenty and woven stuffs, all of which, I thank heaven, lie hidden in a cave. Finally, I came up here at Athene's suggestion so that we could discuss the destruction of our enemies. And now I want you to run through their names for me one by one, so that I may know exactly who and how many they are. Then I will face the problem boldly and decide whether we two could deal with them by ourselves or whether we should seek assistance.'

'Father,' Telemachus replied with his usual prudence, 'I have always heard of your great reputation as a soldier who could use his brains as well as his hands. But this time you have over-reached yourself. You appal me! Two men couldn't possibly take on so many, and such good fighters into the bargain. There are not a mere dozen Suitors, nor a couple of dozen, but many times more than that. I can tell you their strength here and now. Dulichium has sent fifty-two, the pick of her young men, with six valets in tow. From Same there are twenty-four, and from Zacynthus twenty noblemen; while Ithaca itself has contri-buted a dozen of its best, and with them Medon the herald, and an excellent minstrel, besides two servants used to carving. If we meet them at the house in full force, I am afraid it may be you who pay a cruel and a ghastly price for the crimes you have come to avenge. So if you can think of any possible allies, consider the people most likely to fight heart and soul on our side.'

'I will indeed,' said the all-daring Odysseus. 'Hear what I think; and ask yourself whether Athene with Father Zeus will serve our purpose, or whether I need cudgel my brains for any further allies.'

'Your champions are an excellent couple, I'm sure,' said Telemachus. 'They may sit up there in the clouds, but they rule the whole world of men and gods.'

'And so,' said Odysseus, 'when the scene is set in the palace for ordeal by battle between us and the Suitors, it will not be long before those two are in the thick of the fight. However, at the first sign of dawn, I wish you to go home and show yourself to these rascally Suitors. Later, the swineherd will bring me down to the city disguised as a wretched old beggar. If I meet with insolence in the house, you must steel your heart to my maltreatment, and even if they haul me out of the place by the feet or let fly at me with their weapons, you will have to look on and bear it. You can, of course, take them politely to task and try to make them behave more sensibly; but they simply won't listen to you: their day of judgement is at hand. And here is another part of my plan that I must impress on your mind. When that great strategist, Athene, tells me that the time has come, I shall give you a nod. Directly you see the signal gather up the warlike weapons that are lying about in the hall and stow them away in a corner of the strong-room. See that you take them all, and when the Suitors miss them and ask you what has happened, you must lull their suspicions with some plausible tale. You can say: "I rescued them from the smoke, having noticed how different they looked from when Odysseus left them and sailed for Troy. The fire had got at them and damaged them badly. It also occurred to me – and this was more serious – that, since the very presence of a weapon provokes a man to use it, you might start quarrelling in your cups and wound each other, thus spoiling your festivities and disgracing yourselves as suitors."

'Just for us two, leave a couple of swords and spears and two leather shields ready to hand, where we can make a dash and pick them up. Pallas Athene and Zeus will distract the Suitors' attention when the time comes.

'One more word; and this is most important. If you really are my son and have our blood in your veins, see that not a soul hears that Odysseus is back. Tell neither Laertes, nor the swine-herd, nor any of the household staff, nor Penelope herself. You and I alone will discover which way the women are heading. And we might also sound one or two of the men-servants, to find out which are loyal and respect us, and which have for-gotten their duty to the fine prince they have in you.'

But his noble son had an objection to raise. 'Father,' said he, 'my own mettle, I am sure, you will come to know in due course: I am not in the habit of behaving like a light-headed fool. But I do feel that we should gain nothing by acting as you propose, and I urge you to think once more. You would waste a lot of time going round the various farms and sounding the ser-vants one by one, while the Suitors are enjoying themselves in our house and eating up our stores in their disgusting way, with-out sparing a thing. I certainly think you ought to find out which of the women-servants are guilty or innocent of dis-loyalty towards you; but as far as the men are concerned, I, personally, vote that we do not go round the farms to sound them, but postpone that till later, if it is really true that you have had some intimation of the will of Zeus.'

While father and son were thus discussing the situation, the good ship that had brought Telemachus and his men from Pylos was making the port. They sailed the black craft into the deep water of the harbour and then dragged her up on the beach. Their eager squires carried off their gear and removed the valu-able gifts to Clytius' house. They then dispatched a messenger to Odysseus' palace to tell the wise Penelope that Telemachus had gone up-country and ordered them to sail round to the city, so that the good queen might not take alarm and let the tear-drops fall. As it happened, this messenger and the worthy swine-herd, conveying the same news to the lady, met on the way. But when they reached the royal palace, the messenger no sooner found himself surrounded by the women-servants than he blurted out his news: 'A message for the Queen! Her son is back!' Whereas the swineherd sought Penelope's own ear and told her everything her son had instructed him to say. His message faithfully delivered, he turned his back on the palace and its precincts and returned to his pigs.

To the Suitors the news came as a shock which cast a gloom over their spirits. They streamed out of the hall along the great wall of the courtyard, and there in front of the gates they held a meeting, which was opened by Eurymachus, son of Polybus.

'My friends,' he said, 'Telemachus, in his impudence, has certainly scored a success by safely bringing off this expedition that we swore should come to nothing. I can only suggest that we should now launch the best available ship, collect a crew of able seamen, and quickly send word to our friends out there that they must come home at once.'

He was still speaking when Amphinomus, happening to turn round, caught sight of their ship from where he sat. She was riding in the harbour and he could see them furling sail and handling the oars. He gave a merry laugh and called out to the rest: 'No need to send a message now! Our friends are back. Some god must have sent them word, or they themselves saw Telemachus' boat slip by and couldn't catch her.'

Hereupon the whole company rose and went down to the beach, where they made haste to drag the black ship up onto the shore, while eager squires relieved the crew of their gear. The Suitors then repaired in a body to the place of assembly, where they allowed no one else, young or old, to join them. And there Antinous, Eupeithes' son, made his report. 'Damnation take the man,' he said, 'but by god's help he saved his skin. All day long we had scouts posted along the windy heights and kept reinforcing them. We never slept ashore at night, but as soon as the sun set we went on board and kept afloat till dawn in the hope of catching Telemachus and finishing him off. Meanwhile some spirit brought him home. Telemachus, I say, must not escape us, but here and now we must think out some way of destroying him. For I contend that while he lives we shall never bring this business of ours to a satisfactory end. The man is clever and he knows how to use his brains, while the people no longer look on us with any favour at all. I suggest action, therefore, before he can call a general Assembly. For mark my words, he won't be slow to do so, and it will be an angry man who rises up to denounce us and tell them all how we plotted his murder and then missed him. They certainly won't applaud this recital of our misdeeds. In fact they may take a strong line and send us into banishment among the foreigners abroad. We must forestall such a move and catch him either in the country well away from town or on the road. We should then have his income and estates, which we would divide fairly between us, while we might let his mother and her new husband keep the house. But if you disapprove of my proposal and would rather see him alive and in possession of all his inheritance, I suggest that we no longer forgather here to eat his excellent dinners, but that each of us court the Queen and make his bridal offers from his own house. She could then marry the man who bid highest and was picked out by fate to be her husband.'

A dead silence followed this speech. It was broken at last by Amphinomus, son of King Nisus and grandson of Aretias, the master-spirit among the Suitors from the corn and grass lands of Dulichium. He was a man of intelligence, whose behaviour had singled him out for Penelope's special approval; and the advice he now gave showed that he had their best interests at heart.

'My friends,' he said, 'you must not regard *me* as ready to put Telemachus to death, it is a dreadful thing to spill the blood of princes. Before all else, let us learn the gods' will. If the oracles of almighty Zeus approve the deed, I shall not only second you all, I will be his executioner myself. But if the gods say no to it I advise you to hold your hands.'

Amphinomus carried the day and the meeting adjourned

without further debate. They all retired into the palace and sat down once more on their chairs of polished wood.

It was at this moment that Penelope gave way to a sudden impulse to confront these Suitors of hers, now that they had shown to what extremes they were prepared to go. She knew well enough that her son's murder had been canvassed in the palace, for Medon the herald had overheard their debate and warned her. So now she gathered her ladies round her and went down to the hall. With queenly dignity she approached the young men, and drawing a fold of her bright head-dress across her cheeks, took her stand by a pillar of the massive roof, where she rounded on Antinous and called him bluntly to account:

'They say in Ithaca that there is no one of your age so wise and eloquent as you, Antinous. You have proved them wrong; and I denounce you for the double-dealing ruffian that you are. Madman! How dare you plot against Telemachus' life and dishonour the obligations that a past act of mercy imposes – bonds that are ratified by Zeus himself and make all enmity between you two a sacrilege? Or have you forgotten that your father once sought refuge here from the fury of the mob, when their blood was up because he had joined the Taphian pirates in a raid on the Thesprotians, who were at peace with us? They would have killed him and had his heart out, quite apart from the seizure of his handsome income, had not Odysseus intervened and controlled their violence – Odysseus, at whose expense you are living free of charge, whose wife you are courting, and whose son you propose to kill, whatever torture you may cause to me. I command you now to put an end to this and make the rest obey you.'

It was Eurymachus son of Polybus who took it on himself to deal with the Queen. 'Penelope,' he said, 'wise daughter of Icarius, have no fear. Dismiss these terrors from your mind. The man is not born and never will be, who shall lay violent hands on Telemachus your son, so long as I live and am on earth to see the light of day. I am making no idle boast but telling you the solemn truth, when I say that his black blood would soon be pouring from my spear. Didn't Odysseus, the sacker of cities, befriend me too and often take me on his knees to put a piece of roast meat in my fingers and lift the red wine to my mouth? That makes Telemachus my dearest friend on earth, and I assure him he need have no fears whatever for his life. We shall not kill him. If the gods decree his death, that is another matter and there's no escape.'

So said Eurymachus to soothe the mother's fears, while all the time he had murder for the son in his heart. But Penelope withdrew to her splendid apartment on the upper floor, and there she wept for Odysseus her beloved husband till bright-eyed Athene closed her eyes in grateful sleep.

That same evening the good swineherd returned to Odysseus and his son. They were engaged in the routine of preparing supper, having slaughtered a yearling pig, when Athene came up to Odysseus and touched him with her wand, changing him once more into an old man in filthy clothes. She was afraid that the swineherd would recognize him if he saw him undisguised, and being unable to keep the secret run down to tell Penelope the news.

It was Telemachus who greeted him: 'So here you are, my good Eumaeus! What news in the town? Are my gallant lords back from their ambuscade? Or are they still watching for me in the same spot on my way home?'

'I didn't care,' said Eumaeus, 'to go down to the town and make inquiries about that, I was in too much of a hurry to deliver my message and get back here, and I had been joined on my way by a messenger whom your crew had sent running off to the palace. Actually he was the first to convey the news to your mother. But there's something that I *can* tell you, for I saw it with my own eyes. I had climbed up above the town as far as Hermes' Hill when I spied a ship coming into our harbour. She had a crowd of men on board and a whole armoury of shields and two-edged spears. I took it to be their party, but I cannot say for certain.'

When Prince Telemachus heard this he glanced at his father with a smile which he was careful to hide from Eumaeus.

Their work was finished now and the meal prepared. So they sat down with a good appetite and ate their supper together. When their thirst and hunger were satisfied they began to think kindly of their beds and were soon enjoying the boon of sleep.

XVII

ODYSSEUS GOES TO TOWN

THE tender Dawn, flecking the East with red, found King Odysseus' son Telemachus eager to set out for the city. He bound his strong sandals on his feet, and had a word with his swineherd as he picked up his big well-balanced spear.

'Uncle,' he said, 'I am going to town now, as you see, to show myself to my mother, who, I am sure, won't stop weeping and lamenting till she sees me in the flesh. Here are my instructions for you. Take that unhappy visitor of ours to the city and let him beg there for his meals. He is sure to find charitable souls who will give him a crust and a cup of water. I myself cannot possibly cope with all and sundry: I have too many troubles on my mind. And if the stranger takes this in bad part, so much the worse for him. I admit I believe in plain speaking.'

'My good sir,' Odysseus here put in, 'do not think that I am anxious to be left behind. Town is a better place than the country for a man to beg his food in; and I shall find charity there. For I am unsuited by my age to live on a farm at a master's beck and call. So go your way; and presently this man, who already has your orders, will bring me along, when I have warmed myself at the fire and the day grows hot. For these clothes of mine are terribly threadbare and I am afraid the morning frost might be too much for me. It's a long walk to the town, as you have told me.'

Telemachus now went off through the farm and fell into a rapid stride as plans for vengeance on the Suitors took shape in his mind. When he reached the great house he took his spear and leant it against one of the tall pillars, then crossed the stone threshold and went in.

The first to see him was the nurse Eurycleia, who was busy spreading rugs over the curved chairs. With tears in her eyes she ran up to meet him, and soon every maid the stalwart Odysseus possessed was pressing round him and showering affectionate kisses on his head and shoulders. And now the wise Penelope came out from her bedroom, lovely as Artemis or golden Aphrodite, and dissolved in tears as she threw her arms round her son's neck and kissed his forehead and his beautiful eyes. 'So you're back, Telemachus, my darling boy!' she said between her sobs. 'And I thought I should never see you again after you had sailed for Pylos to find out about your dear father – so secretly, so much against my wishes. Come, tell me all you saw.'

'Mother,' Telemachus soberly replied, 'please do not reduce me to tears or play on my emotions when I have just escaped from such a deadly fate. But go upstairs to your room with your ladies, and when you have washed and changed into fresh clothes pray to all the gods, promising them the most perfect offerings if Zeus ever grants us a day of reckoning. I myself am going to the market-place to fetch an acquaintance who accompanied me on my journey back. I sent him ahead of me to town with my good crew and told Peiraeus to take him home and treat him with all care and respect till I should come.'

Telemachus' manner froze the words on her lips. She bathed, changed into fresh clothes, and then addressed herself to the heavenly company, promising them a perfect offering when Zeus should grant her house a day of reckoning.

Meanwhile Telemachus strode across the hall and sallied out, carrying his spear, and with two nimble hounds at his heels. Athene endowed him with such magic grace that all eyes were turned on him in admiration as he approached. The highborn Suitors gathered round him in a throng, with kindly speeches on their lips and evil brewing in their hearts. But he shook them off as they crowded in upon him, and found a seat with Mentor, Antiphus, and Haliserthes, whose friendship for his house was rooted in the past. As these were plying him with questions about his voyage, the spearman Peiraeus came up with Theo-clymenus, whom he had conducted through the streets to the market-place. Telemachus rose to meet him, not faltering for a moment in courtesy towards his guest, but it was Peiraeus who got the first word in and asked him at once to send some women to his house so that he could have Menelaus' gifts conveyed to the palace. Telemachus, however, had his own views on this point. 'No, Peiraeus,' he said. 'None of us can tell what is going to happen. If my lords the Suitors assassinate me in the palace and partition my estate, I should like you or one of my friends here to keep and enjoy the treasures. On the other hand, if I succeed in sending the Suitors to their last account, I am sure you will be as glad to deliver the gifts at my house as I shall be to see them.'

This settled, he led the way home for his travel-worn friend and brought him to the great house, where they threw down their cloaks on settles or chairs, stepped into the polished baths and washed. When the maid-servants had finished bathing them and rubbing them with oil, they gave them tunics and threw warm mantles round their shoulders, and the two left their baths and sat down on chairs. A maid came with water in a fine golden jug and poured it out over a silver basin so that they might rinse their hands. She drew up a wooden table and the staid housekeeper brought some bread and set it by them, together with a choice of dainties, helping them liberally to all she could offer.

Telemachus' mother sat opposite them by a pillar of the hall, reclining in an easy-chair and spinning the delicate thread on her distaff, while they fell to on the good fare laid before them. It was not till they had eaten and drunk their fill that the prudent Penelope broke the silence. Then she said to her son: 'It seems, Telemachus, that I am to retire upstairs and go to my bed – which has been a bed of sorrows stained by my tears ever since Odysseus followed the Atreidae to Ilium – without your having deigned to tell me, before the house is invaded by my noble lovers, just what you may have heard about your father's return.'

'Very well, mother,' said Telemachus; 'you shall hear what I did. We went to Pylos and there visited King Nestor, who received me in his great palace and showed me every hospitality. He might have been my father, and I his long-lost son just back from my travels, so kindly did he and his royal sons look after me. But of the stalwart Odysseus, alive or dead, he said he had not heard a single word from anyone on earth. However, he lent me a fine chariot and pair to take me on to the gallant Menelaus. And there I saw Helen of Argos, for whose sake the Argives and the Trojans by god's will underwent so much. The warrior Menelaus was quick to ask me what had brought me to his pleasant land of Lacedaemon, and when I had explained the whole matter he cried: "For shame! So the cowards want to creep into the brave man's bed? It is just as if a deer had put her little unweaned fawns to sleep in a mighty lion's den and gone to range the high ridges and the grassy dales for pasture. Back comes the lion to his lair, and hideous carnage falls upon them all. But no worse than Odysseus will deal out to that gang! Once, in the pleasant isle of Lesbos I saw him stand up to Philomeleides in a wrestling-match and bring him down with a terrific throw which delighted all his friends. By Father Zeus, Athene and Apollo, that's the Odysseus I should like to see these Suitors meet! A swift death and a sorry wedding there would be for all! But to come to your appeal and the questions you asked me – I have no wish to deceive you or to put you off with evasive answers. On the contrary I shall pass on to you without concealment or reserve every word that I heard myself from the infallible lips of the Old Man of the Sea. He told me that he had seen your father in great distress on an island, in the Nymph Calypso's cavern, where she keeps him prisoner; for without galley or crew to carry him so far across the sea, it is impossible for him to get home." That is all I found out from the gallant Menelaus; so I left him when I had finished my inquiries. Heaven sent me a favourable wind and brought me quickly back to my beloved Ithaca.'

Penelope was deeply moved by what Telemachus had told her. And now the noble Theoclymenus joined in, addressing himself respectfully to Odysseus' queen: 'Believe me, madam, Menelaus has no accurate information. You would do better to listen to me, who will read you the signs exactly and truly. I swear by Zeus before all other gods, and by the board of hospitality, and by the good Odysseus' hearth, which I have reached, that Odysseus is actually in Ithaca at this moment, at rest or afoot, tracing these crimes to their source and scheming revenge on the Suitors – witness the bird of omen which I saw from our good ship and proclaimed to Telemachus.'

'Sir,' said the wise queen, 'may what you say prove true! If it does, you shall learn from my liberality what my friendship means, and the world will envy you your luck.'

While this conversation was going on inside Odysseus' palace, the Suitors, in their usual free and easy way, were amusing themselves outside with quoits and javelin-throwing on the levelled ground where we have seen them at their sports before. When supper-time arrived and the sheep came in from the countryside all round in the charge of the usual drovers, Medon, who was their chosen master of ceremonies and a partner in their junketings, came up to summon them. 'Now that you gentlemen have enjoyed your sports,' he said, 'I suggest that you should come indoors, so that we may get supper ready. There's much to be said for a punctual meal.' The Suitors obediently left their games and flocked into the great house, where they threw down their cloaks on the settles and chairs, and prepared for a banquet by slaughtering some full-grown sheep and goats as well as several fatted hogs and a heifer from the herd.

Meanwhile Odysseus and the loyal swineherd were preparing to come in from the country to the town. It was the excellent herdsman who first proposed a move. 'Friend,' he said, 'I see you are still determined to go to town today, as my master said you should. I myself would rather leave you here to look after the farm. But I respect and fear him. He might scold me presently, and a rebuke from one's master can be a very nasty thing. So now let us be off. The best part of the day is gone and you may well find it chilly towards evening.'

'Understood and agreed,' said Odysseus. 'I recognize sense when I hear it. Let's make a start; and you must lead the way from beginning to end. But do give me a staff to lean on, if you have one cut and ready, for I have gathered from you that it's difficult going.'

As he spoke he hung his mean and tattered knapsack over his shoulders by the strap that supported it, and Eumaeus chose him a staff to suit him. Then the pair set out, leaving the dogs and herdsmen to look after the farm. In this way Eumaeus brought his King to the city, hobbling along with his staff and looking like a wretched old beggar-man in the miserable clothes he was wearing.

Beside the rocky path which they followed down, and not far from the city, there was a public watering-place, where a clear spring ran into a basin of stone that Ithacus, Neritus, and Polyctor had made for the townsfolk. A thicket of alders, flourishing on the moisture, encircled the spot. The cool stream came tumbling down from the rock overhead, and an altar had been erected up above to the Nymphs, where all travellers paid their dues. Here they fell in with one Melantheus son of Dolius, who with two shepherds to help him was driving down some goats for the Suitors' table, the pick of all his herds. This man no sooner set eyes on them than he burst into a torrent of vulgar abuse, which roused Odysseus to fury.

'Ha!' the fellow cried. 'One scapegrace with another in tow – a case of birds of a feather! Tell me, you miserable swineherd, where are you taking this wastrel of yours, this nauseating beggar and killjoy at the feast? Just the sort to lean against all the door-posts and polish them with his shoulders, begging for scraps, but never for work on the pots and pans. Give him to me, to look after the folds, to sweep the pens and carry fodder to the kids, and he might thrive on whey and work his muscles up. But the fellow has taken to bad ways, and work on the farm is the last thing he's looking for. He'd much rather fill his gluttonous belly by touting round the town for alms. You mark my words, and see what happens if he goes to King Odysseus' palace. He'll have a warm reception from the people there – a shower of foot-stools shied at his head and breaking on his ribs.'

With that he passed by and, as he did so, the fool landed a kick on Odysseus' hip, failing, however, to thrust him off the path, so firm was his stance. Odysseus was in two minds whether to let out at the fellow and kill him with his staff or to tackle him by the waist and dash his head on the ground. In the end he had the hardihood to control himself. It was the swineherd who faced up to Melantheus and denounced him.

'Nymphs of the Fountain, Daughters of Zeus,' he cried, raising up his hands in earnest prayer, 'if ever Odysseus made you a burnt-offering of the thighs of rams or kids wrapped up in their rich fat, grant me my wish that he himself may be brought back to us by the hand of heaven. He'd soon cure you, sir, of all the swaggering ways you have picked up since you took to loafing round the town and leaving bad shepherds to ruin your flocks.'

'Hear how the vicious mongrel snarls!' retorted the goatherd Melantheus. 'I'll pack him off one day from Ithaca in a big black ship and make my fortune by him. As for Odysseus, I wish I could make as sure that Telemachus should fall this very day in the palace to Apollo's silver bow or at the Suitors' hands, as I am certain that any chance of his father's coming home has been disposed of far away from here.'

With this last shot he left them to pursue their leisurely way, while he himself stepped out and was soon at the king's house, where he went straight in and joined the Suitors, taking a seat opposite Eurymachus, his favourite. The waiters helped him to the roast, and the staid housekeeper brought bread and gave him some to eat.

Meanwhile Odysseus and his trusty swineherd had arrived; but they paused for a moment outside when the notes from a well-made lyre came to their ears. For Phemius was just preparing to give the company a song. 'Eumaeus,' said Odysseus taking the swineherd by the arm, 'this must surely be Odysseus' palace: it would be easy to pick it out at a glance from any number of houses. There are buildings beyond buildings; the courtyard wall with its battlements is a fine piece of work and those folding doors are true defences. No one could afford to turn up his nose at this. I gather too that a large company is there for dinner: one can smell the roast, and someone is playing the lyre. Music and banquets always go together.'

'You have made no mistake,' said Eumaeus; 'but you are naturally observant. Let us consider our next move. Either you go into the palace first and approach the Suitors while I stay where I am; or, if you prefer it, you wait here and let me be the first to go in. But in that case don't be long, or they may see you here outside and take a shot at you or beat you off. I leave it to you to decide.'

'And rightly too,' said the stalwart Odysseus, 'for I understand the position. You shall go in first while I stay here; for I am quite used to blows and missiles. I have been toughened by what I have suffered in the field and on the sea. After all that, what matters a bit more? But if there is anything that a man can't conceal it is a ravening belly – that utter curse, the cause of so much trouble to mankind, which even prompts them to fit out great ships and sail the barren seas, bringing death and destruction to their enemies.'

Stretched on the ground close to where they stood talking, there lay a dog, who now pricked up his ears and raised his head. Argus was his name. Odysseus himself had owned and trained him, though he had sailed for holy Ilium before he could reap the reward of his patience. In years gone by the young huntsmen had often taken him out after wild goats, deer, and hares. But now, in his owner's absence, he lay abandoned on the heaps of dung from the mules and cattle which lay in profusion at the gate, awaiting removal by Odysseus' servants as manure for his great estate. There, full of vermin, lay Argus the hound. But directly he became aware of Odysseus' presence, he wagged his tail and dropped his ears, though he lacked the strength now to come any nearer to his master. Yet Odysseus saw him out of the corner of his eye, and brushed a tear away without showing any sign of emotion to the swincherd, whom he now proceeded to sound:

'Eumaeus, it is very odd to see a hound like this lying in the dung. He's a beauty, though one cannot really tell whether his looks were matched by his pace, or whether he was just one of those dogs whom their masters feed at table and keep for show.'

'It's plain enough,' said the swineherd Eumaeus, 'that this is a dog whose master has met his death abroad. If you could see him in the heyday of his looks and form, as Odysseus left him when he sailed for Troy, you'd be astonished at his speed and power. No game that he gave chase to could escape him in the forest glades. For beside all else he was a marvel at picking up the scent. But now he's in a bad way; his master far away from home has come to grief, and the women are too careless to groom him. Servants, when their masters are no longer there to order them about, have little will to do their duties as they should. All-seeing Zeus takes half the good out of a man on the day when he becomes a slave.'

With this Eumaeus left him, entered the great house, and passed straight into the hall where the young gallants were assembled. As for Argus, he had no sooner set eyes on Odysseus after those nineteen years than he succumbed to the black hand of Death.

Prince Telemachus was the first to observe the swineherd's approach through the palace, and signalled to him at once to join him. Eumaeus looked about him and picked up a stool which stood there for the steward to sit on when carving meat for the Suitors at their banquets in the hall. This he brought and placed at Telemachus' table, on the far side, and there he sat down. A waiter fetched a portion of meat, which he set before him, and helped him to bread from a basket.

Close on his heels Odysseus entered the buildings. He looked exactly like some ancient and distressful beggar as he limped along with the aid of his staff, and the rags that hung upon him were a filthy sight. He sat down on the wooden threshold just inside the door, with his back against a pillar of cypress smoothed by some carpenter long ago and deftly trued to the line. Telemachus beckoned the swineherd to his side, and selecting a whole loaf from the dainty basket of bread and as much meat as his cupped hands would hold, he said:

'Take this food and give it to the newcomer. And tell him to go the rounds himself and beg from each of the company in turn. For modesty sits ill upon a needy man.'

Thus instructed, the swineherd went up to Odysseus and carefully delivered his message. 'Stranger,' he said, 'Telemachus makes you this gift and tells you to go the rounds and beg from each of the company in turn. For he points out that modesty sits ill upon a beggar-man.'

Odysseus promptly answered with a prayer: 'I pray to you, Lord Zeus, to make Telemachus a happy man and grant him all the wishes of his heart.' He then stretched out both hands to take the food, put it straight down in front of his feet on his shabby wallet and continued to eat as long as the minstrel's song was heard in the hall. He had finished his supper just as the excellent bard was coming to an end, and now, as the company began to fill the hall with uproar, Athene appeared before Odysseus and urged him to go round collecting scraps from the Suitors and learning to distinguish the good from the bad, though this did not mean that in the end she was to save a single one from destruction. So Odysseus set out and began to beg from them one after the other, working from left to right and stretching out his hand to each like one who had been a beggar all his life. They gave him food out of pity, and surprised at his appearance asked each other who he was and where he had come from. This gave the goatherd Melantheus the chance to put in his word: 'My lords and courtiers of our noble queen, I can tell you something of this stranger, for I've seen him before, when the swineherd was bringing him down here. But I really don't know who he is and where he hails from.'

At once Antinous rounded on Eumaeus. 'How typical of our swineherd!' he cried. 'May I ask, sir, why you brought this

fellow to town? Haven't we tramps in plenty to pester us with
their wants and pollute our dinners? Are you so dissatisfied with
the numbers collected here to eat your master's food that you
must ask this extra guest to join the gathering?'

'Antinous,' the swineherd answered him, 'you may be nobly
born but there's nothing handsome in your speech. Who would
take it on himself to press hospitality on a wandering stranger,
unless he were some worker for the public good, a prophet, a
physician, a shipwright, or even a minstrel whose songs might
give pleasure? For all the world over such guests as those are
welcomed, whereas nobody would call a beggar in to eat him
out of house and home. But of all the Suitors you are always the
hardest on Odysseus' servants, and of all of them hardest on me.
However, I care little for that as long as Penelope my wise mistress and the noble Prince Telemachus are alive in the palace.'

'Enough now!' Telemachus prudently interposed. 'I won't
have you bandying words with Antinous, who likes nothing
better than to rouse a man's passion with his evil tongue and egg
the others on to do the same.' Then he turned on Antinous and
spoke his mind to him: 'Antinous, I appreciate your fatherly
concern on my behalf and your anxiety that I should order the
stranger out of the house. God forbid such a thing! Give him
something yourself. I don't grudge it you; indeed I wish you
would. Have no fear, either, of offending my mother or any of
the royal servants by your charity. But there's no such idea in
your head. You'd far sooner eat the food yourself than give it
away!'

'Telemachus, this is nonsense,' said Antinous in his turn. 'You
let your tongue and temper run away with you. If all the Suitors
were to give him as much as I should like to, the place would be
rid of him for three months.'

As he spoke, he seized the stool that supported his dainty feet
as he dined, and brought it into view from under the table where
it lay. But all the rest made their contributions and soon filled
the wallet with bread and meat. It looked as if Odysseus might
now have regained his seat on the threshold without having to

pay for his experiment with the Suitors. But on the way he
paused beside Antinous and addressed him directly.

'Your alms, kind sir!' he said. 'I am sure you are not the mean-
est of these lords. Indeed, I take you for the noblest here, since
you look every inch a king. Good reason why you should give
me a bigger dole than the rest – and I'd sing your praises the wide
world over. Time was when I too was one of the lucky ones
with a rich house to live in, and I have often given alms to such a
vagabond as myself, no matter who he was or what he came for.
Hundreds of servants I had and plenty of all that one needs to live
in luxury and take one's place as a wealthy man. But Zeus – for
some good reason of his own, no doubt – stripped me of all I
had. To wreck my life, he put it into my head to sail for Egypt
with a set of roving buccaneers. And what a way it was! But at
last I brought my curved ships to, in the Nile. There I ordered
my good men to stay by the ships on guard, while I sent out
some scouts to reconnoitre from the heights. But these ran
amuck and in a trice, carried away by their own violence, they
had plundered some of the fine Egyptian farms, borne off the
women and children and killed the men. The hue and cry soon
reached the city, and the townsfolk, roused by the alarm, turned
out at dawn. The whole plain was filled with infantry and
chariots and the glint of arms. Zeus the Thunderer struck abject
panic into my party. Not a man had the spirit to stand and face
the enemy, for we were threatened on all sides. They ended by
cutting down a large part of my force and carrying off the survivors to work for them as slaves. But they let me be taken off to
Cyprus by an ally of theirs whom they fell in with, a man called
Dmetor son of Iasus, the undisputed king of the island. And it's
from Cyprus that I have now made my painful way to this spot.'

'What god,' exclaimed Antinous, 'has inflicted this plague on
us to spoil our dinner? Stand out there in the middle and keep
clear of my table, or I'll give you the sort of Egypt and Cyprus
you won't relish! The audacity and impudence of the rogue!
He has only to pester each man in turn, and they give him food
without a thought. For they all have plenty before them, and

nobody shows restraint or consideration when it comes to being generous with other people's goods.'

Odysseus prudently drew back and said: 'Ah, I was wrong in thinking that your brains might match your looks! You wouldn't give so much as a pinch of salt from your larder to a retainer of your own, you that sit here at another man's table and can't bring yourself to take a bit of his bread and give it to me, though there's plenty there.'

This roused Antinous to real fury. He gave him a black look and did not mince his words. 'After that,' he said, 'I swear you shall not get away from here in triumph. Your insolence has settled it.' And picking up a stool he let fly and struck Odysseus full on the right shoulder where it joins the back. But Odysseus stood firm as a rock and Antinous' missile did not even make him totter. He just shook his head in silence, filled with revengeful thoughts. And so he went back to the threshold, where he sat down, dropped his bulging wallet, and addressed the company:

'Listen to me, you lords that are wooing our illustrious queen! Let me unburden my heart. A knock or two, when a man is fighting for his own property, his oxen or white sheep, is nothing to cry about or be ashamed of. But this blow from Antinous was brought on me by my wretched belly, that cursed thing men have to thank for so much trouble. And if there are any gods and powers that can avenge a beggar, I hope Antinous will be dead before his wedding day.'

'Sit and eat in peace, sir,' Antinous retorted, 'or take yourself elsewhere. Otherwise your freedom of speech will end in our young men dragging you out of the place by the leg or arm and flaying you from head to foot.'

But the rest of them felt the utmost indignation, and the general sense was expressed by one young gallant who said: 'Antinous, you did wrong to strike the wretched vagabond. You're a doomed man if he turns out to be some god from heaven. And the gods do disguise themselves as strangers from abroad, and wander round our towns in every kind of shape to see whether people are behaving themselves or getting out of hand.'

That was the Suitors' view, but Antinous took no notice of what they said, and Telemachus, though he felt the blow like a stab at his own heart, kept the tears back from his eyes, shook his head in silence and nursed vindictive thoughts. But when the wise queen Penelope in due course heard of Antinous' assault on the stranger in her palace she cried, in her maids' hearing: 'Archer Apollo, strike him as he struck!' And the housekeeper Eurynome chimed in: 'Ah, if we could only have our wishes, there's not a man among them who'd see tomorrow's dawn.'

'Good mother,' Penelope went on, 'I hate the whole gang for the wicked plots they hatch, but Antinous is the blackest scoundrel of them all. An unfortunate tramp, constrained by poverty, came wandering through the house and begged for their alms. All the rest were generous and filled his wallet up; but Antinous threw a stool at his back and hit him on the right shoulder.'

While Penelope was discussing the affair with her maids as she sat in her own apartment, the noble Odysseus was eating his supper. And now Penelope summoned her trusty herdsman to her side and said: 'Go, my good Eumaeus, and ask the stranger to come here. I should like to greet him and inquire whether he happens to have heard of my gallant husband or to have seen him with his own eyes. He seems to have travelled far.'

'My Queen,' replied Eumaeus, 'I only wish the young lords would keep quiet. With the tales he can tell, the man would fascinate you. I must explain that as I was the first person he came across after running away from his ship I had him with me for three nights and kept him all three days in my cottage; but even so he couldn't finish the story of his troubled life. To have that man by me at home with his enchanting tales was like sitting with one's eyes fixed on some bard inspired to melt one's heart with song, so that nothing matters but to listen as long as he will sing.

'He claims acquaintance with Odysseus through his family

and says he is a native of Crete, where the Minoans live. Starting from there, like a rolling stone, and after many painful adventures, he has at last come to us; and he is positive that he has heard of Odysseus, that he's near at hand and alive, in the rich Thesprotian country, and bringing home a fortune.'

'Go now and call him,' said the wise queen, 'so that I can hear his story from himself; and let these others sit at our gates or in the house and enjoy themselves. They have nothing to worry them, for their own wealth, their bread and mellow wine, lies untouched at home with no one but their servants to support, while *they* spend their whole time in and out of our place, slaughtering our oxen, our sheep, and our fatted goats, feasting themselves and drinking our sparkling wine, with never a thought for all the riches that are wasted. The truth is that there is nobody like Odysseus in charge to purge the house of this disease. Ah, if Odysseus could only come back to his own country! He and his son would soon pay them out for their crimes.'

As she finished, Telemachus gave a loud sneeze, which echoed round the house in the most alarming fashion. Penelope laughed and turned to Eumaeus. 'Do go,' she said eagerly, 'and bring this stranger here to me. Didn't you notice that my son sneezed a blessing on all I had said? That means death, once for all, to every one of the Suitors: not a man can escape his doom. One more point, and don't forget it. If, when I hear him tell his own story, I am satisfied with its truth, I will fit him out properly in a new cloak and tunic.'

With these instructions the swineherd left her, and approaching the stranger duly delivered his message. 'My friend,' he said, 'the wise Penelope, Telemachus' mother, wishes to see you. Sorrow-stricken as she is, she is anxious to ask you some questions about her husband. If she is satisfied that all you say is true, she will fit you out with a cloak and tunic, which you need more than anything else: and then you can feed yourself by begging your bread in the town, where charitable folk will give you alms.'

'Eumaeus,' answered the stalwart Odysseus, 'I should be glad to give Icarius' daughter, the wise Penelope, all the real news I have. For I am well-informed about Odysseus, whose misfortunes I have shared. But I am frightened of this crowd of mischievous young gallants, whose insolence and violent acts cry out to heaven. Just now when that fellow struck me a painful blow as I was walking harmlessly through the place, neither Telemachus nor anyone else lifted a finger to save me. So urge Penelope to wait indoors and restrain her impatience till sunset, when she can question me about her husband and the date of his return, and can give me a seat nearer in by the fire. For my clothes are mere rags, as you know well, since it was you whom I first approached.'

When he had heard what the other had to say, the swineherd went off and was accosted by Penelope as soon as he crossed the threshold of her room. 'Eumaeus!' she exclaimed. 'You haven't brought him? What does the man mean by this? Is he afraid of someone in particular, or is he just ashamed to linger in the house? Modesty such as that does not make successful beggars.'

'He wants to save himself,' said Eumaeus, 'from the clutches of a set of scoundrels; and there he's right. Anyone else would feel the same. He begs you to wait till sundown, a time which should suit you too, my lady, better, as it will allow you to converse with the man in private.'

'The stranger is no fool,' Penelope answered: 'he has a good idea of what might happen. For in the whole world I don't believe one could find another set of reprobates and miscreants like these.'

His message delivered, the worthy swineherd left her and rejoined the gathering, where he at once sought out Telemachus and whispered urgently in his ear so that the others could not hear him: 'Dear master, I am leaving presently to look after the pigs and farm, your livelihood and mine. It's for you to see to everything here. Look to your own safety first and take care that you don't come to grief. For plenty of the young lords are none too well disposed. Perdition take them all before they do us in!'

'Very well, uncle,' said Telemachus. 'Go when you've had your supper, and in the morning come back with some good beasts for slaughter. Leave things here to Providence and me.'

The swineherd sat down again on the polished settle and when he had satisfied his appetite and thirst went off to rejoin his pigs, leaving the courts and hall full of banqueters dancing and singing to their hearts' content, by the failing light of day.

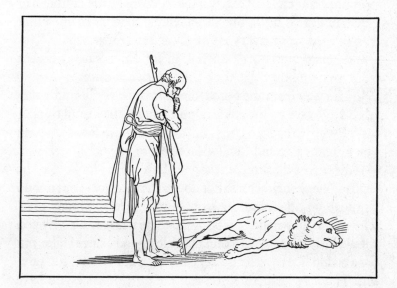

XVIII

THE BEGGAR IN THE PALACE

THERE entered now upon the scene a common vagabond who used to beg for his living in the streets of Ithaca and was notorious for his insatiable greed and his ability to eat and drink all day. He was a big fellow, yet in spite of appearances he had no stamina or muscle. Arnaeus was the name his gentle mother had given him at his birth, but all the young men nicknamed him Irus, since he was at everyone's beck and call for an errand. This was the man who now came up, intent on chasing Odysseus from his own house. He took the offensive at once:

'Make way from the porch, old fellow, or you'll find yourself dragged off by the ankle. Don't you see they're all tipping me the wink to haul you out – not that I should care to? Up with you now, or you and I will soon come to blows.'

Odysseus of the nimble wits gave him a black look. 'Sir,' he replied, 'I have neither said nor done a thing to hurt you; nor do I grudge you the most generous alms that anyone may give. This threshold will hold us both and there is no reason why you should be niggardly with other people's goods, since I take you for a tramp like myself and dependent on Providence for a living. Think twice before you call me out; or once you have roused me, old as I am I'll dye your lips and breast with your own blood, and so, by the way, get a quieter day for myself tomorrow, for I warrant that this palace of Odysseus would never see you back.'

At this the beggar Irus lost his temper. 'Ha!' he cried. 'Slick talk from the glutton! An old cook could do no better. But I've a nasty trick in store for him, a right and left that'll dash all the teeth from his jaws to the ground, like the tusks of a marauding swine. Tuck in your clothes, and let these gentlemen see how we fight – if you really dare to match yourself against a younger man.'

In this way they were whetting each other's fury with a right good will, there on the polished threshold in front of the high doors, when their behaviour caught Antinous' princely eye. He laughed delightedly and called out to the rest of the Suitors:

'My friends, this beats everything. Here is a treat for us blown straight in from heaven. The stranger and Irus are challenging each other to box. Let's make a match of it, quick!'

They all jumped up laughing, and as they crowded round the ragged beggars, Antinous' persuasive voice was heard once more:

'Gentlemen, here's a suggestion. We have some goats' paunches roasting there at the fire, which we stuffed with fat and blood and set aside for supper. I propose that the winner, when he has proved himself the better man, shall come up and take his pick of these. And not only that, he shall join us regularly at dinner, and we'll allow nobody else to beg in this company.'

They all approved Antinous' idea, and the wily Odysseus played up to his part. 'Friends,' he said, 'there's no sense at all in a match between an old fellow worn out by trouble and a younger man. Yet this mischievous belly of mine eggs me on to take my thrashing. So now I ask you all to make me a solemn promise. No one must side with Irus: I don't want to lose to him through a foul blow from one of you.'

They were all prepared to give him their assurance, and when this had been done with due solemnity, Prince Telemachus put in his word:

'Stranger, if you have the heart and pluck to match yourself against this man, you need not be afraid of any of these gentlemen. Whoever strikes you will have others to deal with. I am the host here; and the Prince Antinous and Eurymachus, good judges both, are on my side.'

This met with general applause; so Odysseus tucked up his rags round his middle and bared his great and shapely thighs. His broad shoulders too, and his chest and brawny arms now caught the eye. Indeed Athene herself intervened to increase his royal stature. As a result, all the Suitors were lost in amazement, and significant glances and comments were exchanged. One of them said:

'Under those rags of his, what a thigh the old fellow had! No more errands for Irus! He was looking for trouble and he'll find it.'

This was quite enough for Irus, whose heart failed him completely. But that did not stop the servants from girding up his clothes and dragging him forcibly to the front, though he was in such a state of panic that the flesh quivered on all his limbs. And now he had to listen to a tirade from Antinous.

'You clodhopper!' he shouted at him. 'You may well wish you were dead or had never been born, if you're going to stand quaking there in mortal terror of an old man done in by hardships. I'll be blunt with you, and what I say holds good. If this fellow beats you and shows himself the better man, I'll throw you into a black ship and send you over to the continent to King Echetus the Ogre, who'll have your nose and ears off with his cruel knife and rip away your privy parts to give them as raw meat to dogs.'

The effect of this on Irus was to make him shudder all the more. However, they dragged him into the ring, and the pair put up their hands. Odysseus considered carefully whether he should hit to kill outright or lay him flat with a gentler punch. In the end he decided on the lighter blow, to avoid attracting too much attention from the young lords to himself. Accordingly, when they put up their hands and Irus drove at his right shoulder, Odysseus struck Irus' neck below the ear and smashed in the bones so that the red blood gushed up through his mouth and he fell down in the dust with a groan, grinding his teeth and drumming the earth with his feet. At this the young gallants threw up their hands and nearly died of laughing. But Odysseus seized Irus by the foot and dragged him out through the entrance across the courtyard to the gate of the portico. There he propped him against the courtyard wall, put his stick in his hand and sternly passed sentence upon him: 'Sit there now and keep the pigs and dogs away. And unless you want worse trouble still, drop the part of Beggar-King: it doesn't suit the likes of you.' Then he slung his mean and tattered knapsack over his shoulder by the strap attached to it and returning to the threshold resumed his seat.

The Suitors flocked back into the hall with many a hearty laugh and congratulation for Odysseus. 'Stranger,' they said, 'may Zeus and the other gods grant you the dearest wishes of your heart for having stopped that glutton from begging in Ithaca. Now we'll soon pack him off to the continent, to King Echetus the Ogre.'

Their way of putting it impressed Odysseus as a happy omen for himself; and now Antinous presented him with a large paunch stuffed with fat and blood, while Amphinomus picked out a couple of loaves from a basket, put them down beside him and drank to him from a golden cup. 'Your health, my ancient friend!' he said. 'You are under the weather now; but here's to your future happiness!'

'Amphinomus,' the wise Odysseus answered him, 'you seem to me to be a thoroughly decent fellow, in fact just such a son as I should have looked for from your father, Nisus of Dulichium, whom I have heard well spoken of as a good man and a rich one. Now since he was your father and you strike me as being a gentleman, I am going to be frank with you. Listen to me carefully.

'Of all creatures that breathe and creep about on Mother Earth, there is none so helpless as a man. As long as heaven leaves him in prosperity and health, he never thinks hard times are on their way. Yet when the blessed gods have brought misfortune on his head, he simply has to steel himself and bear it. In fact our outlook upon life here on earth depends entirely on the way in which Providence is treating us at the moment. Look at myself. There was a time when I was marked out to be one of the lucky ones, yet what must I do but let my own strength run away with me and take to a life of lawless violence under the delusion that my father and my brothers would stand by me? Let that be a lesson to every man never to disregard the laws of god but

quietly to enjoy whatever blessings Providence may afford.
The lawlessness I see here is a case in point – these Suitors wasting
the property and insulting the wife of a man who, as I maintain,
will not be kept away much longer from his friends and his own
country. In fact, he is very near; and I only hope that some
power may waft you away to the safety of your own home and
that you may not have to face him on the day that sees him back
on his native soil. For, once he is under his own roof, I have an
idea that blood will be spilt before he and the Suitors see the last
of one another.'

As he finished, Odysseus made his libation and drank the
mellow wine; then returned the cup into the young nobleman's
hands. But Amphinomus went back through the hall heavy at
heart and shaking his head; for he was filled with a foreboding
of disaster. Not that it saved him from his fate, for Athene had
already marked the man out to fall a victim to a spear from Telemachus' hand. Meanwhile, he went back and sat down again
on the chair he had just left.

It was now that Athene, goddess of the flashing eyes, put it
into the wise head of Icarius' daughter Penelope to appear before
the Suitors, with the idea of fanning their ardour to fever heat
and enhancing her value to her husband and her son. Turning
to one of her maids with a forced laugh she said: 'Eurynome,
the spirit moves me, as it never has before, to pay these lovers of
mine a visit – much as I detest them. I should also like to have a
word with my son for his own benefit and warn him not to
spend his whole time with these unruly young men, who may
speak him fair but whose intentions are evil.'

'My child,' said the housekeeper Eurynome, 'you are quite
right. By all means go. And be frank with your son; tell him
what is in your mind. But not before you've washed yourself
and anointed your cheeks. You mustn't go like this, with your
face all stained by tears. It's a bad thing to be for ever weeping,
and never have a change. And you the mother of a fine big
son, whom you've always longed to see with a beard on his
chin!'

'Eurynome,' said Penelope, 'I know your kind heart, but you shouldn't encourage me in this way to have a bath and anoint my cheeks. The gods of Olympus robbed me of any charms I may have had, on the day when my husband took ship and sailed away. However, tell Autonoe and Hippodameia to come here, so that they can attend me in the hall. I am not going to brave that masculine company alone: modesty forbids.'

While the old woman went off through the house to take this message to the maids and send them to their mistress, the goddess Athene carried her scheme a step further by making Penelope so drowsy that her whole body relaxed and she fell back sound asleep on the couch where she was sitting. The great goddess then endowed her with more than human gifts in order that the young lords might be overcome by her beauty. First she cleansed her fair cheeks with a divine cosmetic like that used by Cythereia when she puts on her lovely crown to join the Graces in their delightful dance. Then she gave her the appearance of greater stature and size; and she made her skin whiter than ivory that has just been sawn. When her work was done the goddess withdrew, and the white-armed maids came up from another part of the house. The sound of their voices as they approached woke up Penelope, who rubbed her cheeks with her hands and exclaimed: 'What a wonderful sleep, in spite of all my troubles! I wish holy Artemis would grant me a death as sweet as that, this very moment, and save me from wasting my life in anguish and longing for all the excellences of my dear husband, who was the best man in all Achaea.'

She left her gay apartment and went downstairs, not by herself, but with the two waiting-women in attendance. When she reached her lovers the great lady drew a fold of her bright head-dress across her cheeks and took her stand by a pillar of the massive roof, with one of her faithful maids on either side.

Her appearance staggered the Suitors. Their hearts were melted by desire, and every man among them prayed that he might hold her in his arms. But Penelope turned to her son. 'Telemachus,' she said, 'your wits have deserted you. As a boy you used to have much more sense, but now that you are grown-up and have entered on manhood, and anyone from the outside world, judging by your height and looks, would take you for a rich man's son, you no longer show the same judgement and tact. I am thinking of the scene that the house has just witnessed and of how you allowed this visitor of ours to be so shamefully treated. What if a guest sitting quietly in our hall were to suffer some injury from such rough handling? It is on you that people would lay the blame and the disgrace.'

'Mother,' Telemachus soberly replied, 'I cannot resent your indignation at what happened. In my own heart I can tell right from wrong well enough – I am not the child I was. But it is impossible for me always to take the sensible line. I am prevented by these mischief-makers who surround me here: and there's no one to support me. However, this fight between the stranger and Irus did not go as the Suitors wished, but the stranger won. Ah, Father Zeus, Athene, and Apollo, how I should love, this very day in our palace, to see these Suitors beaten men, scattered about in the courtyard and indoors with their heads lolling on their shoulders and the strength knocked out of all their limbs, just like Irus sitting out there at the courtyard gate, wagging his head like a drunkard and unable to stand up on his feet and find his way home since he's a broken man!'

Eurymachus put an end to this conversation by addressing a compliment to the queen. 'Daughter of Icarius, wise Penelope,' he said, 'if all the Achaeans in Ionian Argos could set eyes on you, these walls of yours would see an even greater gathering of lovers at tomorrow's feast, for in beauty, stature, and sense there is not a woman to touch you.'

'Ah, Eurymachus,' the prudent Penelope replied, 'all merit, grace, or beauty that I had the gods destroyed when the Argives embarked for Ilium and my husband Odysseus joined their ranks. If *he* could return and devote himself to me, my good name might indeed be embellished and enhanced. But I am left to my misery: the powers above have heaped so many troubles on my head. I well remember, when he left this land of his, how he held me by the wrist of my right hand and said: "Wife, one thing is certain – not all our soldiers will return from Troy unhurt. For they say the Trojans are good fighters too, either with javelin and bow, or from the swift horse-chariots that suddenly turn the scale in a pitched battle. So I cannot say whether the gods will let me come back or whether I shall fall on Trojan soil. But I leave everything here in your charge. Look after my father and mother in the house as you do now, or with even greater care when I am gone. And when you see a beard on our boy's chin, marry whomsoever you fancy and leave your home." That is what he said; and now it is all coming true. I see approaching me the night when I must accept a union I shall loathe; heaven has destroyed my happiness and left me forlorn.

'Meanwhile here is something that is causing me the utmost mortification. Yours is by no means the good old way for rivals to conduct their suit for a gentlewoman and a rich man's daughter! Surely it is usual for the suitors to bring in their own cattle and sheep to make a banquet for the lady's friends, and also to give her valuable presents, but *not* to enjoy free meals at someone else's expense.'

Odysseus was delighted at this speech. He liked to see her extorting tribute from her lovers and bewitching them by her coquetry, while all the time her heart was set on quite a different course.

It was Antinous, Eupeithes' son, who answered her. 'Daughter of Icarius, wise Penelope,' he said, 'by all means accept every gift that any of us may arrange to send you – and none could well refuse such a request. But let me add that we will not return to our own estates nor go anywhere else till you marry the best man among us.'

The others agreed and each sent off his squire to fetch a gift. For Antinous they brought a long embroidered robe of the most beautiful material on which were fixed a dozen golden brooches, each fitted with a curved sheath for the pin; and for Eurymachus a golden chain of exquisite workmanship strung with amber beads that gleamed like the sun. For Eurydamas his two squires brought a pair of ear-rings, each a thing of lambent beauty with its cluster of three drops; while from the house of Prince Peisander, Polyctor's son, there came a servant with a necklace which was a lovely piece of jewellery too. Thus each of the young lords contributed his own valuable gift, and presently the lady Penelope withdrew to her upper apartment escorted by her waiting-women, who carried the magnificent presents.

From then till dusk the Suitors gave themselves up to the pleasures of dancing and delights of song. When night fell, it found them making merry still. So they set up three braziers in the hall to give them light, heaped them with faggots of dry wood thoroughly seasoned and newly split, and thrust some burning brands into each pile. The palace maids took it in turns to tend the lights, until King Odysseus himself intervened.

'Away, you masterless maids,' he said, 'to the apartments where you'll find your mistress. Give her the pleasure of seeing you sitting at home, turning the spindle at her side or carding wool with your hands. Meanwhile, I shall provide light for the company, and even if they wish to carry on till the peep of day they won't exhaust me. I am far too tough for that.'

The girls laughed and exchanged glances. But the rosy-cheeked Melantho flared up at him. She was a daughter of Dolius, whom Penelope had reared and looked after as tenderly as her own child, giving her all the playthings she could desire. But her care was not requited: the girl had no sympathy for Penelope's woes; she loved Eurymachus and had become his mistress. Rounding on Odysseus now, she gave him the rough side of her tongue: 'You must be soft in the head, you disreputable old vagabond! Why not go for your night's lodging to the smithy or some other hostel, instead of coming here and airing your views so boldly and disrespectfully before all these gentlemen? The wine has fuddled your wits, or perhaps you talk such nonsense only because they are always like that. Has the drubbing you gave the beggar Irus gone to your head? Look out, I say, or a better man than Irus will stand up to hammer it with his great fists and send you packing with a bloody nose.'

'Brazen hussy,' retorted the great Odysseus, glowering down upon her, 'I shall go straight over and report you to Telemachus for that speech. He'll soon make mincemeat of you.'

His threat scattered the women, who fled through the house, their knees trembling beneath them in alarm, for they had taken him at his word. But Odysseus took his stand by the burning braziers, tending the lights and keeping an eye on them all, though his thoughts were busy elsewhere with schemes that were not doomed to come to nothing.

Athene meanwhile had no intention of allowing the insolent Suitors to abandon their offensive ways; she wished the anguish to bite deeper yet into Odysseus' royal heart. It was Eurymachus' turn to contribute a jibe at the stranger and raise a laugh among his friends. 'Listen!' he cried. 'It has occurred to me–and I really must share this idea with my rivals for our noble Queen –that some divine being must have guided this fellow to Odysseus' palace. At any rate it seems to me that the torch-light emanates from the man himself, in fact from that pate of his, innocent as it seems of the slightest vestige of hair.'

He then turned to Odysseus, the sacker of cities. 'Stranger,' he said, 'I wonder how you'd like to work for me if I took you on as my man, somewhere on an upland farm, at a proper wage of course, building stone dykes and planting trees for timber? I should see that you had regular food and provide you with clothing and footwear. But you've learnt such bad habits that I expect you'll jib at farm-work and prefer to beg in the streets by way of filling your greedy paunch.'

'I only wish, Eurymachus,' replied Odysseus, 'that you and I could compete as labourers in the early summer when the days draw out, in a hayfield somewhere, I with a crooked reaping-hook and you with its fellow, so that we could test each other at work, with nothing to eat till well after dusk and plenty of grass to cut. Or we might have some oxen to drive, tawny great thoroughbreds, bursting with fodder and matched in age and pulling power. It takes a lot to tire a pair like that, and I should choose a four-acre field with a clod that yielded nicely to the share. You'd see then whether I could cut a furrow straight ahead! Or again I wish some fighting could somehow come our way, here and now, and that I had a shield and a couple of spears and a bronze helmet fitting round my forehead. It would be out in the front line that you'd find me then, and you'd have no more quips to make at this paunch of mine. But you, sir, are a braggart with the heart of a bully, who take yourself for a big man and a hero only because the people you meet are so few, and good for nothing at that. Ah, if Odysseus could only come home and show himself you'd soon find that wide doorway there too narrow in your hurry to get safely out!'

Eurymachus' wrath boiled over. With a black look he rounded on Odysseus. 'Rascal,' he cried, 'I'll soon make you pay for your irreverence and public insults. The wine must have got at your wits, or perhaps you talk such trash only because they are always like this. Has the drubbing you gave that beggar Irus gone to your head?' And as he spoke he seized a stool. But Odysseus avoided his attack by sitting down at the knees of Amphinomus of Dulichium, and Eurymachus' missile struck the winesteward on the right hand so that his jug dropped with a clang on the floor and he himself with a groan fell backwards in the dust.

The darkened hall was at once filled with uproar. The Suitors looked at each other in alarm and wished that the vagabond had come to grief elsewhere, before they had seen him, instead of raising all this hubbub in their midst. 'Here we are,' they said, 'at blows about a beggar-man, and our pleasure in an excellent evening's entertainment is going to be spoiled by this outburst of folly.'

But now Telemachus spoke out like a prince. 'Gentlemen,' he said, 'you are out of your senses. It is obvious what the food and wine have done to you. Some power must be stirring you up to trouble. Come now; you have dined well: I suggest you go home to bed at your leisure, though of course I am hustling no one out.'

At this they could only bite their lips and wonder that Telemachus should have the audacity to address them so.

At last Amphinomus took it on himself to reply. This prince was the son of King Nisus, himself the son of Aretias. 'My friends,' he remarked, 'when the right thing has been said, captious criticism is out of place. Let nobody maltreat this stranger or any of the royal servants. Rather, let a wine-steward charge each man's cup so that we can make our offerings and go home to bed, leaving our visitor here in the palace to Tele-machus' care. For after all it is to his house that he has come.'

This was a solution that everyone welcomed. Mulius, a squire from Dulichium in Amphinomus' retinue, mixed them a bowl of wine and then went the rounds and served them all. They poured out their offerings to the blessed gods before drinking up the mellow wine, and when they had made their libations and drunk all they wanted they dispersed to their several homes for the night.

XIX

EURYCLEIA RECOGNIZES ODYSSEUS

KING ODYSSEUS was left in the deserted hall to plot the destruction of the Suitors with Athene's aid. His first step was to give his son some instructions.

'Telemachus,' he said, 'the arms must be stowed away, to the last weapon. When the Suitors miss them and ask you what has happened, you must lull their suspicions with some plausible tale. You can say: "I have rescued them from the smoke, having noticed how different they looked from when Odysseus left them and sailed for Troy. The fire had got at them and damaged them badly. It also occurred to me – and this was more serious – that since the very presence of a weapon provokes a man to use it you might start quarrelling in your cups and wound each other, thus spoiling your festivities and discrediting your suit."'

Acting at once on his father's orders, Telemachus called the nurse Eurycleia to his side and said:

'Good mother, I want you to keep the womenfolk shut up in their quarters till I have stowed away my father's arms in the store-room. They're a fine set, but I've carelessly left them about the place to be tarnished by the smoke ever since my father sailed. I was too small then to know better; but now I have decided to pack them away where the fire won't get at them.'

'My child,' his fond old nurse replied, 'happy the day when you see fit to worry over your house and look after your belongings! But tell me, who is to go along with you and carry a light? The maids would have done it, but you say you won't have them about.'

'This stranger,' Telemachus was quick to reply. 'I keep no man idle who has eaten my bread, however far he may have tramped.'

The old woman could have said more but this silenced her,

and she locked the door of the women's quarters, while Odysseus and the young prince fell to work at their task of stowing away the helmets, the bossed shields, and the pointed spears. Pallas Athene herself took the lead, carrying a golden lamp, which shed a beautiful radiance over the scene. At this, Telemachus could not restrain a sudden exclamation. 'Father!' he cried. 'What is this marvel that I see? The walls of the hall, the panels, the pine-wood beams, and the soaring pillars all stand out as though there were a blazing fire; or so it seems to me. I honestly believe some god from heaven is in the house.'

'Hush!' said the cautious Odysseus. 'Keep your own counsel and ask no questions. The Olympians have ways of their own, and this is an instance. Go to your bed now and leave me here to draw out the maids a little more, and your mother also. In her distress she is sure to cross-examine me thoroughly.'

So Telemachus went off through the hall to bed, and found his way by torchlight to his usual sleeping-quarters, where he now settled down, as on other nights, to sleep till daybreak. Odysseus was left once more in the hall, planning the slaughter of his rivals with Athene's help.

The wise Penelope now came down from her apartment, looking as lovely as Artemis or golden Aphrodite; and they drew up a chair for her in her usual place by the fire. It was overlaid with ivory and silver, and was the work of a craftsman called Icmalius. To the framework itself he had attached a foot-rest, over which a large fleece was spread. Penelope took her seat, and the white-armed maids, issuing from their quarters, began to clear away the remains of the meal, and the tables and cups which the menfolk had used for their debauch. They also raked out the fire from the braziers onto the floor and heaped them high with fresh fuel for light and warmth.

Melantho seized the occasion to scold Odysseus once again. 'Ha! Still here,' she cried, 'to plague us all night long, cruising around the house and ogling the women! Off with you, wretch, and be glad of the supper you had, or you'll find yourself thrown out at the door with a torch about your ears.'

Odysseus of the nimble wits turned on her with a frown. 'My good woman,' he said, 'why set upon me with such spite? Is it because, having no choice in the matter, I go dirty and dressed in rags, and pick up my living from door to door like any other beggar or tramp? If so, let me tell you there was a time when I too was one of the lucky ones with a rich house to live in, and that I've often given alms to such a vagrant as myself, no matter who he was or what he wanted. Hundreds of servants I had, and plenty of all one needs to live in luxury and take one's place as a man of means. But Zeus, no doubt for some good reason of his own, stripped me of everything. So look out for yourself, my girl, or one day you may lose the fine place you have in the household here. Your mistress may fall foul of you, or Odysseus come back. Yes, there's still a chance of that; while, if he's really dead and gone for ever, he has a son by god's grace as good as himself; and there's no mischief any of you women here may do that Telemachus misses. He's past the age for that.'

Penelope, who had listened, rounded in fury on the maid and scolded her for a bold and shameless hussy. 'Make no mistake,' she went on; 'I heard the whole disgraceful affair and you shall pay dearly for what you did. For you knew perfectly well – in fact you heard me say so – that in my great distress I meant to examine this stranger here in my house for any news he might have of my husband.' And turning to Eurynome, the house-keeper, she said: 'Will you bring a settle here, with a rug on it, for my guest to sit on, so that he and I can talk to one another? I wish to have his whole story from the man.'

Eurynome hurried off and came back with a wooden settle, on which she spread a rug. Here the noble and stalwart Odysseus sat down, and Penelope opened their talk by saying: 'Sir, I shall make so bold as to ask you some questions without further ado. Who are you and where do you hail from? What is your city and to what family do you belong?'

'Madam,' answered the resourceful Odysseus, 'there is not a man in the wide world who could take anything amiss from you. For your fame has reached heaven itself, like that of some perfect king, ruling a populous and mighty state with the fear of god in his heart, and upholding the right, so that the dark soil yields its wheat and barley, the trees are laden with ripe fruit, the sheep never fail to bring forth their lambs, nor the sea to provide its fish – all as a result of his good government – and his people prosper under him. Yet just because you are so good, ask me any other questions now that you have me in your house, but do not insist on finding out my lineage and my country, or you will bring fresh sorrow to my heart by making me recall the past. For I have been through many bitter experiences. Yet there is no reason why I should sit moaning and lamenting in someone else's house. It's a bad thing never to stop croaking, and I'm afraid some of your maids here or you yourself might find me a nuisance and conclude that it was the wine that had gone to my head and loosed this flood of tears.'

'Sir,' said Penelope, 'all merit, grace, or beauty that I had, the gods destroyed when the Argives embarked for Ilium and my husband Odysseus joined their fleet. If *he* could return and devote himself to me, my good name might indeed be embellished and enhanced. But I am left to my misery: the powers above have heaped so many troubles on my head. For of all the island chieftains that rule in Dulichium, in Same, and in wooded Zacynthus, or that live here in our own sunny Ithaca, there is not one that is not forcing his unwelcome suit upon me and plundering my house. As a result I neglect my guests, I neglect the beggar at my door, and even the messengers that come on public business. I simply wear my heart out in longing for Odysseus. Meanwhile they are pressing me to name my wedding-day and I have to think out tricks to fool them with. The first was a real inspiration. I set up a great web on my loom here and started weaving a large and delicate robe, saying to my suitors: "I should be grateful to you young lords who are courting me now that King Odysseus is dead, if you could restrain your ardour for my hand till I have done this work, so that the threads I have spun may not be altogether wasted. It is a winding-sheet for Lord Laertes. When he succumbs to the dread hand of Death that stretches all men out at last, I must not risk the scandal there would be among my countrywomen here if one who had amassed such wealth were laid to rest without a shroud." That is what I put to them, and they had the grace to consent. So by day I used to weave at the great web, but every night I had torches set beside it and undid the work. For three years they were taken in by this stratagem of mine. A fourth began and the seasons were already slipping by, when they were given the chance by my maids, those irresponsible wretches, of catching me unawares at my task. They loaded me with reproaches, and I was forced reluctantly to finish the work. And now I can neither evade marriage with one of them nor think of any means of escape, particularly as my parents insist that I should take this step, while the sight of these people eating him out of house and home revolts my son, who realizes well enough what is happening, being a man by now and well qualified to look after a flourishing estate. However, I do press you still to give me an account of yourself, for you certainly did not spring from a tree or a rock, like the man in the old story.'

'Your majesty,' answered the inventive Odysseus, 'will you never be satisfied till I have given you my pedigree? Very well, you shall have it. Yet you will be making me more miserable than I already am – as is only to be expected when a man has spent so long a time away from home as I have, wandering through the world in evil plight from town to town. However, here is my tale and an answer to all your questions.

'Out in the dark blue sea there lies a land called Crete, a rich and lovely land, washed by the waves on every side, densely peopled and boasting ninety cities. Each of the several races of the isle has its own language. First there are the Achaeans; then the genuine Cretans, proud of their native stock; next the Cydonians; the Dorians, with their three clans; and finally the noble Pelasgians. One of the ninety towns is a great city called Cnossus, and there, for nine years, King Minos ruled and enjoyed the friendship of almighty Zeus. He was the father of my father, the great Deucalion, who had two sons, myself and King

Idomcncus. At the time I have in mind, Idomeneus had gone off in his beaked ships to Ilium with the sons of Atreus; so it fell to me, the younger son, Aethon by name, and not so good a man as my elder brother, to meet Odysseus and welcome him to Crete, where he was brought by a gale which had driven him off his course at Cape Malea when bound for Troy. He put in at Amnisus, where the cave of Eileithyie is – a difficult harbour to make; the storm nearly wrecked him. And the first thing he did was to go up to the town and ask for Idomeneus, whom he described as a dear and honoured friend. But nine or ten days had already gone by since Idomeneus had sailed for Ilium in his beaked ships. So I took Odysseus to my house and made him thoroughly welcome. My own wealth at the time enabled me to entertain him lavishly; and as for his following, by drawing on the public store I provided him with corn and wine as well as cattle to slaughter to their hearts' content. The good fellows stayed with me for twelve days, pent up by that northerly gale, which they couldn't even stand up to on dry land, some hostile power made it blow so hard. But on the thirteenth the wind fell and they put out to sea.'

He made all these lying yarns of his so convincing that, as she listened, the tears poured from Penelope's eyes and bedewed her cheeks. As the snow that the west wind has brought melts on the mountain-tops when the east wind thaws it, and, melting, makes the rivers run in spate, so did the tears she shed drench her fair cheeks as she wept for the husband who was sitting at her side. But though Odysseus' heart was wrung by his wife's distress, his eyes, hard as horn or iron, never wavered between their lids, so craftily did he repress his tears.

When Penelope had wept to her heart's content she returned to her interrogation. 'I feel, sir,' she said, 'that it is time I put you to the proof and found out whether you really entertained my husband and his gallant company in your Cretan home as you have stated. Tell me what sort of clothes he was wearing and what he looked like; and describe the men who were with him also.'

'Mistress,' replied Odysseus, 'it is not easy to describe a man when one has not seen him for so long; and nineteen years have passed since Odysseus sailed from my country. However, I'll give you the picture of him that I have in my mind's eye. My lord wore a thick purple cloak folded back on itself and displaying a golden brooch with a pair of sheaths for the pins. There was a device on the face of it: a hound holding down a dappled fawn in his forepaws and ripping it as it struggled. Everyone admired the workmanship, the hound ripping and throttling the fawn, the fawn lashing out with his feet in his efforts to escape – and the whole thing done in gold. I noticed his tunic too. It gleamed on his body like the skin of a dried onion, it was so smooth; and it shone like the sun. I tell you, all the women were fascinated by him. At the same time you must remember that I cannot say whether Odysseus wore these clothes at home, or whether they had been given him by one of his friends when he embarked, or by some acquaintance he visited, for Odysseus was very popular and there were few of his countrymen like him. I myself gave him a bronze sword, a fine purple mantle, and a tunic with a fringe, and I saw him off with all honours on his well-found ship. And here's another thing. He had a squire in his retinue who was a little older than himself. I'll tell you what he looked like too. He was round in the shoulders and had a dark complexion and curly hair. Eurybates was his name, and Odysseus thought more of him than of anyone else in his company, for the squire saw eye to eye with his leader.'

Odysseus' descriptions made Penelope even more disposed to weep, recognizing, as she did, all that he so faithfully portrayed. She found relief in tears once more, then turned to him and said: 'Sir, I pitied you before; but now you shall be a dear and honoured guest in my house. For it was I who gave him those clothes, just as you describe them; I who took them from our store-room; I who folded them and put in the bright brooch as an ornament for him. And now I shall never welcome him home to the land he loved so well. Aye, 'twas an evil day when Odysseus sailed in his hollow ship to that accursed city which I loathe to name.'

'My lady and my Queen,' replied the subtle Odysseus, 'I beg you not to spoil those fair cheeks any more nor to wring your heart by weeping for your husband. Not that I blame you. Any woman mourns when she loses the husband whose love she has enjoyed and whose children she has borne, however poorly that husband might compare with Odysseus, whom people speak about as though he were a god. But dry your tears now and hear what I have to say. I am speaking the truth and nothing but the truth when I tell you that I have news of Odysseus' return, that he's alive and near, actually in the rich land of Thesprotia, and that he's bringing home a great fortune acquired in his dealings abroad. On the other hand he has lost all his company and his good ship on the high seas. This happened soon after they left the island of Thrinacie. Zeus and the Sun-god were infuriated with him because his men had killed the cattle of the Sun; and his whole crew found a watery grave. But he himself clung to the keel of his boat and was cast on shore by the waves in the country of the Phaeacians, who are cousins to the gods. These people in the goodness of their hearts paid him divine honours, showered gifts upon him, and were anxious to see him safely home themselves. Indeed Odysseus would have been here long ago, had he not thought it the more profitable course to travel about in the pursuit of wealth – which shows that in business enterprise he is unsurpassed; in fact not a man alive can rival him. I had all this from Pheidon, the Thesprotian king, who moreover swore in my presence over a drink-offering in his palace that a ship with a crew standing by was waiting on the beach to convey Odysseus to his own country. But Pheidon sent me off before him as a Thesprotian ship happened to be starting for the corn island of Dulichium. He even showed me what wealth Odysseus had amassed. The amount of treasure stored up for him there in the king's house would keep a man and his heirs to the tenth generation.

'Odysseus himself, Pheidon said, had gone to Dodona to find out the will of Zeus from the great oak-tree that is sacred to the god, and to discover how he should approach his own island of

Ithaca after so long an absence, whether to return openly or in disguise.

'So you see that he is safe and will soon be back. Indeed, he is very close. His exile from his friends and country will be ended soon; and whether you ask it or not you shall have my oath to that effect. I swear first by Zeus, the best and greatest of the gods, and then by the good Odysseus' hearth which I have come to, that everything will happen as I foretell. This very year Odysseus will be here, between the waning of the old moon and the waxing of the new.'

'Sir,' the wise queen replied to this, 'may what you say prove true! If it does, you shall learn from my liberality what my friendship means and the world will envy you your luck. But the future that my heart forebodes is different. I neither see Odysseus coming home, nor you securing your passage hence; for we have no one in command here, no leader of men, such as Odysseus (if ever there was such a man), to receive strangers with proper respect and send them on their way. But, come, my maids, you must wash our visitor's feet and spread a bed for him, with mattress, blankets, and clean sheets, so that he may lie in warmth and comfort till Dawn takes her golden throne; and the first thing in the morning you must give him a bath and rub him down with oil so that he may feel ready to take his place beside Telemachus at breakfast in the hall. And if any of those men is spiteful enough to plague our guest, so much the worse for him. His chances of succeeding here will vanish: he can rage and fume as he will. For how are you, sir, to find out whether I really have more sense and forethought than other women, if you sit down to meals unkempt and ill-clad in my house? Man's life is short enough. A churlish fellow with no idea of hospitality earns the whole world's ill-will while he is alive and its contempt when he is dead; whereas when a man does kind things because his heart is in the right place his reputation is spread far and wide by the guests he befriends, and he has no lack of people to sing his praises.'

'Honoured lady,' replied the cautious Odysseus, 'I must

admit that I have taken a dislike to blankets and clean sheets since I sailed off in my galley and said farewell to the snow-capped hills of Crete. So I will lie just as I have often lain and kept vigil in the past. For many's the night I've spent on some unseemly couch, waiting for the gold light of the blessed Dawn. Nor does the prospect of a foot-bath appeal to me much. I shouldn't care for any of your maid-servants here to touch my feet, unless there is some old and respectable dame who has had as much experience in life as I have. If there is such a one, I should not object to her handling my feet.'

To which the wise Penelope replied: 'My dear friend – as I cannot help calling the wisest guest this house has ever wel-comed from abroad, for you put everything so well and you talk so sensibly – I have just such an old woman, a decent soul, who faithfully nursed my unhappy husband and brought him up; in fact she took him in her arms the moment he was born. She shall wash your feet, although she is somewhat past her work. Come, Eurycleia, and do this service for one who is of the same age as your master. Yes, and no doubt Odysseus' hands and feet are like our guest's by now, for men age quickly in mis-fortune.'

At this, the old woman covering her face with her hands burst into tears and gave voice to her grief: 'Alas, my child, that there shouldn't be a thing that I can do for you! Zeus must in-deed have hated you above all men, god-fearing though you were. For no one ever burnt for the Thunderer so many fat pieces from the thigh and such choice sacrifices as you used to offer him when you prayed that you might age in comfort and see your son grow up like a prince. Yet you are the only one of whose home-coming he has said: "It shall not be." I keep think-ing of the women in some foreign land mocking my master when he called at this great house or that, just as you, sir, have been mocked by all these bitches here, whose insolence and vulgar gibes you wished to spare yourself when you refused to let them wash your feet. Well, my wise Queen has given me the task, and I am most willing. I will bathe your feet, both for

Penelope's sake and for your own, since your unhappiness has touched my heart. But hear me out: there's something else I want to say. We have had plenty of wayworn travellers here before, but not one that I have seen has reminded me so strongly of anyone as your looks and your voice and your very feet remind me of Odysseus.'

'My good dame,' said Odysseus, on his guard, 'that is what everyone thinks who has set eyes on us both. They say we are remarkably alike, as you yourself have so shrewdly observed.'

The old woman fetched a clean basin which was used as a foot-bath, poured plenty of cold water in and added warm. Odysseus was sitting at the hearth, but now he swung abruptly round to face the dark, for it had struck him suddenly that in handling him she might notice a certain scar he had, and his secret would be out. Indeed, when Eurycleia came up to her master and began to wash him, she recognized the scar at once.

Years before, Odysseus had received a wound from the white tusk of a boar when on a visit to Autolycus and his sons. This nobleman, his mother's father, was the most accomplished thief and liar of his day. He owed his pre-eminence to the god Hermes himself, whose favour he sought by sacrificing lambs and kids in his honour, and in whom he secured a willing confederate. He went over once to the rich island of Ithaca, where he found that his daughter had just given birth to a son. Eurycleia put the baby on its grandfather's knees as he finished supper, and said: 'Autolycus, perhaps *you* can think of a name to give your daughter's son, whom we have so long been praying for.'

By way of answer, Autolycus turned to his son-in-law and daughter and said: 'Yes, let me be his godfather. In the course of my lifetime I have made enemies of many a man and woman up and down the wide world. So let this child be called Odysseus, "the victim of enmity". And when he has grown up and comes to his mother's old home at Parnassus, where I keep my wordly goods, I will give him a share of them and send him back a happy man.'

This led in due course to a visit from Odysseus, who went

over to receive his grandfather's gifts. Autolycus and his sons gave him a friendly welcome. They shook him warmly by the hand, and his grandmother, Amphithee, threw her arms round his neck and kissed him on the forehead and on both his eyes. Autolycus told his sons to make preparations for a banquet. Nothing loath, they quickly brought in a five-year-old bull, which they flayed and prepared by cutting up the carcass and deftly chopping it into small pieces. These they pierced with spits, carefully roasted, and served in portions. And so they banqueted for the rest of the day till sunset, all sharing alike and all contented with their share. When the sun sank and darkness fell, they went off to their beds to enjoy the blessing of sleep.

Early next day at the first blush of dawn Autolycus' sons accompanied by the good Odysseus set out for the chase with a pack of hounds. Climbing the steep and wooded heights of Parnassus, they soon found themselves on the windswept folds of the mountain; and it was just as the Sun, fresh from the deep and quiet Stream of Ocean, was touching the plough-lands with his first beams that the beaters reached a certain wooded glen. The hounds, hot on a scent, preceded them. Behind came Autolycus' sons, and with them the good Odysseus, close up on the pack and swinging his long spear. It was at this spot that a mighty boar had his lair, in a thicket so dense that when the winds blew moist not a breath could get inside, nor when the Sun shone could his rays penetrate the darkness, nor could the rain soak right through to the ground, which moreover was littered with an abundance of dead leaves. However, the boar heard the footfalls of the men and hounds as they pressed forward in the chase. He sallied out from his den and with bristling back and eyes aflame he faced the hunt. Odysseus was the first to act. Poising his long spear in his great hand, he rushed in, eager to score a hit. But the boar was too quick and caught him above the knee, where he gave him a long flesh-wound with a cross lunge of his tusk, but failed to reach the bone. Odysseus' thrust went home as well. He struck him on the right shoulder, and the point of his bright spear transfixed the boar, who sank to earth with a grunt and there gave up his life. Autolycus' sons took charge of the carcass. They also carefully bandaged the brave young prince's wound, staunching the dark blood with a spell; and before long they were back at home.

Under the care of Autolycus and his sons, Odysseus recovered from his injury and in due course, loaded with presents, was given a happy send-off to his own home in Ithaca. His father and his gentle mother were delighted to see him back. They asked him about all his adventures, in particular how he had come by his scar, and Odysseus told them how in the course of the chase he had been gashed by a boar's tusk on the expedition to Parnassus with Autolycus' sons.

Now, as the old woman passsed her hands over this scar, she recognized the feel of it and abruptly let go her master's foot, which made the metal ring as it dropped against the basin, upsetting it and spilling all the water on the floor. Delight and anguish swept through her heart together; her eyes were filled with tears; her voice was strangled by emotion. She lifted her hand to Odysseus' chin and said, 'Of course, you are Odysseus, my dear child. And to think that I didn't know you till I'd handled all my master's limbs!'

With this she turned her eyes in Penelope's direction, as though to let her know that her own husband was in the room. But Penelope was not prepared to meet her glance or understand it, for Athene had distracted her attention. In the meantime Odysseus' right hand sought and gripped the old woman's throat, while with the other he pulled her closer to him.

'Nurse,' he said, 'do you wish to ruin me, you who reared me at your own breast? I am indeed home after nineteen years of hard adventure. But since by some unlucky chance you have lit on the fact, keep your mouth shut and let not a soul in the house learn the truth. Otherwise I tell you plainly – and you know I make no idle threats – that if I am lucky enough to defeat these love-sick noblemen, I won't spare you, though you're my own nurse, on the day when I put the rest of the maids in my palace to death.'

'My child,' Eurycleia replied in her wisdom, 'no need to talk like that to me. You know well enough how staunch and hard I am. I'll keep silent as a block of stone or iron. Remember this too, that if you have the luck to bring these insolent lordlings down, *I* shall be ready to inform you about all the women in your household and to pick out the disloyal from the innocent.'

'And what,' said the self-reliant Odysseus, 'would be the good of that? I do not need your help, for on my own account I shall take note of each and mark them down. Meanwhile keep all this to yourself and leave the issue to the gods.'

Thus admonished, the old woman went out of the hall to fetch water for his feet, since the whole basinful was spilt. When she had washed and rubbed them with olive-oil, Odysseus drew his settle up to the fire once more in order to get warm, and covered the scar with his rags.

It was Penelope who reopened their talk. 'Sir,' she said, 'I shall venture to detain you yet a while and put another matter to you, and this although I know the time for sleep is drawing near – at least for those whose grief allows them such a sweet reprieve. But in my own case, heaven seems to have set no limit to my misery. For by day my one relief is to weep and sigh as I go about my tasks and supervise the household work; but when night falls and brings all others sleep, I lie down on my bed, and care comes with a thousand stings to prick my heavy heart and turn dejection into torture. You know how Pandareus' daughter, the brown nightingale, perched in the dense foliage of the trees, makes her sweet music when the spring is young, and with how many turns and trills she pours out her full-throated song in sorrow for Itylus her beloved son, King Zethus' child, whom in her careless folly she killed with her own hand. So does my inclination waver, first to this side, then to that. Am I to stay with my son and keep everything intact, my belongings, my servants, and this great house of ours, in loyalty to my husband's bed and deference to public opinion? Or shall I go away now with the best and most generous of my suitors here in the palace? For I must tell you that my son, while still an irresponsible child, made it out of the question for me to leave my husband's house and marry again. But now that he has grown up and entered on manhood, he actually implores me to take myself off, so concerned is he for his estate, which he sees the young lords eating up.

'But enough. Let me ask you to interpret a dream of mine which I shall now describe. I keep a flock of twenty geese in the place. They come in from the pond to pick up their grain and I delight in watching them. In my dream I saw a great eagle swoop down from the hills and break their necks with his crooked beak, killing them all. There they lay in a heap on the floor while he vanished in the open sky. I wept and cried aloud, though it was only a dream, and Achaean ladies gathering about me found me sobbing my heart out because the eagle had slaughtered my geese. But the bird came back. He perched on a jutting timber of the roof, and breaking into human speech he checked my tears. "Take heart," he said, "daughter of the noble Icarius. This is not a dream but a happy reality which you shall see fulfilled. The geese were your lovers, and I that played the eagle's part am now your husband, home again and ready to deal out grim punishment to every man among them." At this point I awoke. I looked around me and there I saw the geese in the yard pecking their grain at the trough in their accustomed place.'

'Lady,' replied the subtle Odysseus, 'nobody could force any other meaning on this dream; you have learnt from Odysseus himself how he will translate it into fact. Clearly, the Suitors are all of them doomed: there is not one who will get away alive.'

'Dreams, sir,' said the cautious Penelope, 'are awkward and confusing things: not all that people see in them comes true. For there are two gates through which these insubstantial visions reach us; one is of horn and the other of ivory. Those that come through the ivory gate cheat us with empty promises that never see fulfilment; while those that issue from the gate of burnished horn inform the dreamer what will really happen. But I fear it was not from this source that my own strange dream took wing, much as I and my son should rejoice if it proved so.

'However, I meant to tell you something else that will give you matter for thought. The hateful day is drawing very near which is to tear me from Odysseus' house. For I intend shortly to propose a trial of strength, using the very axes which he sometimes set up here at home, twelve in a row like the props under a new keel. Standing a good way off, he could shoot an arrow through them all. And now I am going to make the Suitors compete in the same test of skill. Whichever proves the handiest at stringing the bow and shoots an arrow through each of the twelve axes, with that man I will go, bidding goodbye to this house that welcomed me as a bride, this lovely house so full of all good things, this home which even in my dreams I never shall forget.'

'Royal lady,' Odysseus answered, with subtle intent, 'the sooner you hold this contest in the palace the better, for that arch-contriver Odysseus himself will be here long before those fellows have fumbled the string onto that fine bow of his and shot an arrow through the iron marks.'

'Ah, my friend,' said the wise Penelope, 'if you would only sit here at my side in the hall and entertain me, my eyes would never close in drowsiness. But no one can do without sleep for ever. It has its allotted place in our daily lives, like everything else. So now I shall withdraw upstairs to lie down on what has always been for me a bed of sorrows, watered by my perpetual tears, since the day when Odysseus sailed away to that accursed city which I loathe to name. So much for me. And as for you, whether you spread yourself something on the floor or let them make you a proper bed, the house is at your disposal for the night.'

So Penelope went up to her beautiful room, escorted by the ladies in attendance. But as soon as they were all upstairs, she broke down and wept for Odysseus, her beloved husband, till Athene brought her the sweet gift of sleep.

XX

PRELUDE TO THE CRISIS

MEANWHILE Odysseus prepared himself for sleep in the portico. He spread an untanned oxhide on the floor and piled it up with plenty of fleeces, from sheep that the young lords had slaughtered as their habit was; and Eurynome cast a mantle over him when he had settled down. As he lay there brewing trouble for his rivals and unable to sleep, a party of womenfolk, the Suitors' mistresses, came trooping out of the house with many a laugh and interchange of pleasantries. Odysseus' gorge rose within him. Yet he was quite uncertain what to do and he debated long. Should he dash after them and put them all to death; or should he let them spend this one last night in the arms of their profligate lovers? The thought made him snarl with repressed fury, like a bitch that snarls and shows fight as she takes her stand above her helpless puppies when a stranger comes by. So did Odysseus growl to himself in sheer revolt at these licentious ways. But in the end he brought his fist down on his heart and called it to order. 'Patience, my heart!' he said. 'You had a far more loathsome thing than this to put up with when the savage Cyclops devoured those gallant men. And yet you managed to hold out, till cunning got you clear of the cave where you had thought your end had come.'

But though he was able by such self-rebuke to quell all mutiny in his heart and steel it to endure, Odysseus nevertheless could not help tossing to and fro on his bed, just as a paunch stuffed with fat and blood is tossed this way and that in the blaze of the fire by a cook who wants to get it quickly roasted. Twisting and turning thus to one side and the other, he was wondering how single-handed against such odds he should come to grips with his unprincipled rivals, when Athene descended from heaven and approached him in the form of a woman. She leant over his head and spoke to him: 'Sleepless again, poor wretch? And why? Is not this house your home? Is not your wife inside it, and your son as well, a lad whom any man might wish his son to match?'

'Goddess,' replied Odysseus with his usual forethought, 'all that you say is true. And yet I am in some perplexity. How on earth am I to attack these young profligates? I am alone, whereas they always stick together in a crowd when they are here. And there's another and still graver matter on my mind. If by Zeus' grace and yours I bring about their deaths, to what safe refuge can I fly? These are the problems I should like you to consider.'

'How hard you are to please!' exclaimed the bright-eyed goddess. 'Most people are content to put their trust in far less powerful allies, mere men and not equipped with wisdom such as mine. But I that have never ceased to watch over you in all your adventures am a goddess. Will *this* make you understand? If you and I were surrounded by fifty companies of men-at-arms, all thirsting for your blood, you could drive away their cows and sheep beneath their very noses. Come now, give yourself up to sleep. It is mere vexation to lie awake and watch the whole night through; and presently you'll rise above your troubles.' With which the lady goddess closed his eyes in sleep and withdrew to Olympus.

But sleep had no sooner come to Odysseus, resolving all his cares as it relaxed his limbs, than his faithful wife awoke, and sitting up in her soft bed gave way to tears; then, tired of weeping, she had recourse to prayer. 'Great Artemis, Daughter of Zeus,' she prayed, for it was to Artemis that the noble lady's thoughts had flown, 'oh for an arrow from your bow to pierce my heart and take away my spirit in this very hour! Or let the Storm-wind snatch me up and vanish with me down the ways of darkness to drop me where the sea runs into the circling Stream of Ocean – just as the daughters of Pandareus were rapt away by the Demons of the Storm. The gods had robbed them of their parents and left them orphaned in their home; and yet they lived, and flourished on the cheese, the sweet honey, and the mellow wine that Aphrodite brought them, while Here made them beautiful and wise beyond all other women, chaste Artemis increased their stature, and Athene taught them the skilled handicrafts that are a woman's pride. But there came a day when the Lady Aphrodite, eager to make happy marriages for them all, went up to high Olympus to consult with Zeus the Thunderer, who knows so well what good and evil is allotted to each one of us on earth – and on that very day the Storm-Fiends snatched them up and gave them to the hateful Erinyes to serve their beck and call. Gods of Olympus, blot me out like that; or strike me dead, fair Artemis, so that I may sink into the very bowels of the earth with Odysseus' image in my heart, rather than serve the pleasures of a lesser man.

'Ah, it is hard but not beyond endurance, when sick at heart one weeps the whole day long but is possessed by sleep at night, sleep which the moment that it seals one's eyes drives out all consciousness of good and bad alike. But even the dreams that heaven inflicts on *me* are evil. This very night again I thought I saw Odysseus by me in the bed, looking exactly as he looked when he sailed away with the fleet; and my heart leapt up, since I took it for no dream but actual fact.'

Close on her prayers came Dawn and filled the East with gold. Odysseus was disturbed by the sounds of Penelope's distress. He recognized her voice and in a waking dream he seemed to see her beside him with the light of recognition in her eyes. He took the cloak and sheepskins from his bed and put them on a chair indoors, carried the oxhide out and laid it down, then lifted up his hands in prayer: 'O Father Zeus, if it is true that after all your persecution you gods by your grace brought me home over dry land and sea to my own country, let someone in the house, where they are waking now, utter a lucky word for me and let some other sign be given out of doors.'

No sooner had he made his prayer than Zeus the Counsellor thundered in answer from his throne above the mists on the dazzling heights of Olympus. Royal Odysseus rejoiced; and close upon this came the precious words he wanted, from a female slave in a building near by, where the King's hand-mills stood. Twelve women had to toil away at these mills, grinding the barley and the wheat into meal for the household bread. At the moment they had all ground their share and gone off to sleep, all except one not so vigorous as the rest, who had not yet finished her task. This woman stopped her mill now and uttered the words that meant so much to her master: 'Zeus, lord of heaven and earth, what thunder from a starry sky! And never a cloud in sight! You *must* have meant it for some lucky man. Listen to poor me too, and let my wish come true. Here 'tis. Let this very day see the end of these junketings in the palace. Terrible work this, grinding the meal for the young lords. They've broken my back. May this be their last dinner, say I.'

The woman's ominous words combined with the clap of thunder to make Odysseus a happy man. He felt that revenge on the miscreants was in his hands.

By this time the palace maid-servants had assembled for work and were making up the fire which never quite died down on the hearth. Telemachus put on his clothes and got up from his bed, fresh as a young god. He slung his sharp sword from his shoulder, bound a stout pair of sandals on his comely feet, picked up his great bronze-pointed spear, and made his way to the threshold, where he paused for a word with Eurycleia.

'My dear nurse,' he said, 'did you women attend properly to our visitor here, in the matter of food and bedding? Or did you leave him to sleep as best he could? That would be just like my mother, who for all her wisdom is far too ready to make much of a ne'er-do-well and send a better man packing.'

'Come, my child,' said Eurycleia reasonably, 'don't blame her when there is no cause. The man sat and drank as long as he wished; while, as for food, he said he had no appetite for more. Your mother asked him; and when the time came to think of sleep, she told the servants to spread him a proper bed. But like a poor fellow utterly down on his luck, he refused to sleep between blankets on a bed, and lay down instead on an undressed hide and some sheepskins in the portico. The mantle over him was due to us.'

When he had heard this, Telemachus set out from the hall, swinging his spear, and with a couple of dogs trotting beside him made his way to the market-place to join his fellow-countrymen. Meanwhile Eurycleia, as befitted her gentle birth – she was the daughter of Ops, Peisenor's son – issued her orders to the rest of the staff.

'To work!' she called. 'You there, sweep and sprinkle the floors. Look sharp about it, and don't forget to spread the purple coverings on the chairs. And you, sponge all the tables down, and wash the wine-bowls and the best two-handled cups. And you others, run off to the well and fetch us some water as quick as you can. For we shall soon have the young lords in the place. They're coming early: today's a public holiday.'

The girls flew to their duties. Twenty went off to draw water from the depths of the well, while the rest got on with the work indoors like well-trained maids. The gentlemen's men-servants next appeared, and chopped up the fire-wood in a neat and businesslike manner. The womenfolk soon came back from the well, and were joined by the swineherd, who drove up three fatted hogs, the pick of all his beasts. He left the animals to nose around for food in the ample courtyard, and came up to Odysseus, whom he greeted affably: 'Well, friend, are you in better odour with the young lords, or do they still turn up their noses at you here?'

'Ah, Eumaeus,' answered Odysseus, 'how I hope that the gods may some day pay the villains out for their insolence and intolerable behaviour in another man's house! They have not a shred of decency among them.'

While the two were chatting together, up came Melanthius the goatherd, driving in the choice goats from his flocks for the Suitors' table. There were two other herdsmen with him. They tied up the goats under the echoing portico, and Melanthius began baiting Odysseus once more: 'What, you still here? Still set on begging from the gentlemen and upsetting the whole house, rather than pack yourself off? I fancy that you and I will have to sample each other's fists before we say goodbye. For I don't like your way of begging. And anyhow this house is not the only one where people dine.'

Odysseus was prudent enough to give him back not a single word. He merely shook his head in silence, though his heart seethed with evil thoughts.

A third new arrival was the master-herdsman Philoetius, who was driving in a heifer and some fatted goats for the Suitors. These beasts had been brought over from the mainland by the ferrymen who run a service for any travellers that turn up. Philoetius carefully tethered his animals under the echoing portico, and came up to the swineherd with a question. 'Who is this stranger,' he asked, 'that has just come to our house? Where does he hail from according to his own account? Who might his people be, and what is his native place? He seems down on his luck, and yet he has the bearing of a royal prince. But the gods spoil a man's looks, even though he was born in a palace, when they force him to the wretched life of the road.'

With this, he went up to Odysseus, proffered his hand and greeted him with warmth. 'A welcome to you, my ancient friend! You are under the weather now; but here's to your future happiness! Father Zeus, what a cruel god you are! There is none harder. In dealing out misfortunes, misery, and suffering to us men, no sense of mercy holds you back; yet it was you who caused us to be born. Sir, when I looked at you just now, the sweat broke out on me and my eyes were filled with tears. You had brought Odysseus to my mind; for I reckon that he too, in just such rags as you have on, must be a wanderer on the face of the earth, if indeed he is alive and can see the sunshine still. If not, if he has gone below, then here's a sigh for the good Odysseus, who set me over his cattle in the Cephallenian country when I was only a lad. And now those broad-browed herds of mine have multiplied beyond belief, like the ripening corn. Short of a miracle, one couldn't hope for more. But as things are, new masters order me to bring these cattle in, just for themselves to eat, caring no more for the prince's presence in the house than they fear the baleful eye of god. Indeed the king has been away so long that nothing will content them now but to share out his goods. And what a quandary for me! I keep turning it over and over in my mind. With a son of his alive, it seems a poor way out for me to flit elsewhere and take myself and all my herds to foreign parts. Yet it's harder still to stay here and stick to the miserable job of tending cattle that have passed to other hands. I'd have run away long ago and found some great prince to protect me, since things have come to such a pass that I can't bear it; but I still have hopes of my unhappy master; I still think he may blow in some day and send these Suitors flying through the palace.'

'Herdsman,' replied the quick-witted Odysseus, 'you talk like a man of sense and goodwill. I have come to my own conclusions and believe in your discretion. So here's a piece of news for you which I vouch for with my solemn oath. I swear by Zeus before all other gods and by the board of hospitality and by the good Odysseus' hearth which I have reached, that before ever you leave Ithaca Odysseus will be back, and if you wish, you shall see with your own eyes the killing of these gallants who play the part of master here.'

'Sir,' said the cowman in reply to this, 'god grant that all you say may happen! You'd soon know *my* mettle and what I can do with my hands!' And Eumaeus chimed in with a prayer to all the gods that the wise Odysseus might see his home again.

Meanwhile the Suitors whom they had been discussing were once more canvassing ways and means for Telemachus' murder, when, lo and behold, a bird of omen appeared on their left, a soaring eagle with a terrified dove in his talons. Amphinomus rose at once, warned his friends that their plot to kill Telemachus was doomed to miscarry, and proposed a move to dinner. His suggestion pleased them well enough and they adjourned to Odysseus' palace, where they threw down their cloaks on settles or chairs and proceeded to slaughter the big sheep, the fatted goats and porkers, and the heifer from the herd as well. They roasted and served the inner parts and mixed themselves wine in the bowls; the swineherd laid a cup for each man; the master-herdsman Philoetius served them with bread in dainty baskets; Melanthius went round with the wine; and they fell to on the good fare spread before them.

Telemachus deliberately chose Odysseus a spot by the stone threshold, just within the great hall, where he placed a shabby stool for him and a small table. He helped him to the entrails, poured him some wine in a golden cup, and told him he could sit there and drink with the gentlemen. 'You can rely on me,' he added, 'to protect you from any insolence or blows from them. This is not an inn but the palace of Odysseus, which has come into my hands from his. And I ask you, gentlemen, to refrain from all provocation and violence, so that we may have no brawls or wrangling here.'

It amazed them that Telemachus should have the audacity to address them in this style. They all bit their lips, and the only comment came from Antinous, Eupeithes' son, who said: 'Well, sirs, offensive as it is, I suppose we must put up with this pronouncement from Telemachus, in spite of the menacing tone he has adopted. Our plan, you see, was interfered with by the powers above. Otherwise, we should have arranged by now that these walls should hear that silvery voice no more.'

Antinous had his say. But Telemachus took not the slightest notice of him.

Meanwhile, in the town, the beasts destined for sacrifice on this holy day were being led by stewards through the streets; and the long-haired Achaean townsfolk were congregating in the shady grove of Apollo the Archer. But the party in the palace, after the outer flesh had been roasted, withdrawn from the spits, and carved up, devoted themselves to the pleasures of the table. The serving-men gave Odysseus his fair share, which was as generous a helping as they got themselves. Telemachus, his son and heir, had given them orders to this effect. But Athene had no intention of letting the arrogant Suitors abandon their attitude of galling insolence: she wished the anguish to bite deeper yet into Odysseus' royal heart.

They had among them a man called Ctesippus, an unruly spirit who had come over from his home in Same, imbued with a simple faith in his fabulous wealth, to woo the wife of the long-absent king. He now insisted on making himself heard by his uproarious boon companions while he delivered himself of a jest. 'My lords,' he said, 'our guest has already been served with an ample helping, as is only proper, for it would be neither good manners nor common decency to stint any friends of Telemachus who come to the house. But look! I am going to make him a present on my own account, so that he may have something to pass on to the bath attendant or one of the other servants in the royal palace.'

With this, he laid his great hand on a cow's hoof that was in the dish and hurled it at him. But Odysseus avoided it by simply ducking to one side, and the quiet smile he permitted himself as the missile struck the solid wall was sardonic indeed. Telemachus pounced on Ctesippus at once: 'It was well for you, Ctesippus, that you didn't hit my guest, even if your miss was due to him. For if you had, I'd have run you through with my spear, and your father would have held a funeral here instead of a wedding. Understand, I won't have this unseemly conduct from anyone in my house. I have learnt to use my brains by now and to know right from wrong: my childhood is a thing of the past. And although I must and do put up with the sight of your orgies, the slaughtered sheep, the wine and bread consumed, since I could hardly stop you all single-handed, I do ask you to refrain from these outrages, which are aimed against myself. But if you have reached the point where nothing short of my murder will content you, well, I should prefer it so and think it a far better thing to die than day after day to look on while disgraceful things like this are done, my guests are bullied, and my maids are hauled about this lovely house for your foul purposes.'

A long and complete silence followed Telemachus' outburst.

It was broken at last by Agelaus, son of Damastor.

'My friends,' he remarked, 'when the proper thing has been said, captious objections would be out of place. Let there be no bullying of this stranger or of any of the royal servants. And now I have a suggestion to make to Telemachus and his mother. It is kindly meant and I hope that both will take it in good part. As long, Telemachus, as you and your mother could still cherish the hope that your wise father would one day come home, no one could blame you for waiting and holding your ground against the Suitors here. It seemed the better course, and would have proved so, had Odysseus really succeeded in finding his way back. But it is obvious by now that he is not destined to do so. I ask you, therefore, to seek your mother out and put the whole case before her. Let her marry the best and most generous man among us; and as a sequel you shall enjoy your inheritance at ease, with plenty to eat and drink, while she looks after her new husband's house.'

'I swear to you, Agelaus,' the wise youth replied, 'I swear by Zeus and by the sufferings of my father, dead far from Ithaca or wandering yet, that I have no wish whatever to postpone my mother's marriage, that I actually urge her to make her choice and wed again, and that I have promised her a most generous settlement too. But to say the final word that would drive her from the house against her will goes clean against my conscience. God save me from that!'

Pallas Athene had fuddled the Suitors' wits to such effect that they greeted Telemachus' reply with peal after peal of helpless merriment. But before long their laughing faces took on a strained and alien look. Blood, so it seemed to them, was spattered on the food they ate. Tears filled their eyes, and maudlin sentiment their hearts.

And now the voice of the noble Theoclymenus was heard. 'Unhappy men,' he cried, 'what blight is this that has descended on you? Your heads, your faces, and your knees are veiled in night. There is a sound of mourning in the air; I see cheeks wet with tears. And look, the panels and the walls are splashed with blood. The porch is filled with ghosts. So is the court – ghosts hurrying down to darkness and to Hell. The sun is blotted out from heaven and a malignant mist has crept upon the world.'

They laughed at him. They laughed delightedly, with one accord; and Polybus' son, Eurymachus, got up and shouted: 'Our new friend's wits have suffered on his journey from abroad. Quick, you fellows, show him out and direct him to the market-place, since he finds it so dark in here.'

'Eurymachus,' the seer replied, 'I want no help from you to find my way. I have eyes and ears and two feet of my own, as well as a pretty sound head on my shoulders – quite enough to get me out of doors, where I am going now. For I see advancing on you all a catastrophe which you cannot hope to survive or shun, no, not a single one of you who spend your time insulting folk and running riot in King Odysseus' house.' And with that he strode from the palace and sought out Peiraeus, who received him kindly.

But the Suitors, after exchanging a few encouraging glances, began one and all to bait Telemachus by holding up his guests to ridicule.

'Telemachus,' said one young blade, and his sally was typical of the rest, 'you really are most unfortunate in your hospitality. Look at this tramp now, whom you have dragged in here to entertain. All *he* wants is food and drink. He has never heard of a hard day's work; in fact he is just a burden on the earth. And as if that weren't enough, up jumps another and must play the seer. You'd much better take my advice and let us clap these friends of yours on board a galley bound for Sicily, where you could make a profit on the deal.'

But this and all their other jibes provoked Telemachus to no rejoinder. He kept his mouth shut and his eyes fixed on his father, always watching for the moment when Odysseus should be ready to attack the graceless crew. As for Penelope, that prudent lady had placed her best chair for herself at a point of vantage from which she was able to hear what was said by everyone in the hall.

It was certainly a rich and savoury dinner that they had managed, for all their merriment, to prepare, since they had
slaughtered freely. But as for their supper, nothing less palatable
could be imagined than the fare which a goddess and a strong
man were soon to spread before them, since the first step in
villainy had been theirs.

XXI

THE GREAT BOW

ATHENE, goddess of the flashing eyes, now prompted that wise lady, Penelope, to confront the Suitors in the palace with the bow and the great iron axes that were to test their skill and lead to their destruction. She descended the high staircase from her own apartments and with her shapely hand picked up a well-made copper key which had an ivory handle, then made her way with her ladies to a store-room in a distant corner of the house where the King's treasure was kept. Here, with his stocks of bronze, of gold, and of wrought iron, lay the incurved bow and quiver full of deadly arrows which had been given to him by his friend Iphitus, of heroic fame, when they met in Lacedaemon. The two came across each other at Ortilochus' house in Messene. Odysseus had come over to recover a public debt, some Messenians having lifted three hundred sheep from Ithaca, shepherds and all, and carried them off in their galleys. This was the business that brought Odysseus so far afield, though a mere lad at the time. His father and the other elders had entrusted him with the mission. Iphitus, for his part, had come in search of a dozen mares he had lost, with the sturdy little mules that they had foaled. In the sequel these horses led to his death in a fatal encounter with Heracles, the lion-hearted Child of Zeus and hero of the mighty Labours. For Heracles killed him in his own house, though he was Iphitus' host, caring no more in that cruel heart of his for the vengeful eye of god than for the hospitality he had given him – feasted the man first, then killed him, took the mares himself, and put them in his own stables.

It was on his quest for these animals that Iphitus met Odysseus and gave him the bow, which in years gone by the great Eurytus, his father, had carried and at his death bequeathed him in his palace. In return, Odysseus gave Iphitus a sharp sword and a stout spear as earnest of a friendship that he hoped to cherish. But before the two could meet as host and guest, the Son of Zeus had killed the heroic Iphitus, the giver of the bow. This bow Odyseus never took on board with him when he sailed to the wars but laid it up at home in memory of a treasured friend, though he did use it on his own estate.

The Queen reached the store-room and mounted the oaken threshold – the work of some carpenter of bygone days, whose adze had smoothed it well and trued it to the line, and whose hands had fixed the doorposts too in their sockets and hung the polished doors upon them. She quickly undid the thong attached to the door-knob, passed the key through the hole, and with a well-aimed thrust shot back the bolt. The key did its work. With a groan like the roar of a bull at grass in a meadow, the doors flew open before her, and she stepped onto the raised boarding of the floor. Here stood the chests where clothing was laid by in scented herbs. But Penelope, rising on tiptoe, fetched the bow down from its peg in the shining case that covered it. And there she sat down with the case on her knees and burst into sobs as she drew out her husband's bow. But when the abundance of her tears had brought its own relief, she set out for the hall to face the proud lords who were courting her, carrying the bow and the quiver with its deadly load of arrows in her arms, while the women followed with a box full of the iron and bronze implements that their master had employed for games of skill. Then, veiling her cheeks with a fold of her bright headdress, the noble lady took her stand by a pillar of the massive roof and without further ado issued her challenge to the Suitors:

'Listen, my lords. You have fastened on this house, in the long absence of its master, as the scene of your perpetual feasts, and you could offer no better pretext for your conduct than your wish to win my hand in marriage. That being the prize, come forward now, my gallant lords; for I challenge you to try your skill on the great bow of King Odysseus. And whichever man among you proves the handiest at stringing the bow and shoots an arrow through every one of these twelve axes, with that man

I will go, bidding goodbye to this house which welcomed me as a bride, this lovely house so full of all good things, this home that even in my dreams I never shall forget.'

She then turned to the good swineherd Eumaeus and told him to hand over the bow and the iron tools to the Suitors. As he took them from her and set them down, Eumaeus gave way to tears, while from the cowman beyond him there also came a sob when he saw his master's bow. Antinous fell foul of them at once. 'The stupid yokels,' he exclaimed, 'who can't see further than their noses! You miserable pair, what are you standing there for, snivelling and upsetting your mistress, as though the loss of her beloved husband weren't trouble enough? Sit down and eat your food in silence; or else clear out of here and cry outside. You can leave the bow where it is, to settle this matter between us, as it certainly will. For I don't think that pretty weapon will prove easy to string! There's not a man in this whole company as good as Odysseus was. I saw him myself; and I have a good memory, though I was only a child at the time.'

In spite of what he said, Antinous nursed a secret hope that he himself might string the bow and shoot through all the marks, though actually, when it came to shooting, he was to be the first to feel an arrow from the hands of the peerless Odysseus, whom he had just been insulting, and encouraging all his friends to insult, as he sat in the man's own house.

But the young prince Telemachus had a word to say too. 'I'm afraid I must be a born fool!' he laughingly exclaimed. 'My dear mother, wise as she is, says she will leave this house to marry again, and here I am, smiling and chuckling to myself like an idiot. Well, gentlemen all, come forward. Here is your prize – a lady whose like you will not find today in all Achaea, no, not in sacred Pylos, nor in Argos, nor Mycene, nor in Ithaca itself, nor on the dark mainland. But you know this well enough. What need for me to sing my mother's praises? So come along! No false excuses or delays! Make up your minds to face the thing, and let us see you string it. Why, I shouldn't mind trying myself. And if I string the bow and shoot an arrow through the axes, my mother can say goodbye to this house and go off with another man, for all I care, leaving me here, satisfied that at last I am equal to handling my father's formidable toys.'

As he finished, Telemachus leapt from his seat, thrust the purple cloak off his shoulders and removed his sword. He proceeded to dig a single long trench for all the axes; then he planted them in it, checked their alignment and stamped down the earth around them. The men watching him could not help admiring the neat way in which he set them up though he had never seen it done before. Then he took his stance on the threshold and addressed himself to the bow. Three times he made it quiver in his efforts to bend it, but every time he gave the struggle up, though not the hope that he might still succeed in drawing on the string and shooting through the iron marks. And the fourth time he put such pressure on the bow that he might well have strung it yet, if Odysseus had not put an end to his attempts with a shake of the head.

'Ah well,' the young prince sighed, 'I suppose I shall always be a craven and a weakling. Or perhaps I'm too young, not sure enough yet of my own strength to take on anyone who may care to pick a quarrel with me. Well, sirs, it is now up to you, who are stronger men than I, to try the bow and see who comes off best.'

With this he put the bow down on the ground, propping the tip against the polished woodwork of the door with the arrow resting close beside it. Then he resumed his seat. Antinous, in his persuasive way, proposed that they should all take their turn, working from left to right, the way the wine went round. This was agreed, with the result that the first man to get up was Leodes son of Oenops, who used to officiate at their sacrifices and always sat by the great wine-bowl in the far corner. Unlike the rest, he abhorred violence, and their conduct filled him with indignation. Rising now to take the first turn, he picked up the bow and arrow, took his stand on the threshold and addressed himself to the bow. But long before he could string it, the effort of bending it tired out his delicate, unhardened hands.

He turned to the Suitors. 'My friends,' he said, 'I shall never string it; let the next man try. Believe me, this bow will break the heart and be the death of many a champion here. And a good thing too: far better to die than to live on and miss the prize that lures us all here every day and keeps us always hoping. There are some of you at this moment who still think they may have their desire and win Queen Penelope's hand. Let them try the bow and see! They'll soon transfer their love and lay their gifts at the feet of some other Achaean beauty. And so Penelope will be able to marry the man who offers most and is her destined mate.'

Leodes relinquished the bow, propping the tip against the polished woodwork of the door with the arrow leaning close beside it; and so resumed his seat. But Antinous took him to task with asperity: 'Leodes! What a preposterous speech! It's an outrage, which I strongly resent, to suggest that this bow will "break the hearts and be the death of the best men here" – just because you cannot string it yourself. Which is really your mother's fault – you were never born to be a bowman. However, there are others in this noble company who will string it soon enough.' Then he turned to Melanthius the goatherd. 'Look sharp, Melanthius,' he ordered, 'and make a fire in the hall, draw up a big stool with a fleece on it, and bring a large round of tallow from the stores, so that we young men may thaw and grease the bow before we try it and settle the match.'

Melanthius quickly made up the fire, which was still glowing, drew up a stool, on which he spread a rug, and fetched a large round of tallow from the store. The young men greased the bow with hot tallow and did their best. But they failed to string it all the same; in fact they were not nearly strong enough. Antinous, however, and Prince Eurymachus held off for the time being – and they were the leaders of the party and by far the best men it could boast.

Meanwhile the two king's men, the cowman and the swineherd, had joined forces and slipped out of the house. Odysseus himself followed them, and when they had passed through the door and the courtyard, he called out, 'Cowman! And you there, the swineherd!' and then proceeded tactfully to sound them: 'Shall I out with it, or shall I hold my tongue? No, I feel I must speak. If it came to fighting for Odysseus, what line would you men take – supposing he were to blow in from somewhere, suddenly, just like that? Would you be on the Suitors' side or his? Tell me which way your real feelings lie.'

'I wish to god,' the cowman said, 'some power would only bring him home. You'd soon know my mettle and what I can do with my hands.' And Eumaeus chimed in with a prayer to all the gods that their wise master might see his home again.

Odysseus, thus assured of their genuine feelings, took the next step. 'Well, here I am!' he said. 'Yes, I myself, home again in my own country after nineteen years of suffering. I realize that you are the only two of all my men who will be glad to see me back, for I have not heard a single one of the others put up a prayer for my return. So I'm going to tell you two exactly what I am prepared to do for you in the future. If the powers above let me suppress this gang of bullies, I'll get you each a wife, make you a grant, and build you houses near to mine; and from that day I shall regard you both as Telemachus' friends and brothers. I have said I am Odysseus – let me give you proof positive of the fact, so that you may know me for certain and be convinced in your hearts. Look at this scar, where I was struck by a boar's tusk when I went to Parnassus with Autolycus' sons.'

As he spoke, he drew his rags aside and exposed the long scar. The two men looked, and examined it carefully. Then they burst into tears, flung their arms round Odysseus' neck, and kissed him fondly on the head and shoulders. Odysseus, equally moved, kissed their heads and hands; and the tender scene might well have been prolonged till sunset, had Odysseus not decided to bring it to an end. 'Stop crying,' he said, 'or someone coming from the house may notice us and tell the people indoors. Go in now, one after the other, not in company. I shall go first; and you must follow. And here's your cue. The others, I mean that gang of Suitors, will refuse to let me have the bow and quiver.

When that happens, my good Eumaeus, bring the bow down the hall and put it in my hands. Also, tell the women to lock that tight-fitting door which leads to their rooms, and say that if they hear groans or any other noise from the men's part of the house, they are not to stir from their quarters but to stay quietly where they are and get on with their work. The job of bolting and roping the courtyard gate, I give to you, my good Philoetius. Fasten it tight!'

When he had given them these instructions Odysseus went back into the palace and sat down once more on his stool. The two royal servants followed him in.

By now the bow had come into the hands of Eurymachus, who was shifting it about in the firelight to warm it. But he failed to string it for all that, and the man's proud heart rebelled. 'Damnation take the thing!' he cried in his rage. 'I feel this bitterly, not for myself alone but for us all. The miscarriage of our wedding plans I certainly regret, but not so very much – there are plenty of women left in our island here and in the other towns. What does grieve me is the thought that our failure with his bow proves us such weaklings compared with the godlike Odysseus. The disgrace will stick to our names for ever.'

But Antinous, plausible as always, would have none of this. 'Eurymachus,' he said, 'that is quite the wrong view to take; you know it yourself. Today is a public holiday in honour of the Archer god. Is that a time for bending bows? Put the thing down and forget it. And why not leave the axes standing where they are? I'm sure nobody's going to break into the royal palace and steal them. Come, let the wine-steward go round and pour a little in each cup. We'll make our offerings and give archery a rest. And tell the goatherd Melanthius in the morning to bring in the very best goats from all his flocks, so that we can sacrifice to the great Archer, Apollo, and *then* try the bow and see who wins.'

This was very much to their liking. Accordingly their squires came and sprinkled their hands with water, while the lads filled the mixing bowls to the brim with drink, and then, after pour-

ing a little first in each man's cup, they served them all with
wine. When they had made their libations and satisfied their
thirst, the crafty Odysseus came out with a seemingly guileless
suggestion.

'Hear me,' he said, 'you gentlemen that are courting our
famous queen. I feel moved to beg a favour of you all, and in
particular of Eurymachus, and Prince Antinous, who so wisely
proposed that you should let the bow be for the moment and
leave the issue to heaven, confident that tomorrow the Archer
god will make his favourite win. Now what I ask is that you
should let me have the bow, so that you may see me test the
strength of my hands and find out whether there's any power
left in these limbs that were once so supple, or whether a roving
and comfortless life has robbed me of it all by now.'

His request annoyed them beyond measure, for they really
feared that he might string the bow; and Antinous took him up
sharply: 'A pest on you, sir! When will you learn sense? Aren't
you content to dine in peace with your betters, to get your share
of every dish and to listen to our talk, which no other visitor or
tramp is privileged to hear? Your trouble is this mellow wine,
which always does for a man when he gulps it down instead of
drinking in moderation. Remember Eurytion the Centaur! It
was the wine that got at *his* wits, in King Peirithous' house,
when he was visiting the Lapithae. Fuddled with drink, what
must he do but run amuck in the palace? His hosts leapt up in
anger, dragged him to the porch, and threw him out of doors;
but not before they had sliced his ears and nose off with a knife.
Away went the maddened brute, with his woes heavy on his
silly soul; and so the feud started between Centaurs and men.
But he was the first to suffer, and he brought his troubles on himself by getting drunk. And you, sir, I warn you, will come to
grief in much the same way, if you string this bow. You will be
given no quarter in our part of the country, but we'll pack you
off in a black ship to King Echetus, the Ogre; and nothing will
get you out of his clutches! So drink in peace, and don't attempt
to compete with men younger than yourself.'

But here the prudent Penelope intervened: 'Antinous, it is neither good manners nor common decency to show such meanness to people who come to this house as Telemachus' guests. Do you imagine that if this stranger has enough faith in his own strength to bend the great bow of Odysseus he is going to carry me home with him and make me his wife? I don't believe he ever thought of such a thing himself. So do not let that spoil anyone's dinner here. The idea is preposterous!'

Eurymachus now took a part in the argument: 'Our wise Queen Penelope must realize that we are not afraid that this man will win her hand. That is out of the question. What we shrink from is the name that men and women will give us. We don't want the common folk to be saying things like this: "A poor lot, these; not up to the fine gentleman whose wife they want to marry! *They* can't string his bow! But in comes some casual tramp, strings the bow with the greatest ease, and shoots through all the marks!" That is the sort of thing they will say; and our reputation might suffer.'

'Eurymachus,' Penelope retorted, 'no one who cynically supports himself at his prince's expense can possibly stand well with the people. But why take this affair as a reflection on yourselves? Our guest here is a very big and well-built man, who can also claim to be of noble birth. So give him the bow now and let us see what happens. I promise – and these are no idle words – that if by Apollo's favour he succeeds in stringing it I shall fit him out in a fine new coat and tunic, I shall give him a sharp javelin to keep off dogs and men, and a two-edged sword, as well as sandals for his feet, and I shall see him safe wherever he wants to go.'

'About that bow, mother –' Telemachus interposed, 'there is not a man in the whole country who has a better right than I to give it or refuse it as I like. And that applies to every chieftain here in rugged Ithaca or in the isles off Elis where the horses graze. There is not one of them who could override my decision, even if I made up my mind to give this bow to my guest once and for all and let him take it away. So go to your quarters now and attend to your own work, the loom and the spindle, and see that the servants get on with theirs. The bow is the men's concern, and mine above all; for I am master in this house.'

Penelope was taken aback and retired to her own apartments digesting the wisdom of her son's rebuke. Attended by her maids she went upstairs to her bedroom, where she gave way to tears for Odysseus, her beloved husband, till bright-eyed Athene closed her eyes in grateful sleep.

Meanwhile the worthy swineherd had picked up the curved bow and was taking it along, when protests rang out from all the Suitors in the hall. He could hear one of the young bloods yelling at him: 'Where are you taking that bow, wretched swineherd and vagabond? If we could have our way, the very dogs you've bred would tear you to pieces, out there among your pigs where no one goes.'

The torrent of abuse brought Eumaeus to a standstill, and cowed by the angry crowd in the hall he dropped the bow. But now Telemachus' voice came loud and menacing from the other side. 'Forward there with the bow, old fellow! You'll soon find that you can't obey us all. Take care I don't chase you up the fields with a shower of stones. I may be young, but I'm a brawnier man than you. And if only I had the same advantage in muscle over all the hangers-on in the place, I'd soon be throwing them out on their ears from this house of mine where they hatch their ugly plots.'

The Suitors greeted this effusion with roars of merry laughter, which took the edge off their resentment against Telemachus. The swineherd picked up the bow, carried it down the hall to Odysseus and put it in his able hands. He then called the nurse Eurycleia from her quarters and told her what to do. 'Eurycleia,' he said, 'you have a wise head on your shoulders. Telemachus wants you to lock that close-fitting door to the women's rooms. And if they hear groans or any other noise from the men's part of the house, they are not to stir from their quarters, but must stay quietly where they are and get on with their work.'

Too awestruck to argue, Eurycleia went and locked the door leading out of the great hall. At the same time Philoetius slipped quietly out and barred the door leading into the courtyard, which he made fast with a ship's hawser of papyrus that was lying under the colonnade. This done, he went in and sat down on the stool he had left, with his eyes fixed on Odysseus.

Odysseus now had the bow in his hands and was twisting it about, testing it this way and that, for fear that the worms might have eaten into the horn in the long absence of its owner. The Suitors glanced at one another and gave vent to some typical comments: 'Ha! Quite the expert, with a critic's eye for bows! No doubt he collects them at home or wants to start a factory, judging by the way he twists it about, just as though he had learnt something useful in his life on the road!' And this from another of the young gallants: 'Little good may he get from it – as little as his chance of ever stringing the bow!'

Amid all their banter, the cool-headed Odysseus had poised the great bow and given it a final inspection. And now, as easily as a musician who knows his lyre strings the cord on a new peg after looping the twisted sheep-gut at both ends, he strung the great bow without effort or haste and with his right hand proved the string, which gave a lovely sound in answer like a swallow's note. The Suitors were confounded. The colour faded from their cheeks; while to mark the signal moment there came a thunderclap from Zeus, and Odysseus' long-suffering heart leapt up for joy at this sign of favour from the Son of Cronos of the crooked ways.

One arrow lay exposed on the table beside him, the rest, which the Achaean lords were soon to feel, being still inside their hollow quiver. He picked up this shaft, set it against the bridge of the bow, drew back the grooved end and the string together, all without rising from his stool, and aiming straight ahead he shot. Not a single axe did he miss. From the first haft, right through them all and out at the last, the arrow sped with its burden of bronze. Odysseus turned to his son. 'Telemachus,' he said, 'the stranger sitting in your hall has not disgraced you. I scored no miss, nor made hard work of stringing the bow. My powers are unimpaired, and these gentlemen were mistaken when they scornfully rated them so low. But the time has come now to get their supper ready, while it is light, and after that to pass on to the further pleasures of music and dancing, without which no banquet is complete.'

As he finished, Odysseus gave a nod. Whereupon his son and heir, Prince Telemachus, slung on his sharp-edged sword and gripping his spear took his stand by the chair at his father's side, armed with resplendent bronze.

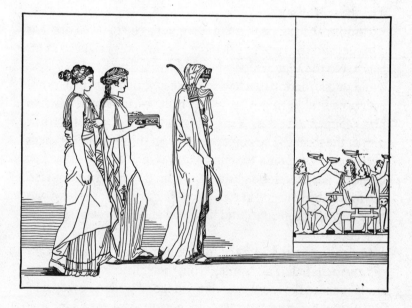

XXII

THE BATTLE IN THE HALL

SHEDDING his rags, the indomitable Odysseus leapt onto the great threshold with his bow and his full quiver, and poured out the winged arrows at his feet.

'That match is played and won!' he shouted to the Suitors. 'Now for another target! No man has hit it yet; but with Apollo's help I'll try.' And with that he levelled a deadly shaft straight at Antinous.

Antinous had just reached for his golden cup to take a draught of wine, and the rich, two-handled beaker was balanced in his hands. No thought of bloodshed had entered his head. For who could guess, there in that festive company, that one man, however powerful he might be, would bring calamity and death to him against such odds? Yet Odysseus shot his bolt and struck him in the throat. The point passed clean through the soft flesh of his neck. Dropping the cup as he was hit, he lurched over to one side. His life-blood gushed from his nostrils in a turbid jet. His foot lashed out and kicked the table from him; the food was scattered on the ground, and his bread and meat were smeared with gore.

When the Suitors saw the man collapse, there was an angry outcry in the hall. They sprang from their chairs and rushed distraught about the room, searching the solid walls on every side. But not a shield or sturdy spear did they see to lay their hands on. They rounded in fury on Odysseus: 'Stranger, men make a dangerous target; you have played your last match. Now you shall surely die. You have killed the greatest nobleman in Ithaca: the vultures of Ithaca shall eat you.'

They laboured each and all under the delusion that he had killed the man by accident. It had not dawned upon the fools that every one of them was marked for slaughter too.

The unconquerable Odysseus looked down on them with a scowl. 'You curs!' he cried. 'You never thought to see me back from Troy. So you ate me out of house and home; you raped my maids; you wooed my wife on the sly though I was alive – with no more fear of the gods in heaven than of the human vengeance that might come. I tell you, one and all, your doom is sealed.'

Fear drained the colour from their cheeks and each man peered round to find some sanctuary from sudden death. Eurymachus alone was able to reply: 'If Odysseus of Ithaca is home and you are the man, then what you say of all the villainous things we have done, here in your house and on your lands, is justified. But the man who was responsible for all lies dead already, Antinous there, the prime mover in these misdeeds, inspired not so much by any wish or need to marry as by a very different aim, in which the powers above have thwarted him. And that was to make himself king of the fair city and land of Ithaca, after setting a trap for your son and putting him to death. But he has got his deserts now and been killed. So spare us, who are your own people. And afterwards we will make amends to you by a public levy for all the food and drink that has been consumed in your house. We will each bring a contribution to the value of twenty oxen, and repay you in bronze and gold, till you relent. Meanwhile, there is every excuse for your anger.'

Odysseus glared at him and said: 'Eurymachus, not if you made over your whole estates to me, with all you stand possessed of or could raise elsewhere, would I keep my hands from killing till you gallants had paid for all your crimes. The choice now lies before you, either to face me and fight, or else to run and see if you can save your skins, though I fancy some of you may fail to get away alive.'

When they heard this, their hearts quaked and their knees shook underneath them. But once again Eurymachus spoke up. 'My friends,' he said, 'there's no quarter coming from those ruthless hands. He has got the strong bow and the quiver and will shoot from the threshold floor till he has killed us all. Let's

make the best of it and fight! Out with your swords; hold up
the tables to keep off his murderous shots, and advance on him
in a body. Who knows but we may oust him from the threshold
and the door, and sally through the town, where there would
quickly be a hue and cry? He'd soon find out that his last bolt
was shot!'

As he spoke, he drew his sharp and two-edged sword of
bronze, and leapt at Odysseus with a terrible shout. But at the
same moment the brave Odysseus let an arrow fly, which struck
him by the nipple on his breast with such force that it pierced his
liver. The sword dropped from his hand. Lurching across the
table, he crumpled up and tumbled with it, hurling the food and
wine-cup to the floor. In agony he dashed his forehead on the
ground; his feet lashed out and overthrew the chair, and the fog
of death descended on his eyes.

Amphinomus was the next to attack the illustrious Odysseus,
making straight at him, sword in hand, to force him somehow
from the door. But before he could close, Telemachus had
smitten him from behind, midway between the shoulders, with
a spear-cast that transfixed his breast. He fell with a crash and
struck the ground full with his forehead. Telemachus leapt aside,
leaving the long spear planted in Amphinomus' body, for he
was much afraid that one of the enemy might dash in and strike
him with a sword as he pulled at the long shaft or stooped above
the corpse. So he ran off quickly to rejoin Odysseus and whispered anxiously in his ear: 'Listen, father, I am going to fetch
you a shield now and a couple of spears and a bronze helmet to
fit round your temples. I shall equip myself too when I come
back, and do the same for the swineherd and the drover. It
would improve our chances to have armour on.'

'Run,' said the imperturbable Odysseus, 'and bring the arms
while I have arrows left for my defence, or they may drive me
from the doorway while I stand alone.'

Telemachus took his father's advice and hurried off to the
store-room where they kept their weapons of war. There he
picked out four shields, eight spears, and four bronze helmets

topped with horsehair plumes, and carrying these made all haste to his father's side, where he at once proceeded to arm himself. The two servants equipped themselves in the same way and took their stand by Odysseus, their wise, resourceful leader.

As long as he had arrows to fight with, Odysseus kept picking off the Suitors one by one in the hall till the dead lay in piles. But the time came when the arrows failed the archer. So he propped his bow between one of the door-posts of the great hall and the burnished side of the porch, hung a shield of fourfold hide on his shoulder, put a strong helmet on his sturdy head, with the horsehair plume nodding defiantly above, and finally picked up two stout bronze-pointed spears.

Let into the solid masonry of the wall there was a raised postern, guarded by closely-fitting doors. Here a way led, past the threshold of the great hall at its upper level, into an outside alley. Odysseus told the swineherd to stand on guard by this postern, to which there was only one approach. But Agelaus too had a word to say about this. 'Friends,' he called to them all, 'can't somebody climb to the postern and tell the people what is going on? We should have help in a trice; and our friend here would soon find he'd shot his last bolt!'

'Impossible, my lord Agelaus,' answered the goatherd Melanthius. 'The big door into the courtyard is terribly near, and the mouth of the alley is an awkward place, where one stout fellow could keep us all back single-handed. But let me fetch you armour to put on from the arsenal. For I have an idea that the arms are in the house and that Odysseus and the prince have not hidden them far afield.'

So Melanthius the goatherd went up by devious ways through the palace to the store-room of Odysseus, where he helped himself to a dozen shields and spears and an equal number of bronze helmets topped with horsehair plumes. He set out with these and had soon handed them over to the Suitors. When Odysseus saw them putting armour on and brandishing great spears in their hands, his knees quaked and his heart failed him. The affair, he felt, was taking a disastrous turn. He swung round to his son and said in dismay: 'Telemachus, I am certain that one of the women here is responsible for this warlike display against us. Or else it's Melanthius' work.'

'Father,' Telemachus wisely confessed, 'the mistake was mine, and no one else is to blame. I left the strong door of the store-room open, and they kept a sharper look out than we did. Quick, my good Eumaeus, go and shut the arsenal door. See too whether it's one of the women who has done the mischief, or Melanthius, Dolius' brat, as I suspect.'

As they were talking, Melanthius the goatherd set out once more to fetch another fine load of armour from the store-room. But the worthy swineherd spied him and at once said to Odysseus, who was close at hand: 'My royal master, the very scoundrel we suspected is off to the armoury again. What are your orders? If I can overpower him, shall I kill him or shall I bring him to you here to pay for all his misdeeds in your house?'

To which Odysseus replied: 'Telemachus and I will keep these lovelorn gentlemen pent up within the four walls of this hall, however hard they fight. You two are to bind Melanthius' hands and feet behind his back and throw him into the armoury, locking the door when you have done. Tie a rope round his body and hoist him up a pillar to the roof, so that he may hang alive in torment for a while.'

Only too ready to obey, they set out at once for the arsenal. Melanthius was already there but did not see them come, as he was hunting round for arms in a corner of the room. The two men stood by the doorposts on either side and waited, till the goatherd came out across the threshold with a fine helmet in one hand and the other burdened with a large and ancient shield spotted with mildew, which had been borne by the lord Laertes as a young soldier, but had lain by for some time with the seams of its straps rotted. The two men pounced upon him, dragged him in by the hair and threw the unhappy wretch on the floor, where they tied his hands and feet together with biting knots, relentlessly forcing the limbs till they met behind him, as their royal master had ordained. Finally they made a rope fast round his body and hauled him aloft up a pillar till he nearly touched the roof. Then Eumaeus the swineherd mocked at his victim.

'A long, long watch for you, Melanthius, lying all night on the downy bed that you deserve. Nor will the young Dawn catch you napping as she comes up in gold from Ocean's Stream, about the time when you drive in the goats for the Suitors' table in the palace.' And there Melanthius was left, racked in the grip of those deadly cords, while the pair resumed their armour, closed the polished door, and returned to Odysseus, their wise and inscrutable master.

It was at this point, when the two parties were breathing defiance at each other, the four on the threshold facing the large and formidable body in the hall, that Zeus' Daughter Athene assumed Mentor's voice and appearance to visit the scene. Odysseus hailed her with joy. 'To the rescue, Mentor!' he cried. 'Remember your old friend and the good turns I've done you in the past. Why, you and I were boys together!'

He had a shrewd idea, when he said this, that he was addressing the warrior goddess, whose arrival, meanwhile, had been greeted on the Suitors' part by a chorus of abuse. Out of this tumult came the menacing voice of Agelaus, son of Damastor. 'Mentor,' he cried, 'don't let Odysseus talk you round and make you fight for him against the Suitors. I'll tell you just how *we* intend to finish this affair. When we put these men to death – and we mean to kill both father and son – you too shall join them and shall die for what you now propose to do in this house. With your own head you shall pay the price. And when our swords have disposed of you and your friends, we shall throw in all you possess, indoors or out, with Odysseus' estate. We shan't let son or daughter of yours live in your house, and your good wife won't dare to show herself in the streets of Ithaca.'

This outburst served only to exasperate Athene, who rounded on Odysseus and rated him sharply: 'Where is your spirit, Odysseus? Where is your prowess gone? You are not the man you were when for nine relentless years you fought the Trojans for the white arms of highborn Helen, killing your man in battle time and time again, and planning the stratagem that captured Priam's spacious town. You are home now among your own possessions. Why then deplore your lack of courage to confront that crew? Come, my old friend, stand by my side and watch a deed of arms, to learn how Mentor son of Alcimus repays past kindness in the thick of battle.'

In spite of this, Athene did not yet throw all her powers in, to give him victory, but continued to put the strength and courage of both Odysseus and his noble son on trial, while she herself withdrew, taking the shape of a swallow and darting aloft to perch on the smoky main beam of the hall.

An attempt to rally the Suitors was now made by six of their number – Agelaus son of Damastor, Eurynomus, Amphimedon, Demoptolemus, Peisander son of Polyctor, and the able Polybus – who stood out as the bravest among those left alive to fight for their existence, many having already succumbed to the arrows that had hailed on them from the bow. Agelaus took command and called out to the survivors: 'Comrades, the invincible Odysseus shows signs of weakening at last! See how Mentor deserted him after his idle boast, and the four of them are left alone in the entrance. Don't cast your long spears all together, but let us six throw first on the off chance of hitting Odysseus and covering ourselves with glory. The others won't count, once he has fallen.'

The six took their cue from him and cast with all their might. But Athene made the whole discharge miscarry. One man hit the doorpost of the great hall, one the solid door, while a third landed his six foot of ash and heavy bronze against the wall. The party on the threshold, unscathed by this volley from the Suitors, now heard the indomitable Odysseus give his orders: 'Friends, it is my turn now to give the word, and ours to shoot. Cast into the thick of that gang, who are adding to their other crimes by this attempt to butcher us.'

They all took careful aim and four sharp lances left their hands, with the result that Odysseus killed Demoptolemus, and

Telemachus, Euryades, while Elatus fell to the swineherd, and Peisander to the man who kept the cows. Four men had bitten the dust together. The Suitors retreated to the far corner of the hall, while Odysseus' party dashed in and withdrew their weapons from the dead.

Once more the Suitors fiercely hurled their spears; but for the most part in vain – Athene saw to that. One hit the doorpost of the great hall, another the solid door, while a third struck the wall with the massive bronze point of his ashen pole. But Amphimedon did succeed in catching Telemachus on the wrist – a glancing blow, the bronze just grazed the skin. And a long lance from Ctesippus, flying over Eumaeus' shield, scratched his shoulder before it passed beyond and fell to the ground. Again Odysseus, cool and collected, discharged a volley with his men into the thick of the enemy. This time Eurydamas fell to the Sacker of Cities, Telemachus killed Amphimedon, the swineherd accounted for Polybus, and finally the cowman struck Ctesippus in the breast and exulted over his foe: 'You foul-mouthed son of a braggart, I'll teach you to control your fatuous tongue and not to talk so big, but to leave judgement to the gods, who are far wiser than you. Take that in return for the cow's hoof you gave King Odysseus when he begged in the hall.' And so the humble drover had his triumph.

Next, Odysseus rushed in and wounded Agelaus with his great spear, while Telemachus struck Euenor's son Leiocritus right in the flank with a lance, driving the point clean through the man, who fell face down and struck the ground full with his forehead. And now, high in the roof above their heads, Athene raised her deadly aegis. The Suitors were scared out of their senses. They scattered through the hall like a herd of cattle whom the dancing gadfly has attacked and stampeded, in the spring-time when the long days come in. But the others swooped down on them, as vultures from the hills, with curving claws and crooked beak, swoop down upon the smaller birds, who though they shun the upper air and scour the ground find no help there and no escape, for the vultures pounce on them

and kill, while people looking on applaud the sport. So did
Odysseus' party chase the Suitors pell-mell through the hall and
hack them down. Skulls cracked, the hideous groans of dying
men were heard, and the whole floor ran with blood.

Leodes rushed forward, clasped Odysseus' knees and burst
into an anguished appeal: 'I throw myself on your mercy,
Odysseus. Have some regard and pity for me. I swear to you
that never, by word or deed, have I done wrong to a woman in
the house. In fact I did my best to hold them all back from such
evil courses. But they wouldn't listen when I told them to keep
their hands from mischief, and their own iniquities have
brought them to this awful pass. But I was only their priest; I
did nothing. And now I am to share their fate! That is all the
thanks one gets for the goodness one has shown.'

Odysseus looked at him with disgust. 'You say you were their
priest,' he answered. 'How often, then, you must have prayed in
this hall that the happy day of my return might be put off, and
that my dear wife might be yours and bear your children. For
that, nothing shall save you from the bitterness of death.' And he
laid his great hand on a sword dropped on the ground by Agelaus as he died, and with it struck Leodes full in the neck, so
that his head met the dust before he ceased to speak.

The minstrel Phemius, Terpius' son, who served as their unwilling bard, had so far managed to escape destruction. He stood
now close to the postern door. His lyre lay silent in his hands,
and he was debating in his mind whether to slip out of the hall
and seat himself at the great altar in the court, scene of so many
burnt-offerings from Laertes and Odysseus to their Household
Zeus, or to come forward and plead for mercy at Odysseus' feet.
He weighed the two courses and decided to make a direct appeal
for mercy to the King. So he laid the hollow instrument on the
ground half-way between the mixing-bowl and the silver-
studded chair, and then ran up to Odysseus, flung his arms round
his knees and poured out his plea: 'I throw myself on your
mercy, Odysseus. Respect and pity me. You will repent it later
if you kill a minstrel like me, who sing for gods and men. I had

no teacher but myself. All kinds of song spring unpremeditated to my lips; and I feel that I could sing for you as I could sing for a god. Think twice, therefore, before you cut my throat. Besides, your own son Telemachus could tell you that I never came to your house of my own free will or for pay to sing at the Suitors' banquets, but only because brute force and numbers dragged me there.'

Prince Telemachus was near enough to Odysseus to overhear this appeal and quickly called out to his father: 'Stop! The man is innocent. Don't put him to the sword. And Medon the herald, who always looked after me at home when I was a boy, is another we must spare, unless indeed he has already been killed by Philoetius or the swineherd, or met you as you stormed through the hall.'

His words reached the herald's ears. For Medon, wise in his generation, had wrapped himself up in the fresh hide of an ox and lay cowering under a high chair, where he had retired to escape destruction. He promptly emerged from this refuge and throwing off the hide made a dash for Telemachus, whom he clasped by the knees and implored for mercy: 'My dear lad, here I am. Spare me, and speak for me to your father. Don't let him kill me with that cruel sword, irresistible as he is and maddened by this gang who ate him out of house and home and hadn't even the sense to treat you with respect.'

Odysseus in his wisdom smiled at the man and said: 'Dismiss your fears. My son has saved you from the jaws of death to teach you the lesson, which I hope you'll take to heart and preach, that virtue is a better policy than vice. Now quit the hall, you and the songful music-maker. Into the court with you out of this carnage, and sit there till I've done the work I have to do indoors.'

The two made off at once out of the hall into the open air and seated themselves at the altar of Zeus, peering about on every side and still expecting sudden death. Odysseus also took a good look round his house to see whether any survivors were hiding to escape their fate. But he found the whole company dead.

They lay in heaps in the blood and dust, like fish that the fishermen have dragged out of the grey surf in the meshes of their net onto a bend of the beach, to lie in masses on the sand gasping for the salt sea water till the bright sun ends their lives. Thus, like a catch of fish, the Suitors lay there heaped upon each other.

'Telemachus,' said Odysseus to his son, 'will you send the nurse Eurycleia to me here? There is something I wish to tell her.'

Telemachus obediently went off, shook the door of the women's quarters and called out to Eurycleia, the old dame, telling her to come at once as his father wished to speak to her, and reminding her of her position as matron of the women-servants in the palace.

His summons left Eurycleia speechless, but she opened the door of the apartments, came out and hurried along in Telemachus' wake. She found Odysseus among the corpses of the fallen, spattered with blood and filth, like a lion when he comes from feeding on some farmer's bullock, with the blood dripping from his breast and jaws on either side, a fearsome spectacle. That was how Odysseus looked, with the gore thick on his legs and arms. But when Eurycleia saw the dead men and that sea of blood her instinct was to raise a yell of triumph at the mighty achievement that confronted her. Odysseus, however, checked her exuberance with a sharp rebuke: 'Restrain yourself, old dame, and gloat in silence. I'll have no jubilation here. It is an impious thing to exult over the slain. These men fell victims to the hand of heaven and their own infamy. They paid respect to no one who came near them – good men and bad were all alike to them. And now their own insensate wickedness has brought them to this awful end. But what of the women-servants in the house? Tell me which have been disloyal to me and which are honest.'

'My child,' his fond old nurse replied, 'I'll tell you exactly. Your have fifty women serving in your palace, whom we have trained in household work and to card wool and make the best of slavery. Of these there are twelve all told who have taken to vicious ways and snap their fingers at me and Penelope herself. Telemachus has only just grown up and his mother wouldn't allow him to order the maids about. But let me go upstairs now to my lady's apartments and give her the news. As luck would have it she has fallen asleep.'

'Don't wake her yet,' said the wise Odysseus. 'But tell the women who have disgraced themselves to come here.'

The old dame left the hall to inform the women that they must report themselves, while Odysseus called Telemachus and the two herdsmen to his side and gave them his immediate orders: 'Start carrying out the dead and make the women help you. Then clean the tables and our best chairs here with sponges soaked in water. When the whole place is tidied up, take the women out of the hall between the round-house and the great wall of the courtyard, and use your long swords on them, till none are left alive to remember their loves and the hours they stole in these young gallants' arms.

Wailing bitterly, with the tears streaming down their cheeks, the women all arrived together. Their first task was to remove the bodies of the slain, which they laid under the portico of the walled courtyard, propping them one against the other. Odysseus himself took charge and hounded them on till they had finished their unwilling work.

Next they washed down the tables and the beautiful chairs with sponges and water, after which Telemachus and the two herdsmen scraped the floor of the great hall with spades, while the maids removed the scrapings and got rid of them outside. Finally, when the whole house had been set in order, they took the women out of the building, and herded them between the round-house and the great courtyard wall in a narrow space from which there was no escape. Then Telemachus spoke.

'I swear I will not give a decent death,' he said, 'to women who have heaped dishonour on my head and on my mother's, and slept with members of this gang.'

With that he took a hawser which had seen service on a blue-bowed ship, made one end fast to a high column in the portico, threw the other over the round-house, and pulled it taut at such a level as would keep their feet from touching earth. And then, like doves or long-winged thrushes caught in a net across the thicket where they come to roost, and meeting death where they had only looked for sleep, the women held their heads out in a row, and a noose was cast round each one's neck to dispatch them in the most miserable way. For a little while their feet kicked out, but not for very long.

Next Melanthius was dragged out across the court and through the gate. There with a sharp knife they sliced his nose and ears off; they ripped away his privy parts as raw meat for the dogs, and in their fury they lopped off his hands and feet. Then, after washing their own hands and feet, they went back indoors to Odysseus and the business was finished.

Odysseus turned now to his fond old nurse. 'Eurycleia,' he said, 'bring me some disinfectant sulphur, and make me a fire so that I can fumigate the house. Also, ask Penelope to come here with her ladies-in-waiting and tell all the maids to come through into the hall.'

'My child,' said the doting old dame, 'all that is right and proper. But let me bring you a cloak and tunic to put on, and don't stand about like that in the house with your broad shoulders wrapped in rags, or people will be shocked.'

But Odysseus knew his own mind. 'The first thing I want,' he retorted, 'is a fire in this hall.'

Eurycleia did not disobey him. She made him a fire and brought the sulphur, with which Odysseus thoroughly fumigated the hall, the house, and the courtyard outside.

Meanwhile the old lady went off through the royal palace to give the other women the news and tell them to come. They flocked out of their quarters, torch in hand, and welcomed Odysseus by flinging their arms round his neck, showering affectionate kisses on his head and shoulders, and seizing both his hands. As for him, overwhelmed by tender feelings he broke down and sobbed. There was not one he failed to recognize.

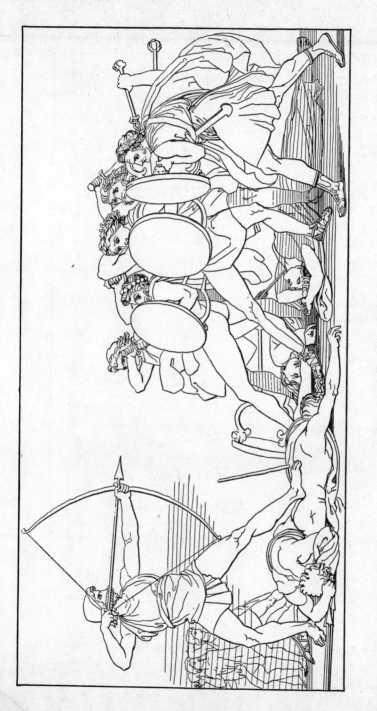

Odysseus killing the suitors.

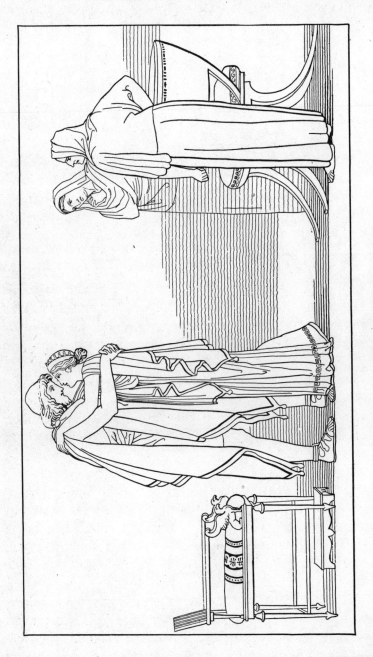

The meeting of Odysseus and Penelope.

XXIII

ODYSSEUS AND PENELOPE

CHUCKLING as she went, the old woman bustled upstairs to tell her mistress that her beloved husband was in the house. Her legs could hardly carry her fast enough, and her feet twinkled in their haste. As she reached the head of the bedstead, she cried: 'Wake up, Penelope, dear child, and see a sight you've longed for all these many days. Odysseus has come home, and high time too! And he's killed the rogues who turned his whole house inside out, ate up his wealth, and bullied his son.'

Penelope was not caught off her guard. 'My dear nurse,' she said, 'the gods have made you daft. It's as easy for them to rob the wisest of their wits as to make stupid people wise. And now they've addled *your* brains, which used to be so sound. How dare you make sport of my distress by waking me when I had closed my eyes for a comfortable nap, only to tell me this nonsense? Never have I slept so soundly since Odysseus sailed away to that accursed place I cannot bring myself to mention. Off with you now downstairs and back into your quarters! If any of the other maids had come and awakened me to listen to such stuff, I'd soon have packed her off to her own place with a box on the ears. You can thank your age for saving you from that.'

But this did not silence the old nurse. 'I am not making fun of you, dear child,' she said. 'Odysseus really has come home, just as I told you. He's the stranger whom they all scoffed at in the hall. Telemachus has known for some time that he was back, but had the sense to keep his father's plans a secret till he'd made those upstarts pay for their villainy.'

Penelope's heart leapt up. She sprang from the bed and clung to the old woman, with the tears streaming from her eyes and the eager words from her lips. 'Dear nurse,' she cried, 'I beg you for the truth! If he is really home, as you say, how on earth did he manage single-handed against that rascally crew who always hang about the house in a pack?'

'I never saw a thing,' said Eurycleia. 'I knew nothing about it. All I heard was the groans of dying men. We sat petrified in a corner of our quarters, with the doors shut tightly on us, till your son Telemachus shouted to me to come out. His father had sent him to fetch me. And then I found Odysseus standing among the bodies of the dead. They lay round him in heaps all over the hard floor. It would have done you good to see him, spattered with blood and filth like a lion. By now all the corpses have been gathered together at the courtyard gate, while he has had a big fire made and is fumigating the palace. He sent me to call you to him. So come with me now, so that you two may enter into your happiness together after all the sorrows you have had. The hope you cherished so long is fulfilled for you today. Odysseus has come back to his own hearth alive; he has found both you and his son in the home, and he has had his revenge in his own palace on every one of the Suitors who were doing him such wrong.'

'Don't laugh too soon, dear nurse; don't boast about them yet,' said Penelope in her prudence. 'You know how everyone at home would welcome the sight of him, and nobody more than myself and the son we brought into the world. But this tale of yours does not ring true. It must be one of the immortal gods that has killed the young lords, provoked, no doubt, by their galling insolence and wicked ways. For they respected nobody they met – good men and bad were all the same to them. And now their iniquities have brought them to this pass. Meanwhile Odysseus in some distant land has lost his chance of ever getting home, and with it lost his life.'

'My child,' her old nurse exclaimed, 'how can you say such things! Here is your husband at his own fireside, and you declare he never will get home. What little faith you have always had! But let me tell you something else – a fact that proves the truth. You know the scar he had where he was wounded long ago by the white tusk of a boar? I saw that very scar when I was washing him, and would have told you of it, if Odysseus, for his own crafty purposes, hadn't seized me by the throat and prevented me. Come with me now. I'll stake my life upon it. If I've played you false, then kill me in the cruellest way you can.'

'Dear nurse,' Penelope replied, 'you are a very wise old woman, but even you cannot probe into the minds of the everlasting gods. However, let us go to my son, so that I can see my suitors dead, together with the man who killed them.'

As she spoke she left her room and made her way downstairs, a prey to indecision. Should she remain aloof as she questioned her husband, or go straight up to him and kiss his head and hands? What she actually did, when she had crossed the stone threshold into the hall, was to take a chair in the firelight by the wall, on the opposite side to Odysseus, who was sitting by one of the great columns with his eyes on the ground, waiting to see whether his good wife would say anything to him when she saw him. For a long while Penelope, overwhelmed by wonder, sat there without a word. But her eyes were busy, at one moment resting full on his face, and at the next falling on the ragged clothes that made him seem a stranger once again. It was Telemachus who broke the silence, but only to rebuke her.

'Mother,' he said, 'you strange, hard-hearted mother of mine, why do you keep so far from my father? Why aren't you sitting at his side, talking and asking questions all the while? No other woman would have had the perversity to hold out like this against a husband she had just got back after nineteen years of misadventure. But then your heart was always harder than flint.'

'My child, the shock has numbed it,' she admitted. 'I cannot find a word to say to him; I cannot ask him anything at all; I cannot even look him in the face. But if it really is Odysseus home again, we two shall surely recognize each other, and in an even better way; for there are tokens between us which only we two know and no one else has heard of.'

Patient Odysseus smiled, then turning briskly to his son he said: 'Telemachus, leave your mother to put me to the proof here in our home. She will soon come to a better mind. At the moment, because I'm dirty and in rags, she gives me the cold shoulder and won't admit that I'm Odysseus. But you and I must consider what is best to be done. When a man has killed a fellow-citizen, just one, with hardly any friends to carry on the feud, he is outlawed, he leaves his kith and kin and flies the country. But we have killed the pick of the Ithacan nobility, the mainstay of our state. There is a problem for you.'

'One you must grapple with yourself, dear father,' Telemachus shrewdly rejoined. 'For at getting out of a difficulty you are held to be the best man in the world, with no one else to touch you. We will follow your lead with alacrity, and I may say with no lack of courage either, so far as in us lies.'

Odysseus was not at a loss. 'As I see it, then,' he said, 'our best plan will be this. Wash yourselves first, put on your tunics, and tell the maids in the house to get dressed. Then let our excellent minstrel strike up a merry dance-tune for us, loud as his lyre can play, so that if the music is heard outside by anyone passing in the road or by one of our neighbours, they may imagine there is a wedding-feast. That will prevent the news of the Suitors' death from spreading through the town before we can beat a retreat to our farm among the orchards. Once there, we shall see. Providence may play into our hands.'

They promptly put his idea into practice. The men washed and donned their tunics, while the women decked themselves out. The admirable bard took up his hollow lyre and had them soon intent on nothing but the melodies of song and the niceties of the dance. They made the great hall echo round them to the feet of dancing men and women richly clad. 'Ah!' said the passers-by as the sounds reached their ears. 'Somebody has married our much-courted queen. The heartless creature! Too fickle to keep patient watch over the great house till her lawful husband should come back!' Which shows how little they knew what had really happened.

Meanwhile the great Odysseus, in his own home again, had himself bathed and rubbed with oil by the housekeeper Eurynome, and was fitted out by her in a beautiful cloak and tunic.

Athene also played her part by enhancing his comeliness from head to foot. She made him look taller and sturdier than ever; she caused the bushy locks to hang from his head thick as the petals of the hyacinth in bloom; and just as a craftsman trained by Hephaestus and herself in the secrets of his art takes pains to put a graceful finish to his work by overlaying silver-ware with gold, she finished now by endowing his head and shoulders with an added beauty. He came out from the bath looking like one of the everlasting gods, then went and sat down once more in the chair opposite his wife.

'What a strange creature!' he exclaimed. 'Heaven made you as you are, but for sheer obstinacy you put all the rest of your sex in the shade. No other wife could have steeled herself to keep so long out of the arms of a husband she had just got back after nineteen years of misadventure. Well, nurse, make a bed for me to sleep alone in. For my wife's heart is just about as hard as iron.'

'You too are strange,' said the cautious Penelope. 'I am not being haughty or indifferent. I am not even unduly surprised. But I have too clear a picture of you in my mind as you were when you sailed from Ithaca in your long-oared ship. Come, Eurycleia, make him a comfortable bed outside the bedroom that he built so well himself. Place the big bed out there, and make it up with rugs and blankets, and with laundered sheets.'

This was her way of putting her husband to the test. But Odysseus flared up at once and rounded on his loyal wife. 'Penelope,' he cried, 'you exasperate me! Who, if you please, has moved my bed elsewhere? Short of a miracle, it would be hard even for a skilled workman to shift it somewhere else, and the strongest young fellow alive would have a job to budge it. For a great secret went into the making of that complicated bed; and it was my work and mine alone. Inside the court there was a long-leaved olive-tree, which had grown to full height with a stem as thick as a pillar. Round this I built my room of close-set stone-work, and when that was finished, I roofed it over thoroughly, and put in a solid, neatly fitted, double door. Next I lopped all the twigs off the olive, trimmed the stem from the root up, rounded it smoothly and carefully with my adze and trued it to the line, to make my bedpost. This I drilled through where necessary, and used as a basis for the bed itself, which I worked away at till that too was done, when I finished it off with an inlay of gold, silver, and ivory, and fixed a set of purple straps across the frame.

'There is our secret, and I have shown you that I know it. What I don't know, madam, is whether my bedstead stands where it did, or whether someone has cut the tree-trunk through and shifted it elsewhere.'

Her knees began to tremble as she realized the complete fidelity of his description. All at once her heart melted. Bursting into tears she ran up to Odysseus, threw her arms round his neck and kissed his head. 'Odysseus,' she cried, 'do not be cross with me, you who were always the most reasonable of men. All our unhappiness is due to the gods, who couldn't bear to see us share the joys of youth and reach the threshold of old age together. But don't be angry with me now, or hurt because the moment when I saw you first I did not kiss you as I kiss you now. For I had always had the cold fear in my heart that somebody might come here and bewitch me with his talk. There are plenty of rogues who would seize such a chance; and though Argive Helen would never have slept in her foreign lover's arms had she known that her countrymen would go to war to fetch her back to Argos, even she, the daughter of Zeus, was tempted by the goddess and fell, though the idea of such madness had never entered her head till that moment, which was so fateful for the world and proved the starting-point of all our sorrows too. But now all's well. You have faithfully described our token, the secret of our bed, which no one ever saw but you and I and one maid, Actoris, who was my father's gift when first I came to you, and sat as sentry at our bedroom door. You have convinced your unbelieving wife.'

Penelope's surrender melted Odysseus' heart, and he wept as he held his dear wife in his arms, so loyal and so true. Sweet moment too for her, sweet as the sight of land to sailors struggling in the sea, when the Sea-god by dint of wind and wave has wrecked their gallant ship. What happiness for the few swimmers that have fought their way through the white surf to the shore, when, caked with brine but safe and sound, they tread on solid earth! If that is bliss, what bliss it was for her to see her husband once again! She kept her white arms round his neck and never quite let go. Dawn with her roses would have caught them at their tears, had not Athene of the flashing eyes bestirred herself on their behalf. She held the long night lingering in the West, and in the East at Ocean's Stream she kept Dawn waiting by her golden throne, and would not let her yoke the nimble steeds who bring us light, Lampus and Phaethon, the colts that draw the chariot of Day.

But there was one thing which Odysseus had the wisdom soon to tell his wife. 'My dear,' he said, 'we have not yet come to the end of our trials. There lies before me still a great and hazardous adventure, which I must see through to the very end however far that end may be. That was what Teiresias' soul predicted for me when I went down to the House of Hades to find a way home for my followers and myself. So come to bed now, my dear wife, and let us comfort ourselves while we can with a sweet sleep in each other's arms.'

Prudent Penelope answered: 'Your bed shall be ready the moment you wish to use it, now that the gods have brought you back to your own country and your lovely home. But since it did occur to you to speak of this new ordeal, please tell me all about it; for I shall certainly find out later, and it could be no worse to hear at once.'

'Why drag it out of me?' he asked reproachfully. 'Well, you shall hear the whole tale. I'll make no secret of it. Not that you'll find it to your liking! I am not pleased myself. For he told me to take a well-cut oar and wander on from city to city, till I came to a people who know nothing of the sea, and never use salt with their food, so that our crimson-painted ships and the long oars that serve those ships as wings are quite beyond their ken. Of this, he said that I should find conclusive proof, as you shall hear, when I met some other traveller who spoke of the "winnowing-fan" I was carrying on my shoulder. Then, he said, the time would have come for me to plant my oar in the earth and offer the Lord Poseidon the rich sacrifice of a ram, a bull, and a breeding boar. After that I was to go back home and make ceremonial sacrifices to the everlasting gods who live in the far-flung heavens, to all of them, this time, in due precedence. As for my end, he said that Death would come to me in his gentlest form out of the sea, and that when he took me I should be worn out after an easy old age and surrounded by a prosperous folk. He swore that I should find all this come true.'

'Well then,' Penelope sagely replied, 'if Providence plans to make you happier in old age, you can always be confident of escaping from your troubles.'

While they were talking, Eurynome and the nurse, by the light of torches, were putting soft bedclothes for them on their bed. When the work was done and the bed lay comfortably spread, the old woman went back into her own quarters for the night, and the housekeeper Eurynome, with a torch in her hands, lit them on their way to bed, taking her leave when she had brought them to their room. And glad indeed they were to lie once more together in the bed that had known them long ago. Meanwhile Telemachus, the cowman, and the swineherd brought their dancing feet to rest, made the women finish too, and lay down for the night in the darkened hall.

But Odysseus and Penelope, after their love had taken its sweet course, turned to the fresh delights of talk, and interchanged their news. He heard this noble wife tell of all she had put up with in his home, watching that gang of wreckers at their work, of all the cattle and fat sheep that they had slaughtered for her sake, of all the vessels they had emptied of their wine. And in his turn, royal Odysseus told her of all the discomfiture he had inflicted on his foes and all the miseries which he himself had undergone. She listened spellbound, and her eyelids never closed in sleep till the whole tale was finished.

He began with his first victory over the Cicones and his visit to the fertile land where the Lotus-eaters live. He spoke of what the Cyclops did, and the price he had made him pay for the gallant men he ruthlessly devoured. He told her of his stay with Aeolus, so friendly when he came and helpful when he left; and how the gale, since Providence would not let him reach his home so soon, had caught him up once more and driven him in misery down the highways of the fish. Next came his call at Telepylus on the Laestrygonian coast, where the savages destroyed his fleet and all his fighting men, the black ship that carried him being the only one to get away. He spoke of Circe and her magic arts; of how he sailed across the seas to the mouldering Halls of Hades to consult the soul of Theban Teiresias, and saw all his former comrades and the mother who had borne him and nursed him as a child. He told her how he had listened to the rich music of the Sirens' song; how he had sailed by the Wandering Rocks, by dread Charybdis, and by Scylla, whom no sailors pass unscathed; how his men had killed the cattle of the Sun; how Zeus the Thunderer had struck his good ship with a flaming bolt, and all his loyal band had been killed at one fell swoop, though he escaped their dreadful fate himself. He described his arrival at the Isle of Ogygia and his reception by the Nymph Calypso, who had so much desired to marry him that she kept him in her cavern home, a pampered guest, tempted by promises of immortality and ageless youth, but inwardly rebellious to the end. Finally he came to his disastrous voyage to Scherie, where the kind-hearted Phaeacians had treated him like a god and sent him home by ship with generous gifts of bronze ware and of gold, and woven stuffs. He had just finished this last tale, when sleep came suddenly upon him, relaxing all his limbs as it resolved his cares.

Once more Athene of the flashing eyes took thought on his behalf. Not till she was satisfied that he had had his fill of love and sleep in his wife's arms, did she arouse the lazy Dawn to leave her golden throne by Ocean Stream and to bring daylight to the world. At last Odysseus rose from that soft bed of his and told Penelope his plans. 'Dear wife,' he said, 'the pair of us have had our share of trials, you here in tears because misfortune dogged each step I took to reach you, and I yearning to get back to Ithaca but kept in cheerless exile by Zeus and all the gods there are. Nevertheless we have had what we desired, a night spent in each other's arms. So now I leave the house and my belongings in your care. As for the ravages that gang of profligates have made among my flocks, I shall repair the greater part by raiding on my own, and the people must contribute too, till they have filled up all my folds again. But at the moment I am going to our orchard farm, to see my good father, who has been so miserable on my account. And this, my dear, is what I wish you to do, though you are too wise to need my instructions. Since it will be common knowledge, as soon as the sun is up, that I have killed the Suitors in the palace, go with your ladies-in-waiting to your room upstairs and stay quietly there, see nobody, and ask no questions.'

Odysseus donned his splendid body-armour, woke up Tele-machus, the cowman, and the swineherd, and told them all to arm themselves with weapons. They carried out his orders and were soon equipped in bronze. Then they opened the doors and sallied out with Odysseus at their head. It was broad daylight already, but Athene hid them in darkness and soon had them clear of the town.

XXIV

THE FEUD IS ENDED

MEANWHILE Cyllenian Hermes was gathering in the souls of the Suitors, armed with the splendid golden wand that he can use at will to cast a spell on our eyes or wake us from the soundest sleep. He roused them up and marshalled them with this, and they obeyed his summons gibbering like bats that squeak and flutter in the depths of some mysterious cave when one of them has fallen from the rocky roof, losing his hold on his clustered friends. With such shrill discord the company set out in Hermes' charge, following the Deliverer down the dark paths of decay. Past Ocean Stream, past the White Rock, past the Gates of the Sun and the region of dreams they went, and before long they reached the meadow of asphodel, which is the dwelling-place of souls, the disembodied wraiths of men.

Here they encountered the souls of Peleus' son Achilles, of Patroclus, of the noble Antilochus, and of Aias, who in stature and in manly grace was second to none of the Danaans but the peerless son of Peleus. These had forgathered with Achilles' soul, and now they were joined by that of Agamemnon, Atreus' son, who came to them still plunged in grief and still surrounded by the souls of all that met their doom and died with him in Aegisthus' house. Achilles' soul spoke first. 'Agamemnon,' he said to him, 'we used to think of you, among all our princes, as the lifelong favourite of Zeus the Thunderer, because of the great and gallant army you commanded in Troyland when we Achaeans fought those hard campaigns. But you too were to be visited in your prime by that fell power whom no man born can evade. How I wish you could have met your fate and died at Troy in the full enjoyment of your royal state. For then the whole nation would have joined in building you a mound and you would have left a great name for your son to inherit. But as things were, you were doomed to die a most appalling death.'

'Illustrious Prince Achilles,' the soul of Atreus' son replied, 'yours was the happy death, in Troyland far away from Argos, with the flower of the Trojan and Achaean forces falling round you in the battle for your corpse. There in a whirl of dust you lay, great even in your fall, thinking no longer of a charioteer's delights. And the whole day long we fought. Indeed we never would have ceased had Zeus not stopped us with a storm. Then we carried you off from the battlefield to the ships, cleaned your fair flesh with warm water and unguents, and laid you on a bed. Your countrymen gathered round you; hot tears were shed, and many locks of hair were cut. Your mother, when she heard the news, came up from the sea with the deathless Sea-Nymphs, and a mysterious wailing rose from the waters. The whole army was seized by panic and would have fled on board the ships, if one man, Nestor, had not used his knowledge of our ancient lore. And it was not the first time that his wisdom triumphed. He came forward and checked them in his friendly way. "Halt, Argives!" he shouted. "Achaeans, stand your ground! This is Achilles' mother who has come out of the sea with her immortal Nymphs to see her dead son's face." He stopped the panic, and the troops plucked up their hearts. They saw the Daughters of the Old Sea-god, dressed in the robes of immortality and shedding bitter tears, take up their stand around your corpse. The Nine Muses too were there, chanting your dirge in sweet antiphony, till not a dry eye was to be seen in all the Argive force, so poignant was the Muses' song.

'For seventeen days and seventeen nights we mourned for you, immortal gods and mortal men alike; and on the eighteenth day we committed you to the flames, with a rich sacrifice of fatted sheep and shambling cattle at your pyre. You were burnt in the clothing of the gods, in lavish unguents and sweet honey; and an armed company of Achaean nobles, on foot or in their chariots, moved in procession round the pyre where you were burning and filled the air with sound. When the sacred flames had consumed you, we gathered your white bones at dawn, Achilles, and laid them by in unmixed wine and oil. Then your mother gave us a golden urn, a gift, she said, from Dionysus, made by the great Hephaestus. In this your white bones lie, my lord Achilles, and mingled with them the bones of Menoetius' son Patroclus, dead before you, and separately those of Antilochus, who was your closest friend after Patroclus' death. Over them all, we soldiers of the mighty Argive force built up a great and glorious mound, on a foreland jutting out over the broad waters of the Hellespont, so that it might be seen far out at sea by the sailors of today and future ages. Then, in the middle of the lists where the Achaean champions were to test their skill, your mother placed the magnificent prizes she had asked the gods to give. You must often have attended royal funerals yourself, when the young men strip and make ready for the games by which they honour their dead king, but the splendid prizes offered in *your* honour by the divine Thetis of the Silver Feet would have struck you as the most wonderful you had ever seen. For the gods loved you very dearly. Thus even death, Achilles, did not destroy your glory and the whole world will honour you for ever. But what satisfaction is there now for me in having brought the war to a successful close? For on my very journey home Zeus planned a miserable end for me, at the hands of Aegisthus and my unconscionable wife.'

Their talk was interrupted now by the near approach of Hermes the Giant-slayer, ushering into the world below the ghosts of the Suitors whom Odysseus had killed. Astonished at the sight of all these newcomers, the pair moved quickly up, and the soul of Agamemnon was able to recognize the noble Amphimedon, Melaneus' son, who had entertained him in his home in Ithaca. Agamemnon's soul did not wait for him to speak, but greeted him at once. 'Amphimedon,' he said, 'what catastrophe has brought you down into the bowels of the earth with this chosen band of men of your own age, as carefully picked as though one had gone round and taken the very flower of some city's best? Did Poseidon catch your ships in a gale and overwhelm you in the heavy seas? Or did you fall to some hostile tribe on land as you were lifting their cattle and their flocks, or fighting with them for their town and women? Pray tell me, for you and I have been host and guest. Or have you forgotten the time when I came over to your house in Ithaca with King Menelaus to persuade Odysseus to join forces with me in the naval expedition against Ilium? It was a full month after that before we had made the long sea passage, so hard did we find it to win over the man who now is styled the Sacker of Cities.'

'August and imperial Agamemnon,' the soul of Amphimedon replied, 'I well remember all that your majesty has referred to, and will give you a full and honest account of the events that culminated in our tragic death.

'In the prolonged absence of Odysseus we began to pay our addresses to his wife. These proved distasteful to her, but instead of refusing us outright or taking the final step, she schemed to bring about our downfall and our death. Here is a sample of the woman's guile. On her loom at home she set up a great web and began weaving a large and delicate piece of work. And she said to us: "I should be grateful to you young lords who are courting me now that King Odysseus is dead, if you could restrain your ardour for my hand till I have done this work, so that the threads I have spun may not be utterly wasted. It is a winding-sheet for Lord Laertes. When he succumbs to the dread hand of Death, which stretches all men out at last, I must not risk the scandal there would be among my countrywomen here, if one who had amassed such wealth were put to rest without a shroud." That is how she talked, and we, like gentlemen, let her persuade us, with the result that by day she wove at the great web, but every night had torches set beside it and undid the work. For three years she fooled us with this trick. A fourth began, and the seasons were already slipping by, when one of her women, who knew all about it, gave her mistress away. We caught her unravelling her beautiful work, and she was forced reluctantly to complete it. But no sooner had she woven the great web, laundered the robe and shown it to us gleaming like the sun or moon,

than the powers of evil landed Odysseus out of the blue in a
distant corner of his estate where the swineherd had his cabin.
His son, Prince Telemachus, just back from sandy Pylos in his
ship, made for the same spot too. They put their heads together,
planned our assassination, and made their way to the city of
Ithaca, or rather, Telemachus served as vanguard and Odysseus
followed later. The swineherd brought him down disguised in
rags, and looking like a wretched old beggar as he hobbled
along with his staff. He was so disreputably dressed that not a
man in our party, not even the older members, could realize
that this was Odysseus when he suddenly appeared among us.
In fact we gave him the rough side of our tongues and threw
things at his head. For a while he had the self-control to put up
patiently with this man-handling and abuse in his own palace.
But presently the spirit stirred within him. With Telemachus'
help he removed the excellent weapons they possessed and
stowed them in the arsenal behind locked doors. Then, for his
own cunning purposes, he prevailed on his wife to challenge our
skill with a bow and some grey iron axes, toys that were to play
a leading part in the slaughter of my unhappy company. Not
one of us could string the mighty weapon; indeed we were too
weak by far. But when it came to handing the great bow to
Odysseus, we all protested loudly that he shouldn't have it,
however much he argued. Telemachus was the only one who encouraged him to take it. And so that great and reckless man got
his hands on the bow, which he strung without effort, and shot
through the iron marks. Then he leapt onto the threshold and
with murder in his eye poured out his arrows, and shot Prince
Antinous down; after which, aiming straight in every case, he
let fly at the rest of us with his deadly shafts. We fell thick and
fast; and it was obvious that some god was on their side. For
presently their fury gave them confidence to charge through
the hall and they hacked us down right and left. Skulls cracked,
the hideous groans of dying men were heard, and the whole
floor ran with blood.

'That, Agamemnon, is how we were destroyed. And our

corpses still lie uncared for in Odysseus' house, since the news has not yet reached our several homes and brought our friends to wash the dark blood from our wounds, to lay our bodies out and mourn for us, as is a dead man's right.'

'Unconquerable Odysseus!' the soul of Agamemnon cried. 'Ah, happy prince, blessed in Icarius' daughter with a wife in whom all virtues meet, flawless Penelope, who has proved herself so good and wise, so faithful to her wedded love! Her glory will not fade with the years, but the deathless gods themselves will make a song for mortal ears, to grace Penelope the constant queen. What a contrast with Clytaemnestra and the infamy she sank to when she killed her wedded lord! Her name will be cursed wherever she is sung. She has branded all her sex, with every honest woman in it.'

While the souls stood there in Hades' Halls, conversing in the bowels of the earth, Odysseus' party left the town behind, and before long had reached the rich and well-run farmlands of Laertes, which he had wrested from their natural state by his own exertions long ago. Here was his cottage, surrounded by outbuildings, where the serfs that laboured for him had their meals and sat and slept. An old Sicilian woman lived in the cottage, devoting all her care to the old man's comfort in this rural retreat.

When they reached the spot, Odysseus said to Telemachus and his men: 'Go into the main building now and make haste to kill the best pig you can find for our midday meal. Meanwhile I shall try an experiment with my father, to find out whether he will remember me and realize who it is when he sees me, or fail to know me after so long an absence.'

As he spoke, he handed his weapons of war to the servants, who then went straight into the house, while Odysseus moved off towards the luxuriant vineyard intent on his experiment. As he made his way down into the great orchard, he fell in neither with Dolius nor with any of the serfs or Dolius' sons, who had all gone with the old man at their head to gather stones for the vineyard wall. Thus he found his father alone on the vineyard terrace digging round a plant. He was wearing a filthy, patched, and disreputable tunic, a pair of stitched leather gaiters strapped round his shins to protect them from scratches, and gloves to save his hands from the brambles; while to crown all, and by way of emphasizing his misery, he had a hat of goatskin on his head. When the gallant Odysseus saw how old and worn his father looked and realized how miserable he was, he halted under a tall pear-tree and the tears came into his eyes. Nor could he make up his mind at once whether to hug and kiss his father, and tell him the whole story of his own return to Ithaca, or first to question him and find out what he thought. In the end he decided to start by assuming a brusque manner in order to draw the old man out, and with this purpose in view he now went straight up to his father.

Laertes was still hoeing round his plant with his head down, as his famous son came up and accosted him.

'Old man,' said Odysseus, 'you have everything so tidy here that I can see there is little about gardening that you do not know. There is nothing, not a green thing in the whole enclosure, not a fig, olive, vine, pear, or vegetable bed that does not show signs of your care. On the other hand I cannot help remarking, I hope without offence, that you don't look after yourself very well; in fact, what with your squalor and your wretched clothes, old age has hit you very hard. Yet it can't be on account of any laziness that your master neglects you, nor is there anything in your build and size to suggest the slave. You look more like a man of royal blood, the sort of person who enjoys the privilege of age, and sleeps on a soft bed when he has had his bath and dined. However, tell me whose serf you are. And whose is this garden you look after? The truth, if you please. And there's another point you can clear up for me. Am I really in Ithaca? A fellow I met on my way up here just now assured me that I was. But he was not very intelligent, for he wouldn't deign to answer me properly or listen to what I said, when I mentioned a friend of mine and asked him whether he was still in the land of the living or dead and gone by now. You shall learn about this friend yourself if you pay attention to what I say. Some time ago in my own country I befriended a stranger who turned up at our place and proved the most attractive visitor I have ever entertained from abroad. He said he was an Ithacan, and that Arceisius' son Laertes was his father. I took him in, made him thoroughly welcome and gave him every hospitality that my rich house could afford, including presents worthy of his rank. Seven talents of wrought gold he had from me, a solid silver wine-bowl with a floral design, twelve single-folded cloaks, twelve rugs, twelve splendid mantles and as many tunics too, and besides all this, four women as skilled in fine handicraft as they were good to look at. I let him choose them for himself.'

'Sir,' said his father to Odysseus, with tears on his cheeks, 'I can assure you that you're in the place you asked for; but it's in the hands of rogues and criminals. The gifts you lavished on your friend were given in vain, though, had you found him alive in Ithaca, he would never have let you go before he had made you an ample return in presents and hospitality, as is right when such an example has been set. But pray tell me exactly how long ago it was that you befriended the unfortunate man, for that guest of yours was my unhappy son – if ever I had one – my son, who far from friends and home has been devoured by fishes in the sea or fallen a prey, maybe, to the wild beasts and birds on land. Dead people have their dues, but not Odysseus. We had no chance, we two that brought him into the world, to wrap his body up and wail for him, nor had his richly dowered wife, constant Penelope, the chance to close her husband's eyes and give him on his bier the seemly tribute of a dirge.

'But you have made me curious about yourself. Who are you, sir? What is your native town? And where might she be moored, the good ship that brought you here with your gallant crew? Or were you travelling as a passenger on someone else's ship, which landed you and sailed away?'

'I am quite willing,' said the resourceful Odysseus, 'to tell you all you wish to know. I come from Alybas. My home is in the

palace there, for my father is King Apheidas, Polypemon's son.
My own name is Eperitus. I had no intention of putting in here
when I left Sicania, but had the misfortune to be driven out of
my course; and my ship is riding yonder by the open coast some
way from the port. As for Odysseus, it is four years and more
since he bade me farewell and left my country – to fall on evil
days, it seems. And yet the omens when he left were good, birds
on the right, which pleased me as I said goodbye, and cheered
him as he started out. We both had every hope that we should
meet again as host and guest and give each other splendid gifts.'

When Laertes heard this, he sank into the black depths of despair. Groaning heavily, he picked the black dust up in both his
hands and poured it on the grey hairs of his head. Odysseus'
heart was stirred, and suddenly, as he watched his dear father,
poignant compassion forced its way through his nostrils. He
rushed forward, flung his arms round his neck, and kissed him.
'Father,' he cried, 'here I am, the very man you asked about,
home in my own land after nineteen years. But this is no time
for tears and lamentation. For I have news to tell you, and heaven
knows there is need for haste. I have killed that gang of Suitors
in our palace. I have paid them out for their insulting gibes and
all their crimes.'

Laertes answered him: 'If you that have come here are indeed
my son Odysseus, give me some definite proof to make me
sure.'

Odysseus was ready for this. 'To begin with,' he said, 'cast
your eye on this scar, where I was wounded by the white tusk of
a boar when I went to Parnassus. You and my mother had sent
me to my grandfather Autolycus, to fetch the gifts he solemnly
promised me when he came to visit us. Then again, I can tell you
all the trees you gave me one day on this garden terrace. I was
only a little boy at the time, trotting after you through the orchard, begging for this and that, and as we wound our way
through these very trees you told me all their names. You gave
me thirteen pear-, ten apple-, and forty fig-trees, and at the same
time you pointed out the fifty rows of vines that were to be

mine. Each ripened at a different time, so that the bunches on them were at various stages when the branches felt their weight under the summer skies.'

Laertes realized at once that Odysseus' evidence had proved his claim. With trembling knees and bursting heart he flung his arms round the neck of his beloved son, and stalwart Odysseus caught him fainting to his breast. The first words he uttered as he rallied and his consciousness returned were in reply to the news his son had given him. 'By Father Zeus,' he cried, 'you gods are still in your heaven, if those Suitors have really paid the price for their iniquitous presumption! But I have a horrible fear now that the whole forces of Ithaca will soon be on us here, and that they will send urgent messages for help to every town in Cephallenia.'

'Have no fear,' said his resourceful son, 'and don't trouble your head about that; but come with me to the farmhouse here by the orchard, where I sent on Telemachus with the cowman and swineherd to prepare a meal as quickly as they could.'

Accordingly the pair set out for the house, and there in the pleasant homestead they found Telemachus and the two herds-men carving lavish portions of meat and mixing the sparkling wine. The lord Laertes made use of his own house to have him-self bathed, anointed, and decked out in a fine mantle by his Sicilian maid-servant, and Athene herself intervened to increase his royal stature. As he stepped out of the bath she made him seem taller and sturdier than before, so that his own son was amazed when he saw him looking like an immortal god. He could not repress his astonishment. 'Father!' he exclaimed. 'I do believe some god has made you handsomer and taller than ever!' To which the wise old man replied: 'By Father Zeus, Athene, and Apollo, if only I could have been the man I was when as King of the Cephallenians I took the stronghold of Nericus on the mainland cape, and could have stood by you yesterday in our palace, clothed in mail, to help you beat those rascals off! I warrant I'd have brought them down in plenty and delighted your heart!'

While they were talking to one another, the others finished their work and prepared the meal. They had just taken their seats at table and were falling to, when the old man Dolius came up with his sons, weary after their work, from which they had been called in by their mother, the old Sicilian, who saw to their food and looked after their old father with unfailing devotion now that his years sat heavily upon him. When they set eyes on Odysseus and realized who he was, they stopped short in amazement half-way across the room. Odysseus greeted them with friendly chaff. 'Old man,' he said, 'sit down to your lunch. And the rest of you, don't stand gaping there! We have been hard put to it to keep our hands off the food in here, waiting all this time and expecting you every minute.'

Dolius ran up with outstretched arms, seized Odysseus by the hand, and kissed him on the wrist. 'So you have come back to us, my dear master,' he said with emotion, 'and fulfilled our dearest wishes! We had given up hope, but heaven itself must have led you home. Here's health and happiness, and may the gods shower their blessings on you! But tell me this, for I am anxious – has our wise queen Penelope heard of your arrival here, or shall we send someone to tell her?'

'She knows already, my old friend,' Odysseus answered 'Don't you trouble your head about that.'

Dolius sat down again on his wooden stool, and now it was his sons' turn to gather round the famous Odysseus, make him speeches of welcome, and shake him by the hand. Then they all took their seats by Dolius their father.

But while Odysseus' party were discussing their meal in the farmhouse, whispering Rumour flew like wildfire through the town, with the fateful news of the Suitors' hideous death. As a result, a murmuring throng of mourners, coming in from all sides with one accord, gathered at Odysseus' gate. They carried out the corpses and each buried their dead, while those from the other towns were put on ships and dispatched in the crews' care to their several homes. The disconsolate Ithacans then trooped out to the meeting-place, and there, when the Assembly was

complete, Eupeithes rose to address them, overcome by grief
for his son Antinous, the first of the great Odysseus' victims.
'Friends,' he began, and tears for his son were streaming down
his cheeks, 'I denounce Odysseus as the inveterate enemy of our
race. Where is the gallant company he sailed away with? Lost
by him, every one; and our good ships lost as well! And now he
comes home and slaughters the very pick of the Cephallenians!
Quick, I say. Before he can fly to Pylos or to Elis where the
Epeians rule, let us make a move, or we'll never be able to hold
up our heads again. Our names will stink in the nostrils of our
descendants if we do not avenge ourselves on the murderers of
our sons and brothers. I, for one, should find no further pleasure
in living, but should prefer to finish now and join the dead. To
action then, or they may be across the seas before we move.'

His tearful appeal stirred all his countrymen to pity. But at
this moment Medon and the minstrel appeared on the scene. On
waking, they had come straight from the palace, and now took
their stand in the centre of the assembly. Everyone wondered
what this meant, but Medon, who was by no means a fool, en-
lightened them at once. 'Listen, my fellow-Ithacans,' he said,
'and you will understand that in acting as he did Odysseus was
not without the guiding hand of heaven. With my own eyes I
saw an immortal, who looked exactly like Mentor, standing at
his side. And some divine being could be seen, at one moment
ahead of Odysseus, cheering him on, and at the next charging
down the hall and striking panic into the Suitors, who fell in
heaps before him.'

Medon's disclosure drained the blood from their cheeks; and
now the aged lord Halitherses, the only man there who could
look into the future as into the past, rose up to administer a well-
meant rebuke. 'Ithacans,' he cried, 'I beg for your attention.
Your own wickedness, my friends, is to blame for what has happened. You would not listen to me or to your leader Mentor,
when we urged you to check your sons in their career of folly.
They threw all restraint to the winds, and in plundering the
estate and insulting the wife of a prince whom they counted on

never seeing here again, they were guilty of a flagrant offence. I hope therefore that you will be persuaded by me when I propose that we should take no action; or else I fear that some of you may bring your own doom on your heads.'

At the end of this speech, more than half the audience, bursting into uproar, leapt to their feet, though a fair number remained in their seats. The old lord's plain speaking had proved unpalatable; Eupeithes won the day. They rushed to arms, equipped themselves in their gleaming bronze and mustered in an open space beside the town. Eupeithes in his folly took command. He saw himself avenging his son's death, though in fact he was never to come back alive but to meet his own fate on the selfsame day.

Athene now decided to consult with Zeus. 'Father of ours,' she said to him, 'Son of Cronos, King of Kings, will you reveal to me the thoughts that are hidden in your heart? Are you planning to prolong this strife, with the horrors and turmoil it entails, or to establish peace between the warring sides?'

To which the Cloud-gatherer replied: 'My child, why come to me with such questions? Was it not your own idea that Odysseus should return and avenge himself on his enemies? Act as you please, though this is what I think most suitable myself. Since the admirable Odysseus has had his revenge on the Suitors, let them make a treaty of peace to establish him as king in perpetuity, with an act of oblivion, on our part, for the slaughter of their sons and brothers. Let the mutual goodwill of the old days be restored, and let peace and plenty prevail.'

With this encouragement from Zeus, Athene, who had already set her heart on action, sped down at once from the peaks of Olympus.

In the farmhouse, meanwhile, they had enjoyed a satisfying meal, when the gallant Odysseus suggested that someone should go out and discover whether the enemy were not yet in sight. One of Dolius' sons jumped up and went to the threshold. Standing there, he saw the whole hostile force at no great distance, and called excitedly to Odysseus: 'See! They are on us.

Get ready, quick!' Whereupon they leapt up and put their armour on. Odysseus and his followers made four; Dolius' sons another six; and to them Laertes and Dolius himself must be added, for they armed themselves too, grey-headed though they were and forced by circumstance to fight. When all were clad in gleaming bronze they opened the gates and sallied out under Odysseus' leadership.

They were now joined by Athene, Daughter of Zeus, who had assumed Mentor's appearance and voice for the occasion. The stalwart Odysseus was overjoyed to see her. He turned at once to his dear son and said: 'Telemachus, when you find yourself in the thick of battle, where the best men prove their mettle, I am sure you will know how not to shame your father's house. In all the world there has been none like ours for valour and for manly strength.' And the wise Telemachus replied: 'As you have said, dear father, in this present mood of mine your line will not be put to shame by me. You shall see that for yourself.'

Laertes was delighted. 'Dear gods!' he exclaimed. 'What a day this is to warm my heart! My son and my grandson are competing in valour.'

Athene of the flashing eyes came up to him now and said: 'Laertes, dearest of all my friends, pray to the Lady of the flashing eyes and to Father Zeus; then quickly swing your long spear back and let it fly.'

As she spoke Pallas Athene breathed daring into the old man, who, with a prayer to the Daughter of Zeus, poised his long spear at once and hurled it. He struck Eupeithes on the bronze cheek-guard of his helmet. The helmet failed to stop the spear, the point burst through, and with a clang of armour Eupeithes crashed to earth. Then Odysseus and his noble son fell on the front rank of the enemy and smote them with their swords and double-pointed spears. They would have destroyed them all and seen that none went home alive, if Athene, Daughter of aegis-wearing Zeus, had not raised a great cry and checked the whole of the contending forces: 'Ithacans, stop this disastrous fight and separate at once before more blood is shed.'

Athene's cry struck panic into the Ithacans, who let their weapons go, in their terror at the goddess' voice. The arms all fell to earth, and the men turned citywards, intent on their own salvation. The indomitable Odysseus raised a terrible war-cry, gathered himself together and pounced on them like a swooping eagle. But at this moment Zeus let fly a flaming bolt, which fell in front of the bright-eyed Daughter of that formidable Sire. Athene called out at once to Odysseus by his royal titles, commanding him to hold his hand and bring this civil strife to a finish, for fear of offending the ever-watchful Zeus.

Odysseus obeyed her, with a happy heart. And presently Pallas Athene, Daughter of aegis-wearing Zeus, still using Mentor's form and voice for her disguise, established peace between the two contending forces.

GREEK GODS IN THE ODYSSEY

Name	Relationship to Zeus	Functions
APHRODITE (Venus)	Daughter of Zeus and Dione	Goddess of Love
APOLLO (Apollo)	Son of Zeus and Leto	God of light, music, archery, prophecy
ARES (Mars)	Son of Zeus and Here	God of war
ARTEMIS (Diana)	Daughter of Zeus and Leto; twin sister of Apollo	Goddess of wild life, hunting, maidens
ATHENE (Minerva)	Daughter of Zeus	Goddess of defensive war, wisdom, arts of peace; patroness of Odysseus
CALYPSO	Daughter of Atlas	Nymph who kept Odysseus with her for seven years
EOS (Aurora)	Parentage doubtful	Goddess of Dawn
ERINYES (Furies)		Avengers of impiety and other crimes
HADES (Pluto, Dis)	Brother of Zeus	God of the underworld and the dead
HEPHAESTUS (Vulcan)	Son of Zeus and Here	God of fire and metal work; lame smith of gods
HERE (Juno)	Sister and wife of Zeus	Goddess of marriage and wives; Queen of heaven
HERMES (Mercury)	Son of Zeus and Maia	God of travellers, thieves, scholars; messenger of the gods

HYPERION	One of the Titans	God of the sun
INO LEUKOTHEE (Ino)	Daughter of Cadmus	A minor sea-goddess, who rescues Odysseus
PHOEBUS	See under Apollo	
POSEIDON (Neptune)	Brother of Zeus	God of the sea and of horses
ZEUS (Jupiter, Jove)	Son of Cronos and Rhea	God of sky, weather; King of gods; protector of strangers

*The Roman equivalents are given in parentheses